THE ARC OF THE MORAL UNIVERSE

THE
ARC
OF THE
MORAL
UNIVERSE

and Other Essays

JOSHUA COHEN

HARVARD UNIVERSITY PRESS
Cambridge, Massachusetts, and London, England
2010

Library of Congress Cataloging-in-Publication Data

Cohen, Joshua, 1951–
The arc of the moral universe and other essays / Joshua Cohen.
    p.   cm.
Includes bibliographical references and index.
ISBN 978-0-674-05560-5 (alk. paper)
1. Democracy.   2. Political science—Philosophy.   I. Title.
JC423.C6473   2010
320.01—dc22   2010010348

For Jack

CONTENTS

CONTENTS

THE ARC OF THE MORAL UNIVERSE

INTRODUCTION

In *Philosophy, Politics, Democracy*,[1] I collected a set of my essays focused on an ideal of democracy. A democracy, according to that ideal, is a political society of equals, in which the justification of institutions—as well as laws and policies addressed to consequential problems—involves public argument based on the common reason of members, who regard one another as equals. The essays I have selected for this book locate these ideas about democracy in a wider context. More precisely, I consider three wider contexts: I explore some issues about the relationship between democratic values and history (Part I), discuss the account of democracy in connection with the views of a few theorists in the democratic tradition (Part II), and examine the place of democratic ideals in a global setting (Part III).

My description of the three contexts is very general because these essays are only loosely linked, not written as parts of an unfolding plan. To the extent that the pieces hang together, they are linked by an outlook and an aim.[2]

The outlook is that political philosophy is a practical subject. It is obviously practical in its focus, on institutions, practices, and conduct. But it is also practical in one of its central purposes. That purpose is to orient and guide conduct in the social world, not only to understand the social world, or to judge its moral quality. In the *Critique of Pure Reason*, Kant says that the three great philosophical questions are: "What can I know?" "What should I do?" and "What may I hope?"[3] Political philosophy is importantly animated by Kant's second and third questions, about action and hope (to be distinguished from wish or expectation).

I am grateful to Rob Reich for helpful comments on an earlier draft of this Introduction.

1. (Cambridge, MA: Harvard University Press, 2009).

2. For a fuller discussion, see the Introduction to *Philosophy, Politics, Democracy*.

3. Immanuel Kant, *Critique of Pure Reason*, trans. Paul Guyer and Allen Wood (Cambridge: Cambridge University Press, 1998), A805–B833.

In saying that political philosophy is a practical subject, I am not offering a definition or an argument but simply declaring a position. The position explains why the essays collected here mix moral, social-scientific, and historical argument. Without that mix, we cannot hope to have the orientation and guidance that is central to the work of political philosophy.

The aim is to understand better the place in the world of democratic self-government. At Gettysburg, President Lincoln expressed concern about whether a society, conceived in liberty and dedicated to the proposition that we are all equals, could long endure. He expressed as well the hope that the fight for democracy's endurance would succeed. He was right to be concerned. I would like to think that the essays in this volume—along with the companion collection on *Philosophy, Politics, Democracy*— suggest some reasons for thinking that the hope for such endurance is not unreasonable.

1. History

Political philosophy is a normative inquiry. It is about how the social-political world ought to be and how it would be good for it to be, not how the social-political world is. But anyone who thinks about norms and ideals wonders at some point, perhaps early and often, about their relationship to the world as it is, about the relationship, in Hegel's terms, of the reasonable to the actual.[4]

That concern is often expressed by asking whether some proposed political ideal or norm—an ideal of equality, for example, or of self-government— is merely good in theory, or if it is also workable in practice, given human nature and the demands of social order. Thus Rousseau wondered whether legitimate government was possible, "taking men as they are and the laws as they can be."[5]

The opening essay, "The Arc of the Moral Universe," addresses a different, less familiar question about the relations between actual fact and reasonable norm. I ask about the use of norms not in judging the world, or guiding its reform, but in *explaining* its course. Abraham Lincoln speculated

---

4. G. W. F. Hegel, *Elements of the Philosophy of Right*, ed. Allen W. Wood, trans. H. B. Nisbet (Cambridge: Cambridge University Press, 1991), 20. See also the editorial note at 389–390.
5. Jean-Jacques Rousseau, *Of the Social Contract*, in *The Social Contract and Other Later Political Writings*, ed. and trans. Victor Gourevitch (Cambridge: Cambridge University Press, 1997), 41.

in his 1860 Cooper Union address that "right makes might," and Plato thought that the "objects of knowledge" owe not only their being-known but also their *very being* "to the Good."[6] Mae West disagreed.[7] In response to praise for her jewelry—"goodness, what lovely diamonds"—she said, "goodness had nothing to do with it."

When I began working on this topic (in 1984), I shared Mae West's skepticism. I had been writing in criticism of the optimism associated with Marx's historical materialism and was drawn to a Gramscian mix of optimism of the will, pessimism of the intellect.[8] To test this mix, I decided to write about slavery, which struck me as a hard case for a sharp dualism of fact and norm. Slavery is unjust. As Lincoln said, if slavery is not unjust, then nothing is unjust. And I accepted (perhaps too quickly) that slavery had been abolished, not only in the United States, but in the world. Was it really so plausible, then, that the injustice of slavery "had nothing to do with it"? Or did the injustice of slavery—that it is objectively unjust, not simply thought to be unjust—create troubles for slavery?

My initial skepticism about the connection between the injustice of slavery and its demise gave way, for two reasons. First, the very same conflict between slavery and the basic interests of slaves as human agents—interests in material well-being, autonomy, and dignity—that made slavery so grossly unjust also seemed to have limited its viability. Second, I came to see the question in a different light. As I read in the history, I realized that lots of people—the essay quotes an ex-slave named William Williams, Unitarian abolitionist Theodore Parker, as well as Lincoln—used norms in explanations and predictions and said in particular that slavery would not last *because it was wrong:* "Its Nature of wickedness," Parker said, "is its manifest Destiny of Ruin."[9] So I was not simply addressing a question in historical sociology—what explains the demise of slavery?—and considering whether historical sociologists should incorporate moral norms into their answers to that question. Instead, I was starting

6. Plato, *Republic*, trans. G. M. A. Grube (Indianapolis: Hackett, 1974), 509B.

7. I owe the Mae West reference to Alan Garfinkel, with whom I discussed the issues about norm and fact in the mid-1970s.

8. This mix was at work in an unpublished paper (c. 1979) on Marx's theory of the state, "Trouble in Paradise"; in my review of G. A. Cohen's *Karl Marx's Theory of History: A Defence*, in *Journal of Philosophy* (May 1982): 253–273; and in Joshua Cohen and Joel Rogers, *On Democracy* (Middlesex, UK: Penguin, 1983).

9. Theodore Parker, *The Relation of Slavery to a Republican Form of Government* (Boston: William Kent and Company, 1858), 20.

within a moral outlook on the social world—an outlook comprising moral explanations as well as moral judgments—and aiming to assess its plausibility. The issue was whether Williams, Parker, Lincoln, and Martin Luther King Jr. were saying something sensible and defensible, something that could plausibly be regarded as an exercise of practical reason, or whether reflective philosophical and social-scientific thought condemned their views as a mix of rhetoric and wishful thinking.

To be sure, Parker, Lincoln, King, and Williams all understood the world in religious terms. They drew strength from their conviction that the world has a moral author whose judgments "are true and righteous altogether."[10] But I concluded that a secular case could be made for a modest version of their sense of hope—their hope for a world that would not so relentlessly and radically deny the equality of persons that is essential to democracy.

2. Democratic Thought

Part II includes a series of essays that engage more directly with democratic ideas and their implications by exploring the views of a few important political theorists in the democratic tradition: John Locke, John Rawls, Noam Chomsky, Jürgen Habermas, and Susan Moller Okin.

Locke forcefully asserts the equal freedom of human beings, and their rational powers, central ideas in the democratic tradition. But he also defends a class state in which political power belongs to property owners. How does he arrive at this surprising conjunction of ideas? We can criticize the question by arguing that Locke really was a democrat who denied the legitimacy of a class state, or by locating some sleight-of-hand in Locke's assertion that we are all free and equal. But both criticisms are interpretively implausible and obscure the distinctive features of Lockean views.

To address the puzzle, I ask (in Chapter 2): Why would free and equal individuals rationally consent to a state in which only some members share in political authority? Although initially surprising, this agreement makes good sense once we focus on the fact that Locke—like many classical liberals—thought of individual property as prior to political society. So when individuals form a state by freely and rationally consenting to a

---

10. Lincoln quoted this passage from Psalm 19:9 in his Second Inaugural Address.

common authority, they do so not simply as free and equal persons, but as owners, and as owners of potentially vastly unequal amounts of wealth. These pre-political inequalities then carry over through the social contract into inequalities of political rights, which can serve to reinforce the pre-political inequalities. I conclude by contrasting this Lockean perspective— which locates formal freedom and equality against a background of inequality and associated differences of interest—with a Rousseauean view, on which freedom and equality are less formal, more fundamental, and expressed in the democratic ideal of a free community of equals.[11]

This argument about Locke resonates with a common stylization in political theory. Liberals are said to favor rights and the philosophical reasoning that supports rights but to be anxious about democracy, which they want to restrict through bills of rights, written constitutions, courts with final interpretive power over a constitution, and other devices that are designed to discipline mind and body and limit politics. Liberals, according to this characterization, undervalue political autonomy—people resolving fundamental issues themselves rather than having those fundamentals settled in advance and deposited in a scheme of rights and constitutional limits. Moreover, they lack Lincoln's "patient confidence in the ultimate justice of the people."

Although it fits some elements of Locke's view, this stylization is misguided as an interpretation of democracy and of liberalism and exaggerates the tensions between them.[12] In three essays on Rawls, I explore these issues by focusing on the role of ideas about democracy in Rawls's conception of justice. Rawls was certainly a liberal. He was a powerful exponent of personal and political liberties, and an opponent of communitarian conceptions of political society, which make strong social solidarity a precondition of justice or a value lying beyond its limited reach. But Rawls also rejects the Lockean view about freedom and equality. And a concern about democracy played a central role in shaping his conception of justice.

In his doctoral dissertation (1950), Rawls distinguishes authoritarian and positivistic views about ethical knowledge.[13] These views, despite their many differences, share the conviction that "reasoning in moral questions

11. See Joshua Cohen, *Rousseau: A Free Community of Equals* (Oxford: Oxford University Press, 2010).
12. For discussion of these themes, see *Philosophy, Politics, Democracy*, chaps. 4, 5, 7–9.
13. The discussion that follows draws on John Rawls, "A Study in the Grounds of Ethical Knowledge: Considered with Reference to Judgments on the Moral Worth of Character"

[is] to no effect." This anti-rationalism, he says, has troubling implications for democracy:

> The democratic conception of government looks to the law and not to the state as the primary source of authority; and it views the law as the outcome of public discussions as to what rules can be voluntarily consented to as binding upon the government and the citizens. . . . Rational discussion . . . constitutes an essential precondition of reasonable law. Democratic theory and practice must consider the process of reasoning as one of the crucial points in its whole program. It is *because* [the authoritarian and positivistic views about moral thought] strike at *what is essential in democratic theory* that the question about the rational foundation of ethical principles is *worthy of our attention.*

Rawls here traces his concern about reason's place in *moral* argument to a conception of legitimate democratic lawmaking. From the start, then, he was focused on political justification in a democracy. The three essays on Rawls aim to bring out the role of democratic ideas in shaping his views.

"Democratic Equality" (Chapter 3) explores Rawls's *difference principle*. A controversial standard of distributive justice, this principle permits inequalities only if they work to the maximum advantage of the least advantaged. Rawls presents the principle as part of a conception of "democratic equality," as a specifically "democratic interpretation" of the widely shared idea that justifiable inequalities should work to "everyone's advantage."[14] What does democracy have to do with it?

The idea, I argue, is not that the difference principle helps to make the political process itself more democratic. Instead, the content and rationale of the principle are shaped by democratic ideas. In particular, the difference principle is animated by the view that we are equals in virtue of possessing certain moral-political capacities—for individual self-government and for participation in collective self-government on reasonable terms. That conception of equality, in turn, is embedded in the settled institu-

---

(PhD diss., Princeton University, 1950), 7–8. Available from UMI Dissertation Services, Ann Arbor, Michigan.

14. See John Rawls, *A Theory of Justice*, rev. ed. (Cambridge, MA: Harvard University Press, 1999), 65–73, 280–281 (on the difference principle and the "ethos of a democratic society").

tions of a democracy, where citizens have equal standing as bearers of personal and political liberties, regardless of differences in social background, native ability, moral and religious conviction, or race and gender. The difference principle interprets "everyone's advantage" in light of this idea of equality. This strategy of taking a conception of persons as equals from democracy and extending its reach to the distribution of resources underscores Rawls's distance from the Lockean view, with its assumption of pre-political inequalities that shape the terms of a political compact.

"A More Democratic Liberalism" (Chapter 4) interprets Rawls's shift from the philosophical liberalism of A *Theory of Justice* to his later "political liberalism" as a response to a problem about democracy. Essential to this understanding is the idea that democracy is an enterprise of reasoning together—reasoning on the basis of values and principles that can be shared by equals—and not only a system with equal political rights or an electorally disciplined contest for power. Suppose we accept this picture of democracy, are concerned about inclusion in the practice of public reasoning, and understand that members of democratic societies disagree deeply on fundamental moral, religious, and philosophical questions. The central ideas of Rawls's political liberalism then fall generally into place. Political conceptions of justice and of the person, as well as public reason and overlapping consensus—they are what democracy requires, once we accept profound disagreement on fundamentals, and seek to avoid sectarian political exclusion by finding terms of mutual political justification among equals.[15]

"For a Democratic Society" (Chapter 5) distinguishes three ideas about democracy: a *democratic* society, as a society of equals; a *political democracy*, as a system with equal political rights and fair elections; and a *deliberative* democracy, as a political democracy in which the exercise of power is backed by argument founded on ideas of justice that are suited to a society of equals. We need all three ideas to understand why Rawls supposed that his conception of justice as fairness, with its two principles of justice, provides "the most appropriate moral basis for a democratic society."[16] Democracy, once more, is not simply a regulated contest for power;

15. I add the idea of a political conception of truth in *Philosophy, Politics, Democracy*, chap. 11.
16. Rawls, A *Theory of Justice*, xviii.

it is also a public argument about how to exercise public power. Thus Rawls's principles of justice (and the reasoning for those principles) are proposed, then, as terms of public deliberation about institutions, laws, and policies; they are suited in their content to a democratic society (see Chapter 3); and citizens in such a society can use them as a basis for political judgment when they exercise their political liberties. The idea, then, in presenting a theory of justice is not to substitute philosophical reasoning about justice for democratic politics or to limit the scope of politics by resolving the fundamentals in advance of democratic self-government. The aim instead is to contribute to democracy by offering a conception of justice founded on democratic ideas that might engage with and shape public judgment and argument.

The final three essays in Part II discuss three political theorists who all arguably belong to a radical-democratic tradition with expansive hopes for democracy.

Chomsky's radical-democratic impulse is expressed in his emphasis on the role of mobilized and informed citizens in disrupting social privilege, his account of the importance of ideological manipulation to "manufacture consent" in political systems that do not coercively repress all opposition, and his anarchist's skepticism about the need for a state and political authority in a free society. In Chapter 6, Joel Rogers and I explore the roots of these views in Chomsky's conception of human nature, which mixes Rationalist ideas about the intrinsic structures of the human mind with Romanticism's emphasis on creativity (within the bounds fixed by those intrinsic structures). This conception of human nature shapes Chomsky's views about language, the hopefulness that has guided his political engagement, and his suspicions about states. We are unconvinced, however, by his efforts to link the conception with anarchism. Although there are very good reasons for resisting the glorification of states, and for challenging exaggerated expectations about their capacity to solve problems, we find the anarchist idea of state-free cooperation on a large scale hard to grasp, and, to the extent that it has definite content, to be of very uncertain benefit.[17]

Habermas identifies himself as a radical democrat who takes his inspiration from the ideal of "a self-organizing community of free and equal citizens," coordinating their collective affairs through their common reason

---

17. Some skepticism about state capacity does, however, inform the arguments in *Philosophy, Politics, Democracy*, especially chapters 3, 6, and 10.

(Chapter 7). He proposes a distinctive way to think about the implications of that ideal under modern conditions of social complexity. What is essential to achieving the democratic promise under modern conditions is not the direct participation of citizens in the formal exercise of authority, as if the Athenian assembly could be restored at modern political scale. Instead, we need to ensure that democratic lawmaking, and the administrative agencies responsible for implementing those laws, maintain their links with the informal, dispersed, non-technical, open-ended explorations of values, principles, and policies by citizens and the associations of civil society. And we need, too, to preserve the autonomy of those explorations from commercial or administrative control.

These ideas about the "public sphere" strike me as essential to an understanding of the possibilities of mass democracy. The conception of democracy as an interplay between a dispersed and open public discussion and deliberative political decision is a powerful corrective to the idea that we face a choice between democracy as a scheme of electoral competition disconnected from public discussion and democracy as direct citizen participation in lawmaking. At the same time, I suggest two criticisms, corresponding to two positive lines of argument in *Philosophy, Politics, Democracy*. I argue, first, that Habermas' view lacks a sufficiently compelling story about democracy and individual rights, because he does not sufficiently appreciate the implications of deep pluralism for democracy's public reason. And second, I argue that his hopes for democracy may be unnecessarily truncated by an overly mechanical conception of modern administration. By treating much consequential policy-making in the administrative state as the downstream implementation of legislative directives, his conception unnecessarily and implausibly limits the political role of public discussion.[18] If Chomsky's radical democratic ideas are implausibly anarchist, Habermas' may be too wedded to the state.

The designation of Okin as a radical democrat is somewhat unconventional. Her work was not generally about democracy, but about justice and gender, in particular about the importance of understanding that the reach of justice extends to the domestic sphere. But the designation is suggested by her emphasis (the focus of one part of Chapter 8) on the

---

18. I address issues of pluralism and liberties in chapters 4, 5, 7, and 9 of *Philosophy, Politics, Democracy*; concerns about democracy in the administrative state frame the discussion in chapters 3, 6, and 10.

public-private distinction as preserving the subordination of women, thus undermining the equal treatment they are owed. The roots of gender subordination lie in the family, so there is no hope of achieving justice, once we designate the family as a sphere of private ordering, outside the scope of politics. The critique of the public-private distinction (not to be confused with its rejection) thus corresponds to a more expansive view of democracy, which extends its reach into the informal, domestic arena.

Okin was right to worry about the role of the public-private distinction in limiting our capacity to achieve democracy's promise. And she was right, too, to think (as I believe she did) that some sort of public-private distinction is essential to any democracy worthy of our allegiance, even if Lockean ideas about pre-political property and pre-political domesticity do not have it right. Okin did not offer a compelling way to navigate the tension between these two convictions—that a public-private distinction is both problematic for and an important element of a compelling conception of democracy. But she identified and left us with an essential task for democratic theory.[19]

3. Global Justice

Part III addresses issues about political norms and values outside the context of a state. The three essays suggest an idea of "global public reason"—a terrain of political justification in global politics, different in content from democracy's public reason, in which an idea of equality plays an essential role.

The essays are critical of two temptations in thinking about global justice. One view, call it "minimalism," says that when we move outside the state, claims of justice lose their grip. Normative demands contract to a (massively violated) humanitarian morality condemning such extremes as torture, genocide, and starvation. A second, "maximalist" view is that political boundaries and differences of political tradition are normatively irrelevant, that standards of justice associated with the democratic tradition are required everywhere. This is expressed, inter alia, in the view that there is a human right to democracy and that democracy is the rule for legitimate global institutions as well as for domestic political societies.

---

19. I suggest an angle of approach in chapter 9 of *Philosophy, Politics, Democracy.*

Chapters 9 and 11 are directed against two different versions of the minimalist temptation, which offer different reasons for thinking that normative demands markedly diminish when we move outside the context of a state. A first version is founded on a commitment to the value of toleration and an associated aim of presenting a conception of human rights and justice that is suited to global politics and thus cannot depend on specifically liberal political ideas. Once the idea of human rights is separated from its liberal moorings, so it is argued, we are left only with a very basic core of human rights, confined to protections of persons against the most egregious forms of abuse and mistreatment—to some core civil and political rights, and not to economic and social rights.

I share the commitment to toleration and the associated aim, which are both essential to global public reason. But I argue in Chapter 9 that an account of human rights can be tolerant, in providing a common ground of argument that can be occupied by adherents of very different moral and religious traditions, without being substantively minimal. I offer a conception of human rights in which an idea of inclusion plays a central role, show how that conception could be endorsed as part of global public reason by competing ethical and religious views, and explain why it is not substantively minimal.

Another version of minimalism argues that a political authority must—because of its coercive impositions—meet particularly exacting normative standards, perhaps the normative standards associated with egalitarian justice. But then, because there is no global state, thus no global coercive imposition, the normative standards outside the state are correspondingly less demanding. More precisely, outside the state there is no justice (*extra rempublicam nulla justitia*). We are led to minimalism not by value of toleration but by the absence of coercion.

In Chapter 11, Charles Sabel and I argue that political relations in the context of global politics—of interdependence, cooperation, and institutional responsibility—are sufficiently developed to undermine the plausibility of this statist conception of justice. Even if the normative demands of global public reason are less stringent than the demands associated with democracy's public reason, they do not collapse to the humanitarian minimum.

Chapter 10, focused on the idea of a human right to democracy, addresses the maximalist temptation, to treat political boundaries and differences of political tradition as normatively irrelevant. I accept that democracy is a requirement of justice. But I deny that legitimate authority, which ensures essential rights to all, must be democratic, and thus deny the idea of a human right to democracy. Legitimate authority must meet a weaker standard, by respecting conditions of collective self-determination. Democracy is one form of collective self-determination, associated with an idea of members as equals. But other forms of collective self-determination are possible, and they ought to be respected.

Although I deny a human right to democracy, I agree that democracy and its conditions of equal standing are conditions of justice. In defending this conjunction of views, I am not turning my back on the moral importance of democracy. Instead, I am expressing confidence in the capacity of people to understand what justice demands and to make, over history's long arc, the concerted efforts needed to meet those demands. That confidence is associated in turn with skepticism about the view that the relevant normative insights are culturally or geographically confined or that they can be achieved through imposition.

The views expressed in the title essay to this volume partially underwrite this concluding judgment about the arc, its direction and length, and its roots in human capacities. They suggest some force in Hegel's double proposition, that the reasonable is actual and the actual is reasonable. But that proposition must be taken in the right way: as affirming grounds for hope that efforts to achieve moral progress will bear fruit, not as counseling a complacently optimistic fatalism in the face of the world's course.

I

JUSTICE IN HISTORY

1

THE ARC OF THE MORAL UNIVERSE

Through all the sorrow of the Sorrow Songs there breathes a
hope—a faith in the ultimate justice of things. The minor ca-
dences of despair change often to triumph and calm confidence. Sometimes it is faith in life, sometimes a faith in death,
sometimes assurance of boundless justice in some fair world
beyond. But whichever it is, the meaning is always clear: that
sometime, somewhere, men will judge men by their souls and
not by their skins. Is such a hope justified? Do the Sorrow
Songs sing true?

—W. E. B. DU BOIS, "The Sorrow Songs"

1. *Ethical Explanation*

William Williams was born into slavery in Salisbury, North Carolina. He
escaped to Canada in 1849, where he was later interviewed by the American abolitionist Samuel Gridley Howe. It was two years into the American

This essay is drawn from a larger book project that I worked on between 1985 and 1992. I
put the book project aside because I was persuaded that completing it would require a level of
historical knowledge, especially about African history, that was beyond my professional reach.
I concluded, too, that the main line of argument could be stated without the historical depth
that the book would have required. I published roughly half of the manuscript (edited of
course for the purposes of separate publication) as an article in 1997. In preparing the version
for this collection, I restored about a third of the material that had been originally cut and
made some other small editorial changes. However, I have not gone back and read the historical literature published after 1992. I wrote the first draft for a 1986 symposium on "Moral Realism" at the annual meeting of the American Political Science Association, and I presented
subsequent versions to philosophy colloquia at Carnegie-Mellon University and Columbia
University, the Western Canadian Philosophical Association, the Harvard Government
Department's political theory colloquium, New York University Law School, the Pacific Division meetings of the American Philosophical Association, the Bay Area Group on Philosophy
and Political Economy, the Society for Ethical and Legal Philosophy, an Olin Conference on

Civil War, and Williams said: "I think the North will whip the South, because I believe they are in the right."[1]

Williams's remark provides a striking example of an ethical explanation. Generally speaking, ethical explanations cite ethical norms—for example, norms of justice—in explaining why some specific social facts obtain, or, as in Williams's case, can be expected to obtain. The norms are offered in explanations of social facts, not only in appraisals of them. Williams not only hopes the North will win; he expects the North to win; and he expects the North to win because it is in the right.[2] Similarly, the great abolitionist minister Theodore Parker predicted defeat for the "slave power" because it was wrong. Speaking to the New England Anti-Slavery Convention in 1858, he said of the slave power: "Its Nature of wickedness is its manifest Destiny of Ruin."[3]

Political Economy at Stanford University, the A. E. Havens Center for the Study of Social Structure and Social Change (University of Wisconsin, Madison), and the Universidade Federal Fluminens in Niterói. I am grateful to audiences at each of these occasions for their comments and criticisms. I especially wish to thank Robert Brenner, David Brink, Robert Cooter, Michael Hardimon, Paul Horwich, Frances Kamm, George Kateb, Ira Katznelson, Harvey Mansfield, Amelie Rorty, Charles Sabel, Michael Sandel, T. M. Scanlon, Samuel Scheffler, Anne-Marie Smith, Laura Stoker, and Erik Olin Wright for helpful suggestions. Karen Jacobsen, Anne-Marie Smith, and Katia Vania provided invaluable research assistance. I received research support from a National Endowment for the Humanities summer fellowship, and MIT's Levitan Prize in the Humanities, generously supported by James and Ruth Levitan. Epigraph source: W. E. B. Du Bois, *The Souls of Black Folk* (New York: Vintage, 1990), 188.

1. Cited in John W. Blassingame, ed., *Slave Testimony* (Baton Rouge: Louisiana State University Press, 1977), 437.

2. For philosophical endorsement of ethical explanations, see Plato, *Republic*, trans. Allan Bloom (New York: Basic Books, 1968), 509B; G. W. F. Hegel, *Lesser Logic*, trans. William Wallace (Oxford: Oxford University Press, 1892), para. 234. Contemporary philosophical discussion of ethical explanations is set within the context of debates about moral realism and moral objectivity. See, among much else, Gilbert Harman, *The Nature of Morality* (Oxford: Oxford University Press, 1977), esp. chap. 1; Nicholas Sturgeon, "Moral Explanations," in David Copp and David Zimmerman, eds., *Morality, Reason, and Truth: New Essays on the Foundations of Ethics* (Totowa, NJ: Rowman and Allanheld, 1985), 49–78; Peter Railton, "Moral Realism," *Philosophical Review* 95, 2 (April 1986): 163–207; Warren Quinn, "Truth and Explanation in Ethics," *Ethics* 96 (April 1986): 522–544; Thomas Nagel, *The View from Nowhere* (Oxford: Oxford University Press, 1986), 144ff.; David Brink, *Moral Realism and the Foundations of Ethics* (Cambridge: Cambridge University Press, 1989); Crispin Wright, *Truth and Objectivity* (Cambridge, MA: Harvard University Press, 1992), chap. 5; Judith Jarvis Thomson, "Moral Objectivity," in Gilbert Harman and Judith Jarvis Thomson, *Moral Relativism and Moral Objectivity* (Cambridge: Blackwell, 1996).

3. Theodore Parker, *The Relation of Slavery to a Republican Form of Government* (Boston: William Kent and Company, 1858), 20. Strictly speaking, Williams and Parker make ethical predictions: they predict a change in a world and base the predictions on norms of rightness. No doubt that they would have embraced the claim that the North won because it was in the right.

Philosophers, historians, and social scientists often recoil from ethical explanations: How could slavery's injustice contribute to explaining its demise? Or the injustice of sexual subordination to explaining the instability of systems that subordinate women? Or the injustice of exclusion from the suffrage to explaining twentieth-century suffrage extension? Or the injustice of permitting life chances to be fixed by the accidents of birth to the emergence of social insurance? Such explanations seem both too relaxed about distinctions between fact and value and too Panglossian. Is it sensible to share Lincoln's "faith that right makes might"?

Still, ethical explanations play an important role in certain commonsense schemes of social and historical understanding: they are elements of certain folk moralities, so to speak. Martin Luther King Jr. said "the arc of the moral universe is long but it bends toward justice."[4] If there is an arc, King is right about its length. But is there one that bends toward justice? Do the Sorrow Songs sing true? More immediately, do ethical explanations withstand reflective examination, or are they simply collages of empirical rumination and reified hope, held together by rhetorical flourish?

I think that some ethical explanations—for example, about slavery, sexual subordination, and suffrage extension—have force. That force derives from the general claim that the injustice of a social arrangement limits its viability. This general claim rests in turn on the role played by the notion of a voluntary system of social cooperation in plausible accounts of both justice and the long-term viability of social forms. Social arrangements

4. The phrase "arc of the moral universe" or variants on it occur throughout King's writing and speeches. See Martin Luther King Jr., *A Testament of Hope: The Essential Writings of Martin Luther King, Jr.*, ed. James Washington (San Francisco: Harper & Row, 1986), 141, 207, 230, 277, 438. King took the phrase from Theodore Parker's 1853 sermon on "Justice and the Conscience." Parker said: "Look at the facts of the world. You see a continual and progressive triumph of the right. I do not pretend to understand the moral universe, the arc is a long one, my eye reaches but little ways. I cannot calculate the curve and complete the figure by the experience of sight; I can divine it by conscience. But from what I see I am sure it bends towards justice. Things refuse to be mismanaged long. Jefferson trembled when he thought of slavery and remembered that God is just." Parker added that this optimism should not be taken as a counsel of quietism: "in human affairs, the justice of God must work by human means," and "you and I can help forward that work" of creating a "kingdom—no, a Commonwealth—of justice on the earth." See Theodore Parker, *Ten Sermons of Religion* (Boston: Crosby, Nichols, and Company; New York: Charles Francis and Company, 1853), 84–85, 100.

better able to elicit voluntary cooperation have both moral and practical advantages over their more coercive counterparts.[5]

This theme lies at the basis of Enlightenment theories of history: Adam Smith's account of the pressures that encourage the emergence of a system of natural liberty,[6] Hegel's account of the instabilities of social systems that enable only incomplete forms of human self-consciousness,[7] and Marx's thesis that exploitative social relations ultimately give way because of the constraints they impose on the free development of human powers.[8] Enlightenment historical sociology was too sanguine about the importance of the connection between justice and viability in accounting for historical evolution, insufficiently attentive to the grim side of historical progress, and of course unaware of (and unprepared for) this century's carnage. Nevertheless, there may be something to the connection.

To argue the case that there is, I will sketch, in very spare terms, an argument for a thesis that is broader than William Williams's claim about the outcome of the American Civil War, but not quite so sweeping as the general claim about the connections between justice and viability: that the injustice of slavery contributed to its demise. I will defend this claim by arguing for the following four:

> Thesis One: The basic structure of slavery as a system of power stands in sharp conflict with fundamental slave interests in material well-being, autonomy, and dignity.
>
> Thesis Two: Slavery is unjust because the relative powerlessness of slaves, reflected in the conflict between slavery and slave interests, implies that it could not be the object of a free, reasonable, and informed agreement.
>
> Thesis Three: The conflict between slavery and the interests of slaves is an important source of the limited viability of slavery.

---

5. For suggestive discussion, see Jürgen Habermas, *Legitimation Crisis*, trans. Thomas McCarthy (Boston: Beacon Press, 1975), Part 3; and Jürgen Habermas, *Communication and the Evolution of Society*, trans. Thomas McCarthy (Boston: Beacon Press, 1979).

6. Adam Smith, *The Wealth of Nations* (New York: Random House, 1965), Book 3.

7. G. W. F. Hegel, *Philosophy of History*, trans. J. Sibree (New York: Dover, 1900).

8. Karl Marx, "Preface" to *A Contribution to the Critique of Political Economy*, and Karl Marx and Frederick Engels, *German Ideology*, in Robert Tucker, ed., *The Marx-Engels Reader*, 2nd ed. (New York: Norton, 1978), 4–5, 146–200.

Thesis Four: Characterizing slavery as unjust conveys information relevant to explaining the demise of slavery that is not conveyed simply by noting that slavery conflicts with the interests of slaves.

I will start by setting out some background claims about the nature of slavery and the bases of its reproduction as a system (section 2). Then I present a defense of the ethical explanation by advancing some considerations in support of these four theses (section 3). The presentation throughout is relatively bloodless and highly abstract: I am largely inattentive to the sheer murderousness of slavery, the gruesome slave trade, and the infinite variety of forms of slavery. These qualities are dictated in part by the problem of squeezing a large claim into a relatively small space, but they also reflect the content of my principal thesis, which requires that I work with a very general characterization of slavery. I know that such abstractness has costs, but the remarks of Williams, Parker, King, and Du Bois persuade me that the claim is sufficiently important to outweigh those costs.

Before getting to the argument, however, I want to clarify its aims by distinguishing my concerns from those in two related debates, one in history, the other in philosophy. First, my focus here is on the role (if any) played by the injustice of slavery in explaining the ultimate demise of slavery. Slavery is unjust—as Lincoln said, "If slavery is not wrong, nothing is wrong"[9]—and it has been abolished. But did its wrongness contribute to its demise? Historians continue to debate the role of moral convictions about the injustice of slavery—held, for example, by Quakers—in accounting for the abolition of slavery.[10] I do not doubt the causal importance of these convictions, much less their sincerity. Indeed, I will eventually make them

9. Quoted in David Potter, *The Impending Crisis: 1848–1861*, completed and ed. Don E. Fehrenbacher (New York: Harper & Row, 1976), 342. The passage comes from Lincoln's letter to Albert G. Hodges (April 4, 1864).

10. For criticism of explanations of the decline of ancient slavery in which religious morality plays a central role, see Keith Bradley, *Slavery and Society at Rome* (Cambridge: Cambridge University Press, 1994), chap. 8; Pierre Dockès, *Medieval Slavery and Liberation*, trans. Arthur Goldhammer (Chicago: University of Chicago Press, 1982), 145–149; G. E. M. de Ste. Croix, *The Class Struggle in the Ancient Greek World* (London: Duckworth, 1981). For recent debate on the complexities of assessing the contribution of moral convictions to modern abolitionism, see the debate among John Ashworth, David Brion Davis, and Thomas Haskell in Thomas Bender, ed., *The Antislavery Debate: Capitalism and Abolitionism as a Problem in Historical Interpretation* (Berkeley: University of California Press, 1992).

part of the story about how the injustice of slavery contributed to its demise. But my topic is different. I am not concerned principally with the causal importance of moral convictions in the decline of slavery but the importance of the injustice itself in accounting for that demise. In short, I am concerned with the consequences of slavery's injustice—whether "its Nature of wickedness is its manifest Destiny of Ruin"—and not simply the consequences of the fact that some people came to think of it as wrong.

Second, some philosophers—they might be called "scientific moral realists"—argue that moral discourse is objective if and only if there are substantial moral facts. Moreover, making a case that there are such facts requires showing that they have a role in the causal explanation of human behavior, moral beliefs, social evolution, or some other nonmoral facts about the world.[11] Scientific moral realism seems to me a mistaken view about moral facts, truth, and objectivity. But I will not argue this claim here because my concerns are more or less orthogonal to the debate about its merits. My aim is not to defend morality, to show that slavery was immoral, or to argue for any particular philosophical theory about morality or moral objectivity. Instead, I begin from within morality, premise slavery's injustice, note the practice of ethical explanation, and ask whether there is anything to the claim—made by Williams and Parker, among others—that slavery's being unjust contributed to its demise. What is at stake is not the appropriate moral attitude toward slavery or philosophical outlook on morality, but rather the appropriate attitude toward the social world. How accommodating is the social world to injustice? Is it reasonable, from a moral point of view, to hate the world?

Having drawn this distinction, however, I need to supplement it with two observations—one about the assumptions of my argument, one about its implications—that do bear on debates about moral realism. First, a defense of ethical explanations is not necessary to showing that some moral claims are true, or, correspondingly, that there are moral facts. So when I assume that some moral claims are true—in particular, that "slavery is unjust" states a truth and expresses a fact—I am not begging any questions against the critic of ethical explanations. Second, the ethical explanation I will defend is consistent with a minimalist outlook in morality,

11. On scientific moral realism, see Sturgeon, "Moral Explanations"; Brink, *Moral Realism*; and especially Railton's excellent "Moral Realism."

according to which moral claims can be assessed as true or false, and true moral claims correspond, as a matter of platitude, to moral facts. No more substantial commitment to moral realism is required, nor is any implied.[12] Thus a defense of ethical explanations is neither necessary for moral truth nor sufficient for establishing a robust form of moral realism.

2. *Slavery*

My argument that the injustice of slavery contributed to its demise depends on several background ideas about slavery and slave interests. Briefly summarized, I propose that slavery is a distinctive distribution of de facto power, that this distribution was reproduced through both force and "consent," and that patterns in the use of force and strategies for inducing consent provide a basis for attributing to slaves basic interests in material well-being, autonomy, and dignity. These ideas are not uncontroversial, and I am unable here to defend them properly. But I need to say something about them—about slavery as a framework, and slaves as agents—both to explain the terms of the argument, and to make it plausible.

First, however, a few observations on the complexity of the historical problem. The problem is to explain the demise of slavery: the nearly complete and apparently stable elimination of a social relation of broad historical reach and importance. Any such explanation must be attentive to the variety of circumstances in which slavery has existed, the distinctive features of different slaveries, and the diverse paths to its elimination.

Slavery was not restricted to any religious group. Although Islamic law condemned the enslavement of fellow believers, this stricture was often violated and provided no bar to enslaving non-believers.[13] And whereas slavery was construed in Islamic law as a means of conversion, and manumission encouraged as an act of piety, no condemnation of the general

---

12. Here I follow Crispin Wright's discussion of moral explanations and minimalism in *Truth and Objectivity*, chap. 5.

13. For discussion of this practice, see Orlando Patterson, *Slavery and Social Death* (Cambridge, MA: Harvard University Press, 1982); Paul Lovejoy, "Slavery in the Sokoto Caliphate," in Paul Lovejoy, ed., *The Ideology of Slavery in Africa* (Beverly Hills, CA: Sage, 1981), 211. But enslavement of free Muslims could have a significant cost. The *jihad* that consolidated the Sokoto caliphate in the central Sudan in the first half of the nineteenth century resulted in part from the enslavement of free Muslims. See Lovejoy, "Problems of Slave Control in the Sokoto Caliphate," in Paul Lovejoy, ed., *Africans in Bondage: Studies in Slavery and the Slave Trade* (Madison: University of Wisconsin Press, 1986), 245.

practice of slavery was implied or suggested by that encouragement.[14] Similar accommodations to the practice of slavery were found in the other major salvation religions as well.[15] Nor, of course, was this sanctioning restricted to monotheistic religions.[16]

Slaves were not restricted to any particular position in the division of labor—not, for example, to the unskilled gang labor associated with New World plantations, Roman latifundia, or Athenian silver mines. Even in the U.S. case, some slaves performed some skilled labor.[17] The labor on East African clove plantations was more skilled than the labor on sugar and cotton plantations.[18] And in other cases—for example, ancient Roman and Athenian slavery—skilled slaves were not at all uncommon.

Furthermore, slaves have not served simply as productive laborers. Together with freedmen, they were the highest officials (apart from the emperor) in late imperial Rome. They provided the bulk of the police in Athens (the 300 Scythian archers).[19] And in a wide variety of Islamic states, slaves played a significant military role.[20] Slaves served as concubines, and

14. Allan G. B. Fisher and Humphrey J. Fisher, *Slavery and Muslim Society in Africa: The Institution in Saharan and Sudanic Africa and the Trans-Saharan Trade* (London: C. Hurt and Co., 1970), 43–51.

15. David Brion Davis, *The Problem of Slavery in Western Culture* (Ithaca: Cornell University Press, 1966), chaps. 3, 4.

16. On Greek and Roman religious sanctions of slavery, see Patterson, *Slavery and Social Death*, 66–76.

17. Fogel and Engerman estimated that more than 26 percent of male slaves were craftsmen, semi-skilled workers, or "professional-managerial" workers. Robert W. Fogel and Stanley L. Engerman, *Time on the Cross*, 2 vols. (Boston: Little, Brown, 1974), 38–41. For doubts about the estimate, see Paul David, Herbert Gutman, Richard Sutch, Peter Temin, Gavin Wright, *Reckoning with Slavery* (New York: Oxford University Press, 1976), 344. Genovese's account of drivers and skilled workers gives no percentages, and importantly emphasizes both the declining numbers of skilled slaves in the nineteenth century and the prominence of the skilled among runaways: "all the measures encouraging their economic performance had the disadvantage of making them considerably less servile than slaves were supposed to be." Eugene D. Genovese, *Roll, Jordan, Roll* (New York: Pantheon, 1974), 393, and in general 327–398; on the tensions between skill and servility see Stefano Fenoaltea, "Slavery and Supervision in Comparative Perspective: A Model," *Journal of Economic History* 44, 3 (September 1984): 635–668.

18. Frederick Cooper, *Plantation Slavery on the East Coast of Africa* (New Haven: Yale University Press, 1977), 157–159.

19. Moses Finley, *Economy and Society in Ancient Greece* (Harmondsworth, UK: Penguin, 1983), 122.

20. For discussion of the military role of slaves, see Patterson, *Slavery and Social Death*, 308, and, in general, chap. 11.

in the more "open" forms of slavery associated with Africa, such concubines played an important role in sustaining the free population.[21]

Nor was slavery restricted by historical period, region, climate, or racial or ethnic group. In short, slavery is a "ubiquitous" historical presence.[22]

Because of this diversity of slaveries, it is hard to provide a useful, general characterization of slavery, and to present a general account of its demise. A general characterization must be sensitive to the significant variations across forms of slavery, and an explanation of its elimination must account for the fact that a very widespread social phenomenon, widely believed to be reasonable and natural, and (less widely but still) commonly thought to be just, came to be abolished and morally condemned. A full explanation of the demise of slavery (if a "full" explanation makes sense) would need to be much more attentive to historical context than I can be—to the ways that the end of imperial expansion, taxes imposed by the Roman state, barbarian invasions, and the uncertain position of the coloni contributed to the decline of slavery in the late Roman Empire; to the role of evangelicals, Quakers, and the economic interests of the British during the Napoleonic Wars in abolishing the slave trade in the early nineteenth century; to the interaction between that abolition and the eventual elimination of New World plantation slavery; to the links between the peculiari-

21. See Igor Kopytoff and Suzanne Miers, "African Slavery as an Institution of Marginality," in Suzanne Miers and Igor Kopytoff, eds., *Slavery in Africa: Historical and Anthropological Perspectives* (Madison: University of Wisconsin Press, 1977), 30–39, 61–66; James Watson, ed., *Asian and African Systems of Slavery* (Berkeley: University of California Press, 1980), 9–13; Patterson, *Slavery and Social Death*, 137–138. On the diversity of social roles of slaves in the African context in particular, see Kopytoff and Miers, "African Slavery," 55–59. Apart from their role in production and reproduction, slaves were "domestics, messengers, trading agents, retailers, and experts in literacy, as retainers at the courts of rulers and high officials, as officers of state, bureaucrats, and warriors and military commanders, whose duties included the capture of others" (55–56). For criticisms of this (over)emphasis on non-economic uses of slaves in the African context, see Martin Klein, "Review Article: The Study of Slavery in Africa," *Journal of African History* 19, 4 (1978): 606–607; Frederick Cooper, "Review Article: The Problem of Slavery in African Studies," *Journal of African History* 20, 1 (1979): 106–107; and Paul Lovejoy, *Transformations in Slavery: A History of Slavery in Africa* (Cambridge: Cambridge University Press, 1983), esp. chaps. 1, 12. For an illuminating discussion of the remarkable phenomenon of palatine slavery, see Patterson, *Slavery and Social Death*, chap. 11.

22. Patterson, *Slavery and Social Death*, vii. For detailed accounts of the extent of slavery, see H. J. Nieboer, *Slavery as an Industrial System*, 2nd ed. (New York: Burt Franklin, 1910 [1971 reprint]), 41–166; Patterson, *Slavery and Social Death*, esp. appendices B and C; Jack Goody, "Slavery in Time and Space," in James Watson, ed., *Asian and African Systems of Slavery* (Berkeley: University of California Press, 1980), 16–42.

ties of U.S. political history and the defeat of Southern plantation slavery; and to the complicated ties between Western colonialism and the abolition of indigenous African slavery.

That said, I will be assuming here that the great diversity of slaveries neither precludes an informative general characterization of slavery and its injustice (Theses 1 and 2), nor undermines the plausibility of the claim (in Thesis Three) that slavery faces general problems of viability, nor defeats the claim (in Thesis Four) that those general problems are linked to the injustice of slavery.

Power

Slavery is sometimes said to be a condition in which some human beings are treated as things lacking a will of their own, as extensions of the will of others, or in which some human beings are treated as the property of others. Both accounts capture something important, but both are misleading, and in similar ways.

According to the "extension of will" conception, a slave is an instrument (instrumentum vocale, Varro said) that lacks a capacity for deliberate, independent action. This conception conforms to a standard interpretation and justification of slavery in slave societies.[23] And this interpretation and justification are both important to understanding the phenomenon of slavery. But the interpretation is also a badly distorted representation of slaves and their conditions. One of the great challenges in understanding slavery and its evolution is to appreciate the ways in which slaves exercised their will and contributed as agents to their own history under highly constrained circumstances, where one of the many constraints upon them was precisely the denial in the public culture of their capacity for deliberate action.

The ownership conception faces a parallel difficulty. Ownership is a legal notion. Focusing on the legal category directs our attention to the interpretation of the position of slaves in law and customary morality—to legal and cultural representations of the nature of slaves and their social position—and away from the relations of power between slaves and masters that are sustained in part by those interpretations. But for the purposes of investigating the evolution and demise of slavery, we need a characterization of the slave condition that is more attentive to relations of

---

23. See, for example, Aristotle, *Politics*, trans. Benjamin Jowett, in *The Complete Works of Aristotle*, ed. Jonathan Barnes, vol. 2 (Princeton: Princeton University Press, 1984), 1254b20ff.

power between human beings than it is to the (frequently misleading) representation of those relations in legal, moral, and religious ideas in societies with slavery.

I propose, then, that slavery is best understood in terms of the notion of de facto power, rather than in terms of familiar cultural or legal representations of slaves—as extensions of the will of masters, or as property.[24] To be specific: a slave is, in the first instance, someone largely lacking the power to dispose of his or her physical and mental powers, including the capacity to produce and control the body more generally (extending to sexuality and reproduction); the power to dispose of the means of production; the power to select a place of residence; the power to associate with others and establish stable bonds; the power to decide on the manner in which one's children will be raised; and the (political) power to fix the rules governing the affairs of the state in which one resides. Slaves are distinguished from of other groups—helots, serfs, sharecroppers, poor but propertied peasants, and property-less proletarians—by the combination of the breadth and the depth of the limits on their powers. The limits extend over all aspects of life, the restrictions cut deeply into each aspect, and there is a corresponding breadth and depth to the powers that others have over them.

When I say that these powers of slaves were greatly confined, I mean to indicate that there were a wide range of activities (including those using the powers just enumerated) in which slaves were required to engage if the master sought to require them (e.g., sexual intercourse); or were de facto prevented from pursuing if their master wished to prevent them; or, if given some possibility of pursuing activities against the will of their master (e.g., selecting a place of residence by running away, withdrawing labor power by feigning illness, fixing the rules of association by establishing an

24. For general discussions of the nature of slavery see de Ste. Croix, *Class Struggle in the Ancient Greek World*, esp. 135, where he discusses the definition of slavery in the 1926 Slavery Convention organized by the League of Nations; Nieboer, *Slavery as an Industrial System*, part I, chap. 1; Patterson, *Slavery and Social Death*, chaps. 1–3; Dockès, *Medieval Slavery*, 4–8; Moses Finley, *Ancient Slavery and Modern Ideology* (Harmondsworth, UK: Penguin, 1980), chap. 2; Finley, *Economy and Society in Ancient Greece*, chaps. 6–9; Kopytoff and Miers, "African Slavery," 3–81; James Watson, "Slavery as an Institution: Open and Closed Systems," in James Watson, ed., *Asian and African Systems of Slavery* (Berkeley: University of California Press, 1980); Paul Lovejoy, *Transformations in Slavery: A History of Slavery in Africa* (Cambridge: Cambridge University Press, 1983), chap. 1; James Oakes, *Slavery and Freedom: An Interpretation of the Old South* (New York: Alfred Knopf, 1990), chap. 1. The conception of slavery I present in the text draws as well on the discussion of "property relations" in G. A. Cohen, *Karl Marx's Theory of History: A Defense* (Princeton: Princeton University Press, 1978), 219–222.

independent "maroon" community, or selecting a sexual partner by saying "no"), faced a small likelihood of success and very great costs of failure (public humiliation, corporal punishment, death). According to this conception of slavery, focused on de facto power, some individuals who were legally slaves were not actually slaves, because the relations of power did not sustain the category. But this feature strikes me as an advantage of the view, and as a natural extension of common usage. Thus consider a remark made by a federal judge presiding at a state constitutional convention in New Orleans in 1864: "If you think that slavery exists, go out in the streets and see if you can get your slave to obey you."[25]

But slaves were not entirely powerless—mere extensions and instruments of another's will.[26] To be sure, their power was highly confined, dangerous to exercise, and nearly always insufficient to overturn slavery itself. But slaves did not, as a general matter, lack all forms of power, and sometimes they asserted their power to improve their conditions and shape the terms of order within the framework of slavery.[27] As an ex-slave and blacksmith named J. W. Lindsay put it in an 1863 interview with the Freedman's Inquiry Commission, "Of course, they treated me pretty well, for the reason that I would not allow them to treat me in any other way. If they attempted to use any barbarity, I would walk off before their faces."[28] Lindsay's remark is almost certainly

25. Cited in Eric Foner, *Reconstruction: America's Unfinished Revolution, 1863–1877* (New York: Harper & Row, 1988), 49.

26. Keith Bradley says, "To live in slavery . . . was to be utterly disempowered." He backs this assertion with observations about the absence of slave rights and master obligations, apparently running together the relations of power with legal-cultural representations. See Bradley, *Slavery and Society*, 27.

27. Hobbes offers an extreme version of the powerlessness conception, characterizing a slave as a captive who is "kept in prison or bonds." Thomas Hobbes, *Leviathan* (Harmondsworth, UK: Penguin, 1968), 255. Unable to run away if they desire to, slaves lack all "corporal liberty," and therefore nothing they do can be construed as giving consent or undertaking an obligation to obey. Variants of this view are quite common. Although Adam Smith and Karl Marx (see note 80 below) did not think that slaves lacked all corporal liberty, they did think (wrongly) that slaves were "condemned to be revolutionary"—that there was nothing that they could do to improve their conditions within the framework of slavery. In modern literature on slavery, Stanley Elkins represented slaves in the United States (in contrast with Latin America) as virtually powerless—comparing plantations with Nazi concentration camps—and, as having developed, in consequence of their powerlessness, a "Sambo" personality. For critical discussion, see, for example, Eugene D. Genovese, "Rebelliousness and Docility in the Negro Slave: A Critique of the Elkins Thesis," *Civil War History* 13 (1967): 293–314; and George M. Frederickson and Christopher Lasch, "Resistance to Slavery," *Civil War History* 13 (1967): 315–329. The Elkins Thesis provoked a generation of creative refutation.

28. Blassingame, *Slave Testimony*, 397.

an exaggeration, and certainly not a plausible generalization. Still, it captures a truth put more subtly by Harriet Jacobs, who said: "My master had power and law on his side; I had a determined will. There is might in each."[29]

The power of slaves was most clearly in evidence in the range of activities commonly grouped together as "slave resistance."[30]

First, there were a variety of forms of resistance that could be pursued individually without directly threatening the institution of slavery, including "taking" from masters (masters called it "stealing"[31]); lying; feigning illness; slowing down the pace of work; damaging tools and animals; self-mutilating; committing suicide, infanticide, abortion, or arson; murdering the master; and running away. Running away was particularly important as a display of power. It showed the costs that slaves could impose on masters, who lost a considerable capital investment and needed to increase their investment in enforcement. Moreover, running away could be a collective enterprise, sometimes indistinguishable in its effects on the sustainability of slavery from rebellions, as in the case of the massive exoduses of slaves (especially plantation slaves) in French West Africa beginning in 1895,[32] or in the massive fleeing of so-called contraband slaves

---

29. Cited in Elizabeth Fox-Genovese, *Within the Plantation Household: Black and White Women of the Old South* (Chapel Hill: University of North Carolina Press, 1988), 290.

30. For discussion, see Keith R. Bradley, *Slavery and Rebellion in the Roman World 140 B.C.– 70 B.C.* (Bloomington: Indiana University Press, 1989); Pierre Dockès, *Medieval Slavery and Liberation*, trans. Arthur Goldhammer (Chicago: University of Chicago Press, 1982), 210–211; Orlando Patterson, *The Sociology of Slavery: An Analysis of the Origins, Development and Structure of Negro Slave Society in Jamaica* (London: MacGibbon and Kee, 1967), chap. 9; Raymond A. Bauer and Alice H. Bauer, "Day to Day Resistance to Slavery," *Journal of Negro History* 27 (October 1942): 388–419; Genovese *Roll, Jordan, Roll*, book 4; Eugene D. Genovese, *From Rebellion to Revolution: Afro-American Slave Revolts in the Making of the New World* (New York: Vintage, 1979); Mary Karasch, *Slave Life in Rio de Janeiro 1808–1850* (Princeton: Princeton University Press, 1987), chap. 10; Barbara Bush, *Slave Women in Caribbean Society 1650–1838* (Kingston: Heineman Publishers, 1990), chap. 5; Isaac Mendelsohn, *Slavery in the Ancient Near East* (New York: Oxford University Press, 1949), 66, 121; Ruth Mazo Karra, *Slavery and Society in Medieval Scandinavia* (New Haven: Yale University Press, 1988), 123–127; Frederick Cooper, *Plantation Slavery on the East Coast of Africa*, 200–210; Richard Roberts and Martin A. Klein, "The Banamba Slave Exodus of 1905 and the Decline of Slavery in the Western Sudan," *Journal of African History* 21 (1980): 375–394; Paul Lovejoy, *Transformations in Slavery: A History of Slavery in Africa* (Cambridge: Cambridge University Press, 1983), chap. 11; Paul Lovejoy, ed., *Africans in Bondage: Studies in Slavery and the Slave Trade* (Madison: University of Wisconsin Press, 1986); Suzanne Miers and Richard Roberts, eds., *The End of Slavery in Africa* (Madison: University of Wisconsin Press, 1988), chaps. 3, 6, 9, 13. For some skeptical remarks, see Finley, *Ancient Slavery and Modern Ideology*, 111–116.

31. On stealing and resistance, see Genovese, *Roll, Jordan, Roll*, 599–612.

32. See Roberts and Klein, "Banamba Slave Exodus"; Lovejoy, *Transformations*, 266ff. For doubts about the extent of desertions in the period of African abolition, see Richard Roberts

during the American Civil War, or in the flight of more than 20,000 slaves from Deceleia in the final decade of the Peloponnesian War.

A second form of resistance—less frequent, but also more collective and threatening—was the widespread phenomenon of "maroon" communities.[33] Established by runaway slaves, some maroon communities were quite small—the Hanglip community near Cape Town; the watoro communities on the Swahili coast; the various Western African cases of maroon activity in the eighteenth and nineteenth centuries; and the many maroon colonies in the southern United States (particularly in the eighteenth century), some based on Indian-black alliances. Others were large-scale and long-standing—including the Jamaican communities established in the 1650s, consolidated through the first Maroon War of 1725–1740 and recognized by a treaty with the British in 1738, and several of the Brazilian quilombos, in particular the quilombo of Palmares, an African state in Pernambuco and Alagoas, which lasted for nearly a century (from c. 1605 to 1695), included (on some estimates) as many as 20,000–30,000 slaves, and fought off some eighteen Dutch and Portuguese expeditions over a period of more than fifty years.

Finally, most dramatically, there were slave revolts: three major rebellions in Italy and Sicily between 140 and 70 B.C., the first of which involved some 200,000 rebels, and the last (led by Spartacus in 73–71 B.C.) involving as many as 150,000 rebels; the fourteen-year war of the Zanj against the Abassid Empire in the mid-ninth century; the one significant slave rebellion per decade in the Guineas in the eighteenth and early nineteenth centuries (one of which involved some 10,000–20,000 slaves); and the revolution in Saint Dominique stimulated by the French Revolution.[34]

---

and Suzanne Miers, "The End of Slavery in Africa," in Suzanne Miers and Richard Roberts, eds., *The End of Slavery in Africa* (Madison: University of Wisconsin Press, 1988), 27–33.

33. On maroon activity, see Patterson, *Sociology of Slavery*, 266–273; Cooper, *Plantation Slavery*, 200–210; Fisher and Fisher, *Slavery and Muslim Society in Africa*, 94; and Genovese, *From Rebellion to Revolution*, chap. 2.

34. For discussions of these and other slave rebellions see C. L. R. James, *The Black Jacobins: Toussaint L'Ouverture and the San Domingo Revolution* (New York: Random House, 1963); Genovese, *Roll, Jordan, Roll*, 587–598; Genovese, *From Rebellion to Revolution*; John W. Blassingame, *The Slave Community: Plantation Life in the Antebellum South*, 2nd ed. (New York: Oxford University Press, 1979), 125–131; David Brion Davis, *Slavery and Human Progress* (Oxford: Oxford University Press, 1984), 5–8; Moses Finley, *The Ancient Economy* (Berkeley: University of California Press, 1973), 89, 92; P. A. Brunt, *Social Conflicts in the Roman Republic* (New York: Norton, 1971), 114–115; Dockès, *Medieval Slavery*, chap. 4; Patterson, *Sociology of Slavery*, 266–273; Bradley, *Slavery and Rebellion*. For references on and discussion

These examples underscore the limits of the extension-of-will and owner-ship conceptions of slavery. To appreciate the power of slaves we must distinguish real from legal disabilities and from the public interpretation of those disabilities. Slaves suffered from legal disabilities, of course, which both codified and contributed to their lack of power. But their general lack of legally codified or publicly acknowledged rights also exaggerated their real situation. Thus slaves were commonly able to do what the law denied them the right to do.

For example, slave "marriages" were not recognized at law, but more or less stable unions were part of the practice of virtually all slave societies.[35] And although slaves had no legal right to control the pace of their work, they had, as a general matter, some power—highly qualified, limited, and always dangerous to exercise—to help to shape it through various forms of resistance and threats of resistance. Whereas the actual terms of association among slaves themselves and between slaves and masters reflected the need to find a stable accommodation between agents with vastly different powers, then, the legal and moral representation of those relations denied that need, emphasizing instead the unilateral dictation of terms and conditions by masters and the absence of a capacity for independent action on the part of slaves.

In response to these points about the power of slaves, it might be objected that slave marriages and efforts by slaves to control the pace of their work provide no evidence about their power. Underlying the objection is the correct observation that power is a matter of capability, not success; someone who is powerless may still have the remarkably good fortune of getting everything she wants. Power is about the ability to advance one's interests even in the face of opposition. So, the objection says, masters may sometimes have permitted slaves to establish families or control the pace of their work. But had the masters decided otherwise, they would have been able to get their way.

---

of African cases, see Cooper, *Plantation Slavery*, 202–203; Cooper, "Review Article: The Problem of Slavery in African Studies," 103–125; Roberts and Klein, "Banamba Slave Exodus"; Lovejoy, *Transformations in Slavery*.

35. See Patterson, *Slavery and Social Death*, 186: "In 97 percent of the societies falling in the sample of world cultures, masters recognized the unions of slaves. In not a single case, however, did such recognition imply custodial powers over children." On the U.S. case, see Genovese, *Roll, Jordan, Roll*, 433–535; Herbert Gutman, *The Black Family in Slavery and Freedom, 1750–1925* (New York: Vintage, 1977).

For example, referring to slave dealers in Rio de Janeiro, Karasch says "besides feeding the Africans, treating their diseases, and vaccinating them, dealers attempted to improve their mental health and prevent suicides."[36] In so doing, they were not responding to the power of slaves, but rather were seeking to improve slave conditions in the face of threats to the value of their human "property." Slaves, we can assume, wanted the medical treatment, but the treatment was not a result of their power. More generally, Moses Finley argues, "The failure of any individual slaveowner to exercise all his rights over his slave-property was always a unilateral act on his part, never binding, *always revocable*. That is a critical fact [emphasis added]. So is its reverse, the equally unilateral, always revocable grant by a slaveowner of a specific privilege or benevolence." By way of illustration, he points out that slaveowners "frequently offered slaves the incentive of eventual manumission through various arrangements which automatically brought into being a chain of behavior and expectations that affected the master, too. Although in law *and in fact* [emphasis added] he could always revoke the offer, the material gains to be derived from slavery would have been sharply reduced if such arrangements were not as a rule honored."[37]

Finley's point about revocability—"he could always revoke the offer"— seems misleading, arguably a result of conflating the de facto conditions of slaves with their conditions as represented in law and public morality. The fact that owners would, as Finley observes, have suffered losses as a consequence of violating slave expectations requires some qualification to the flat claim that masters could "in fact" revoke their offers of manumission and other grants of "privilege." Such revocations were not without costs, in part because slaves would have resisted the violation of traditional norms and expectations. For this reason, the "failure to exercise all his rights" was not simply a unilateral act on the part of the master, whatever the legal or cultural representation may have been.

It is certainly true that masters, and the legal systems that codified their advantages, characteristically represented benefits to slaves as privileges, as revocable grants, and as unilateral expressions of benevolence.[38] It is true, too, that those representations codified and helped to sustain their consider-

---

36. Karasch, *Slave Life in Rio de Janeiro*, 40.
37. Finley, *Ancient Slavery and Modern Ideology*, 74.
38. Genovese, *Roll, Jordan, Roll*, book 1.

able power. But slaves—I will return to this point later—characteristically rejected this construal, and in some cases they were able to give practical force to that rejection. All of which suggests that Hegel was onto something when he suggested that, in the end, the advantage in self-consciousness belonged to slaves, not masters.

Force and Consent

Premising this conception of slavery as a distinctive form of power, we come now to the question: How was slavery reproduced?

First, through force. Force plays a central role in the initial enslavement of individuals and groups. Voluntary enslavement is quite rare in the history of slavery. War and kidnapping, in contrast, are among the most familiar means for initially enslaving non-slave populations, although most slaves were born into the condition.[39] Furthermore, masters themselves, or their agents (drivers, overseers, etc.) commonly deployed force—in particular, the force of the lash[40]—directly against slaves. Throughout antiquity, slaves alone were subject to corporal punishment, and they were permitted to give evidence only under torture.[41] Greek and Roman slave owners had the right to punish and torture their own slaves for offenses committed against the master and on his property.[42] And Orlando Patterson estimates that in 75 percent of slave societies, masters received either negligible or mild punishment for killing slaves.[43]

But the use of force against slaves was not simply a common feature of slavery. According to a seventeenth-century Brazilian saying, "Whoever wants to profit from his Blacks must maintain them, make them work well, and beat them even better; without this there will be no service or gain."[44] Force, that is, was an essential feature whose role can be explained in terms of the basic properties of slavery.

39. See Patterson, *Slavery and Social Death*, chaps. 4, 5 for discussion of the frequency of different forms of enslavement.

40. Thus Patterson says "there is no known slaveholding society where the whip was not considered an indispensable instrument." *Slavery and Social Death*, 4. For some vivid details, see Bradley, *Slavery and Society*, 165–173, and Karasch, *Slave Life in Rio de Janeiro*, 113–125.

41. Finley, *Ancient Slavery and Modern Ideology*, 93–94; Thomas Wiedemann, *Greek and Roman Slavery* (Baltimore: Johns Hopkins University Press, 1981), 74, 166–169.

42. Edward Peters, *Torture* (Oxford: Blackwell, 1985), 18ff.

43. Patterson, *Slavery and Social Death*, 193.

44. Cited in Stuart B. Schwartz, *Sugar Plantations in the Formation of Brazilian Society: Bahia, 1550–1835* (Cambridge: Cambridge University Press, 1985), 133.

To see how explanation goes, let us distinguish symbolic, distributive, and productive uses of force. Force is used symbolically when masters use it to exemplify or express the public understanding of slaves as fully subordinate to them, analogous to the practice of giving slaves new names or requiring them to wear special forms of clothing. I will put this symbolic use to the side here, principally because we are not able to understand the central role of violence in slave systems, or the patterns in the use of violence against slaves, in terms of the role of force as a symbol of domination and emblem of servitude.

Force is used distributively when it is deployed to ensure a favorable distribution of the benefits of social order—to ensure, that is, a greater share of the benefits than one would be able to secure through bargaining on equal terms. The importance of the distributive use of force can be underscored by noting that slavery commonly emerges under conditions of labor scarcity.[45] With labor relatively scarce, owners of land and other non-human resources would face a relatively unfavorable bargaining position, if they had to bargain. As a Dr. Collins, a planter in the West Indies, wrote in an 1811 treatise, "the sugar colonies, in their present state of slender population, can only be wrought by slaves, or by persons so much at our command, as to be obliged to labor whether they will or not." Drawing the natural consequence about the use of force as a way to ensure that slaves fulfill their obligations, he says, "Where slavery is established, and the proportion of slaves outnumbers their masters ten to one, terror must operate to keep them in subjection, and terror can only be produced by occasional examples of severity."[46]

But the distributive use, too, does not explain the patterns in the use of force in different slave systems, in particular the especially high levels of force used against slaves who are involved in plantation agriculture and mining. This pattern suggests that force did not serve simply to symbolize or preserve inequalities of power, but was also deployed as a means of eliciting effort. I refer to this as "the productive use of force." Force is used productively, then, when it is employed to provide incentives to increase

---

45. For discussion of this "Nieboer-Domar hypothesis," see Evsey D. Domar, "The Causes of Slavery or Serfdom: A Hypothesis," *Journal of Economic History* 30, 1 (March 1970): 18–32.

46. Dr. Collins, *Practical Rules for the Managment and Medical Treatment of Negro Slaves in the Sugar Colonies* (London: J. Barfield, 1811), 33, 36.

the level of output (for example, by increasing labor intensity), rather than simply to ensure a favorable distribution of a fixed output.

The productive use has a familiar economic rationale. Limited in their power, slaves drew limited benefits from social cooperation, and, since they did not have to sell their labor to gain their subsistence, such benefits as they did receive were importantly independent from their activity. So masters faced problems in motivating slaves to work. Force was one solution (we will come to the others). As Adam Smith put it, "A person who can acquire no property, can have no other interest but to eat as much, and to labor as little as possible. Whatever work he does beyond what is sufficient to purchase his own maintenance, can be squeezed out of him by violence only, and not by any interest of his own."[47] Smith's contention about "violence only" is overstated, in ways that will become clear when I discuss the use of positive incentives. But it does capture an important problem for masters, and provides a good characterization of the basis of the productive use of force.

Appreciating the scope and limits of the productive use of force requires attention to the costs (to masters) of using force as distinct from other incentives.[48] It might require a staff of overseers, or some other diversion of resources from more productive uses, and might cause damage to the human beings one is seeking to "motivate." Those costs would be worth incurring, however, if they were low relative to the benefits generated by the use of force.

Two conditions help to produce such a violence-generating cost-benefit structure. First, the costs of enforcement depend in part on the nature of the activities being enforced. And the costs of using force are likely to be relatively low when—as in important areas of agriculture and mining—performance is easy to monitor (the tasks are straightforward, can be performed in groups or gangs, and have easily measurable outcomes), and the work is sufficiently distasteful that considerable material incentives would be required to motivate its performance.

47. Smith, *The Wealth of Nations*, 365.

48. The discussion that follows draws on Stefano Fenoaltea, "Slavery and Supervision in Comparative Perspective: A Model," *Journal of Economic History* 44, 3 (September 1984): 635–668; also Ronald Findlay, "Slavery, Incentives, and Manumission: A Theoretical Model," *Journal of Political Economy* 83, 5 (1975): 923–933; Giorgio Canarella and John A. Tomaske, "The Optimal Utilization of Slaves," *The Journal of Economic History* 35 (September 1975): 621–629.

The benefit side depends on the responsiveness of slaves to force as against compensation. Force will be encouraged if slaves have a "target" income beyond which they are relatively unresponsive to further material incentives, and if the tasks they are expected to perform require intensive effort rather than high levels of skill and attention. The reason is that intensive effort can plausibly be motivated by threats of pain rather than promises of reward.

This cost-benefit structure is characteristic of work in agriculture and mining. And, as I indicated, we do see force playing an especially central role in slavery when slaves are integrated into the economy, more particularly when they work in mines and on plantations (more so with cotton than tobacco), and, in the case of sugar, more in planting and harvesting cane than in milling it.[49] Under such circumstances, as Dr. Collins put it, "a system of remuneration alone is inadequate, for the reward must ever be incommensurate to the service, where labour is misery, and rest, happiness."[50] In contrast, we find other means to elicit effort from slaves who were more skilled, or located in urban settings.

The maintenance of slavery could not, then, proceed through force alone.[51] Masters wanted to elicit greater effort; slaves typically faced impossible odds if they sought their own emancipation. The result was superficially more consensual forms of servitude. Abstracting from endless varieties of compromise and accommodation, varying across time and place, we can distinguish two broad ways to make servitude (superficially) more voluntary.

First, masters deployed positive incentives—what Dockès has called the "paraphernalia of 'voluntary' servitude"[52]—including material rewards, authority, autonomy, family security, and manumission.

The importance of the strategic use of material incentives is a common theme in ancient and modern treatises on slave management. Chief among the material incentives was the peculium, a (legally) temporary

---

49. Writing about Bahian sugar plantations, for example, Schwartz claims that none of the "commentators on the engenho operations speaks of drivers or the whip being used inside the fabrica." See *Sugar Plantations*, 154, and the subsequent discussion of the need for incentives, 155–159.

50. Collins, *Practical Rules*, 170.

51. For a valuable summary of the evolving literature on this issue in the case of American slavery, see Robert W. Fogel, *Without Consent or Contract: The Rise and Fall of American Slavery* (New York: Norton, 1989), chap. 6.

52. Dockès, *Medieval Slavery*, 208.

grant to a slave of the power to use and enjoy a certain portion of the master's property.[53] A key feature of the peculium was that it could be used to purchase liberty. More broadly, the peculium enabled slaves to improve their material conditions within the confines of slavery and provided an incentive for diligence within those limits. Other forms of material incentive were also used to elicit more willing subordination. In certain periods in the United States, for example, slaves had and were encouraged to cultivate their own plots (so-called kitchen gardens), paralleling the Caribbean practice of providing "provision grounds." Genovese quotes an overseer making the strategic case for permitting slaves to pursue private cultivation: "Every means are used to encourage them, and impress on their minds the advantage of holding property, and the disgrace attached to idleness. Surely, if industrious for themselves, they will be so for their masters, and no Negro, with a well-stocked poultry house, a small crop advancing, a canoe partly finished, or a few tubs unsold, all of which he calculates soon to enjoy, will ever run away. In ten years I have lost by absconding, forty-seven days, out of nearly six hundred Negroes."[54] Similarly, a Brazilian advice book instructs planters in Rio de Janeiro that: "Their gardens and what they produce in them cause them to acquire a certain love of country, distract them a bit from slavery,

53. I am using the term "peculium" here to refer to any arrangement in which a slave is granted the power to use and enjoy property. The term originates in the Roman law of persons, according to which only the *paterfamilias* could own any property. Fathers would thus permit their sons the use and enjoyment of some of their property, that is, grant them a peculium. At law the peculium remained the property of the father; he could legally take it back at his pleasure, and it reverted to the father's estate upon his death. The same arrangement was used with slaves as well, and it provided the basis for the accumulation of personal holdings by slaves and also for the conduct by slaves of the businesses of their masters. With slaves, as well as children, the legal status of the peculium was at best an imperfect guide to the practices. Thus the normal expectation was that the peculium would not be withdrawn and that it would remain in the hands of the grantee after the death of the owner. For discussion of the Roman law background see Barry Nicholas, *An Introduction to Roman Law* (Oxford: Oxford University Press, 1962), 68–71. On the use of the peculium, see Patterson, *Slavery and Social Death*, 182–186 (emphasizing its role as an incentive); Keith Hopkins, *Conquerors and Slaves* (Cambridge: Cambridge University Press, 1978), 126; Mendelsohn, *Slavery in the Ancient Near East*, 66–74; Finley, *The Ancient Economy*, 64–65.

54. Genovese, *Roll, Jordan, Roll*, 539. On private cultivation as an incentive in other settings, see Rebecca Scott, *Slave Emancipation in Cuba: The Transition to Free Labor, 1860–1899* (Princeton: Princeton University Press, 1985), 15; John Edwin Mason, "Fortunate Slaves and Artful Masters: Labor Relations in the Rural Cape Colony during the Era of Emancipation, ca. 1825–1838," in *Slavery in South Africa: Captive Labor on the Dutch Frontier*, ed. Elizabeth A. Eldredge and Fred Morton (Boulder, CO: Westview Press, 1994), 67–91.

and delude them into believing they have a small right to property. . . . Extreme discomfort dries up their hearts, hardens them, and inclines them to evil."[55]

It was also not uncommon for slaves to fill positions of authority and perform skilled labor, although the frequency of this practice varied across systems. It was, for example, commonplace in Rome, but less typical in the United States. When slaves did fill such positions, they characteristically received material benefits and the greater autonomy that is associated with skilled labor and positions of authority. Autonomy, in the form of time free from labor, for example, was distributed with similar aims. A West Indian planter summarized this strategy: "The best way of rewarding them . . . is to assign them a task, regulated by [a] given quantity, and to require as much from them every day, leaving them to effect it at what hours they please, and let them enjoy to their own use, whatever time they do it in less. This will encourage every negro to make his utmost exertion, in consequence of which, the work of twelve hours will be dispatched in ten, and with much more satisfaction to themselves."[56]

Provision grounds and kitchen gardens also provided greater autonomy; and holidays played a similar role in motivating slave cooperation by ensuring greater autonomy. Rome had at least one holiday exclusively for slaves, and Frederick Douglass said that holidays were among the "most effective means in the hands of the slaveholder in keeping down the spirit of insurrection. . . . The holidays serve as conductors or safety valves, to carry off the rebellious spirit of enslaved humanity." Emphasizing the role of holidays as an incentive, he says that they are "part and parcel of the gross fraud, wrong, and inhumanity of slavery. They are professedly a custom established by the benevolence of the slaveholders; but I undertake to say that, it is the result of selfishness. . . . They do not give the slaves this time because they would not like to have their work during its continuance, but because they know it would be unsafe to deprive them of it."[57]

Masters also sometimes permitted and even encouraged more stable and independent slave families. They did so in part with the expectation

55. Cited in Robert Conrad, *Children of God's Fire: A Documentary History of Black Slavery in Brazil* (Princeton: Princeton University Press, 1983), 78.

56. Collins, *Practical Rules*, 152.

57. Frederick Douglass, *Narrative of the Life of Frederick Douglass, An American Slave*, in Henry Louis Gates Jr., ed., *The Classic Slave Narratives* (New York: Signet, 1987), 300.

that greater stability would encourage a biologically reproductive slave population, of particular importance in the absence of a slave trade, and in part because family ties would dampen enthusiasm for resistance or rebellion. Thus a Peripatetic treatise on household management urges that "one ought to bind slaves to one's service by letting them have children."[58] Frederick Douglass underscores the force of such binding in the U.S. context: although he put the odds of successful escape from slavery at "ten chances of defeat to one of victory," Douglass thought that "thousands would escape from slavery . . . but for the strong cords of affection that bind them to their families, relatives, and friends."[59] Henry Bibb's autobiography, *Narrative of the Life and Adventures of Henry Bibb, An American Slave*, poignantly reinforces this point. He says that leaving his family was "one of the most self-denying acts of my whole life, to take leave of an affectionate wife, who stood before me on my departure, with dear little Frances in her arms, and with tears of sorrow in her eyes as she bid me a long farewell. It required all the moral courage that I was master of to suppress my feelings while taking leave of my little family."[60] Similarly, a nineteenth-century Brazilian manual on farm management encourages owners to foster slave families because "of all ties it is the bonds of family that most closely link a man to his obligations."[61]

A majority of slave systems relied as well on practices of manumission through which slaves were individually emancipated by their masters, although rates of manumission varied greatly across different slave systems.[62] The practice might take the form of self-purchase, with the slave using his or her peculium to pay for freedom (the Cuban *coartación* and Islamic *murgu* both involved gradual self-purchase). Other standard processes included the freeing of concubines, the emancipation of the chil-

58. Aristotle, *Economics*, trans. E. S. Forster, in *The Complete Works of Aristotle*, ed. Jonathan Barnes, vol. 2 (Princeton: Princeton University Press, 1984), 1344b18. This treatise was written by a member of Aristotle's school, not by Aristotle himself. See Christos Baloglou, "Hellenistic Economic Thought," in *Ancient and Medieval Economic Ideas and Concepts of Social Justice*, ed. S. Todd Lowry and Barry Gordon (Leiden: Brill, 1998), 105–106.

59. Gates, *Classic Slave Narratives*, 319; Blassingame, *Slave Community*, 198, 200.

60. Cited in Blassingame, *Slave Community*, 199.

61. Cited in Schwartz, *Sugar Plantations in the Formation of Brazilian Society*, 380.

62. See Patterson, *Slavery and Social Death*, chaps. 8–10; Hopkins, *Conquerors and Slaves*, 117–118, 126, 128, 131, 147; Cooper, *Plantation Slavery*, 242–252; Frederick Cooper, "Islam and Cultural Hegemony," in Paul Lovejoy, ed., *The Ideology of Slavery in Africa* (Beverly Hills, CA: Sage, 1981), 287–288.

dren of concubines, and the manumission of slaves as displays of piety in Islamic societies. A central motivating idea behind the practice of manumission is stated clearly in a Peripatetic treatise on economics: "All [slaves] ought to have a definite end (telos) in view. For it is just and beneficial to offer slaves their freedom as a prize, for they are willing to work when a prize is set before them and a limit of time is defined."[63] Aristotle, too, notes in the *Politics* that "it is expedient that liberty should always be held out to [slaves] as the reward of their services."[64]

Considering Aristotle's official views about slavery, this strategy of holding out manumission as a long-term reward is puzzling. Book One of Aristotle's *Politics* tells us that some human beings are naturally slaves. The natural slaves lack the capacity for deliberation and so are appropriately subordinated to those possessed of adequate deliberative powers. More particularly, natural masters have the capacity to foresee by exercising their minds, whereas natural slaves have only the power to implement such foresight with their bodies. But to say that slaves will work willingly when they have a goal and can see the connections between present actions and the achievement of that goal suggests that slaves have greater deliberative powers and powers of foresight than this justification permits. Here we see a characteristic tension between the practices associated with slavery and its public justifications, tensions I will emphasize in my later discussion of slave interests and the injustice of slavery.

More immediately, I want to emphasize the rationality of the use of manumission as an incentive, which is indicated by patterns in the practice of manumission. In particular, manumission seems to have been an especially important prize or incentive in the case of slaves for whom pain was an implausible motivator. So although there were low rates of manumission in plantation systems, and, as a general matter, among slaves involved in mining, rates tended to be high among slaves involved in more skilled activities, presumably because the appropriate sorts of effort could not be elicited by force. Furthermore, reflecting this higher rate among more skilled slaves, we also find that rates of manumission tended to be higher among urban slaves rather than among rural slaves.

63. Aristotle, *Economics*, 1344b12–22.
64. Ibid., 1330a33ff.

Thus we see a widespread and self-conscious use of positive incentives to address the problem of motivating a relatively powerless group that is officially understood as (although apparently did not act as) an extension of the master's will and some evidence, at least in the case of manumission, of a highly discriminating use of such incentives. Although we learn something about masters from their use of these incentives, what will be more important is what we learn about slaves. But first I want to complete the picture of consent.

Alongside positive incentives, then, cultural representations of slavery as reasonable—religious and ethical representations justifying slavery—are a further factor that helps to explain more willing compliance.

Rousseau's *Social Contract* emphasizes what has come to be a commonplace of modern social theory: that the "strongest is never strong enough to be master all the time, unless he transforms force into right and obedience into duty."[65] The thought is that existing power is made more powerful by public ideas that represent it as a necessity, make a virtue of such necessity, and thereby suggest that the terms of order are an object of common consent and the subjects of that order willingly comply. It seems indisputable that slavery was sustained in part by the acceptance on the part of slaves of religious and ethical views that present their status as suitable for them and by the more willing compliance resulting from such acceptance: though vast inequalities of power typically excluded determined resistance, the phenomenology of compliance was not simply one of strategic accommodation to those inequalities. But three qualifications are equally important.

First, slaves typically did not simply embrace the dominant religious and ethical interpretations of their nature and their condition. More commonly, they either developed syncretic religious views, combining religious conceptions and practices formed prior to enslavement with distinctive interpretations of the dominant religious tradition—as in the case of Afro-Baptist conceptions of the soul,[66] or in the reported case of a reli-

65. Jean-Jacques Rousseau, *On the Social Contract, with Geneva Manuscript and Political Economy*, ed. Roger D. Masters, trans. Judith R. Masters (New York: St. Martin's Press, 1978), 48. The literature on the subject is vast. For an especially illuminating discussion, see James C. Scott, *Domination and the Arts of Resistance: Hidden Transcripts* (New Haven: Yale University Press, 1990), esp. chaps. 3, 4.

66. Mechal Sobel, *Trabelin' On: The Slave Journey to an Afro-Baptist Faith* (Princeton: Princeton University Press, 1988), 105.

gious confraternity in Salvador, Brazil, called "Confraternity of our Lady of the Good Death"[67]—or pursued dual systems of religious belief and practice, as with the simultaneous embrace by Brazilian slaves of Bantu and Yoruban cults as well as Christianity. Syncretism and dualism provided frameworks for incorporating themes favorable to the interests of slaves into slave religions.[68]

American Afro-Baptism, for example, rejected doctrines of original sin and predestination and emphasized Old Testament themes of earthly deliverance, comparing the situation and prospects of slaves with the deliverance of the Jews from bondage in Egypt.[69] Thus the Freedman's Hymn: "Shout the glad tidings o'er Egypt's Dark Sea; Jehovah has triumphed, his people are free." According to Frederick Douglass, the spirituals "breathed the prayer and complaint of souls boiling over with the bitterest anguish. Every tone was a testimony against slavery, and a prayer to God for deliverance from chains." And when slaves sang "O Canaan, sweet Canaan, I am bound for the land of Canaan," by "Canaan" they meant the North.[70] Similarly, the religious views characteristic of East African coastal slaves blended hinterland beliefs and practices with a distinctive form of Islam, which rejected the dominant conception of sharp divisions within God's creation in favor of an emphasis on the importance of love for the Prophet and possibility of attaining religious purity through that love.[71]

Second, even when slave understandings served as a basis for an accommodation to slavery, the fact that they were not fully accommodations turned them into potential sources of "internal normative criticism" and resistance. By "internal normative criticism" (sometimes called "restorationist" or "traditionalist" criticism) I mean the criticism of practices by appeal to understandings, norms, and values that are, at some level of generality, widely shared.

67. Katia M. de Queiros Mattoso, *To Be a Slave in Brazil, 1550–1888*, trans. Arthur Gold-hammer (New Brunswick, NJ: Rutgers University Press, 1986).

68. For an alternative view in the case of Cariocan slave religion—as essentially continuing flexible Central African traditions, rather than as syncretic or dualistic—see Karasch, *Slave Life in Rio de Janeiro*, chap. 9.

69. Genovese, *Roll, Jordan, Roll*, 232–255; for qualifications, see Patterson, *Slavery and Social Death*, 73–76. On the importance of deliverance in slave spirituals, see Blassingame, *Slave Community*, 141–145.

70. Douglass, *Narrative*, 263.

71. Cooper, *Plantation Slavery*, 236–242, and "Islam and Cultural Hegemony," 291–293.

So, for example, we find cases in which slaves appear to embrace the language and moral ideals of a dominant paternalistic conception of the relations between masters and slaves, thus describing and evaluating their own position on the model of relations between parents and children.[72] The practical correlates of this paternalism—what gave it experiential resonance— were the various positive incentives that I just discussed. But whereas masters would characterize their paternalist "obligations" to provide such incentives and the various actions undertaken in fulfillment of those obligations as expressions of their own benevolence, and the benefits they conferred on slaves as grants of privilege revocable at will, slaves appear to have interpreted them in terms of masters' obligations and/or slaves' rights.

Such slave interpretations served in turn as bases for resisting unilateral shifts in the traditional terms of relation between masters and slaves—for example, in Confederate states during the Civil War, or in areas of French West Africa, Coastal Guinea, and the East African coast that experienced large scale slave exoduses in the late nineteenth and early twentieth centuries.[73] Whereas masters might have taken such shifts to be legitimate revocations of privilege, the slaves took them to be infringements of obligations and violations of entitlements. Similarly, we find slave resistance in the mid- and late nineteenth century in the Sokoto Caliphate in the Central Sudan organized around millennial interpretations of dominant Islamic ideals, ideals that had served earlier in the century to mobilize slaves to join in the *jihad* that had established the caliphate.[74]

Finally, no sharp and useful distinction can be drawn between the use of internal norms to criticize practices and more radical forms of criticism that reject those norms in favor of other norms. And the views of some slaves—how many we will never know—seem most plausibly character-

72. Genovese, *Roll, Jordan, Roll.*

73. See Leon F. Litwack, *Been in the Storm So Long: The Aftermath of Slavery* (New York: Vintage, 1979), 5–6; Martin A. Klein, "Slave Resistance and Slave Emancipation in Coastal Guinea," in Suzanne Miers and Richard Roberts, eds., *The End of Slavery in Africa* (Madison: University of Wisconsin Press, 1988), 203–219.

74. For detailed discussion of this important range of issues and cases, see Genovese, *Roll, Jordan, Roll*; Cooper, "Islam and Cultural Hegemony"; Richard Roberts, "Ideology, Slavery, and Social Formation: The Evolution of Maraka Slavery in the Middle Niger Valley," in Paul Lovejoy, ed., *The Ideology of Slavery in Africa* (Beverly Hills, CA: Sage, 1981), 171–199; Dockès, *Medieval Slavery*, 212–215; Lovejoy, "Problems of Slave Control in the Sokoto Caliphate," in Paul Lovejoy, ed., *Africans in Bondage: Studies in Slavery and the Slave Trade* (Madison: University of Wisconsin Press, 1986), 262–264.

ized as continuing internal normative criticism to the point where it
passes into external criticism.

Consider a few examples. Frederick Douglass tells the story of bringing his weekly wages of six dollars to his master, and sometimes being
given six cents to "encourage" him. But, Douglass says, this "had the
opposite effect. I regarded it as a sort of admission of my right to the
whole. The fact that he gave me any part of my wages was proof, to my
mind, that he believed me entitled to the whole of them."[75] Or consider
what is sometimes referred to as the "antinomianism" of American slaves,
reflected for example in the willingness of slaves to endorse theft from
masters—they referred to such "theft" as "taking" not "stealing"—while
acknowledging the wrong of theft from other slaves.[76] Commenting on
this willingness, Thomas Jefferson observes: "That disposition to theft,
with which [slaves] have been branded, must be ascribed to their situation, and not to any depravity of the moral sense. The man in whose
favor no laws of property exist, probably feels himself less bound to respect those made in favor of others. When arguing for ourselves, we lay
it down as fundamental, that laws, to be just, must give reciprocation of
right; that without this, they are mere arbitrary rules, founded in force,
and not in conscience, and it is a problem which I give the master to
solve, whether the religious precepts against the violation of property
were not framed for him as well as his slave? and whether the slave may
not justifiably take a little from one who has taken all from him, as he
may slay one who would slay him?"[77] Similarly, there is a song that
slaves in Brazil are reported to have sung:

> The white man says: the black man steals
> The black man steals for good reason.
> Mister white man also steals
> When he makes us slave.[78]

---

75. Douglass, *Narrative*, 317.

76. Blassingame, *Slave Testimony*, 374. For a detailed discussion of theft and its implications for the moral rejection of slavery and the development of a "counter-morality," see
Alex Lichtenstein, "'That Disposition to Theft, With Which They Have Been Branded':
Moral Economy, Slave Management, and the Law," *Journal of Social History* 21 (1988):
413–440.

77. Quoted in Lichtenstein, "'That Disposition to Theft,'" 413.

78. Mattoso, *To Be a Slave*, 137.

Are these cases in which slaves embrace such plausibly widespread internal norms as that people may legitimately take back what has been stolen from them, or steal in cases of extreme need, or own what they make? Or does the fact that they apply those norms to themselves as slaves show that they are advancing a divergent interpretation of widely accepted norms? What seems most plausible is that the very idea that these norms apply to slaves as well as non-slaves, and the attendant suggestion of the moral equality of masters and slaves, is such a departure from dominant understandings—such a distinctive interpretation of the moral community covered by the norms—that we have now passed from internal to external criticism. At the same time, this expansion of the moral community and the associated passage from internal to external criticism is arguably anticipated when the internal norms are presented to slaves as considerations they should recognize as binding and by appeals to reciprocity in justifications of slavery.[79] In any case, it seems clear that no crisp line can be drawn between different forms of normative criticism and that the pursuit of one can lead by easy steps to the pursuit of the other.

Whereas the claim that moral acceptance leads to compliance has some force, then, that force is limited. Its limits are not to be found (at least not exclusively) in the rejection by slaves of moral ideas, or their failure to take moral notions seriously. To the contrary, they are marked by the fact that regnant norms and alternative interpretations of those norms can themselves serve as bases for moral criticism of social arrangements and by the fact that internal criticism can pass over into more radical forms of moral criticism that appeal to a distinctive set of moral ideals. But if we are to understand better the critical use of norms, the development of alternative interpretations of norms, the uses slaves made of their power, and the importance and prevalence of positive incentives, we need an account of the interests of slaves.

One final point to conclude the discussion of slavery. In using the phrase "paraphernalia of voluntary servitude," I do not mean to suggest that masters deployed incentives—material reward, autonomy, family security, and freedom—simply as a strategy to control slaves by disguising their chains—the chains were unmistakable—or that the incentives func-

79. See the suggestive remarks on unanimity in Scott, *Domination*, 55–58; on the importance of reciprocity in shaping public justifications of power, see Barrington Moore, *Injustice: The Social Bases of Obedience and Revolt* (White Plains, NY: M. E. Sharpe, 1987).

tioned exclusively to increase that control. Their etiology and their consequences were more complicated and more double-sided than that.

The incentives did reflect the strategic judgments of masters about how to
control slaves and seem to have had some measure of success from this point
of view. The positive incentives increased the returns to obedience and hard
work by providing routes to individual improvement within the framework of
slavery, thus raising the costs of resistance by increasing the losses that might
follow from resistance. Slaves, in short, had more to lose than their chains.[80]
The incentives also divided slaves from one another by fostering cooperation
with masters. And by providing avenues of individual exit from slavery,
manumission in particular discouraged the pursuit of more collective exits.

But these efforts to elicit more voluntary cooperation through positive
incentives and moral justifications were the homage paid by domination
to human aspirations. By providing incentives to slaves, and by encouraging the idea that slavery stands in need of justification, masters acknowledged and encouraged slaves to recognize and to pursue a variety of interests that the basic structure of slavery did not and could not adequately
accommodate, including an interest in material well-being, an interest in
greater control over the circumstances of life and work (i.e., an interest in
autonomy), and an interest in securing the conditions for a dignified life.

---

80. For this reason the account of slavery in Adam Smith and Marx exaggerates the contrast
with other forms of labor. For Smith, see *The Wealth of Nations*, 363–367. In fact, there is an
interesting tension within Marx's account. In places, Marx suggests that slaves are impelled
only by fear, and that they lack conceptions of liberty, responsibility, and self-control. Elsewhere, however, he suggests that the basis of the decline of slavery is "the slave's awareness
[*Bewusstsein*] that he *cannot* be the property of another, . . . his consciousness of himself as a
person." Karl Marx, *Grundrisse*, trans. Martin Nicolaus (New York: Random House, 1973),
463. These two views are consistent if one can argue, along the lines suggested by Hegel's
discussion of master and slave, that this awareness is itself a product of work under conditions
of servitude, and not a constant feature of it. G. W. F. Hegel, *Phenomenology of Spirit*, trans.
A. V. Miller (Oxford: Oxford University Press, 1977), 117–119. Elsewhere, however, Marx suggests that it, or something like it, *is* a constant feature. In a discussion of Varro's distinction
between the slave (an *instrumentum vocale*), animal (an *instrumentum semi-vocale*), and implement (an *instrumentum mutum*), he notes that the slave "himself takes care to let both beast
and implement feel that he is none of them. He gives himself the satisfaction of knowing that
he is different by treating the one with brutality and damaging the other *con amore*. Hence the
economic principle, universally applied in this mode of production, of employing only the
rudest and heaviest implements, which are difficult to damage owing to their very clumsi-
ness." And he offers this as one of the conditions that "make production based on slavery more
expensive." Marx, *Capital*, vol. 1, trans. Ben Fowkes (Harmondsworth, UK: Penguin, 1976),
303–304n18. This last comment suggests that it may not be so easy to account for the self-
consciousness Marx appeals to in explaining the demise of slavery as a product of the evolution of slavery: perhaps it is a constant feature.

Interests

Slaves had interests in material well-being, autonomy, and dignity. Perhaps that goes without saying. But the enterprise of attributing interests to people may seem arbitrary, and attributions of these interests to slaves may seem anachronistic, romantic, ideologically blinded, or simply ignorant. These interests, however, play two roles in my argument: the case for both the injustice of slavery and its limited viability turns on the claim that slavery conflicts with the legitimate interests of slaves in material well-being, autonomy, and dignity. So I need to say enough about them to explain why that later appeal to them is plausible.

As a general matter, then, a course of action or state of affairs is in a person's interests just in case that course or state is the best way to realize an end that he or she would affirm on reflection—considering his or her life as a whole, conflicts between and among current aims, the strength of various desires, and the conditions that may have engendered current ends—given full information and full imaginative powers.[81] In practice, however, we base attributions of interests on a person's actual ends (abjuring the hypothetical aims that figure in the definition) because we, in effect, assume that reflection would not produce changes in the relevant ends. The burden of proof falls on challengers to attributions based on actual ends; they must provide a reason for thinking that those ends would shift on reflection. Applying these general observations to my comments here, I will sketch some evidence that slaves cared substantially about material well-being, autonomy, and dignity, leaving it to those who doubt the attributions of interests to show that reflection would have dissolved these concerns.

First, then, the phenomena of resistance and revolt support the view that at least some slaves cared greatly about autonomy—enough to accept significant risks (e.g., the risks taken by the 6,000 crucified slaves who lined the road from Capua to Rome after the defeat of the rebellion led by

---

81. The account of interests draws on the discussion of deliberative rationality in John Rawls, *A Theory of Justice*, rev. ed. (Cambridge, MA: Harvard University Press, 1999), sec. 64; Albert O. Hirschman, *The Passions and the Interests: Political Arguments for Capitalism before Its Triumph* (Princeton: Princeton University Press, 1977); Railton, "Moral Realism;" Raymond Geuss, *The Idea of a Critical Theory: Habermas and the Frankfurt School* (Cambridge: Cambridge University Press, 1981), chap. 2; and William Connolly, *The Terms of Political Discourse*, 2nd ed. (Princeton: Princeton University Press, 1983), chap. 2.

Spartacus; 100,000 slaves were killed in this revolt).[82] This willingness is clearest in the case of individual runaways, maroons, and rebels.

Furthermore, this aspiration to autonomy appears to be quite general, extending widely across time and space. Referring to the phenomenon of mass departures by slaves in, for example, Northern Nigeria, Guinea, and the French Sudan between 1895 and 1910, Lovejoy claims that this "exodus was so large that it represents one of the most significant slave revolts in history."[83] Moreover, acknowledging disagreement about the scope of the aspiration to autonomy, he observes as well that "Some scholars [he has in mind the incorporationist analyses of slavery advanced by Kopytoff and Miers; see note 83] have argued that African servility depended on attitudes quite unrelated to the concept of 'freedom.' African thought, they claim, did not consider freedom a desirable or possible status. There can be no mistake about this matter. The massive desertions by slaves throughout the nineteenth century and especially at the end of the century when European conquest was well underway, demonstrates that the views of these scholars are incorrect." But even the less determined forms of resistance indicate a desire for greater control by slaves over the circumstances of their lives.

To be clear, with the exception of the slave revolution in St. Dominique in 1792, none of the rebellions or maroon wars aimed at abolition. The massive rebellions in Italy and Sicily between 140 and 70 B.C., for example, did not aim to eliminate slavery.[84] More characteristic was a 1738 peace treaty in Jamaica that recognized the freedom of one group of maroons while including a provision requiring that group to return future runaways.[85] But these observations do not undercut my claim here, which is

---

82. Finley, *Ancient Slavery and Modern Ideology*, 98; Wiedemann, *Greek and Roman Slavery*, 222, citing a passage from Appian's *Roman History*; Bradley, *Slavery and Rebellion*.

83. Lovejoy, *Transformations in Slavery*, 267. For an alternative view, see Igor Kopytoff, "The Cultural Context of African Abolition," in Suzanne Miers and Richard Roberts, eds., *The End of Slavery in Africa* (Madison: University of Wisconsin Press, 1988), 485–503, especially the illuminating remarks about demarginalization, social dependence, and social belonging, at 494–502.

84. Bradley, *Slavery and Rebellion*; Finley, *The Ancient Economy*, 68; Wiedemann, *Greek and Roman Slavery*, 199–223.

85. For discussion of the British Treaty with Captain Cudjoe, see Patterson, *Sociology of Slavery*, 270–271. Relations between maroons and slaves were not always so uncooperative. For example, the Palmarinos in Brazil took slaves by force from plantations but also provided shelter for runaways. For discussion of the Palmares case and other New World slave-maroon relations see Genovese, *From Rebellion to Revolution*, chap. 2.

that slaves have interests in their own material well-being and autonomy, not that they were abolitionists.

Second, the provision of material incentives and manumission, and the various other paraphernalia of voluntary servitude, indicate that slaves wanted material improvement and autonomy, and that masters, aware of those wants, sought to elicit more cooperative behavior by promising to reward such behavior by satisfying those wants. Earlier I mentioned the passages in the Peripatetic treatise addressing manumission. We find closely parallel arguments in the Roman agricultural treatises of Cato, Varro, and Columella, the last of which mentions the importance of "decent living conditions, of time off from work, the fostering of family life among slaves," and above all the prospect of manumission in encouraging cooperative behavior.[86]

Third, evidence for the desire for autonomy is provided by American slave narratives, and the interviews conducted by both the Freedman's Inquiry Commission and the Works Progress Administration They provide significant testimony on the aspiration to autonomy; indeed, the slave narratives are organized around that aspiration. And they commonly return to the theme suggested by the phenomenon of manumission: that the desire for autonomy is not simply in service of material improvement.

Mary Prince, for example, writes that: "All slaves want to be free—to be free is very sweet. I have been a slave myself—and I know what slaves feel—I can tell by myself what other slaves feel, and by what they have told me. The man that says slaves be quite happy in slavery—that they don't want to be free—that man is either ignorant or a lying person."[87] Writing some 1,800 years earlier, the ex-slave Phaedrus suggested that the classical Roman fable of the dog, who is well fed and has a place to live but who is kept in chains during the day, and the wolf, who is hungry and homeless but free, expresses the slaves' sense of how sweet liberty is.[88] Reverend E. P. Holmes, a clergyman who had been a house servant, testified to Congress in 1883: "Most anyone ought to know that a man is better off free than as a slave, even if he did not have anything. I would rather be free and have my liberty. I fared just as well as any white child could have

86. Keith R. Bradley, *Slaves and Masters in the Roman Empire: A Study in Social Control* (New York: Oxford University Press, 1987), 25.

87. Mary Prince, *History of Mary Prince, a West Indian Slave*, in Henry Louis Gates Jr., ed., *The Classic Slave Narratives* (New York: Signet, 1987), 214.

88. For discussion of the fables, see Bradley, *Slaves and Masters*, 150–153.

fared when I was a slave, and yet I would not give up my freedom."[89] William Williams, the ex-slave I quoted at the outset, said "I could get as much again money as a slave there than I can earn here [in Canada] as a freeman." But, he continued, "the way the laws are here, I would rather live on bread and water here, than live there the way I did."[90] J. D. Lindsay, the blacksmith I quoted earlier, tells a story of being asked: "Don't they treat you pretty well?" To which he responded, "that had nothing to do with my liberty."[91]

Returning to the narratives, my claim that they are organized around the aspiration to freedom is best captured by a passage near the end of Linda Brent's *Incidents in the Life of a Slave Girl.* "Reader," she says, my story ends with freedom; not in the usual way, with marriage. I and my children are now free! We are as free from the power of slaveholders as are the white people of the north; and though that, according to my ideas, is not saying a great deal, it is a vast improvement in my condition."[92]

Fourth, the central role of force in establishing and sustaining slave systems also argues for the presence of interests in material well-being and autonomy. The fact that slave "recruitment" typically involved force indicates that slavery was rarely chosen by slaves—and then only under difficult circumstances—and that observing the conditions of others who had been enslaved did not encourage self-enslavement.[93] Further, the fact that force and threats of force were regular features of the lives of slaves indicates that masters thought that slaves themselves would not consent to the continuation of slavery, given an alternative.

Finally, this claim about interests receives support from the combination of ambiguous acceptance and rejection of the regnant justifications of slavery. The fact that slaves did not fully internalize regnant justifications for slavery, together with the fact that an acceptance of the justifications would have put them at disadvantage in pursuing material well-being and autonomy, provides indirect support for the claim that they had

89. Cited in Eric Foner, *Nothing But Freedom: Emancipation and Its Legacy* (Baton Rouge: Louisiana State University Press, 1983), 7.

90. Blassingame, *Slave Testimony*, 437.

91. Ibid., 396.

92. Linda Brent, *Incidents in the Life of a Slave Girl*, ed. L. Marian Child, in Henry Louis Gates Jr., ed., *The Classic Slave Narratives* (New York: Signet, 1987), 513. Or see Lucy A. Delaney, *From the Darkness Cometh the Light or Struggles for Freedom*, in *Six Women's Slave Narratives* (New York: Oxford University Press, 1988), 58.

93. On self-enslavement, see Patterson, *Slavery and Social Death*, 130–131.

these fundamental interests. Since full acceptance might have disarmed slaves even when the balance of forces turned in their favor, they were led away from it. Lacking the resources to forge wholly independent and distinctive ideals, they developed variants of the dominant views with an affinity to their interests, or embraced alternatives to those dominant ideas. The interests of slaves are, in short, reflected in the content and interpretation of the dominant norms and ideals themselves.

Coming now to dignity: the central feature of dignity for our purposes is its social aspect—that it involves a desire for public recognition of one's worth. Although a person can sustain a sense of self-worth in the face of repeated insults, still, public recognition is related to dignity in two ways: first, persons with a sense of their own worth regard such recognition as an appropriate acknowledgment of that worth; and, second, recognition provides psychological support for that sense, making it easier to sustain. In particular, having a sense of dignity, we want others to recognize that we have aims and aspirations and to acknowledge the worth of those aims and aspirations by, inter alia, providing conditions (opportunities and resources) that enable us to pursue them.

Several considerations support the attribution to slaves of an interest in conditions that support and are appropriate to a sense of dignity. First, when we consider the few oral and written records left by slaves, from the fables collected by Phaedrus to American slave narratives, what we find are repeated assertions of their sense of self-worth and the ways that their conditions violate that sense.[94]

Second, as I already indicated, the normative understandings of slavery held by slaves press the worth of the slaves into focus. This sense of worth is suggested both by the content of those views—for example, by the slave interpretations of regnant norms—and by the very concern that there be a justification for the slave condition. For example, I mentioned earlier the claim that benefits conferred by masters are matters of right, and not privilege. A particularly striking statement of this is provided by an ex-slave named Benjamin Miller. In a Freedman's Inquiry Commission interview, Miller says: "I was in bondage in Missouri, too. I can't say that my treatment was bad. In one respect I say it was not bad, but in another I

94. "There is," according to Patterson, "absolutely no evidence from the long and dismal annals of slavery to suggest that any group of slaves ever internalized the conception of degradation held by their masters." Patterson, *Slavery and Social Death*, 97.

consider it was as bad as could be. I was a slave. That covers it all. I had not the rights of a man."[95]

Third, the desire for dignity is closely linked to a desire for social conditions that support autonomy and decent material circumstances. For such conditions provide support for a sense of dignity, both because maintaining a sense of self-worth without resources is so difficult and because having a decent level of resources (or at least a substantial opportunity to secure them) is itself an index of respect.[96] This connection between material welfare, autonomy, and dignity suggests that the pursuit of welfare and autonomy may in part be animated by a desire for the public affirmation and recognition ingredient in conditions that enable people to secure their autonomy and material welfare.

Taking these remarks about the different interests together, I will hereafter use the term "fundamental interests" as shorthand for the three interests that I have just discussed.

The Perverse Stoic

I said earlier that our attributions of interests can be overturned by showing that the present aims that underlie the attribution would be rejected on reflection. But I also suggested that the burden of proof is on the person who holds that reflection would undermine actual ends. In the case at issue, he or she must provide some account, based on the actual circumstances and motives of slaves, that would support the claim about the transformation of ends under reflection. It is not enough to observe that the outcome of the hypothetical, imaginative, and informed reflection that defines interests is not perfectly determinate and to conclude that slaves might simply have chosen to reject these concerns.

With a view to meeting the burden of proof, a Perverse Stoic might argue that, on reflection, with full information and a vivid grasp of the alternatives, slaves would have lost their concern for well-being, autonomy, and dignity because they would have recognized that a life without a concern for these goods, often unattainable, would be a less frustrating life for them. The Perverse Stoic might argue that, on reflection, slaves would often have wanted to organize their lives and aspirations around the ideal of quiescent obedience. Since obedience is in any case their lot, better to obey without

---

95. Blassingame, *Slave Testimony*, 439.
96. See Rawls's discussion of the social bases of self-respect in A *Theory of Justice*, sec. 67.

frustration than to disobey and suffer for that disobedience, or to obey while wanting something very different. For the Perverse Stoic, then, the fully reflective ideal of a slave is (not always, but often) to be an obedient slave. And what advances the interests of slaves are those actions and conditions that help them to achieve a perfect, unfrustrated obedience, with desires and powers in equilibrium and conduct in conformity with desires.

But Perverse Stoicism is mistaken. The thesis that quiescent obedience is the ideal appears to rest on the view that slaves are completely powerless either to improve their conditions while remaining slaves or to extricate themselves from slavery through manumission, or running away, or revolt. These claims are exaggerated and of a piece with the common exaggeration of the power relations that define slavery.

The Perverse Stoic could respond by arguing that slaves typically were not able to extricate themselves from slavery. And that if those who were not able were to reflect on their ends on the basis of full information (including the information that they could not extricate themselves), it would have been reasonable, at least for them, to give up the end of autonomy, thus sparing themselves the frustration that followed on an inability to achieve it.

This reply seems doubly mistaken. First, slavery itself permits greater and lesser degrees of autonomy and not just greater and lesser levels of material well-being. Slaves, as I indicated earlier, sometimes exercised greater control over their personal and family lives, their religion, and their work. Their abilities to do so were in part a result of the fact that they wanted to and thus acted to increase their autonomy within the framework of slavery. So it is not true that the concern for increased autonomy resulted only in frustration. Even if one knew that one would remain a slave, it would not have been reasonable to give up a desire for autonomy for the sake of avoiding frustration.

Second, the Perverse Stoic's case for a reflective rejection of an interest in autonomy and dignity assumes that the supreme aim of slaves is to avoid frustration, and therefore that an end that will certainly not be achieved is an end best relinquished. We have no reason, though, to suppose that the supreme end of slaves was the avoidance of frustration and therefore no reason to suppose that frustration-avoidance would have controlled their reflective assessment of their lives. Having a desire for autonomy, even knowing that it will go unsatisfied, can serve as a reminder that a slave is not what he or she is said to be. If the lack of autonomy was an important source of the indignity of slavery, then preserving a desire for autonomy could have served to limit that indignity.

3. *Injustice and the Limits of Slavery*

Slavery, I have proposed, is best understood as a particular form of power; that form was reproduced through force, strategic incentives, and moral-religious norms; and slave interests in material improvement, autonomy, and dignity are revealed in the practices that reproduce slavery. With these claims as background, I come to the main argument about the injustice of slavery and its viability, which I will pursue by taking up, in turn, the four theses stated earlier.

Slavery and Slave Interests

Thesis One: The basic structure of slavery as a system of power stands
in sharp conflict with fundamental slave interests in material
well-being, autonomy, and dignity.

Consider, first, the interest in material well-being. The intuitive argument for this aspect of Thesis One is that being a slave is materially undesirable because slaves are relatively powerless. Limited power means limited capacity to bargain for advantage, which means limited capacity to protect basic material interests in nourishment and health. So it seems plausible that it is materially better not to be a slave, even if one is a serf or poor peasant. Given the breadth and depth of the limits that define the condition of slave, one can expect to have more power if one is not a slave and to be able to turn that power to material advantage.

Against this intuitive argument, it has been said—most famously in Fogel and Engerman's *Time on the Cross*[97]—that the relative powerlessness of slaves can work to their material advantage: Because of the limits on their power, slaves can be subjected to the productive use of force. If they are, output per worker increases, enabling slaves themselves to live a materially better life than if they were emancipated. The intuitive idea is straightforward. Suppose two modes of production are in operation: peasant farms worked by family labor and plantations worked by slave gangs. Suppose, too, that output per worker is greater on the plantations than the family farms. Greater output per head in the plantation system permits owners to provide

---

97. Fogel and Engerman, *Time on the Cross*.

a higher standard of living to slaves than is available to the family farmers. But why could families in the small-holding sector not pool their resources to form larger units and reap the benefits of the scale economies? Or if the costs of pooling are too high, why could the small holders not offer their labor to plantation owners for a wage in excess of what they can earn on their own farms? Why is being enslaved essential to reaping the benefits?

The answer lies in the fact that increased output per worker on large plantations is not generated by increasing returns to scale but by high intensity, continuous work imposed by masters in the plantation sector on slaves: Fogel estimates that slaves on medium and large plantations worked 76 percent more intensely per hour than free Southern farmers or slaves on small plantations.[98] Because of the non-pecuniary costs of such intense and continuous labor, no one would willingly perform it without substantial pecuniary compensation. Because slaves were relatively powerless, they could be forced to do it. When they were forced, output per person increased, and slaves themselves ended up consuming more than they would have been able to consume if they were not slaves. As Fogel and Engerman put it, "It was only by applying force that it was possible to get blacks to accept gang labor without having to pay a premium that was in excess of the gains from economies of scale."[99] Why, then, is relative powerlessness not in the slave's material interest?

Two considerations suggest doubts about the force of this argument. First, the argument about material well-being assumes that we can assess the material welfare of a group simply by considering its level of compensation. But what about the interest in not performing intense, undesirable labor? And what about the fact that increased consumption may fail to compensate for the greater expenditures of energy required by such labor? To be materially well-off is in part a matter of being well-nourished. But nourishment is not a function simply of food consumption levels.[100] The same basket of food can produce widely different levels of nourishment depending of such factors as metabolic rates, body size, gender, activity levels, and access to medical services. But the argument that I have been considering assumes that the level of output per person was increased by

---

98. Fogel, *Without Consent or Contract*, 78–79.

99. Fogel and Engerman, *Time on the Cross*, vol. 1, 237.

100. For a discussion and exploration of implications, see Amartya Sen, "Well-Being, Agency, and Freedom," *Journal of Philosophy* 82, 4 (April 1985): 195–200.

imposing conditions of intense labor and pain that presumably decrease the level of nourishment resulting from a fixed quantity of food consumption.[101] To argue, under these conditions, that slavery improves material welfare by enabling an increased level of food consumption is, then, a form of fetishism.[102]

Put otherwise, in the passage I cited earlier, Fogel and Engerman refer to "economies of scale" associated with gang labor. But their argument about the material benefits of powerlessness is, as I have indicated, not really about scale economies, but about the forceable extraction of more intense and continuous labor.[103] Thus Fogel estimates that gang-system plantations in the South had a 39 percent advantage in total factor productivity over free farms but that this advantage was due to "the greater intensity of labor per hour" imposed by the gang system.[104] Acknowledging this, we need to consider whether the added income made available by forced high labor intensity sufficed to compensate for its burdens. Fogel notes some suggestive evidence: while slaves "earned 15 percent income per clock-time hour . . . their income per equal-efficiency hour was 33 percent less than that of free farmers."[105]

Second, the argument requires both that slavery generate increased output per head and that slaves reap some of the gains. But in determining whether slavery is materially beneficial for slaves, we cannot simply include a specified level of compensation in the characterization of the slave condition. I have not included such specification in the characterization of slavery as a form of power. More substantively, because slaves were relatively powerless—not merely subordinate at work, but relatively powerless across the board—they would not have the power to enforce a specified share of

101. Paul David and Peter Temin, "Slavery: The Progressive Institution," in Paul David et al., eds., *Reckoning with Slavery* (New York: Oxford University Press, 1976), 178–186; Yoram Barzel, "An Economic Analysis of Slavery," *The Journal of Law and Economics* 21, 1 (April 1977): 95.

102. I have focused on implications for consumption and nourishment. On health, see Joseph C. Miller, *Way of Death: Merchant Capitalism and the Angolan Slave Trade, 1730–1830* (Madison: University of Wisconsin Press, 1988), chaps. 9, 10; Karasch, *Slave Life in Rio de Janeiro*, chap. 5; Richard Steckel, "A Dreadful Childhood: The Excess Mortality of American Slaves," *Social Science History* 10, 4 (Winter 1986): 427–465; Fogel, *Without Consent or Contract*, chap. 5.

103. I am indebted to Robert Brenner for discussions of this issue.

104. Fogel, *Without Consent or Contract*, 78; see also Stefano Fenoaltea, "The Slavery Debate: A Note from the Sidelines," *Explorations in Economic History* 18 (1981): 304–308.

105. Fogel, *Without Consent or Contract*, 79.

the potential gains. Even if relative powerlessness helps to produce potential material gains, then, such powerlessness makes it unreasonable to expect to benefit in the distribution of those gains. So, the position of slave will, as a general matter, be the most materially disadvantageous social position.

The conflict between slavery and the autonomy interests of slaves is more straightforward. Autonomy is a matter of being able to set and to pursue one's aspirations. To be in a relatively powerless position is on the whole to lack just such power, or to have it as a result of conditions that are more fortuitous in the lives of slaves than they are even in the lives of other socially subordinate groups. This is clear not just in areas of work but (particularly for women slaves) in areas of sexuality as well.[106]

The case of dignity seems equally clear. A characteristic feature of slave systems is that both the organization of power and the symbolic understandings of that organization—especially the pervasive symbolism of social death[107]—deny that slaves have interests that command public respect. Thus the organization of power largely deprived slaves of the powers required for advancing their interests; and the symbolic expression of that organization represents slaves as extensions of the wills of their masters or as their property, as having no legitimate social place, and as legitimately denied the powers required for protecting and advancing their interests.

In his opinion in Dred Scott, Chief Justice Taney said that when the Constitution was written, blacks had "for more than a century been regarded as beings of an inferior order . . . so far inferior that they had no rights which the white man was bound to respect."[108] Because the interest in dignity carries with it an interest in such respect and recognition—both as appropriate to and as supportive of the sense of dignity—both the structure of slavery and the forms of public culture that grow up around it are more sharply at odds with the interests of slaves than alternative systems are with the interests of their members. Emphasizing the concern for dignity, its independent standing, and the hostility of slavery to it, an unidentified former slave said: "We knowed freedom was on us, but we didn't know what was to come with it. We thought we was going to get rich like the white folks. We thought we was going to be richer than the white

---

106. See, for example, Bush, *Slave Women*, 110–118; Karasch, *Slave Life*, 205–210.
107. Patterson, *Slavery and Social Death*.
108. *Dred Scott v. Sanford*, 60 U.S. 393 (1857).

folks, 'cause we was stronger and knowed how to work, and the whites didn't, and we didn't have to work for them any more. But it didn't turn out that way. We soon found out that freedom could make folks proud, but it didn't make 'em rich."[109]

Injustice

Thesis Two: Slavery is unjust because the relative powerlessness of slaves, reflected in the conflict between slavery and slave interests, implies that it could not be the object of a free, reasonable, and informed agreement.

In stating this second thesis, I introduce a particular account of justice, based on an idealized notion of consensus—a free, reasonable, and informed agreement.[110] I will not defend this account of justice here; nor does the argument depend on its details. What matters are the intuitive ideas that the ideal consensus view articulates: that a just arrangement gives due consideration to the interests of all its members, and that we give due consideration when we treat people as equals, taking their good fully into account in our social arrangements. The ideal consensus view articulates this requirement of treating people as equals by asking what arrangements people themselves would agree to, if they looked for arrangements acceptable to all, understood as equals. By a free agreement, then, I mean an agreement reached under conditions in which there are no bargaining advantages. An agreement is reasonable only if it is reached on the basis of interests that can be advanced consistent with the aim of arriving at a free agreement. I will hereafter call such interests "legitimate interests." An informed agreement is one in which the parties correctly understand the consequences of the agreement.

According to this ideal consensus view of justice, then, slavery is unjust because it could not be the object of a free and reasonable agreement. Why not? What features of slavery preclude it from being the object of such an agreement? Given the relative powerlessness that defines the condition of slavery, the force essential to sustaining it, and the public inter-

---

109. Cited in Gutman, *The Black Family in Slavery and Freedom*, 361.

110. I draw, as will be evident, on Rawls, *A Theory of Justice* (Cambridge, MA: Belknap Press of Harvard University Press, 1971); T. M. Scanlon, "Contractualism and Utilitarianism," in Amartya Sen and Bernard Williams, eds., *Utilitarianism and Beyond* (Cambridge: Cambridge University Press, 1982).

pretation of slaves that is encouraged by that distribution of power, it is reasonable for slaves to have very low expectations about the satisfaction of their fundamental interests, lower even than in alternative systems of direct social subordination. Given this low expectation, slaves could only "consent" to their condition if the relations of power between masters and slaves determined the rational course of their conduct. But such power is excluded by the requirement of a free agreement.

This rejection is reasonable because the fundamental slave interests that lie at its foundation are legitimate. Advancing them was consistent with acknowledging that everyone has the fundamental interests and that the structure of the social order ought to accommodate those interests. While a material gain for slaves may well have involved reduced expectations at dominant social positions—I am not assuming that the elimination of slavery must represent a Pareto-improvement over a status quo with slavery—those expectations would still have been considerably greater than the expectations of slaves under slavery. Moreover, a gain in dignity for slaves need imply no loss in dignity for masters. The rejection of slavery would have been reasonable, then, because the elimination of slavery would have improved the conditions of slaves with respect to their fundamental interests; but that improvement need not have imposed on any group a burden at all comparable to that borne by slaves under slavery.[111]

Consider, by contrast, the interest in having slaves—which I suppose at least some masters to have had. This was not a morally legitimate interest, since it could not be advanced as a basis for an agreement consistent with the aim of reaching a free agreement on terms of cooperation. Slavery was in the sharpest conflict with the fundamental interests of slaves. Given that slaves had these interests, masters could only propose slavery if they were not aiming to find mutually acceptable terms of social order but instead seeking to advance their particular interests. And masters could not reasonably expect slaves to agree to terms that conflict with their interests simply because such an agreement would be advantageous to masters— not as part of a free agreement.

---

111. I focus here on the injury of slavery to slaves, not on claims about the general benefits of abolition. For especially eloquent statements of those benefits, see Joaquim Nabuco, *Abolitionism: The Brazilian Antislavery Struggle*, trans. Robert Conrad (Urbana: University of Illinois Press, 1977), esp. 83.

This rejection of slavery would have been an informed rejection in that it turns on the general features of slavery that I sketched earlier: that slaves are relatively powerless; because they are relatively powerless their legitimate interests in material well-being and autonomy are at best marginally and insecurely protected; such protection as they in fact receive results either from the whims of masters or from a precarious and shifting balance of power between masters and slaves; and since their interests are typically not recognized as significant either in the organization of power or in the dominant conceptions of slaves and their social standing, slavery is an insult to their dignity. This argument does not turn on identifying slavery with its most murderous forms or slaves as utterly powerless, nor does it assume that slaves are always and everywhere "worked like animals . . . [and] housed like animals,"[112] living lives of joyless degradation. Relative powerlessness itself suffices.

Limited Viability

Thesis Three: The conflict between slavery and the interests of slaves is an important source of the limited viability of slavery.

Slavery is unjust, then, because it conflicts with certain interests of slaves—interests that are identified as morally legitimate by the ideal consensus view (and no doubt by other views). Does this injustice-making conflict help to account for the demise of slavery? And where, if at all, does the injustice itself enter in? As a first step to answering this question, I defend the third thesis by sketching two sources of the limited viability of slavery—two lines of argument that figure as important strands in plausible accounts of abolition.

The first source emphasizes the recognition of injustice. The idea is that slavery is undermined in part because it was unjust, because that injustice was recognized, and that recognition motivated opposition. Here the injustice of slavery plays an explanatory role, roughly, by virtue of its being cognized and then serving to motivate moral opposition.

Let us separate the contention that recognition of injustice is relevant to explaining the demise of slavery into three components: some consequential opposition to slavery was motivated by moral conviction; the content of those moral convictions can reasonably be represented by the ideal con-

112. James, *Black Jacobins*, 10.

sensus conception of justice that I have presented here; and those moral convictions are themselves explained in part by the injustice of slavery. Without this third point, it would not be the injustice itself that helps to explain the demise but only the belief that slavery is wrong. I will consider the first two points here and return later to the third.

First, then, it seems clear that moral opposition motivated at least some eighteenth- and nineteenth-century abolitionist opponents of slavery who fought against the slave trade and for the abolition of slavery, who objected to slavery on grounds of principle, whose interests are not sufficient to explain their opposition—Quakers being only the most familiar case—and whose opposition was important to abolition.[113] Fogel, who emphasizes the economic success and viability of American slavery, puts the case especially strongly: "[Slavery's] death was an act of 'econocide,' a political execution of an immoral system at its peak of economic success, incited by men ablaze with moral fervor."[114] Moral conviction also provides an explanation of some of the motivations of slaves, particularly those who were animated by external moral criticisms of slavery.

Concerning the second point: Slaves, I have suggested, were motivated to oppose slavery in part by indignation and outrage, and not only by their interests. But this does not suffice to show that they were motivated by a recognition of the injustice of slavery as I have characterized the notion of injustice here. Sometimes—in the case of internal moral criticism—their indignation could be explained by the fact that masters had violated traditional norms and customary understandings. But, as I suggested in my earlier discussion of external criticism, the continuity between internal and external criticism, and the expanded conception of the moral community associated with such criticism, not all slave opposition can be explained in those terms. Among the forms of opposition that cannot be are the views advanced in the course of the Haitian Revolution, in slave petitions in the United States, in Jamaica's 1831 Christmas rebellion, and in the views that animated the participation of ex-slaves in the fight against the Confederacy. In all of these cases, opposition was shaped

113. On the complex background and implications of moral opposition, see David Brion Davis, *The Problem of Slavery in the Age of Revolution, 1770–1823* (Ithaca: Cornell University Press, 1975); Jean R. Soderlund, *Quakers and Slavery: A Divided Spirit* (Princeton: Princeton University Press, 1985).

114. Fogel, *Without Consent or Contract*, 410.

in part by the notions of due consideration and treating people as equals that provide the intuitive foundation of the ideal consensus conception.[115]

More generally, the conception of slavery—and not merely their own individual enslavement or the violations by masters of customary expectations—as unjust helps to explain the late eighteenth-century shift that Genovese has described from restorationist rebellions to revolutionary opposition to slavery.[116] Furthermore, this opposition (particularly the revolution in St. Dominique) was consequential and contributed to the end of slavery by, among other things, helping to limit the expansion of slavery and contributing strength to movements end the slave trade.

The case for the first two aspects of the recognition-of-injustice view seems plausible. Still, we have not yet arrived fully at the recognition of injustice; for that we must also vindicate the claim that there is an explanatory connection between the injustice of slavery and moral beliefs about it. I will discuss this issue later, and respond in particular to the objection that all that matters here are beliefs about injustice and that talk about "recognition" is misplaced.

The second view is what I call the conflicting interests account. This view locates viability problems in slavery directly in the conflict between slavery and the fundamental slave interests, without the mediation of moral beliefs. The contention is that these conflicts are a key source of pressure to move from slave to non-slave systems because they are a source of conflict within slave systems and of disadvantages that slave systems face when they compete economically and conflict militarily with non-slave systems.

To bring out the content of this view, I want to note that it helps to explain the force and limits of the classical economic arguments about the limits of slavery. Those arguments emphasize the costliness of slave labor, deriving from high enforcement costs, constrained productivity, and difficulties of securing a biologically reproductive slave population.[117] Adam

---

115. Davis, *The Problem of Slavery in the Age of Revolution*, 137–151, 276; Genovese, *Rebellion to Revolution*. On the interaction between metropolitan abolitionism and slave resistance, see Seymour Drescher, *Capitalism and Antislavery: British Mobilization in Comparative Perspective* (London: MacMillan, 1986), 100–103.

116. Genovese, *Rebellion to Revolution*.

117. See, for example, Smith, *The Wealth of Nations*, 363–367; Karl Marx, *Capital*, vol. 1, trans. Ben Fowkes (Harmondsworth, UK: Penguin, 1976), 303–304n18. On the problem of biological reproduction, see Max Weber's essay on "Social Causes of the Decline of Ancient Civilization," in Max Weber, *The Agrarian Sociology of Ancient Civilizations*, trans. R. I. Frank

Smith, for example, thought that slave labor was the most costly, and was imposed because of false pride and a desire to dominate, not for sound economic reasons.[118] The conflicting interests view argues that the liabilities of slavery result principally from difficulties in inducing the willing cooperation of slaves and that those problems of motivation in turn reflect the underlying conflict of interests.

The reasons for thinking slavery costly fall into three broad categories. First, there are hidden costs. Several "overhead" costs make slave labor expensive. The need to keep slaves from running away or rebelling imposes high surveillance and enforcement costs on dominant groups, costs that are (only) worth paying if other forms of labor require very high levels of compensation. Moreover, an initial capital outlay is required for purchasing slaves, and that outlay is entirely lost if the slave dies or runs away before reaching a productive age and is partly lost if the slave runs away during his or her productive years. And when slaves are employed on plantations, there is a systematic tendency to underutilization of "capacity" because of the highly seasonal nature of agricultural labor. Although labor requirements are highly seasonal, slaves must be supported throughout the year even when there is little labor to be done. Other sorts of dependent laborers, by contrast, can be required to support themselves for parts of the year.

Second, there are productivity problems. Slaves generally lack reliable incentives for skilled, flexible, and intensive work and therefore are less productive than laborers who are not enslaved. Furthermore, they cannot in general be trusted with expensive, delicate equipment so that owners lack incentives to invest in productivity-enhancing capital equipment. In addition, providing slaves with education and permitting them to live in urban settings may foster runaways and organized rebellion[119] because

---

(London: New Left Books, 1976); Gavin Wright, "The Efficiency of Slavery: Another Interpretation," *American Economic Review* 69, 1 (March 1979): 219–226; de Ste. Croix, *Class Struggle*, 229–237. For criticism of the economic arguments, see Fogel, *Without Consent or Contract*, chaps. 3, 4. For criticisms of de Ste. Croix's argument about conflicts between biological reproduction and full economic exploitation, see Keith R. Bradley, "Wet-Nursing at Rome: A Study in Social Relations," in Beryl Rawson, ed., *The Family in Ancient Rome: New Perspectives* (Ithaca: Cornell University Press, 1986), 211–212.

118. Smith, *The Wealth of Nations*, 365.

119. For qualifications, see Claudia Dale Goldin, "A Model to Explain the Relative Decline of Urban Slavery," in Stanley L. Engerman and Eugene D. Genovese, eds., *Race and Slavery in the Western Hemisphere: Quantitative Studies* (Princeton: Princeton University Press), 427–450.

the organizers of such rebellions characteristically come from the better-educated slaves. Moreover, motivating more-skilled and better-educated slaves requires a higher rate of manumission.

Finally, there are reproduction costs. Slaves are generally not biologically reproductive, and therefore the viability of slavery is typically contingent on the availability of inexpensive external supplies of slaves. As the cases of imperial Rome, the United States, and a number of other New World plantation systems—all with biologically reproductive slave populations—show, this is no law of nature. On the other hand, encouraging reproduction imposes costs, costs that arguably played a central role in the decline of ancient slavery, as limits on slave imports during the principate required the hutting of slaves for the purposes of reproduction and then the enserfment of the free population to compensate for the declining exploitation of the slave class.[120] Among the costs to propertied classes of a reproductive slave class is that it requires reducing the labor time of women. This diminishes one of the chief advantages that slavery would otherwise have, namely, a very high rate of labor force "participation"; for example, the rate of participation in Latin American systems has been estimated at a remarkable 80 percent.[121] And it also imposes the "burden" of high maternal death rates and infant mortality on the slave economy, rather than—as when slaves are largely imported—letting those burdens fall on the source society.

If these considerations have force, then we should expect problems deriving from the conflicting interests to have non-economic manifestations as well—for example, in the form of relative military weakness, overt slave resistance, and in the loss of political confidence by owners.

Consider the military issue. Wars present two problems for slave systems. First, in a wide range of systems, slaves were either not trusted to

120. See de Ste. Croix, *Class Struggle*; Wright, "The Efficiency of Slavery." For criticisms of Ste. Croix's argument about the drop in the rate of female labor force participation resulting from efforts to encourage reproduction, see Keith Bradley, "Wet-Nursing at Rome: A Study In Social Relations," in Beryl Rawson, ed., *The Family in Ancient Rome: New Perspectives* (Ithaca: Cornell University Press, 1986), 211–212. Bradley points to the phenomenon of wet-nurses for infant slaves and suggests that the "*dominus* may thus have considered it far more efficient for the child of one slave woman to be nursed by another who had already given birth . . . so that as small a number of women as possible were 'diverted' from their usual occupations" (212). But Bradley gives no indication of how widespread this phenomenon was.

121. Herbert S. Klein, *African Slavery in Latin America and the Caribbean* (New York: Oxford University Press, 1986), 60–61.

fight or otherwise excluded from fighting. With a segment of the population thus excluded, military potential is diminished. For example, the constraints slavery imposed on military potential became an important issue in the Confederacy in 1863–1864. General Patrick Cleburne said, "Slavery, from being one of our chief sources of strength at the commencement of the war, has now become, from a military point of view, one of our chief sources of weakness." To remedy this weakness, he proposed the recruitment of an army of slaves, and a guarantee of freedom "within a reasonable time to every slave in the South who shall remain true to the Confederacy." But the slave-owning class resisted, and the Confederate Congress did not authorize black enlistment until March 1865. As a Mississippi Congressman put it, "Victory itself would be robbed of its glory if shared with slaves." A Georgian made the even more telling observation that "The day you make soldiers of them is the beginning of the end of the revolution. If slaves will make good soldiers our whole theory of slavery is wrong."[122]

A second, closely related point is that slave societies are constantly threatened by "two-front wars," a problem that Aristotle counted among the chief considerations that make slavery a troublesome affair, thinking of the problems that the Thessalians faced from the Penestae and that the helots gave to the Spartans, "for whose misfortunes they are always lying in wait."[123] In such cases, the slaves either rebel or fight for the other side when the society is under attack.[124]

Because of these problems of limited military potential and two-front wars, military conflicts—including conflicts surrounding Islamic *jihads*—served as one of the principal historical stimuli to emancipation.[125] The Emancipation Proclamation in 1863 is only the most familiar example of

122. Cited in James McPherson, *Battle Cry of Freedom: The Civil War Era* (New York: Oxford University Press, 1988), 832–835.

123. Aristotle, *Politics*, 1268b38. Lovejoy, "Problems of Slave Control," 247 discusses an early nineteenth century example from the Oyo kingdom in the Sudan.

124. On the two-front war in the Confederate case, see Ira Berlin, Barbara J. Fields, Steven F. Miller, Joseph Reidy, and Leslie S. Rowland, "The Destruction of Slavery," in Ira Berlin et al., *Slaves No More: Three Essays on Emancipation and the Civil War* (Cambridge: Cambridge University Press, 1992), 3–76.

125. Patterson, *Slavery and Social Death*, 287–293; Wiedemann, *Greek and Roman Slavery*, 64–68; Lovejoy, "Problems of Slave Control," 246–249. Analogously, military conflict has played an important role in democratization. See Dietrich Rueschemeyer, Evelyne Huber Stephens, and John D. Stephens, *Capitalist Development and Democracy* (Chicago: University of Chicago Press, 1992), 70–71, 279.

military manumission, and the failure of the Confederacy to enlist or manumit is, so to speak, the exception that proves the rule. In explaining his decision to issue the Emancipation Proclamation, Lincoln said in July 1862 that he had concluded that emancipation was "a military necessity, absolutely essential to the preservation of the Union. We must free the slaves or ourselves be subdued. The slaves were undeniably an element of strength to those who had their service, and we must decide that element should be with us or against us."[126] Bolivar and San Martin also used military manumission as a fundamental strategy in the Independence Wars in Spanish America, giving the fight for independence an antislavery cast.[127] And a Roman imperial code compiled in 438 A.D. states that: "Of course we believe that free-born persons are motivated by patriotism; nevertheless we exhort slaves too, by the authority of this edict, to offer themselves for the exertions of war as soon as possible, and if they take up arms as men fit for military service, they are to obtain the reward of freedom."[128]

In general, then, the conflicting interests view contends that the demise of slavery results in part from the practical advantages in competition and conflict available to systems less sharply in conflict with the interests of their members than slavery is—advantages expressed through mechanisms akin to natural selection.

The conflicting interests theory may appear to explain "too much." Although conflicts between slavery and slave interests may have been fundamental and persistent, slavery was not in permanent crisis. But the conflicting interests account does not imply that it would be. That account is not intended to provide a comprehensive explanation of the evolution and demise of slavery, but rather to characterize one important, destabilizing determinant of that evolution. The importance and effects of conflicts between slave interests and slavery, manifest in internal opposition and in disadvantages in economic competition and military conflict, vary widely across systems of slavery and across social environments. More particularly, the pressure away from slavery produced by conflicts of interest are greatest in periods of military conflict; when slaves are used as productive laborers in a system that produces for exter-

126. MacPherson, *Battle Cry*, 504, and more generally, 354, 490–510.

127. Robin Blackburn, *The Overthrow of Colonial Slavery, 1776–1848* (London: Verso, 1988), chap. 9.

128. Wiedemann, *Greek and Roman Slavery*, 67–68.

nal markets, as distinct from cases in which slaves are "accumulated" as luxury goods or as outward displays of status; and when the ratio of slave to free is high, slaves are relatively homogeneous (ethnically and linguistically), and regularly brought into contact with other slaves, thus reducing barriers to collective action.

To expand briefly on this last point: slaves, like other subordinate groups comprising large numbers of people with very limited resources, face severe constraints on their capacity to act collectively. Those constraints are especially severe for slaves, not least because of the vertical dependency of slaves on masters. So, the higher the ratio of slave to free, the more the balance of power tips in favor of slaves. And the more homogeneous the group is ethnically, racially, and linguistically, and the more it is brought together in the normal course of its work and life—the less "atomized" the group is—the easier it is for the group to act collectively, since repeated interactions foster cooperative strategies and plausibly encourage the formation of group allegiances. As Plato, mindful of Spartan troubles with helots, put it, "Those will more easily serve as slaves who aren't compatriots and whose languages are as discordant as possible."[129] Although a remark made by the Governor of Virginia in 1720 serves as a reminder that such barriers to cooperation were not insurmountable: "We are not to depend on either their stupidity, or that Babel of languages among 'em; freedom wears a cap which can without a tongue, call together all those who long to shake off the fetters of slavery."[130]

The importance and effects of conflicts between slave interests and slavery vary widely, then, across systems of slavery and across external

129. Plato, Laws, 777C. See de Ste. Croix, Class Struggle in the Ancient Greek World, 146, for references to a range of Greek and Roman writers who express similar concerns. Roman proposals to mark slaves by requiring that they wear special dress were rejected out of fear that slaves would then recognize their numerical strength. See Hopkins, Conquerors and Slaves, 121, citing a discussion in Seneca's On Mercy. For more general suggestions about the conditions that facilitate collective action by slaves see Patterson, Sociology of Slavery, 274–280; Mendelsohn, Slavery in the Ancient Near East, 121; Genovese, Roll, Jordan, Roll, 590–591; Kopytoff and Miers, "African Slavery as an Institution of Marginality," 48–49. Consider as well the accounts of the evolution of plantation slavery in nineteenth-century Africa, and the intensified problems of social control that resulted, in Roberts and Klein, "The Banamba Slave Exodus;" Roberts, "Ideology, Slavery, and Social Formation;" Lovejoy, "Slavery in the Sokoto Caliphate;" Patrick Manning, "Contours of Slavery and Social Change in Africa," American Historical Review 88, 4 (October 1983): 853–856.

130. Blackburn, The Overthrow of Colonial Slavery, 55.

environments. Absent the kinds of "environmental" factors that I just mentioned, the problems rooted in conflicting interests will be less pressing. Despite such variations, however, slave systems do face viability problems resulting from forces internal to slavery, and those problems are important in understanding what happens in "unfavorable" environments.

Justice and Viability

Thesis Four: Characterizing slavery as unjust conveys information relevant to explaining the demise of slavery that is not conveyed simply by noting that slavery conflicts with the interests of slaves.

Suppose, then, that the conflict between slave interests and slavery limits the viability of slavery. What, then, does injustice have to do with limited viability? Why would the same limits not exist even if slave interests were not legitimate? What force is added to the explanation by noting that slave interests are morally weighty?

I suggest two ways that our understanding of the limits of slavery is aided by noting that moral weight. The first is provided by considerations about the recognition of injustice. Recall where we left the discussion of that recognition: I indicated that moral convictions motivated some consequential opposition to slavery and that the content of those moral convictions can reasonably be characterized by the ideal consensus conception of justice. Still, the injustice of slavery is not perhaps evident in this argument: How does the injustice itself shape the moral motivations of opponents? It might be said that simple beliefs on the part of abolitionists and slaves that slavery is unjust suffice to motivate opposition, quite apart from the actual injustice of slavery.

The objection seems to me not to have much force since it is natural to want an explanation of the moral beliefs as well. Explanations, to be sure, must come to an end somewhere, but this observation about the logic of explanation provides no reason to turn our spades so early in the explanatory game. Part of the explanation for the moral belief is that slaves have interests in material well-being, autonomy, and dignity and are recognized as having them; that slavery sharply conflicts with those interests and is recognized as so conflicting; and that those interests are legitimate and recognized as such. And is this sequence of points not captured by saying that people believe slavery to be unjust in part because it is unjust?

To see why this rendering is appropriate, consider the force of the "because" in "because it is unjust." We can interpret it as follows: Suppose people reason morally about the rightness or wrongness of slavery and pursue that reasoning in light of an understanding of certain facts about slave interests and the conflict between slavery and those interests. Because the reasoning is moral, it is guided by the thought that the interests of slaves need to be given due consideration, as they are, for example, in the requirement of free agreement. Pursuing that reasoning, they will be driven to the conclusion that slavery is wrong: they do not see how slavery could result from a free agreement. (It is not that difficult to see how this might go; after all, we do something like this now when we ask whether slavery is wrong.)

What is essential is to acknowledge that slaves have legitimate interests. And the key to that acknowledgment is to see that slaves have the properties— for example, the interests and the capacity for deliberate action—that others have (masters, or other members of the free population) in virtue of which people are prepared to attribute legitimate interests to those others. (Recall the remark I cited earlier: "The day you make soldiers of them is the beginning of the end of the revolution. If slaves will make good soldiers our whole theory of slavery is wrong.") But this recognition is available to anyone who reflects on the practices that help to sustain slavery, in particular on the practice of providing the incentives that I mentioned earlier. For those incentives are in effect the homage paid by a scheme of domination to fundamental human aspirations; to provide them is in effect to acknowledge that slaves have the relevant interests and capacities.[131]

Recall, for example, my earlier discussion of the tension between the Aristotelian view that slaves lack a substantial capacity to deliberate and the argument that slaves will be made more cooperative by providing them with the prize of freedom. To offer freedom as a goal is to assume that slaves do have powers of foresight and self-control; otherwise the offer of freedom in the distant future would not be expected to shape current action. But this suggests the recognition that slaves have the powers that are relevant to their membership in the moral community, and so they are

---

131. The incentives represent what is sometimes described as the "inherent contradiction" of slavery: its treatment of human beings as though they were mere things. See G. W. F. Hegel, *The Phenomenology of Spirit*, trans. A. V. Miller (Oxford: Oxford University Press, 1977), 111– 119; Karl Marx, *Grundrisse*, trans. Martin Nicolaus (New York: Random House, 1973), 463; Davis, *The Problem of Slavery in Western Culture*, 58–62.

bearers of legitimate interests. To take a more prosaic example, consider the remark of a Wisconsin cavalry officer, made in light of the performance of the largely ex-slave, black soldiers in the Civil War: "I never believed in niggers before, but by Jasus they are hell in fighting."[132] Or, as a former slave named Thomas Long put it, in reflecting on the importance of the black contribution to the Civil War and the moral learning achieved through that contribution: "If we hadn't become sojers, all might have gone back as it was before; our freedom might have slipped through de two houses of Congress and President Linkum's four years might have passed by and notin' been done for us. But now things can neber go back, because we have showed our energy and our courage and our naturally manhood."[133]

Suppose, then, that one comes to understand certain facts, all of which can be recognized independent from the procedures of moral reasoning: that slaves share the natural properties that are sufficient for being subjects of legitimate interests, that they have the fundamental interests, and that slavery sharply conflicts with those interests. Moral reasoning about slavery, proceeding in light of these facts, and giving due consideration to the interests of slaves, is bound to recognize the interests as legitimate and to condemn slavery as unjust. To say, then, that the wrongness of slavery explains the moral belief is to note the following: that moral reasoning mandates the conclusion that slavery is unjust; and that the moral belief is produced in part by that kind of reasoning. And once the injustice is recognized, it is reasonable to expect that that recognition plays some role in motivation, that it contributes to the antagonism of slaves to slavery, that it adds non-slave opponents to the slave opponents, and that, once slavery is abolished, it helps to explain why there are not strong movements to bring it back.

The moral weight also figures implicitly in the conflicting interests view. To see how, keep in mind that an explanation of the demise of slavery is not simply an account of opposition to slavery, or of shifts away from slavery—an account of the evolution of institutional variation—but also an account of the eventual retention of non-slave arrangements, of the absence of "wandering" from slave to non-slave and then back. The competitive disadvantages of slave systems are important to understanding this

132. Litwack, *Been in the Storm So Long*, 101.
133. Ibid., 102.

retention. The conflict of slavery with legitimate slave interests, and the fact that masters' interests in preserving slavery are not legitimate, plausibly helps to "tip the balance" in favor of stable departures from slavery.

To see how, consider a remark from a nineteen-year-old black soldier and ex-slave, who, after the Battle of Nashville, used his furlough to pay a visit to his former mistress. She asked him: "You remember when you were sick and I had to bring you to the house and nurse you." When he replied that he did remember, she responded: "And now you are fighting me." To which the soldier said: "No'm, I ain't fighting you. I'm fighting to get free."[134] To appreciate the bearing of this remark on the issue here, recall that the rejection of slavery was reasonable and slave interests legitimate because the fundamental interests of slaves could be advanced consistent with the aim of reaching a free agreement. The fundamental interests that provide the basis for a reasonable rejection of slavery are shared by masters, and slavery imposes great hardship on slaves while alternatives to slavery do not impose a hardship on any other group comparable to the hardship imposed on slaves by slavery. Alternatives to slavery accommodate the interests of subordinate groups better than slavery does. Moreover, they provide substantial protections of the fundamental interests at the superordinate positions. By contrast, the slaveowner interest in maintaining slavery was not shared by slaves. Because slaves and masters shared the fundamental interests, slaves could reject slavery consistent with extending to masters the same standing that they desired for themselves. But masters could not have advanced their interest in maintaining slavery except by failing to extend to slaves the same recognition that they desired for themselves. These facts about common and conflicting interests are the basis for the moral condemnation of slavery.

Suppose slave interests were not legitimate. Slaves might still have resisted just as much. But the economic and military disadvantages of slavery, the abolition of slavery, and the apparent stability of that abolition, would be more surprising. Suppose in particular that the fundamental interests were not capable of mutual satisfaction. Then we would expect dissatisfaction with abolition leading to struggles for slavery's reimposition. We would also not expect any particular practical advantage to be conferred by the absence of slavery if those other systems conflicted with the

---

134. Cited in ibid., 97.

interests of some of their members as sharply as slavery does with some of its members. For if the conflicts were as sharp, then they would have the same difficulties as slavery in eliciting cooperation. Of course, other systems of social subordination are also unjust. But slavery is on the extreme end of powerlessness; alternatives to it permit greater space for material improvement, increased scope for autonomy, and do not rest on an enslaving denial of dignity. So the sources of conflict and instability in the alternatives to slavery do not tend to produce returns to slavery. And the fact that those replacements are improvements with respect to justice makes the stability of the shift away from slavery less surprising.

Thus the fact that there is not wandering back and forth between slavery and abolition reflects the fact that the fundamental slave interests were shared and so could serve as the basis of an agreement.[135] Stating that slavery is unjust and that slave interests are legitimate interests conveys all these relevant facts about the conflict between slavery and the interests of slaves. It represents a second, distinct reason for citing the injustice in an explanation of the end of slavery. We cite the injustice itself, first, then, to indicate that moral reasoning mandates a certain conclusion, that people arrived at the conclusion because they reasoned, and were motivated to act. And we cite it, second, to convey information about the features of the system and of the alternatives to it in virtue of which the moral reasoning condemns it as unjust and to claim that those very features are a source of instability.

I do not deny that there are other ways of conveying those features. One could simply state the properties of slavery—the conflict between slavery and slave interests—and of the alternatives, without taking a position on whether those properties indeed are what makes slavery unjust; in short (and putting the issue of recognition to the side), the fact that the properties are injustice-making is not itself a part of my argument. Still, they are, and they can unobjectionably be presented via the moral classification. Moreover, that mode of presentation is morally important. For the world looks different if we think that injustice-making features limit the viability of systems that have them.

135. It might be objected that the decline of slavery with the end of the Roman empire and its reemergence with New World plantation slavery represent precisely such abolition and reimposition. But see William D. Phillips, *Slavery From Roman Times to the Early Transatlantic Trade* (Minneapolis: University of Minnesota Press, 1985); Robin Blackburn, *The Making of New World Slavery: From the Baroque to the Modern, 1492–1800* (London: Verso, 1997), chap. 1.

In sum, then, we have no reason to correct William Williams or Theodore Parker. Ethical explanations have some force, given certain plausible background beliefs about the connections between the satisfaction of fundamental interests and the justice of social forms, about the tendency of people to act on their interests and about the relationship between the satisfaction of those interests and the viability of social arrangements (especially when those arrangements operate under conditions of competition and conflict). To be sure, an explanation of the demise of slavery might proceed without embracing the ethical account of that explanation simply by citing the injustice-making properties—the properties moral reasoning singles out in condemning slavery. Injustice, in short, is not indispensable to the explanation.

But this observation is no objection because my aim has not been to argue that slavery is really wrong, nor to demonstrate the objectivity of moral norms by indicating their indispensability to explanation, nor even to persuade people who do not give ethical explanations that they ought to start. Instead, starting from within morality and its concern about the relationship of moral norms to the social world, and premising that we (or some of us) give ethical explanations, I have asked whether more reflective forms of historical and social inquiry condemn that practice and its relaxed attitude to the distinction between fact and value.

My answer is a qualified "No."

One final objection before concluding. Someone might say: "You defend what you call a 'common-sense scheme of social and historical understanding' by drawing on contemporary studies of slavery. But the circle is too narrow. The 'common sense scheme' is simply the detritus in mass consciousness of an Enlightenment conception of justice and history, or of a religiously inspired narrative of salvation. The contemporary studies that you draw on proceed to operate within that same conception of history. So at best you provide a restatement and endorsement of some unreflective prejudices shared by common sense, political philosophy, and historical social science: that slavery is particularly unjust, rather than simply another link in the long chain of schemes of human domination; that human agency and interests transcend contexts of social power; that the notion of a more free society is a coherent and attractive idea. But you have not provided an assessment of the plausibility of the common sense scheme on independent grounds."

This sketch of my argument is pretty nearly correct. I have, for example, endorsed Enlightenment-inflected criticisms of slavery as a paradigm of injustice. (I have never seen a plausible case for the proposition that slavery is simply another form of domination.) I do, however, reject the claim that I fail to assess the plausibility of this complex of convictions on any independent grounds. I have assessed it on the only "independent grounds" there are: the highly fallible instruments of rational argument and historical evidence. What I have not done is to let the Enlightenment resonance of the argument serve as grounds for its rejection.

4. Scaffold and Throne

Appeals to the injustice of slavery can play a role in explaining the demise of slavery. But that role is limited, no greater than the practical advantages conferred by moral improvements. Those limits in turn underscore the length of the arc of the moral universe. King often coupled his reference to that arc with a stanza from James Russell Lowell:

> Truth forever on the scaffold,
> Wrong forever on the throne;
> Yet that scaffold sways the future,
> And behind the dim unknown
> Standeth God within the shadow
> Keeping watch above His own.

Many of us do not share Lowell's faith—or King's—in a God who keeps watch above his own. But even if we do not, we can find some support for the hopeful views of Lowell, King, and William Williams—for Lincoln's "faith that right makes might"—in the human aspirations and powers that shape the arc of our part of the moral universe.

II

REFLECTIONS ON THE
DEMOCRATIC TRADITION

2

STRUCTURE, CHOICE, AND LEGITIMACY: LOCKE'S THEORY OF THE STATE

1. Introduction

Locke held that human beings are by nature rational and equally free.[1] On the basis of that rationality and equal freedom he argued against political absolutism and in defense of a constitutional state. Much more than his distinctive *institutional* views about popular sovereignty, legislative supremacy, or the separation of powers, it was these *foundational* beliefs that distinguished Locke from contemporary constitutionalists.[2]

But Locke also believed in the legitimacy of a class state, that is, in a constitutional state subject to the formal authority, and not just the substantive control, of property owners.[3] In this respect Locke was indistinguishable

I would like to thank Paul Horwich, John Rawls, and the editors of *Philosophy & Public Affairs* for comments on an earlier draft; Robert Brenner for discussions of a number of issues in the essay; and audiences at University of Maryland Law School, Bates College, the University of Massachusetts, the University of Connecticut, McGill University, and Stanford University for raising questions that have helped to clarify the main argument of the essay. Work on the final versions of this essay was supported by a grant from the National Endowment for the Humanities.

1. References to Locke's *Two Treatises of Government*, ed. Peter Laslett (Cambridge: Cambridge University Press, 1960) are abbreviated as follows: "1.123" refers to the *First Treatise*, paragraph 123, "2.18" to the *Second Treatise*, paragraph 18. I have included references parenthetically in the text.

2. "Parliamentary debates and pamphlet controversies involving the law or the constitution were almost invariably carried on either wholly or partially in terms of an appeal to the past made in this way [i.e., with reference to the ancient constitution]; famous antiquaries were treated as authorities of recognized political wisdom; and nearly every thinker noted for his contribution to political theory in its usual sense—Hunton, Milton, Lilburne, Hobbes, Harrington, Filmer, Nevile, Sidney: only Locke appears to be an exception among notable writers—devoted part of his pages to discussing the antiquity of the constitution." J. G. A. Pocock, *The Ancient Constitution and the Feudal Law* (New York: W. W. Norton, 1957), 46; also chap. 9.

3. See 2.140, 2.158, and the reading of these passages in Martin Seliger, *The Liberal Politics of John Locke* (London: George Allen and Unwin, 1968), 283ff. Cf. also John Dunn, *The Political Thought of John Locke* (Cambridge: Cambridge University Press, 1969), 236; and

from virtually all his contemporaries. But are these two views really consistent? Is Locke's foundational commitment to equal freedom and rationality consistent with his institutional belief in the legitimacy of a property owner's state? In view of the intimate connection between Locke's conception of equal freedom and his commitment to a contractual theory of political legitimacy (see below, pp. 87–88), this question can be explicated in a way that will make it more susceptible to a precise answer: Could free and equal parties to a social contract rationally consent to a system of political association featuring the formal inequality of political rights that defines a property owner's state?

First, some terminology. By a "constitutional state" I will mean a political order characterized by: (1) the rule of law. That is, effective restriction on the use of state power to the enforcement of general and public rules: "one rule for rich and poor, for the favourite at court, and the country man at plough" (2.142; see also 2.137). Locke's remark about "rich and poor" suggests that he understood the requirement of generality in a way that would rule out legally codified barriers to interclass mobility;[4] (2) separation of legislative and executive powers; (3) legislative control of taxation; and (4) an independent judiciary. By a "property owner's state" I will mean a constitutional state in which the legislative function is formally controlled by a propertied class. That is: (5) the franchise is re-

---

C. B. MacPherson, *The Political Theory of Possessive Individualism* (Oxford: Oxford University Press, 1962), 195, 251ff. In contrast, James Tully holds that Locke supported universal manhood suffrage. See *A Discourse on Property: John Locke and His Adversaries* (Cambridge: Cambridge University Press, 1980), 173. Tully's case rests on his reading of the last line of 2.158. Locke says there that representation should be based on "just and undeniably equal measures suited to the original frame of the government." Tully holds that these "equal measures suitable to the original constitution cannot but be the natural equality of all men" (2.5). But this reading of the concluding line of 2.158 is not supported by the paragraph as a whole. Earlier in 2.158 Locke argues that the executive should convoke the legislature "observing rather the true proportion, than fashion of representation." Clarifying the phrase "true proportion," Locke says that representation of any "part of the people" should be "in proportion to the assistance which it affords to the public," having already said at 2.140 that appropriate levels of assistance are a function of amounts of taxable estate. The point of the paragraph is that when the executive exercises its legitimate prerogative by reforming the system of representation according to *this* principle, it "cannot be judged to have set up a new legislative, but to have restored the old and true one." Such a system conforms to the "intention of the people, to have a fair and equal representative," and restores representation to the "reasons it was at first established upon" (2.157). The remarks about the "original frame" and "equal measures" in the last line of 2.158 simply summarize these earlier points.

4. See Seliger, *Liberal Politics*, 164–165, 292.

stricted to those with a specified level of property ownership; and (6) eligibility for elected office is restricted to the same propertied group. Whereas (1)–(4) promise *universal* protections of civil rights and liberties, (5) and (6) accord one class special political standing. Finally, I will use the term "democratic state" to mean a constitutional state with universal political rights, a state without the franchise and office-holding restrictions characteristic of the property owner's state. For other purposes it would be important to provide more detailed conditions and to draw further distinctions. But for present purposes, these brief characterizations suffice, and so we can return to the main question: Could free and equal rational agents consent to a property owner's state?

To clarify the terms of the question and the constraints on an acceptable answer, I want to consider two familiar answers: (1) there could be an "agreement," but only if the agreement involved fraud; and (2) there could be an agreement, but only if the "consent" were forced. What we want to know is not *whether* Locke wanted to rule out forced and fraudulent agreements—of course he did—but how he did it, so that we can eventually see if there is an agreement to a property owner's state that satisfies these and other constraints.

A Lockean agreement to a property owner's state would be based on *fraud* if some form of deception of the propertyless were required to secure their agreement to such a state. The propertyless might, for example, be led to believe that their fundamental interests would be best protected under a state controlled by the propertied, when in fact some other arrangement would provide greater protection, and the propertied know this. Locke himself does not address this issue. But there are various ways that such an agreement would not satisfy plausible extensions of Locke's own strictures. Here I will suggest just one, namely, that he would not consider such an agreement *rational*. That is, a rational social contract is not simply a social pact in which the parties maximize expected benefits *given their current beliefs*. Instead, it must also be the case that no one would choose differently if he/she knew the beliefs of others. The parties need not have the same beliefs; they might agree to disagree. And their beliefs need not be true. But it cannot be that the outcome would be different if everyone's beliefs were common knowledge.[5]

---

5. I am much more confident that Locke would want to rule out such agreements than that he would want to do so by building a common knowledge requirement into the notion of a ra-

The second alternative is an agreement based on *force*. In this case, those with property parlay their property advantage into control of the means of violence and use that control to extract consent. But, for Locke, forced consent is no consent at all: "It remains only to be considered, whether promises extorted by force, without right, can be thought consent, and how far they bind. To which I shall say, they bind not at all" (2.186; also 2.1, 2.176). Consent is forced and therefore not binding (or really no consent at all) when it is given as a consequence of a threat—whether direct or indirect—to the preservation of the consenting agent.

Two points about such threats will play a role later on. First, Locke construes indirect threats to preservation very broadly. Any threat either to my liberty or to any of my property counts as a threat to my preservation (2.18). Secondly, Locke will not count the *failure to increase* someone's chances of preservation as a threat to that person's preservation. This point is suggested by Locke's remark that "The only way whereby any one divests himself of his natural liberty, and puts on the bonds of civil society, is by agreeing with other men. This any number of men may do, because it injures not the freedom of the rest; they are left as they were in the liberty of the state of nature" (2.95).

These points about force and fraud are straightforward enough. The reason for entering them is not to endorse Locke's construal of force and fraud, but rather to indicate some requirements on an answer to our question that respects the main lines of Locke's conception (allowing for the moment that there may be no such solution). Specifically, an agreement to a property owner's state justifies that state only if the agreement is based on common beliefs and is not dependent upon direct or indirect threats to preservation.

2. MacPherson's Solution

The most systematic answer to the question that I have raised is provided by C. B. MacPherson in his *Political Theory of Possessive Individualism.*[6]

---

tional agreement. An alternative route would be via the natural duty of "truth and keeping of faith" (2.14). Nothing in my argument depends on the particulars of the solution to this issue.

6. For important (although quite disparate) criticisms see works by Dunn, Seliger, and Tully cited above in footnote 3; Peter Laslett, "Introduction," in Locke, *Two Treatises of Government* (Cambridge: Cambridge University Press, 1960); Alan Ryan, "Locke and the Dictatorship of the Bourgeoisie," *Political Studies* 13, 2 (June 1965;): 219–230; and Neal Wood, *John Locke and Agrarian Capitalism* (Berkeley: University of California Press, 1984), esp. pp. 7–9,

In part because I agree with much that he says, and in part because my own account can be motivated by considering the shortcomings of MacPherson's view, I want to review his reconstruction and suggest a few lines of criticism. Before considering the details, however, I will sketch what I take to be the *intuitive* motivations for his account.

Consider again our question: How could a social contract justify a political order with unequal political rights? Why, in particular, would the propertyless rationally consent to their own political subordination? There is a strong temptation to suppose that they would not consent and to hold, therefore, that a property owner's state could only issue from an (unforced and non-fraudulent) social contract if the propertyless were excluded from that contract. But to justify their exclusion, one would need to argue that they lack rationality and/or freedom, that they lack, that is, the qualifications for giving rational consent. And this is just the view that MacPherson attributes to Locke.

According to MacPherson, Locke: (1) proposes a theory of property that provides non-utilitarian foundations for capitalist property relations, in particular, for the existence of labor markets; (2) construes this defense of capitalist property relations as justifying the claim that there are natural class differentials in *rights* and *rationality*; and (3) concludes that these differences in rights and rationality entail the exclusion of the propertyless from the social contract, and therefore entail that the outcome of that agreement will be a property owner's state, or what MacPherson calls a "joint-stock company whose shareholders [are] the men of property" (195). Some scholarship has challenged MacPherson on point (1), defending both the historical thesis that talk about capitalism in seventeenth-century England is anachronistic and the interpretive claim that close attention to Locke's theory of property indicates that he is in fact a critic of wage labor. My main concern here is with points (2) and (3), and so for the purposes of this essay I will simply assume what I take to be true, namely, that MacPherson is right about point (1).[7]

15–19. My argument in this essay is independent of certain important elements of these criticisms. I do not, for example, wish to dispute Dunn's thesis concerning the importance of the natural law in Locke's conception.

   7. For recent discussion of capitalism in seventeenth-century England, see Robert Brenner's discussion of agrarian capitalism in *The Brenner Debate*, ed. T. H. Aston and C. H. E. Philpin (Cambridge: Cambridge University Press, 1985), chaps. 1, 10. For the view that Locke is a critic of wage labor, see Tully, *Discourse on Property*, 136ff. Tully claims that people confuse Locke's

What of MacPherson's second claim? According to him, Locke holds that there are natural differences between the rights and rationality of propertied and propertyless, *natural* in that they can be accounted for without assuming the existence of a state, and that in justifying political arrangements they provide part of the background of the agreement. Furthermore, he holds that Locke aims to defend this view about natural differences with an argument that takes *equal* rights and rationality as its point of departure.

Here I will consider just the case of differential *rights*.[8] MacPherson argues that Locke begins from a situation in which no one has any jurisdiction or authority over anyone else. He then shows how this equality of jurisdiction is transformed into an inequality of *jurisdiction* between propertied and propertyless prior to the formation of a state. This transformation of equal into unequal natural rights occurs together with the more advanced evolution of property rights. The introduction of money permits what had previously been impermissible—that people own more than they themselves can use. But the resulting accumulation of property by some leads finally to circumstances in which one group owns the land and other conditions of production (call them "the propertied"), while the members of another group (call them "the propertyless") own only their own labor.

But why does this inequality in *kinds of property* imply inequality of *authority*? According to MacPherson:

---

endorsement of master-servant relations with an endorsement of wage labor. But, Tully argues, being a servant is voluntary, and therefore acceptable to Locke, insofar as "the choice not to become a servant is available to him [the servant]" (137). By contrast, wage labor is involuntary, and therefore unacceptable to Locke, because the wage laborer must work for a capitalist and can only choose which one to work for. But this understanding of the voluntariness of the master-servant relation is not supported by Locke's remarks on masters and servants, which are directed primarily to contrasting the position of servants with the position of slaves (esp. 2.85–86). A more plausible reading is that the servant's position is voluntary just in case it satisfies three conditions: that there be a *choice of employers*, that the master-servant contract be *limited in time*, and that the terms and conditions of employment be stated explicitly in the contract itself. The agreement between master and servant, Locke says, "gives the master but a temporary power over him, and no greater, than what is contained in the contract between 'em" (2.85). These conditions are sufficient to distinguish the servant from the slave (and from the "vassals" that Locke mentions at 1.42). But they are also perfectly consistent with wage labor. For a parallel treatment of Tully, see Wood, *John Locke*, 85–92.

8. The evidence for Locke's belief in differential rationality is, I think, very unpersuasive. See MacPherson, *The Political Theory of Possessive Individualism*, 232–238.

> Once the land is all taken up, the fundamental right not to be subject to the jurisdiction of another is so unequal as between owners and non-owners that it is different in kind, not in degree: those without property are, Locke recognizes, dependent for their very livelihood on those with property, and are unable to alter their own circumstances. The initial equality of natural rights, which consisted in no man having jurisdiction over another cannot last after the differentiation of property. To put it another way, the man without property in things loses that full proprietorship of his own person which was the basis of equal natural rights. (231)

MacPherson's conclusion, then, is that the emergence of capitalist property relations is tantamount to a shift from equality of jurisdiction to inequality of jurisdiction. It is not simply that owners live better than nonowners. Rather, the material inequality of propertied and propertyless creates a condition of dependence that undermines the original equality of jurisdiction within the state of nature. Materially dependent on the propertied, the propertyless lack the freedom that is required for participation in the original agreement. And the fact that they do not participate implies their subordination in the state.

There are at least three problems with this view. First, I think that it is a mistake to construe *natural* equality and freedom in a quasihistorical way, as an original equality and freedom that obtains prior to the differentiation into classes and is superceded by that differentiation. And in the discussion below (pp. 87–88), I will present an alternative construal of equal freedom.

Second, MacPherson's account conflicts with Locke's emphasis on the fundamental distinction between property and authority. One of the basic themes of the *Treatises*, and one of the two central lines of criticism of Filmer in the *First Treatise*, is the separation between property and authority.[9] Sharply criticizing the feudal identification of property and authority, Locke argues that property ownership does not even require the

---

9. The other central line of criticism concerns the distinction between family and state (1.2). Both lines reflect the deepest difference between Filmer and Locke, that Filmer denies and Locke endorses the view that human beings are naturally free (1.6).

existence of authority, much less confer it; and that authority is not owned by those who exercise it, but is entrusted to authorities subject to specified conditions.[10] One passage draws this distinction in a way that bears most directly on MacPherson's account. It appears in the fourth chapter of the *First Treatise*, a chapter devoted to criticizing Filmer's explanation of political power in terms of property ownership, ultimately in fact in terms of Adam's ownership of the entire earth. Having completed his case against the thesis that Adam *was* the proprietor of the earth, Locke next argues that *even if he were* the proprietor, still it would not follow that he had any political authority:

> The most specious thing to be said is, that he that is Proprietor of the whole world, may deny all the rest of mankind food, and so at his pleasure starve them, if they will not acknowledge his sovereignty, and obey his will. . . . God the Lord and Father of all has given no one of his children such a property in his peculiar portion of things of this world but that he has given his needy brother a right to the surplusage of his goods; so that it cannot justly be denied him, when his pressing wants call for it. And therefore *no man could ever have a just power over the life of another, by right of property in land or possessions* [emphasis added]; since 'twould always be a sin in any man of estate, to let his brother perish for want of affording him relief out of his plenty . . . ; and a man can no more justly make use of another's necessity, to force him to become his vassal, by withholding that relief . . . than he that has more strength can seize upon a weaker, master him to his obedience and with a dagger at his throat offer him death or slavery. (1.41–1.42)

Thus the use of property advantages to compel submission to authority is an unjust use of that property. It is a direct threat to preservation; such threats being uses of force, they cannot justify the resulting submission (see above, p. 78). Locke now completes the case:

---

10. On the unity of property and authority in English feudalism, as well as the dynamics of their separation, see S. F. C. Milsom, *Historical Foundations of the Common Law*, 2nd ed. (Toronto: Butterworth, 1981); and J. M. W. Bean, *The Decline of English Feudalism, 1215–1540* (Manchester: Manchester University Press, 1968).

> Should anyone make so perverse a use of God's blessings poured
> upon him with a liberal hand [that is, threaten starvation to those
> who don't acknowledge sovereignty]; should anyone be cruel and
> uncharitable to that extremity, *yet all this would not prove that
> propriety in land, even in this case, gave any authority over the
> persons of men, but only that compact might*; since the authority
> of the rich proprietor and the subjection of the needy beggar be-
> gan not from the possession of the land, but *the consent of the
> poor man, who preferred being his subject to starving*. And the
> man he thus submits to, can pretend no more power over him,
> than he has consented to, upon compact. (1.43; emphases added)

So it is wrong to make a person an offer that he or she cannot refuse. But
even if the offer were legitimate, the acceptance of the offer would still
be required to bind the agent. If MacPherson were right, however, Locke's
"needy beggar" would not be capable of giving consent, and would therefore be legitimately excluded from the contractual justification of political
authority. MacPherson thus identifies and has Locke identifying the condition of economic-class subjection with a condition of political subjection.
But in the passage about the beggar, Locke denies precisely this identification. Even in circumstances in which consent is virtually a foregone conclusion, the basis for political authority is consent and not the material dependence that motivates it. For Locke, then, the differentiation of property
holdings does not transform the state of nature from a state of equal jurisdiction to a state of unequal jurisdiction. But, as we shall see shortly, equality of jurisdiction is the only equality that matters to Locke.

This criticism highlights a third problem: because he has Locke identifying property and authority, MacPherson fails to solve a central problem
that he claims to solve.

> The view of Locke's state as in effect a joint-stock company
> whose shareholders were the men of property has won consid-
> erable acceptance. . . . But there is one great difficulty in this
> view. Who were the members of Locke's civil society? If they
> were only the men of property, how could Locke make civil
> society oblige everyone? How could the social contract be an
> adequate basis of political obligation for all men? Yet undoubt-

edly the purpose of the social contract was to find a basis for all-inclusive political obligation. Here is an outstanding difficulty. (195)

MacPherson maintains that his interpretation resolves this "great difficulty":

> The problem inherent in the joint-stock interpretation of Locke's state is now no problem, for we have seen how Locke could consider the state to consist both of property-owners only and of the whole population. He would have no difficulty, therefore, in thinking of the state as a joint-stock company of owners whose majority decision binds not only themselves but also their employees. The laboring class . . . cannot take part in the operations of the company at the same level as the owners. Nevertheless, the laboring class is so *necessary to the operations of the company as to be considered an organic part of it.* (251; emphasis added)

This is no solution at all, and the phrase "organic part" indicates just what is wrong. MacPherson's question was: How could the propertyless have an obligation to comply with the laws of a property owner's state? His answer is that they are an "organic part" of the order, a component required for the proper functioning of the whole. But the central point of Locke's political conception—and the main thrust of his criticisms of Filmer— is that an account of political right must be based on the idea of *voluntary parts,* not *organic parts.* "Nature," he says, "gives paternal power to parents for the benefit of their children," while "voluntary agreement gives . . . political power to governors for the benefit of their subjects" (2.173). Had Locke been satisfied with organic justifications of political authority, he would not have written the *Treatises.* So MacPherson's outstanding difficulty remains outstanding.

Before proposing a solution, I must discharge one final obligation. The criticisms I have made strike me as straightforward and in a way obvious. And I think that when one makes straightforward and obvious criticisms of a work that is as serious as MacPherson's, one owes an account of how the problems might have been overlooked. The reason, I believe, is provided by what I described as the intuitive motivations for MacPherson's account, and I provided those motivations then with a view to discharging this obligation now. The hypothesis is that MacPherson simply thought it obvious that if the propertyless were included in the social contract, then it could not issue in a property owner's state. Believing this, he tried to find a plausibly Lockean argument for excluding the propertyless from the social contract. But the background view is incorrect. And to believe it is to neglect a central point about contracts, social or otherwise. The outcomes of rational agreements depend on the relative positions of the bargainers outside the contract. They depend not just on whether the parties are equal in *some* respects, but on the respects in which they are and are not equal.[11] Attentiveness to this point will indicate a solution to the "outstanding difficulty" that does not require attributing to Locke a belief in differential rationality or differential rights.

3. Equal Freedom and the Social Contract

In order to assess the compatibility of Lockean foundations with Lockean institutions, I want to proceed in three steps. First, I will characterize a Lockean contract situation. Then I will indicate several conditions that must be met by a solution to that collective choice problem. And, finally, I will consider whether a property owner's state plausibly satisfies those three conditions.[12]

Equality, Freedom, and Rationality

The first problem is to embed the Lockean conception of freedom, equality, and rationality in, to use Rawls's term, an "initial choice situation." The way that I set up the choice problem may seem less strained if I preface that setup with a word on states of nature and contractual arguments.

A state of nature is the situation that agents are in when there is no common authority over them. In classical contract theories such states play a variety of roles, two of which are important for my purposes here. First, a state of nature is one of the alternatives faced by the parties to the social contract, a second alternative being the existence of a state. The familiar argument is that the insecurity and uncertainty of the state-free condition

---

11. A simple illustration of this dependence is provided by the Zeuthen-Nash-Harsanyi solution for two-person bargaining games. Those who are better off prior to the game gain the majority of benefits from the game. For discussion, see R. Duncan Luce and Howard Raiffa, *Games and Decisions* (New York: Wiley, 1957), 124–136.

12. In what follows I draw on Rawls's schematization of social contracts in A *Theory of Justice* (Cambridge, MA: Harvard University Press, 1971), secs. 20–25.

gives everyone a reason for expecting their basic interests to be better satisfied in a state (or at least in a state of a certain kind) than in a state of nature. Second, the state of nature is the situation in which individuals
make a social contract that justifies the existence of the state. Thus it is
suggested that because each rationally prefers the existence of a state to
the state of nature, people in a state of nature would contract into a state.

But the thesis that individuals in a state of nature would agree to form a
state seems unnecessary for a social contract argument to have its justifying force. Familiar problems of collective action could stand in the way of
getting together or reaching an agreement in a state of nature, even if it
were true both that the state is collectively preferable to the state of nature
and that it would be agreed to by free, equal, and rational individuals
if they did come together to see if they could reach an agreement. We
should separate the question of what would be agreed to by free, equal,
and rational individuals who are aware of how bad the state of nature would
be from what they would agree to if they were in the state of nature. The
problems about coordination and communication raised by agreements
within the state of nature are not immediately relevant to problems of justification because they are not of immediate relevance to the question of rational and free consent.

So what I want to do is to characterize an initial choice situation that is
not the state of nature but that does explicitly incorporate Locke's notions
of *freedom, equality,* and *rationality,* and thus serves the purposes of
justification.

Equality

Locke provides the following account of natural equality:

> Though I have said above, chap. 2, that all men are by nature
> equal, I cannot be supposed to understand all sorts of equality:
> age or virtue may give men a just precedency: excellency of parts
> or merit may place others above the common level: birth may
> subject some and alliance or benefits others, to pay an obser-
> vance to those to whom nature, gratitude or other respects may
> have made it due; and yet all this consists with the equality,
> which all men are in, *in respect of jurisdiction or dominion one
> over another,* which was the equality I there spoke of, as proper
> to the business in hand, being that equal right that every man

> hath to his natural freedom, without being subjected to the will
> or authority of any other man. (2.54)

Natural equality is, then, simply equality in respect of the natural right to freedom. The problem of characterizing the notion of equality for the purposes of the social contract reduces therefore to the problem of explicating the natural freedom that it qualifies.

Freedom

Human beings, in Locke's view, are naturally in a state of liberty, not license. We are not in a state of license because we are bound by obligations deriving from the fundamental law of nature, and these natural obligations limit natural liberty (2.6). These natural obligations notwithstanding, Locke does think that human beings are naturally free, which he understands to imply something less than moral license and more than the trivial thesis that there are *some* circumstances in which natural obligations do not dictate the choice of a course of action. In fact, he means to highlight a quite specific limit to the natural obligations, a limit that distinguishes his view from Filmer's.

On Filmer's patriarchal theory, political obligations derive from the obligations of children to parents, and therefore derive from the fact of being born. So no human being could exist without having political obligations. Filmer's "great position," Locke says, was that "men are not naturally free. This is the foundation on which his absolute monarchy stands. . . . To prove this grand position of his, he tells us 'Men are born in subjection to their parents,' and therefore *cannot* be free" (1.6; emphasis added). Contrary to Filmer's "great position," Locke held that human beings are naturally free *because* such natural human obligations as those of children to parents are not political obligations nor do they imply the existence of political obligations (1.6; 2.6).[13] In short, to be free by nature *is* to have no natural *political obligations*. As a consequence, the justification of political association must be directed to individuals who *can* conceive of themselves, and who, for the purposes of the justification of the state, *do* conceive of themselves as not being members of or having the rights and

---

13. For recent discussion of the historical shifts in the nature of the family reflected in the disagreements between Locke and Filmer about the relationship between family and state, see Lawrence Stone, *The Family, Sex and Marriage in England 1500–1800* (New York: Harper & Row, 1979).

duties of members of a state. As Locke puts it, if Filmer's "foundation [i.e., no natural freedom] fails, all his fabric falls with it, and governments must be left again to the old way of being made by contrivance, and the consent of men . . . making use of their reason to unite together into society" (1.6).

For present purposes we need not consider Locke's reasons for thinking that we are naturally free. What matters here is only that the thesis that human beings are naturally free can plausibly be explicated in terms of the principle that the justification of political authority is consent. More specifically, Locke's notion of natural freedom supports the views that: (1) political authority requires a consensual justification; (2) the parties to the contract are, as in all post-Hobbesian theories, individuals rather than groups or communities, since it is individuals and not groups that are by nature free; (3) all individuals who are naturally free get an equal vote, since individuals are equally free; and (4) the agreement must be unanimous. The agreement must be unanimous because individuals are naturally free from *all* prior political ties, including the putative political authority of the people or any sort of community. But if individuals are not bound by any such prior ties, then there is no justification, for example, for a rule of majority decision making in the initial agreement, since such a decision rule would embody an antecedent obligation to comply with the decisions of the group.

Rationality

Although they are important, the requirements of equality and freedom do not by themselves constrain the outcome of the contract. To get an agreement the parties to the contract must also have interests. With interests attributed, we can interpret the third main notion, rationality. To suppose that individuals are rational is to suppose that in making an agreement they do so in order to advance these interests. Locke supposes that individuals have a set of basic interests in "life, liberty, health, and indolency of body; and the possession of outward things, such as money, lands, houses, furniture, and the like."[14] Assuming these "civil" interests, a rational agreement is one that each person expects will improve his or her prospects with respect to life, liberty, and goods, for people enter society "only

---

14. Locke, *A Letter Concerning Toleration*, ed. James Tully (Indianapolis: Hackett, 1983), 26. See also 2.2, 2.6, 2.11, and 2.27–28.

with an intention in every one the better to preserve himself his liberty and property; (for no rational creature can be supposed to change his condition with an intention to be worse)" (2.131). Thus each rational individual seeks an agreement that will increase his or her *own level* of civil interest satisfaction.[15]

But the rational interests of different individuals are not fully symmetrical. As MacPherson rightly emphasizes, there are natural differentials in property rights, "men [having] agreed to disproportionate and unequal possession of the earth. . . . This partage of things, in an inequality of private possessions, men have made practicable out of the bounds of society, and without compact, only by putting a value on gold and silver and tacitly agreeing in the use of money" (2.50). I will register this asymmetry in the description of the Lockean choice situation by supposing that the parties enter into the agreement as owners of different amounts and sorts of property. There is, so to speak, no "veil of ignorance" over property holdings. To simplify the argument, we can think of the parties as either land owners or landless laborers, who know their status in the property system, and who assess alternative arrangements in light of these holdings.

The parties to the agreement *are* equal. But they are equal solely with respect to the natural right to freedom, the only sort of equality "proper to the business in hand" (2.54). And they are free, for the facts that enter into the contract do not by themselves imply that any individuals—even the needy beggars—are subject to political obligations. Locke's freedom and equality are fully captured in the *form* of the choice situation by the requirement of unanimous agreement. The *content* of the agreement reflects the civil interests and the different property holdings that individuals bring to the agreement. The question that they will consider is: What arrangements will advantage each of us, given our different starting points?

---

15. To avoid misinterpretation, I should add that I am also assuming that the natural obligations imposed by the natural law—to preserve oneself, and not to harm others in respect of their life, liberty, and property—constrain the choice. In a more complete account of Locke's view, I would incorporate the natural obligations within the conception of rationality, since the motivation for compliance with those laws is to avoid eternal suffering. For discussion of the natural laws and the motivations for compliance with those laws, see *An Essay Concerning Human Understanding* (London: J. M. Dent, 1961), Bk. II, chap. 28, para. 6, 8.

Three Conditions on an Agreement

The way that I have set up the problem suggests (as I will show) that an agreement must satisfy three conditions. Using the terminology of the theory of cooperative games, I will call these conditions "individual rationality," "group rationality," and "coalitional rationality." In considering the appropriateness of these three requirements, it is important to keep in mind that the choice situation is *not* a state of nature. As a result we can abstract from problems of *communication* and *enforcement* of agreements. We are supposing in effect that communication is costless and that the parties will make a binding agreement. Without these assumptions, the cooperative approach to the solution would be misguided.[16]

The first condition is "individual rationality." An agreement satisfies this condition just in case each individual expects to be at least as well off as a result of the agreement as he or she would be if he or she were in the state of nature while all other parties lived in a social order regulated by the terms of the agreement. That an agreement must satisfy this requirement follows directly from the assumption that the parties in the choice situation are rational, together with the requirement of unanimity (see above, pp. 87–88). Everyone must expect to be at least as well off as a result of the agreement, because otherwise they would not make the agreement. And, since I have linked the notion of rationality to civil interests, and am supposing that individuals have definite property rights independently from the social contract—that you *can* take it with you—it is possible to be a bit more precise about these standards of comparison. Each must expect to be at least as well off in terms of life, liberty, and goods as a result of the agreement as he or she would be in the state of nature with his/her property. In short, improvements are measured in specific goods and are relative to the background structure of property. The property owners must be as well off as they would be in the state of nature with their property and the propertyless at least as well off as they would be in the state of nature with their property.

Whereas the individual rationality condition implies that the political order must pareto dominate the state of nature, the second condition—

16. For interesting applications of cooperative game theory to normative issues, see John Roemer, *A General Theory of Exploitation and Class* (Cambridge, MA: Harvard University Press, 1982).

"group rationality"—requires that there be no social state that pareto dominates the state agreed to. That is, there must be no state that makes at least some people better off and none worse off than they would be in the state that is agreed to. This condition is motivated by the construction of the Lockean choice situation in view of the fact that the sole motivation of those entering the contract is the desire to improve *their own level* of civil interest satisfaction. No one, therefore, has any reason to object to a state that improves the situation of others, even if his own conditions are held fixed.[17]

The third condition is "coalitional rationality." This condition requires that there be no subset of the population that would do better by withdrawing (or seceding) than by agreeing to enter a proposed agreement. Here again, we are supposing that groups can withdraw with their property. So for an agreement to be coalitionally rational, it must not be the case that, for example, the entire propertied group would be better off by taking all their property and forming their own state, or that the entire propertyless group would be better off by taking their labor out and forming their own state.

This third condition may seem less motivated than the first two, for at least two reasons. First, there are the obstacles (familiar from discussions of the prisoner's dilemma and other collective irrationality problems) to coalition formation even when the formation of a coalition would produce common benefits. But this first point poses no real objection given the way I have described the initial choice situation. The requirement of coalitional rationality is appropriate in the current context in view of the assumptions of costless communication and enforceable agreements. Given these conditions, and the rational interests of individuals, if a coalition could do better, then it would form and would do better. Thus the choice situation requires that each group must be able to say: given our interests and the current distribution of property, we could not do better in some alternative arrangement.

The second objection to this condition is that its use presupposes that it is legitimate for the members of a society—even the members of a just society—to withdraw from that society. And this might be thought inconsistent with Locke's views about the illegitimacy of such withdrawal, at

17. This condition could be weakened to the requirement that there be no social state that is better for everyone. Nothing in the argument will turn on this difference.

least by those who have given their express consent to social arrangements (2.121). This objection fails because it misconstrues the aim of the present argument. The aim here is to determine which types of state, if any, are just. In order to answer this question, we ask: What sorts of state could be agreed to, given the civil interests and the current distribution of property? If the answer is that, for example, current arrangements could not be agreed to because they are not coalitionally rational, then they are unjust, and consent to an unjust system is not binding. If they could be agreed to, then express consent is permanently binding. But to consider whether or not the existing form of state is coalitionally rational, we need not suppose that it would *in fact be legitimate* to withdraw from a state to which one has given express consent.

Agreeing to a Property Owner's State

With these three conditions in hand, let us now turn to the question of the agreement to a property owner's state. Are there circumstances in which such a state plausibly satisfies the three conditions? In addressing this question, I will suppose that there are four alternatives facing the contractors: (1) live in a state of nature; (2) form a property owner's state; (3) form a single democratic state composed of both propertied and propertyless; and (4) form separate states for propertied and propertyless, with the propertyless forming a democratic state.[18] This restriction on alternatives is in certain respects artificial. To show that the property owner's state would be agreed to—rather than, for example, a system of universal suffrage with plural votes for property owners—would require a more complete account of possibilities and circumstances.[19] But the restriction I have imposed on the set of alternatives permits a more straightforward

18. The original contract, as Locke construes it, does not in fact determine the type of regime but rather forms a people—a collection of individuals governed by the decisions of a majority—who in turn establish the constitution. Thus I am collapsing the two steps into one. For an excellent discussion of the motivations for Locke's two-stage theory, see Julian Franklin, *John Locke and the Theory of Sovereignty* (Cambridge: Cambridge University Press, 1978), esp. chap. 4. My argument would be more complicated by adhering to the two-step structure, but the conclusion would be the same. What would be required is a unanimous agreement to permit the form of regime to be determined by a majority decision of the property owners and for constituent power to return to that group in the face of a dissolution of government. On the consequences of dissolution, see the interesting passage from the radical Whig John Wildman cited in Franklin, *John Locke and the Theory of Sovereignty*, 119.

19. In an earlier draft of this essay I suggested that my argument shows that the property owner's state satisfies the three conditions and is therefore in the core. I would like to thank

account of the structure of Locke's argument and shows how a property owner's state could be chosen over a democratic state even if the property-less are included in the agreement. It thus suffices for my concerns here. What I want to show, then, is *not* that the property owner's state is always the solution, but only that there are plausible conditions in which it would be selected over alternatives (1), (3), and (4).

Since it is easy to see why the propertied would prefer a state controlled by property owners to all the alternatives, I will focus primarily on the as-sessment of these alternatives in terms of the three conditions by the prop-ertyless, with special attention to their assessment of the property owner's state.

Consider first the requirement of individual rationality. Recall that the property owner's state is a constitutional state, with "one rule for rich and poor, for the favorite at court and the countryman at plough" (2.142). So the propertyless could expect greater protection than in the state of nature of their life, their liberty, and such goods as they have. And because of the absence of legal barriers to interclass mobility, they include in their expec-tations some slight probability of gaining property and political rights. It is therefore reasonable to think that the property owner's state satisfies the condition of individual rationality.

To clarify the point, I want to anticipate an issue that properly falls un-der the condition of group rationality. It seems reasonable that a demo-cratic state including both propertied and propertyless would be more likely to adopt redistributive measures favoring the propertyless than that such measures would be adopted in the property owner's state. Abstract-ing from the consequences of such redistribution for economic growth, this difference in likelihood is sufficient for opposition of rational interests of the propertied and propertyless: the propertied prefer the property own-er's state to the democratic state because it is less likely to redistribute; the propertyless prefer the democratic state to the property owner's state be-cause it is more likely to redistribute. This comparison is important. But it is not relevant to the condition of individual rationality. This condition requires only that there be expected civil interest improvements with re-spect to the state of nature (as always, holding the property system fixed). The fact that the propertyless would prefer being in a democratic state

John Ferejohn for emphasizing that I should avoid conveying that impression and should emphasize the restrictions on the set of alternatives.

along with the propertied to being in a state run by the propertied does not imply that it would be irrational for them to agree to the property owner's state. We need to see whether the democratic state with the propertied is a real alternative.

Consider next the condition of coalitional rationality. Here the relevant comparison by the propertyless is between the property owner's state and the democratic state formed by the propertyless alone. Rational agreement to the property owner's state requires that the propertyless *as a group* prefer the property owner's state to their own democratic state. And here again it is plausible to think that *under some circumstances,* and given that the only interests at stake are the civil interests, the propertyless would expect to do better by entering as junior partners in coalition with the propertied than to withdraw and form their own state. There are at least two reasons for this expectation. First, a state composed of the propertyless would be poor, therefore relatively weak, and as a consequence less able to defend itself against external attack. Second, in view of the minimal resources that they control, even the poor members of a rich state might expect a higher level of material well-being than they could expect by living in a poorer state. Locke certainly supposed this. He pointed out that "a king of a large and fruitful territory there [in America], feeds, lodges, and is clad worse than a day-laborer in England" (2.41).

Finally, consider the condition of group rationality. It is plainly not the case that there is an alternative preferred by *everyone* to the property owner's state, since the propertied prefer that state to all other alternatives. Although the propertied and propertyless have opposing preferences on the property owner's state and democratic state (for the reasons indicated earlier, p. 93), the condition of group rationality is nevertheless satisfied.

So the property owner's state does satisfy the three conditions. Everyone prefers it to the state of nature, there is no alternative that everyone prefers to it, and it is not the case that some subset of the population would prefer withdrawal with their property to the property owner's state. But does this distinguish the property owner's state from the democratic state? For it is also plausibly true of the democratic state that it is preferred by all to the state of nature, that there is no alternative that is collectively preferred to it, and that the propertied would prefer the democratic state to forming separate states.

But there is something that distinguishes the two, namely the relative power of the propertied, and associated with that difference a complication in their strategy. Suppose that the propertied threaten that they will not enter into a state with the propertyless unless the state is a property owner's state. Although they would in fact prefer being in a democratic state to being in a state of nature or in separate states, and everyone knows their preferences—recall that the fraud condition disallows agreements that depend on ignorance about the beliefs of others—they are willing to take the chance of having to carry out their threat. That is, they prefer the strategy of insisting on a property owner's state to the strategy of agreeing to a democratic state. For, by virtue of their property, they are stronger than the propertyless. Having greater resources, they can secure protection; being fewer in number, it is easier for them to coordinate. Everyone knows these relative strengths and therefore knows that the propertyless will give in.

It might be objected that such an agreement provides no justification for the property owner's state, since it involves a "threat" by the propertied to the preservation of the propertyless, and as I indicated earlier, consent under threat of force is no consent at all. But this objection fails. For as I also said earlier, there is no obligation to improve the circumstances of others over what they would be in the state of nature. "The only way whereby any one divests himself of his natural liberty, and puts on the bonds of civil society, is by agreeing with other men. . . . This any number of men may do, because it injures not the freedom of the rest; they are left as they were in the liberty of the state of nature" (2.95). In the case under consideration the propertied *offer* a mutually beneficial arrangement to the propertyless. If there is nothing illegitimate about refusing to join together at all, surely there is nothing illegitimate about expressing a willingness to cooperate on mutually beneficial terms—given the different starting points—and then to refuse to cooperate at all if those mutually advantageous terms are rejected.

Simple and Democratic Orders: A Lockean History

The property owner's state is, then, consistent with Lockean foundations.[20] But it is not the only form of state that is consistent with those foundations. The agreement supposes that there are propertied and prop-

20. It is commonly said that Locke is an ahistorical thinker. But that is misleading. He did believe that certain abstract, nonhistorical principles apply across different historical conditions. But perhaps Locke's awareness of the importance and depth of historical change, rather than an inattention to such change, led him away from the more superficially historical modes of argument deployed by those constitutionalists who rested their case on the nature of

ertyless, and that, for example, the propertyless cannot do better in their own democratic state than in a property owner's state. And it is consistent with Locke's theory of property that neither of these conditions obtain. To clarify and elaborate this point, and to preempt a natural misinterpretation of the argument about the property owner's state, I want now to use the general Lockean framework that I sketched above in order to show how, under different background conditions—that is, different property systems and the different rational interests associated with those systems—different forms of state might be agreed to. Here I will consider two alternatives, one that Locke himself discusses and one that is more contemporary.

In the *Second Treatise* Locke briefly discusses the nature of social cooperation before the introduction of money. Since people in the pre-money situation could only legitimately own what they could use, there were significant limits on legitimate inequality. Locke offers the following piece of political sociology about these circumstances: "The equality of a simple poor way of living confining their desires within the narrow bounds of each man's small property made few controversies and so no need of many laws to decide them, or variety of officers to superintend the process, or look after the execution of justice, where there were but few trespasses, and few offenders" (2.107). In this "golden age (before vain ambition, and *amor sceleratus habendi*, evil concupiscence, had corrupted men's minds into a mistake of true power and honor)" (2.111), the chief concern of societies was external aggression, and not internal conflict.[21] Under these conditions of substantial material equality, Locke thought it was reasonable for individuals to agree to a state in which all political authority is held by one person—a first among equals—and placed there primarily for the sake of military leadership. In this simple society, then, the social contract does result in differences of political rights. But those differences do not correspond to differences in property rights.

The second case is an agreement to a democratic state (say, a capitalist democracy). How could this happen? Recall that in agreeing to the property owner's state, the propertyless judge that they would be worse off by

the ancient constitution. Here I agree with David Resnick, "Locke and the Rejection of the Ancient Constitution," *Political Theory* 12, 1 (February 1984): 97–114.

21. For further discussion, see Ronald Meek, *Social Science and the Ignoble Savage* (Cambridge: Cambridge University Press, 1976), chap. 1.

forming their own state than by agreeing to political subordination in a property owner's state (that is, the condition of coalitional rationality was satisfied). But now suppose a point is reached (let us call this point "the late nineteenth century") at which (1) withdrawal by the propertyless is judged preferable to a property owner's state; and (2) it remains true that membership in a democratic state alongside property owners is materially more advantageous than in a democratic state formed just by those without property. The change in expectations might result from changes in both the material resources and organizational capacities of the propertyless, changes that might, for example, be prompted by the growth of large-scale industry within the framework of the property owner's state. In the late nineteenth century, the property owners would still prefer the property owner's state to the democratic state. But they also prefer the democratic state with the propertyless to the withdrawal of the propertyless. Now the propertyless can threaten to withdraw unless there is an extension of suffrage rights. Under these circumstances, the democratic state would be chosen over the property owner's state.

I have introduced these brief examples to illustrate that, on my account, the core commitment of Lockean contractualism is not to a particular form of state. A state controlled by the propertied is consistent with Lockean foundations, even if the propertyless are included in the agreement. Together with the two examples just considered, that consistency underscores that the central commitment is to a way of construing the members of the state and a way to characterize the kind of justification for their political system that members might give to one another. The members are, in the first instance, individuals with specified positions in the property system and with differing rational interests that reflect their divergent positions. And the justifications that they provide must treat these positions and interests as fundamental.

4. Conclusions: Locke and Rousseau

I have tried to indicate what is specific to the notions of freedom, equality, and rationality that figure in Locke's political conception by considering the relationship between the property system and the political order—and particularly by underscoring the fact that the property system serves as part of the background of the agreement in which those notions are embedded, rather than as part of the subject matter of the agreement. The rational interests of the different classes reflect their positions in the property system, and the equal freedom of the members of a social order premises a division between property system and the political order.

By treating the property system as part of the subject matter of the social contract, rather than as part of its background—treating it as social and conventional, not as natural—Rousseau initiated a departure from this Lockean structure of argument. For Rousseau, all features of the social order are subject to public deliberation among equals concerning the requirements of the common good. But if the account I have suggested here is right, that break in the understanding of the relationship between the property system and the political order provides a way of understanding the differences between Lockean and Rousseauean conceptions of freedom, equality, and rationality as well. If the members of the social order do not view themselves and one another as, in the first instance, holders of determinate places in the property system, then they cannot think of their rationality as, in the first instance, a matter of pursuing particular interests that are distinct in known ways from the interests of other members of the order. And without premising the distinction between the property system and the political order, their equal freedom cannot be interpreted simply in terms of a requirement of consent to *political* authority. It must instead be construed in terms of a capacity to enter into public deliberation generally. This view of persons is in one way more abstract than the Lockean view, and yet it suggests the possibility of deeper social bonds. But whether it or the Lockean view is correct depends on how we decide to live our lives.

3

DEMOCRATIC EQUALITY

1. "Guidance Where Guidance Is Needed"

In this essay I examine John Rawls's maximin criterion of distributive equity.[1] According to maximin, social and economic inequalities are just only if they work to the maximum benefit of those in the least advantaged social position.[2] I think that maximin is a reasonable distributive principle, find much that Rawls says in support of it plausible, but believe that that support has not been well understood.[3] So I will present an interpretation, extension, and defense of the arguments for maximin proposed in A *Theory of Justice* (hereafter *TJ*) and in Rawls's more recent papers.[4]

I would like to thank Larry Blum, Paul Horwich, Michael Sandel, and especially Norman Daniels and John Rawls for discussions of some of the issues in this essay, and the editors of this journal for comments on an earlier draft. [*Note added for publication in this collection*: Rawls addresses some of the issues that I discuss in this essay in *Justice as Fairness: A Restatement*, ed. Erin Kelly (Cambridge, MA: Harvard University Press, 2001), 119–130, particularly in his account of the "second fundamental comparison," which assesses his principles in comparison with a mixed conception. Putting the details aside, his thrust is similar to mine: that the "social minimum" at issue in justice as fairness—the minimum defined by the difference principle—is a minimum suited to "the idea of society as a fair system of cooperation between citizens as free and equal," thus suited to an idea of democracy. See 49, 129–130, 132.]

1. Most references to A *Theory of Justice* (*TJ*) are contained in the body of the chapter (Cambridge, MA: Harvard University Press, 1971). [The revised edition of A *Theory of Justice* includes a conversion table that links page numbers in the 1971 edition with page numbers in the 1999 edition. See John Rawls, A *Theory of Justice*, rev. ed. (Cambridge, MA: Harvard University Press, 1999), 517–519.]

2. Throughout I use the term "maximin" rather than "the difference principle."

3. I will not pursue several points on which I disagree with Rawls, including the best interpretation of the ideal of democracy and the implications of that ideal for economic order. See Joshua Cohen and Joel Rogers, *On Democracy: Toward a Transformation of American Society* (Harmondsworth, UK: Penguin, 1983), chaps. 3, 6; Joshua Cohen, "Deliberation and Democratic Legitimacy," in Alan Hamlin and Philip Pettit, eds., *The Good Polity* (Oxford: Blackwell, 1989), 17–34; and Joshua Cohen, "The Economic Basis of Deliberative Democracy," *Social Philosophy and Policy* 6, 2 (Spring 1989): 25–50.

4. Among the many limitations of my discussion are that I do not address problems that arise when "chain-connection" fails, and I say virtually nothing about the problems of characterizing the minimum position or of addressing conflicts among those who are in it.

The essay has three main themes. First, and most important, I emphasize that maximin is a part of a "democratic conception" of equality (75–83). It is a natural consequence of the idea that we should seek to address distributive controversy by "extending" to that controversy the democratic ideal of a political association based on the mutual respect of free and equal citizens.[5] I will come back to this first theme after introducing the second and third.

Second, to present the case for maximin, I will compare Rawls's two principles of justice with three "mixed conceptions" of justice. Like Rawls's conception, each of the mixed views requires equal basic liberties and fair equality of opportunity. But they reject maximin in favor of: (M1) maximizing average utility; (M2) ensuring that no one is below a poverty line, and, subject to that constraint, maximizing average utility; (M3) ensuring that no one is below a poverty line, and subject to that constraint, maximizing average utility discounted by a factor reflecting the degree of income concentration (e.g., the Gini coefficient).[6] To argue the case for maximin, then, I will want to show how considerations of self-respect and stability that provide support for the two principles in preference to utilitarianism (177–183) also carry over to providing reasons for the two principles in preference to the mixed conceptions.[7]

Third, I will present the case for maximin from the point of view of the original position. I will not, however, rely on the maximin rule of choice under ignorance but will emphasize instead that the parties in the original position aim to ensure that their social positions are "acceptable" (see pp. 108–109 below). This account of the original position clarifies and strengthens the arguments for maximin, but it also makes the original position less essential to their statement than one might have thought, an issue that I will revisit at the end of this discussion.

To return now to the first theme, Rawls holds that a reasonable conception of justice should aim to "accommodate our firmest convictions and . . .

5. *TJ*, 319; John Rawls, "Some Reasons for the Maximin Criterion," *American Economic Review, Papers and Proceedings* 64 (1974): 141–146, esp. 144–145; and Rawls, "Reply to Alexander and Musgrave," *Quarterly Journal of Economics* 88 (1974): 633–655, esp. 648.

6. For discussion of this comparison, see *TJ*, sec. 49; Rawls, "Some Reasons for the Maximin Criterion," 141–146; and Rawls, "Reply to Alexander and Musgrave," 646–653. On the motivations for the alternative distributive norms, see below, p. 105.

7. Since the problem is to select a conception of justice that includes a principle regulating the distribution of wealth and authority, and not simply to choose a principle of distribution, such phrases as "reasons for maximin" are shorthand for "reasons for including maximin along with the requirements of equal basic liberties and fair equality of opportunity."

provide guidance where guidance is needed" (20). Justice as fairness accommodates convictions concerning religious toleration, rights of political participation, and racial and sexual discrimination by including an equal right to basic liberties, requiring that positions of social and economic advantage be open to all citizens and affirming that these advantages must operate for the common benefit. To provide guidance, it includes a conception of democratic equality mandating fair equality of opportunity and maximin. Maximin in particular provides needed guidance because it addresses "the correct distribution of wealth and authority," an area in which "we have much less assurance" about what is right than we do on issues of basic liberties, and so "may be looking for a way to remove our doubts" (20).

This lack of "assurance" is fueled in part by the conjunction of two conditions. The first is the intuitive power of certain ideals associated with "the tradition of democratic thought," in particular the fundamental ideal that, as citizens, we are free and equal, however much our social class, our talents, our aspirations, or our fortune may distinguish us and that our institutions should respect our freedom and equality.[8] The second condition is the fact of inequality. Born into different social positions, we have different expectations about the resources we are likely to have over the course of our lives (96). In view of the importance of democratic ideals, it is not surprising that the legitimate extent of these inequalities is controversial. Maximin, when it is understood as addressed to this controversy, has a clear intuitive rationale: If the well-being of the least advantaged is maximized, the least advantaged have no reason to complain. And if the least advantaged have no reason to complain, then how, consistent with accepting the equality of citizens, could anyone have good reason to complain?

So justice as fairness aims both to accommodate and to guide. But as my sketch of the intuitive rationale for maximin indicates, the idea is not simply to supplement principles that accommodate with independent principles that guide. Instead the aim is to guide judgment about the distribution of resources by "extend[ing] the range of some existing consensus"

8. The quote is from John Rawls, "Justice as Fairness: Political Not Metaphysical," *Philosophy and Public Affairs* 14 (1985): 223–251, quote on 233. In general, see Rawls, "Kantian Constructivism in Moral Theory: The Dewey Lectures 1980," *Journal of Philosophy* 72 (1980): 515–572, esp. 517–519; Rawls, "Justice as Fairness," 233–234, 240–244; and Rawls, "The Idea of an Overlapping Consensus," *Oxford Journal of Legal Studies* 7 (1987): 1–25, esp. 2.

(582), in particular by showing that ideals that are ingredient in the democratic tradition, and that are (imperfectly) embodied in modern democracies, provide a *unified rationale* for principles requiring equal liberties, fair equality of opportunity, and maximin. The argument from the original position presents that rationale. Modeling the fundamental ideal of respect for citizens as free and equal, the original position provides (so the argument goes) a justification for the basic liberties associated with citizenship in a democratic state *and* for maximin, thus giving force to the claim that maximin provides a natural extension of democratic ideals.

Whatever its intuitive basis, however, maximin has been the target of three main lines of criticism:[9] that it is an *implausible* principle whose implications are at odds with firm intuitions about just distributions; that choice in the original position is *irrelevant* to justification, and so irrelevant to the justification of maximin in particular; and that maximin would not be the principle of choice in the original position. I will be focusing on the third criticism. Although limits of space prevent me from discussing the implausibility objection in any detail, I do want to sketch one element of it in order to help to motivate the later argument."[10]

Critics of maximin who find some of its implications implausible commonly blame those implications on its "informational poverty" and rigidity.[11] Maximin is impoverished in that it focuses the evaluation of distributions exclusively on the size of their minima, discarding informa-

---

9. The criticisms are stated in a particularly instructive way in Kenneth Arrow, "Some Ordinalist-Utilitarian Notes on Rawls's Theory of Justice," *Journal of Philosophy* 70 (1973): 245–263; Brian Barry, *The Liberal Theory of Justice* (Oxford: Oxford University Press, 1973); Ronald Dworkin, "The Original Position," *University of Chicago Law Review* 40 (1973): 500–533; David Gauthier, *Morals by Agreement* (Oxford: Oxford University Press, 1986), esp. 245–254; John Harsanyi, "Can the Maximin Principle Serve as a Basis for Morality? A Critique of John Rawls's Theory," *American Political Science Review* 69 (1975): 594–606; Thomas Nagel, "Rawls on Justice," *Philosophical Review* 83 (1973): 220–234; Robert Nozick, *Anarchy, State and Utopia* (New York: Basic Books, 1974), chap. 7; Michael Sandel, *Liberalism and the Limits of Justice* (Cambridge: Cambridge University Press, 1982).

10. I do think, however, that many of the cases in which maximin is alleged to have strikingly counterintuitive implications can be addressed by keeping in mind that maximin assumes the operation of the first principle and fair equality of opportunity and is to be applied to the rules of the socioeconomic game and not to particular distributions.

11. I do not discuss Amartya Sen's variant of the informational poverty objection, which emphasizes the problems of focusing on resources rather than human well-being. See "Equality of What?" in Amartya Sen, *Choice, Welfare, and Measurement* (Cambridge, MA: MIT Press, 1982), chap. 16.

tion about, for example, central tendencies and dispersions. It is rigid in that it replaces nuanced judgments about the sufficiency of the minimum (as reflected in, e.g., debates about the location of the poverty line) with the rule that the minimum be maximized.[12] The force of these concerns can be addressed by comparing justice as fairness with the mixed conceptions M_1-M_3, since their distributive components are sensitive to facts that maximin neglects: M_1 considers the mean; M_2 considers the minimum and the mean; and M_3 considers the minimum, the mean, and the dispersion.[13] Furthermore, M_2 and M_3 avoid the rigidity of maximin by rejecting maximization in favor of the less definite requirement of an adequate minimum, namely, a poverty line.[14]

But why pursue this comparison via the original position? Why not simply consider whether these norms, or other more complicated principles, conform to our distributive intuitions and precepts? The reason is that all distributive principles can be expected to conflict with some intuitions and precepts. That is why we need guidance in the first place. The controversy surrounding distribution, and the fact that richness and flexibility may be disadvantages in fundamental distributive norms (see below, p. 120), make it hopeless to pursue that guidance by more thoroughly canvassing our intuitions or by developing richer and more flexible distributive norms in the hope of producing equilibrium between them and a more comprehensive range of distributive intuitions or precepts.

What the implausibility objection really does is to underscore again the importance of the theoretical strategy of looking to more settled ideas outside the sphere of distribution in order to guide judgment within it, of "look[ing] for possible bases of agreement where none seem to exist" (582). This is the aim of an account of democratic equality that addresses the distribution of resources by asking: Which distributive

12. For discussion of the American debates on the location of the poverty line, see James T. Patterson, *America's Struggle against Poverty, 1900–1985* (Cambridge, MA: Harvard University Press, 1986), esp. chap. 5.

13. For variety, I will sometimes use the term "justice as fairness" as a substitute for "the two principles."

14. One can also give additional weight to lower positions by specifying a social welfare function with a parameter that discounts individual utilities as those utilities increase. I will not pursue this idea here since the problem of the arbitrariness in fixing the parameter parallels some of the problems with M_2 and M_3. For discussion, see Rawls, "Reply to Alexander and Musgrave," 643–646; and Anthony B. Atkinson and Joseph E. Stiglitz, *Lectures on Public Economics* (New York: McGraw-Hill, 1980), 339–340.

principles would be chosen by free and equal citizens seeking to choose a full conception of justice that includes principles for liberties and opportunities as well? This strategy for pursuing distributive guidance differs from the approach to questions of distribution that is adopted by Nozick and Gauthier, for example, who do not explain how their views of rights and rational bargaining might account for convictions about the liberty of expression, political liberties, or rights to equal protection of the laws, and that is pursued in the many other approaches to issues of the distribution of resources that do not explicitly incorporate that problem into a wider framework of normative and institutional argument that also accommodates fundamental convictions.[15] An important claim in the argument for maximin, then, is that when we do constrain our evaluation of distributional norms by embedding it in a more comprehensive argument for principles of justice that must also "accommodate our firmest convictions," we will see the reasonable motivations for maximin's (superficially implausible) guidance and its austere informational basis.

2. Original Position and Social Equilibrium

In this section I will clarify the *strategy* of the argument for maximin. I begin by sketching the structure of Rawls's argument for the two principles over average utility.[16] Then I discuss the extension of that structure to the argument for justice as fairness over the mixed conceptions, emphasizing the importance in that argument of the social ideal of a well-ordered society.

The Argument in *TJ*

A central aim of *TJ* is to defend the two principles in preference to utilitarianism (150). The virtues of maximin are relevant to that defense, but they play only a supporting role in the arguments, which turn principally on the uncertain implications of utilitarianism for basic liberties. So the case for maximin itself is not clear. Still, by sketching the argument for the two principles over average utility, we will be in a better position to understand the case for the two principles over the mixed conceptions:

---

15. See, e.g., Nozick, *Anarchy, State, and Utopia*; Gauthier, *Morals by Agreement*.
16. See Steven Strasnick, "Review of Robert Paul Wolff's *Understanding Rawls: A Reconstruction and Critique of 'A Theory of Justice,'*" *Journal of Philosophy* 76 (1979): sec. 5.

ARGUMENT A: TWO PRINCIPLES AND AVERAGE UTILITY

A1. Each party in the original position must seek to ensure that his or her position is satisfactory (or adequate).

A2. The two principles of justice ensure a "satisfactory minimum" (156; also, 175).

A3. Because the two principles ensure a satisfactory minimum, they also ensure satisfactory positions above the minimum.[17]

A4. Average utility does not ensure a satisfactory minimum and may in fact impose "hardship" on some that will be "intolerable" (175).

A5. The gains above the minimum guaranteed by choosing the two principles that might result from choosing average utility (assuming one lands in a position above the minimum) are highly uncertain as to likelihood and magnitude.

A6. Given A1–A5, it is rational to choose the two principles over average utility.[18]

Two points about Argument A are important here. First, the choice of average utility threatens "intolerable" conditions (A4) principally because it provides uncertain support for basic liberties (156). But the liberties and fair equality are protected under the mixed conceptions, and M2 and M3 also put a floor under income and wealth. In considering the choice between the two principles and the mixed conceptions, then, we must drop the claim about intolerable hardships, thus making the arguments less straightforward.

Second, Argument A appeals to the idea that the positions under the two principles, and in particular the minimum position, are satisfactory. Later I

---

17. I make this point explicit in order to address concerns stated by Nozick, *Anarchy, State, and Utopia*, 192; and Gauthier, *Morals by Agreement*, 247.

18. Argument A follows Rawls's claim that the original position exhibits to a high degree the conditions that make the maximin rule of choice suitable—conditions of extreme ignorance, involving grave risks, in which "the person choosing has a conception of the good such that he cares very little if anything, for what he might gain above the minimum stipend that he can, in fact, be sure of by following the maximin rule" (*TJ*, 154). A5 corresponds to the extreme ignorance condition, A4 to the grave risks condition, and A1–A3 to the "cares very little" condition. Note that the "cares very little" passage is not offered as a characterization of the parties in the original position but as a statement of one of the conditions that make the maximin choice rational. What needs to be shown is that an analogous situation obtains in the original position. If A1–A3 obtain, then there is such an analogy. Although the parties represent individuals who do care about getting more than the minimum (they prefer more primary goods to less), they must act to ensure that positions are acceptable. Since getting to an acceptable position is much more important than getting past that position, the analogy obtains.

will present an interpretation of the relevant notion of "satisfactory." Here I want only to enter a point that will be relevant to that interpretation, namely, that much of *TJ* aims to defend the thesis about satisfactory positions. For example, virtually all of Part 3, including the arguments about self-respect and stability, is intended to show that the two principles provide a satisfactory minimum (A2) and thus support the choice of justice as fairness over average utility. There is no formal derivation of the principles that proceeds independently from these "informal" arguments[19] but only the relatively straightforward point (A6) that, if the informal arguments are right, then it is rational to make the conservative choice. So when I present a case for maximin in terms of self-respect and stability, I mean to be providing a case parallel to the argument for the two principles over average utility.

The Argument with the Mixed Conceptions

I will begin the discussion of the reasons favoring the two principles of justice over M1–M3 by sketching an argument modeled on Argument A:

ARGUMENT B: TWO PRINCIPLES AND MIXED CONCEPTIONS

B1. Each party in the original position must seek to ensure that his or her position, whatever it is, is satisfactory (or adequate).

B2. The two principles of justice ensure a satisfactory minimum.

B3. Because the two principles ensure a satisfactory minimum, they also ensure satisfactory positions above the minimum.

B4. M1–M3 do not ensure a satisfactory minimum.

B5. The gains above the minimum guaranteed by the two principles that might result from choosing a mixed conception (assuming one lands in a position above the minimum) are highly uncertain as to likelihood and magnitude.

B6. Given B1–B5, it is rational to choose the two principles over the mixed conceptions.

Argument B differs from A in part because it drops the claim about "intolerable" outcomes (compare A4 and B4). To see whether the balance of reasons still supports justice as fairness, we need a better grip on B1–B4.

19. As is suggested by, among many others, T. M. Scanlon, "Contractualism and Utilitarianism," in A. Sen and B. Williams, eds., *Utilitarianism and Beyond* (Cambridge: Cambridge University Press, 1982), 125–127.

So first I will discuss the notion of a satisfactory position. Then I will show how B1 falls into place. Finally, in the next section, I will present arguments for maximin that aim to provide support for B2–B4, in light of B5.

There are two ways to interpret the notion of an adequate minimum. The first, which I call the "natural threshold interpretation" (NTI), holds that there is a threshold level of primary goods such that any human being with a rational life plan attaches infinite value to attaining that level and a finite value (if any value at all) to getting over it.[20] So a conception of justice ensures a satisfactory minimum if and only if it ensures that everyone gets over the natural threshold. One virtue of NTI is that, by defining a satisfactory position as a position over the threshold, it explains why the parties in the original position are concerned to ensure satisfactory positions (B1). In addition, it shows the special importance of an adequate minimum (B2), since if any positions are below the threshold, the minimum position will be. And finally it explains why the adequacy of the minimum implies the adequacy of all positions (B3), since a minimum above the threshold implies that all positions are over it.

But if NTI is right, then Rawls's argument is transparently wrong.[21] First, it is implausible that rationality and human nature do combine to yield a definite threshold that is uniform across people and circumstances. Second, the existence of a threshold does not support the two principles but requires only that everyone ought to get to the threshold before anyone goes over it. Beyond the threshold, the requirements of equity would remain indeterminate. Third, given that the threshold is assigned infinite utility, any of M1–M3 would do equally well in ensuring the threshold, since average utility will always increase more by pulling people to the threshold than by pushing people over it. The transparency of these difficulties suggests (correctly, I think) that NTI is misguided. But rather than arguing that case, I will propose an alternative account of the adequate minimum that does not assume a natural threshold.

I will call this alternative the "social equilibrium interpretation" (SEI).[22] The SEI begins from the fact that the parties in the original position are

---

20. Brian Barry was, I think, the first interpreter to endorse NTI. Many followed him. See Barry, *The Liberal Theory of Justice*, 97.

21. On the difficulties noted in this paragraph, see ibid., chap. 9.

22. In thinking about SEI I have benefited from Scanlon's "Contractualism," esp. 119–128; and from Edward F. McLennen, "Justice and the Problem of Stability," *Philosophy and Public Affairs* 18 (1989): 3–30.

choosing principles for a well-ordered society with a number of distinct social positions. A conception of justice provides a satisfactory minimum, then, just in case those who occupy the minimum social position in a society regulated by the conception can reasonably expect to find that position acceptable. To explicate the notion of an acceptable social position, I need to say something about the idea of a well-ordered society.

Justice as fairness, as Rawls has emphasized, is addressed to a "modern democratic society" and seeks principles suited to a well-ordered society.[23] These two points are connected in that the notion of a well-ordered society is meant to capture certain aspects of the fundamental democratic ideal of a system of social cooperation among citizens who recognize each other as free and equal and who share an understanding of fair terms of association. Focusing, then, on the notion of a well-ordered society, two features of it play an important role in interpreting the notion of an acceptable position. First, the members of a well-ordered society share a conception of justice, and it is common knowledge that the basic institutions of the society conform to that conception. Recognizing the role of the institutions in shaping their powers, opportunities, and aspirations, those members affirm the legitimacy of those institutions and accept the effects on their powers, opportunities, and aspirations as reasonable. Second, each member has a conception of the good that he or she takes to be worth pursuing. Using that conception as a point of departure, each would arrive at the conclusion that it is rational to have the shared conception of justice, given that others have it as well; each would conclude that justice and goodness are "congruent" (456).

In a well-ordered society, then, each person recognizes the justice of the society and on the basis of that recognition willingly complies with the terms of association and recognizes that his or her conception of justice is rational and, on the basis of that recognition, willingly endorses the conception of justice that leads all members to comply. The question, then, is the following: Are there principles suited to such a society? Are there principles such that (1) if institutions satisfy the principles, and are known by members to satisfy them, then over time new members would

23. On addressing a "democratic society," see *TJ*, viii; Rawls, "Some Reasons for the Maximin Criterion," 142; Rawls, "Kantian Constructivism in Moral Theory," 518; Rawls, "Justice as Fairness," sec. 2; and Rawls, "The Idea of an Overlapping Consensus," secs. 1–2. On the notion of a well-ordered society, see *TJ*, 4, sec. 69; Rawls, "Reply to Alexander and Musgrave," sec. 1; and Rawls, "Kantian Constructivism in Moral Theory," 535–540.

come to understand the principles, to develop an allegiance to them, and to accept the institutions as just because of their conformity to the principles; and (2) each would develop a conception of the good that is worth pursuing and that is congruent with his or her sense of justice? If principles meet these two conditions, then a social order that satisfies them is supported by both moral and prudential reasons, and each position in the order is an acceptable position.

The SEI interprets the notion of a satisfactory position in Argument B in terms of this conception of an acceptable social position in a well-ordered society. Thus a position is satisfactory just in case a person in that position can be expected to acquire a sense of justice that affirms the legitimacy of the system of positions and a conception of the good that they take to be worth pursuing and that supports their sense of justice. Rawls emphasizes that the parties in the original position concentrate on the acceptability of the minimum position (B2). But this concentration is explained by the fact that the minimum position is most likely to be a problem. More fundamentally, the parties aim to ensure that their position is acceptable, whatever it is. And so in my discussion of the choice of principles, I will consider acceptability at positions above the minimum as well as acceptability at the minimum (B3). But before coming to that discussion, I need to consider one final preliminary issue.

Having identified a satisfactory position with an acceptable social position, I need to explain why the parties in the original position conservatively focus on the *acceptability* of positions (B1). The simple answer is that the original position is set up to force them to be conservative, whatever their natural predilections in matters of risk-taking (172). But this simple answer gives rise to two further questions.

First, *why* set up the original position to force a conservative choice? The answer lies in the ethical idea that underlies the design of the original position. The point of the original position is to find principles for a well-ordered society, and the ideal of universal acceptability is one of the features that defines such a society. A variant of the initial situation in which the parties did not seek to ensure the acceptability of their position would be flawed. Put otherwise, the conservativism reflects the fact that the original position is designed to choose principles for a society on the assumption that it is well ordered and not to evaluate the ethical ideal of a well-ordered society itself.

Second, *how* is the original position set up to ensure that the parties focus on acceptability? The requirement that the parties are to *make an agreement* that is *final* requires that they come to terms that they expect to be able to keep; "no one is permitted to agree to a principle if they have reason to doubt that they will be able to honor the consequences of its consistent application."[24] So the parties look for arrangements that are acceptable, since the combination of moral and prudential reasons that make up acceptability should minimize noncompliance, resistance, and efforts at renegotiation. In this way the motivation for the contractual requirement in the original position "lies in its correspondence with the features of a well-ordered society," in particular with the condition of general acceptability.[25] Furthermore, the veil of ignorance prevents knowledge about the likelihood of being in an unacceptable position, if there are any unacceptable positions. And this means that no one can agree to a principle if there is reason to doubt that anyone, in any position, will be able to "honor the consequences of its consistent application." By choosing principles that are generally acceptable, the parties do their best to meet this requirement.

3. Arguments

I now come to the choice between the two principles and the mixed conceptions. Following the structure of Argument B, we need to show that: B2, the minimum position under the two principles is acceptable; B3, the other positions are acceptable given that the minimum is; and B4, the minimum under the alternatives may be unacceptable.

Using this structure to organize the presentation, I will present the case for maximin by showing how the considerations of self-respect and stability that Rawls uses to defend justice as fairness against utilitarianism also provide reasons for preferring it to the mixed conceptions, thus substantiating the claim that maximin is a natural extension of democratic ideas.

Self-Respect

The argument from self-respect is animated by three principal ideas. First, since self-respect is a fundamental good, whose presence is almost

24. Rawls, "Reply to Alexander and Musgrave," 652; see also *TJ*, 175, 183.
25. Rawls, "Reply to Alexander and Musgrave," 651.

certainly required for acceptability (440), the parties must ensure conditions favorable to their self-respect. So important support for maximin would be provided if it were shown that the two principles support self-respect at the minimum position (B2) as well as above the minimum (B3), whereas the mixed conceptions may not support self-respect at the minimum (B4). The rationality of ensuring self-respect is reinforced by B5, that is, by the ignorance surrounding the magnitude of the gains that one may forgo in seeking to ensure self-respect.

While self-respect is not itself subject to public distribution, the second animating idea is that certain supporting conditions or "social bases" of self-respect are. Among those conditions are both the resources (including liberties and opportunities, as well as wealth) that enable us to develop and to pursue our aspirations with self-confidence and the recognition by others (who are themselves respected) of our worth.[26] I will call these the "resource" and "recognitional" bases of self-respect.

A third point aims to give content and plausibility to the idea that self-respect has social foundations by distinguishing two types of social foundation. I will call the first the "associational conditions" for self-respect, the conditions that bear more or less directly on "what we do in everyday life" (441). Self-respect typically requires activity in association with others, including friends, or co-workers, or intimates, or those with whom we share political, intellectual, or spiritual ideals. Such association contributes to both the resource and recognitional foundations of self-respect. But when the basic framework of social and political institutions is unfavorable, these associational conditions may be absent or may fail to have their desired effects. For example, political obstacles may formally restrict the formation of associations; the distribution of wealth may effectively prevent some citizens from advancing their aims; some associations that are formally permitted may nevertheless be subject to public condemnation; and, in the absence of bases of mutual respect that extend across different associations and communities, comparisons across those separate groups may put citizens at odds and weaken the support for self-respect that those associations and communities would otherwise provide. To secure the foundations of self-respect, then, it is important that the framework of institutions and associated forms of public argument—what I will

26. On the importance of recognition to the sense of self, see G. W. F. Hegel, *The Phenomenology of Spirit*, trans. A. V. Miller (Oxford: Oxford University Press, 1977), 111–119.

call the "framework conditions" of self-respect—support and foster the associational conditions.[27]

The parties in the original position must, therefore, assess the effects of different principles on both the resource and recognitional foundations of self-respect, taking into account both associational and framework conditions. Thus they support the liberties of conscience, association, and expression in part because these liberties help to establish a framework that enables citizens to form and to sustain the associations that support their self-respect.[28] They are concerned about their level of resources because they want to be able to use their liberties to pursue their aims with self-confidence.[29] Further, they reject perfectionist principles in favor of "democracy in judging each other's aims" (442, 527), in part because perfectionist norms would likely run counter to the values pursued in at least some associations and thereby undermine the experience of respect in those associations. They embrace the notion of a *right* to liberties because the public understanding that liberties are a matter of right provides a clear affirmation of the worth of each that extends across the plurality of associations, thus enhancing the experience of respect within them. And they require a fair value for political liberty in part because of the public recognition that comes from political equality.[30]

Thus far justice as fairness and M_1–M_3 are in agreement. But they part company over the proper distribution of resources. To make a case for maximin, one needs to show how the considerations of self-respect that support the points of agreement (the right to basic liberties, the fair value of political liberty, the rejection of perfectionism, and some acceptable level of resources) can be extended to provide support for maximin. More specifically, we need to show that maximin assures the foundations of self-respect at the minimum position, that it will ensure those foundations

27. On the associational conditions, see *TJ*, 441–442; on the framework conditions, see *TJ*, 178–180; on their combined operation, see *TJ*, 234, 442.

28. See *TJ*, 536, 543–546; Rawls, "The Basic Liberties and Their Priority," in John Rawls et al., *Tanner Lectures on Human Values*, vol. 3 (Salt Lake City: University of Utah Press, 1982), 32–34.

29. Whereas *TJ*, 543–46, ties self-respect exclusively to the basic liberties, elsewhere maximin is said to contribute to the foundations for self-respect (see *TJ*, 179, 180, 499, 536; Rawls, "Some Reasons for the Maximin Criterion," 145; Rawls, "The Basic Liberties and Their Priority," 32, 34).

30. On self-respect and the fair value of political liberties, see *TJ*, 234; Rawls, "The Basic Liberties and Their Priority," 32.

above the minimum as well, and that M1–M3 will not assure the foundations of self-respect at the minimum position. Let us take up these points in turn.

Consider first the adequacy of justice as fairness in supporting self-respect at the minimum position. Maximin only permits inequalities that contribute to lifetime expectations at the least well-off position. Smaller inequalities would reduce expectations, as would greater inequalities. Let us assume that the value of liberties to a person depends on the level of resources available to the person. (While this seems implausible for the case of the political liberties, their worth is ensured by a proviso in the first principle requiring the fair value of political liberty.)[31] So the minimum value of the liberties under maximin is greater than the minimum value under the alternative principles.[32] Self-respect depends, in turn, on the value of the liberties, since a greater value enables a more confident pursuit of one's aims. Justice as fairness, then, builds strong resource support for self-respect at the minimum position into the framework of association.

Furthermore, this guarantee of the maximal worth of the liberties is part of a *public understanding* about the nature and limits of legitimate inequalities. That understanding identifies an acceptable minimum position as a maximized minimum and so represents a commitment to ensure advantages irrespective of the particulars of social position, natural endowment, and good fortune that distinguish the free and equal members of a well-ordered society. To forgo possible advantages because the changes in public rules required to provide them would also reduce expectations at the minimum is to express respect for those at the minimum and fully to affirm their worth. Given the importance of self-respect, it is rational to build such public recognition of worth into the framework of association

---

31. *TJ*, 224–227, 277–278; Rawls, "The Basic Liberties and Their Priority," 42–45, 72–79.

32. See *TJ*, 204–205, and the more qualified formulation in Rawls, "The Basic Liberties and Their Priority," 40–41. Norman Daniels criticizes this account of the value of liberties in his "Equal Liberty and Unequal Worth of Liberty," in Norman Daniels, ed., *Reading Rawls* (New York: Basic Books, 1975), 253–281. He holds that the value of a liberty to a person is a function of that person's relative position in the distribution of resources (271). In arguing for this thesis he considers only the case of political liberty, where the argument is strongest because the nature of politics makes the value of the liberties competitive. The requirement of a fair value for the political liberties reflects this fact (see Rawls, "The Basic Liberties and Their Priority," secs. 7, 12). But extended to liberties more generally, Daniels's point does not seem right because the use of other liberties is not, as a general matter, competitive.

by choosing maximin, thereby supporting the recognitional bases of re-spect in more particular associations.

So the choice of maximin strengthens the foundations of self-respect. Although the primary support for self-respect may be provided by the as-sociational conditions, the principles of justice and the institutions that satisfy them strengthen the effects of the associations in terms of resources, by ensuring that the minimum level is as large as possible, and in terms of recognition, by providing a framework of public rules and terms of public argument that support a sense of self-worth (234, 442–443).

I now consider a complication in this argument.[33] Maximin is formu-lated in terms of the expectations at the minimum *position,* not in terms of the expectations of the *occupants* of that position (64). Suppose that some farmers are in the minimum position in a maximin system with no agricultural price supports. Introducing price supports might move the farmers out of the minimum, while reducing the minimum expectation by increasing food prices. When this move is rejected as a violation of maximin, farmers cannot be told that their well-being is fully affirmed under maximin because they would be less well off under an alternative principle. The argument instead must be that respect for the farmers is expressed by maximizing the expectation at their position.

But this seems plausible, since it shows no disrespect for the farmers to refuse to improve their condition when such improvement would make another group worse off than the farmers were when they were at the mini-mum. Or at least this argument has force on condition that the farmers do not embrace the idea that there is something especially inappropriate about *farmers* being in the minimum position. And they are committed to rejecting this if they accept the idea that citizens are equals, regardless of social position or aspirations. This is an important qualification, which I will return to below.

We come now to the adequacy of maximin for self-respect at positions above the minimum. Nozick states the problem this way: "No doubt, the difference principle presents terms on the basis of which those less well-endowed would be willing to cooperate. (What *better* terms could they

---

33. After writing the first draft of this article, I read an essay by Brian Barry, "In Defense of the Difference Principle" (paper presented at American Political Science Association annual meeting, Washington, DC, August 1985), which makes the points in this paragraph. I would like to thank John Rawls for bringing Barry's paper to my attention.

propose for themselves?) But is this a fair agreement on the basis of which those *worse* endowed could expect the willing cooperation of others?"[34] Applied to the foundations of self-respect, Nozick's question may appear purely rhetorical. Those in the minimum position have the social bases of self-respect secured in part *by the fact that they are doing as well as they are*. So how could maximin threaten the self-respect of those who are doing *even better?*

One answer is that those who are better off might focus their attention on the transfers and other forms of government activity required by maximin and find the foundations of their self-respect weakened by the fact that those highly visible forms of state action are explicitly keyed to the benefits of those in other positions. But this is a very weak reason. Although the activities of the "transfer branch" (276–277) are not themselves aimed at the benefit of those above the minimum, the social arrangement as a whole is more advantageous to their position than it is to the minimum position. Although the better off are not as well off as they would like to be, the problem, as Nozick's remark indicates, is not to ensure that all citizens are as well off as they would like to be but to find a fair basis for willing cooperation. Furthermore, since maximin imposes no absolute ceiling on the magnitude of the top position, the further success of those who are better off is never treated as worthless. This, too, affirms the foundations of self-respect above the minimum.

But these responses are not satisfactory as they stand because they skirt around the most important difficulty. In particular, they assume that equality is the proper baseline or benchmark for judging advantages. Given that premise, it follows that positions above the minimum are more advantaged *by social cooperation* than those at the minimum. Although those above the minimum prefer still greater advantages, they will not take the fact that their position could be higher under M_1, for example, as a threat to their self-respect under maximin. They accept that if the foundations of self-respect are secure at the minimum position, then they are secure above the minimum.

But why should agents behind the veil of ignorance suppose that they will construe an equal distribution as a reasonable benchmark, if they should occupy a position above the minimum? They might affirm

34. Nozick, *Anarchy, State, and Utopia*, 192.

the ethical relevance of conceptions of the good and natural assets. And if they did, then it would be natural for them to hold that the relevant baseline is a state of nature in which people accumulate property in pursuit of their aspirations and on the basis of their natural assets.[35] But with that baseline, a comparison of positions in the distribution of resources in society provides inconclusive evidence about the relative benefits that flow *from social cooperation*. To accept the state of nature baseline is to reject the claim that advantages *in* society derive *from* social cooperation. Those who are better off might hold that maximin forces absolute concessions on them, or at least that their benefits relative to the relevant baseline are not as great as are the relative benefits for those at the minimum. Even though they are better off, the social order as a whole fails to affirm their worth as fully as the worth of those at the minimum. Concerned to secure their self-respect, they have reason to reject maximin in favor of, for example, maximax, or Gauthier's minimax relative concession, or a principle requiring Pareto improvements over the state of nature.

Of course if they did select one of these alternatives, they might find themselves in a pretty grim minimum. So the conclusion to draw may not be that some alternative to maximin is the principle of choice. Instead it might be that there is no way to secure self-respect at every position and that there does not exist a social equilibrium for a well-ordered society.

In responding to this objection, we need to keep in mind that M_1–M_3 as well as justice as fairness include requirements of equal basic liberties, the fair value of political liberty, and fair equality of opportunity. The parties have already agreed to these principles, having seen their rationale and now are considering distributive norms for a society regulated by them. But then they must assume that whatever more particular position they hold, they are committed to accepting the understanding that the members are basically equal and, in particular, to accepting that social class, natural endowments, and conceptions of the good are all ethical contin-

35. See, e.g., ibid.; Gauthier, *Morals by Agreement*; and James Buchanan, *The Limits of Liberty: Between Anarchy and Leviathan* (Chicago: University of Chicago Press, 1975). For a critical appraisal of such accounts of the social contract, consider Jean-Jacques Rousseau's *Discourse on Inequality*, trans. Victor Gourevitch (New York: Harper & Row, 1986), 183, along with his *On the Social Contract, with Geneva Manuscript and Political Economy*, ed. Roger D. Masters, trans. Judith R. Masters (New York: St. Martin's Press, 1978), bk. 1, chap. 6, paras. 6–7.

gencies that provide no reasons for differential treatment. If they do not accept that view, then it is not clear why they would accept the equal right to liberties of conscience, of expression, and of participation, the fair value of political liberty, and fair equality of opportunity. But if they do accept it, then it is reasonable for them to regard equality as the benchmark for determining advantages. For to advance an alternative would be to assume that some people, or some aims, or some talents, or some contributions are more important than others. But given a benchmark of equality, securing the social foundations of self-respect at the minimum position does secure them above the minimum. So the background assumption of equality provides a rationale for focusing on the bottom position and for supposing that secure foundations of self-respect at the minimum imply secure foundations above the minimum.

Suppose instead that they were to take the position that natural assets and conceptions of the good are relevant. To give content to this view, they imagine a state of nature in which individuals, guided by their aspirations, use their assets to accumulate resources. And they seek to assess the value of social cooperation to individuals by reference to this baseline. Putting to the side the problems of thinking of current aspirations and abilities as the aspirations and abilities people would have in a state of nature, it seems implausible that this line of thought would lead to any of M_1–M_3. In fact, it appears to provide a rationale for rejecting the requirements of fair equality of opportunity as well as the principle of equal political liberty. For once it is agreed that the baseline is a state of nature with differential holdings of property, then a rational social contract only requires improvements with respect to the inequalities of that preinstitutional situation. And such improvements might be secured through a system of constitutional government with inherited differences in real opportunities or in which political rights correspond to property ownership, or gender, or race.[36] So M_1–M_3 seem to be unstable alternatives to maximin. And at least some theories that reject maximin seem also to provide reasons for rejecting the equality of basic liberties and fair equality of opportunity as well, thus promising distributional guidance without accommodating more fundamental convictions.

36. For discussion, see Joshua Cohen, "Structure, Choice, and Legitimacy: Locke's Theory of the State," *Philosophy and Public Affairs* 15 (1986): 301–324 (reprinted as Chapter 2 in this volume).

We now come to the sufficiency of the minimum under the mixed conceptions (B4). Consider first M_1. M_1 provides weaker assurance of the social bases of self-respect than maximin does. Although the adherents of M_1 accept the equality of basic liberties and the need for a fair value of political liberty, they reject the idea of maximizing the minimum value of the liberties. Because the resource minimum may be lower, those who are in the minimum position may end up less able to pursue their aims than the occupants of the minimum position under maximin. And this lower value of the liberties weakens the resource support for self-respect, although the extent of that weakening is uncertain.

Furthermore, in view of the recognitional bases of self-respect, it is important to consider the justification of the magnitude of the minimum and not simply its level. And under M_1, no one can say, "The inequalities cannot go farther than this because of the losses to those in my position." Because of publicity, each knows that *no* loss either of resources or of utility at his or her position ever provides a sufficient reason for rejecting a policy. A policy of loose labor markets, for example, with its predictable distributional implications, might then be supported *because* the combination of utility gains above the minimum and utility losses at the minimum produces an increase in average utility. And this is a weaker guarantee of the recognitional bases of respect than is available with maximin.

The support for self-respect also is weaker under M_2 and M_3 than under maximin, even though both include a minimum requirement. Thus, suppose that distributional institutions satisfy maximin and that I am in the minimum position. Still, my situation is adequate from the point of view of self-respect. As the economy grows, suppose that there is an announced shift to M_2 or M_3 under a transition rule that initially fixes the minimum at a level equal to the minimum expectation under maximin. Thereafter, however, the minimum will not be maximized. But since it never falls below what we assume to be an adequate level, how could the new minimum fail to be adequate?

This line of thought has considerable force on NTI. If everyone were above the threshold under maximin, M_2 or M_3 would by stipulation maintain people above that threshold. But the threshold notion is not a suitable understanding of the foundations of self-respect. It is public knowledge under M_2 and M_3 that the rules of the economic game do not work over time to maximize the minimum. So if I am in the minimum position, then I know that I could do better if those who are better off were prepared to forgo some of their advantages. And I know that this loss of advantage to me is not just for a stretch of time but covers the course of my entire life. Others know this, and know that I know it, and so on. Still they accept the advantages. This is a manifestly weaker affirmation of worth than is provided by maximin. How much weaker depends on where exactly the minimum is fixed under M2 or M3. A political determination of the adequate minimum might match its principled maximization under maximin. If the parties are counting on this, they might just as well choose the more rigid maximin principle. But since this matching seems unlikely, the maximizing specification has advantages over M2 and M3.

In sum, maximin provides stronger support for self-respect than M1–M3. Self-respect might be widespread under the alternatives to maximin; even at the minimum, the associational conditions may be sufficient, especially with the support from the fair value of political liberty and fair equality of opportunity. But the background institutional support is less firm. In view of the importance of self-respect, justice as fairness is preferable.

Stability

We come now to the second argument, which parallels and extends Rawls's account of the stability of the two principles relative to utilitarianism (177–178, 496–504). The core of Rawls's argument is that a society is *stably just* only if there exists a social mechanism that preserves just conditions (should they obtain); that the most plausible mechanism is a shared sense of justice, and in particular a shared sense of justice that is rational for each citizen to affirm on reflection (454–458); and that a sense of justice organized around the two principles could more plausibly play this role than the average utility principle.

Why, however, would the parties, who are assumed not to be moved by considerations of justice at all, be so concerned with the stability of the conception that they choose? The earlier discussion of the ethical ideal of a well-ordered society provides the basis for an answer. What *makes* a conception of justice stable is that a society that conforms to it meets the two conditions I discussed earlier in the account of the acceptability of positions in a well-ordered society: Assuming a society that conforms to the conception of justice, the members of the society *acquire* the conception to which institutions conform; and that sense of justice is congruent with their good. So what underlies the concern with stability in the original position is the concern with acceptability. Assuming this latter concern, then, and following the structure of Argument B, the parties need to consider acquisition and congruence for maximin at the minimum position (B2) and for positions above the minimum (B3), and then the suitability of the mixed conceptions from the minimum standpoint (B4).

The problem of *acquisition* is to find principles such that individuals who are brought up in a well-ordered society regulated by those principles can be expected to acquire them in the normal course of their maturation. Acquisition has both cognitive and motivational aspects (485, 494–495). I will start with the cognitive.

The principles of justice must be learned, their content and implications understood. So it is important to choose principles that are "perspicuous to reason" (499). Since each person occupies the position of equal citizen, this issue, I will assume, can be addressed without special reference to more particular positions. The main issue, then, is the relative ease with which different principles and their implications can be understood. So consider a society whose institutions are regulated by the two principles. The institutions conform to those principles—and conform to them in part because the members seek to preserve that conformity. In this society, the principles, as well as the conceptions of the person and social association that animate them, are learned in part as a consequence of the fact that they are expressed in certain obvious features of public institutions—for example, equality before the law, political liberties, public support for education, and tax and transfer policies aimed at ensuring that inequalities benefit the least advantaged. Acting within those institutions, citizens learn about their obligations and legitimate expectations, and about the features of individuals that are relevant to public argument.[37] Furthermore, the principles are acquired as a consequence of their role in providing the terms of public argument and justification among equal citizens (472–473).

Considered from the point of view of these processes of acquisition, maximin has the advantage of *relative* ease of understanding. Compared to other principles, maximin is relatively simple, the information on which it depends is relatively accessible, and its rigidity makes its implications relatively definite. Relative clarity and ease of understanding should help

---

37. On the idea that citizens acquire norms by participating in institutions that conform to them, see Rousseau, *On the Social Contract*, bk. 3, chaps. 12–15; and G. W. F. Hegel, *The Philosophy of Right*, trans. T. M. Knox (Oxford: Oxford University Press, 1952).

to smooth the way to acquisition and to support a common understanding of the principles despite the differences in the circumstances in which they are learned.

These points about relative ease of understanding are weakest against M_1 because it is simpler than M_2 or M_3. But M_1-M_3 all require relatively inaccessible utility information and cardinal interpersonal comparisons of utility (320–324). M_2 and M_3 (even if they are reformulated in terms of resources instead of utility) are also more complex than maximin, and both are less determinate (rigid) in their specification of the minimum. In short, the informational poverty of maximin, and the limits that its rigidity places on the role of political judgment in defining an acceptable minimum, have a point once when we take into account the importance of perspicuousness to reason. Since these advantages are shared by maximax, they are certainly not decisive. But we are looking to see how the "balance of reasons" (183) comes out and not to find a single decisive reason.

A natural objection is that questions about the implications of distributional principles are not well understood, and so this appeal to relative ease of understanding is spurious. Applying maximin requires, for example, a definition of the least well-off group and judgments about the kind of transfer scheme best suited to maximizing those expectations and the level of government at which it should be implemented. So even with public agreement about maximin, considerable public disagreement would likely remain. This objection correctly highlights that principles of justice can never eliminate the need for judgment. But it does not undermine the point that I am urging here, which concerns the *relative* simplicity, accessibility of information, and determinateness of maximin. Like all principles, maximin leaves considerable room for disagreements about its proper interpretation. But leaving room for disagreement is consistent with providing greater focus and guidance for public debate on distributional issues. And that is the only issue here.

This brings me to the motivational issue. Acquisition requires that citizens develop a disposition to judge and to act with the guidance of the principles, and the feelings (guilt, indignation) that are appropriate to them. Rawls emphasizes, plausibly I think, that reciprocity plays a central role in the formation of moral motivations: when others display a concern for our good, we develop a disposition to respond in kind (485, 494–495). What, then, are the implications of this psychological thesis for the assessment of principles?

I will begin by considering whether maximin contributes to acquisition at the minimum (B_2). Thus suppose that citizens in the minimum position do learn the principles and recognize the commitment to their good reflected in those principles. As we saw in the discussion of self-respect, justice as fairness expresses that commitment by requiring both that inequalities work to the maximum advantage of the least well-off and that public argument proceed in terms of that advantage. Understanding this, those at the minimum position recognize that they (and those to whom they have attachments) benefit from the fact that others act on maximin. The tendency to reciprocate then leads those at the minimum position to develop a sense of justice whose content is given in part by maximin. For my having such a sense of justice is tantamount to my having a commitment to the good of each of those others who acts for my good. So when other citizens act from maximin they display a concern for my good and the good of those to whom I am attached. Responding in kind, I develop a concern for their good, and express this concern in part through an allegiance to the principles, including maximin.

The force of this point about motivation formation is supported by features of maximin that I mentioned in the discussion of the cognitive side of acquisition. Since maximin relies on more accessible information, it reduces temptations to manipulation and thus helps to establish trust. And by rigidly requiring that the minimum be maximized, and not simply that it be "suitable" or "decent," it provides added assurance of the willingness to reciprocate on the part of those in the minimum position.

In all of these respects, M_1–M_3 are less satisfactory (B_4). The bonds of trust, for example, are weakened by the reliance on more manipulable information. But more important, assuming the importance of reciprocity to acquisition, the mixed conceptions are less likely to be acquired than maximin. Those conceptions may require sacrifices at the minimum for the benefit of positions above the minimum. In the case of M_1, the absence of a minimum requirement makes this clear enough. With M_2 and M_3, there is a minimum requirement, but it is weaker. And this makes acquisition at the minimum less likely since affirming the distributive norms would be tantamount to affirming the good of those who do not fully respect one's good.

It may be objected that this appeal to the sacrifices imposed at the minimum by M_1–M_3 is indefensible. I propose to elaborate on the objection and to respond to it by considering the problem of acquisition at positions above the minimum (B3). The objection arises in response to the suggestion that the alternatives to maximin are weaker triggers to reciprocity because of the "sacrifices" they impose at the minimum. In response, it may be said that maximin is equally weak because of the sacrifices it imposes above the minimum. Positions above the minimum could (virtually) always be improved by the departures from the maximin point required by M1—M3. If sacrifices lead to problems of acquisition at the minimum under M1–M3, then there ought also to be obstacles to acquisition at positions above the minimum under maximin. Put otherwise, the argument about acquisition at the minimum may suggest that the only way to trigger reciprocity at *any* position is to maximize the expectation at that position. Then, however, the acceptability of the minimum position under maximin will conflict with the acceptability of other positions, thus undermining B3.

This difficulty cannot be answered by reference to the intrinsic characteristics of reciprocity. It is a commonplace of social psychology that reciprocity is a universal norm. But the content of reciprocity depends on shifting understandings of which values are "equivalent."[38] For example, when capitalists pay more than market-clearing wages, workers often respond by increasing the intensity of their labor. Akerlof has proposed that this response reflects workers' background understanding of the compensation that they can reasonably expect, namely, market-clearing wages.[39] So when capitalists pay above market-clearing wages, workers respond with the "gift" of additional effort. If, by contrast, workers took themselves to be entitled to the higher wage, there would be no such gift exchange. Similarly, consider those whose understanding of entitlements assumes as a background the distribution of natural assets and the accumulations of wealth that would result from that distribution in a notional state of nature. They are unlikely to hold the view that treatment in accordance with maximin displays a concern for their good that ought to be reciprocated with a concern for the good of others as expressed in maximin. Instead, they can be expected to construe such "concern" as the moral equivalent of armed robbery.

38. For both commonplaces, see Roger Brown, *Social Psychology*, 2nd ed. (New York: Free Press, 1986), chap. 2, esp. 48–53, 60–63. Rawls's view is stronger than the near-consensus position, which concerns the regularity of behavioral reciprocity and not the role of reciprocity in the formation of new motives, which is Rawls's concern in *TJ*.

39. George Akerlof, "Labor Contracts as Partial Gift Exchange," *Quarterly Journal of Economics* 87 (1982): 543–569.

In addressing this issue, we come back again to points that I discussed in connection with self-respect at positions above the minimum (see pp. 114–117 above). Agreement has already been reached on equal liberties and fair equality of opportunity. Everyone sees the rationale for those principles; the problem is to choose distributive norms for a society that is regulated by them and that embodies the conception of equality expressed in them. But the fact that the parties accept one another as equals supports the view that equality is the benchmark. And if it is, then they must reject the view that maximin imposes sacrifices above the minimum, since those above the minimum are already doing better relative to the relevant benchmark than others whose position is supposed to be acceptable. So given the background democratic understanding that equality is the benchmark, considerations of reciprocity do support acquisition of maximin at the minimum and at positions above the minimum.

We come now to *congruence*. The problem of congruence arises once we assume that the members of the society have acquired a sense of justice defined by the basic norms that govern their society. The issue that remains is whether it is rational for them to have that sense of justice, given its content and its role in regulating judgment, action, and feeling. More specifically, we need to consider the rational response by a member of a well-ordered society to the fact that other members have a sense of justice (568). If it is rational to respond by embracing the sense of justice that one has acquired, then the principles meet the test of congruence, thus contributing to the argument for them.

My discussion of congruence will be limited in two important ways. First, I will not consider the overall likelihood of congruence, but only whether the choice of the two principles rather than M1–M3 strengthens the case for congruence. So I put to the side issues about congruence that raise difficulties for all the conceptions that I have been examining—for example, the potential conflicts between conscientious convictions and the principles of justice. Second, I will concentrate exclusively on a case for congruence that draws on the "Aristotelian principle" and the idea of a just society as a "social union of social unions" (571).[40] Rawls argues that, in virtue of the Aristotelian principle, membership in a just society is a "great good" (571). But he does not discuss the role of maximin in making

40. See also Rawls, "The Basic Liberties and Their Priority," 34–38.

it such a good.[41] That will be my focus here. I will begin with three background remarks about this argument for congruence.

First, on each of the conceptions of justice that we have considered, a just society provides a framework that encourages the expression of a wide range of human powers. The liberties and fair equality of opportunity formally enable individuals and associations to deploy their powers in pursuit of a plurality of aspirations. The rejection of perfectionism and the embrace of a pluralism of ideas of the good encourage variety in the forms of human expression. And each of the distributive principles provides some support to the pursuit of those diverse aims.

Second, a natural consequence of this first point is that citizens who share a sense of justice share the aim of coordinating their activities in ways that encourage the expression of human powers; they endorse the ideal of securing a framework of conditions in which a plurality of human goods can flourish. Sharing in that aim, they identify with (do not experience alienation from) the aspirations and activities of others who pursue aims and develop powers that they cannot pursue and develop themselves.

Third, there is a pair of psychological ideas. The first is the Aristotelian principle, according to which the enjoyment of our own activities is a function of (among other things) the complexity of those activities (426). The second, the "companion effect" of the Aristotelian principle, states that we enjoy the self-realizing activities of others (426, 428), at least when we are able to develop and to express our own powers as well (523).

These three points together provide some support for congruence on M1–M3 as well as justice as fairness. Thus to have a sense of justice is to have the aim of coordinating action in ways that provide favorable conditions for the expression of a wide range of human powers in pursuit of a plurality of aims. Bringing such coordination out of this diversity of forms of human expression is an activity of great complexity (528). So if the enjoyment of one's own activities depends in part on their complexity, then there is some reason for embracing the common aim by affirming the sense of justice. For it is in virtue of that affirmation that one's own actions are guided by the aim of maintaining the scheme, and being so guided contributes to their complexity.

41. Maximin does not play an explicit role in any of the arguments for congruence in *TJ*, sec. 86.

Further, having a sense of justice, we take an interest in the interests and activities of others; we respect them as free and equal citizens and have among our aims the provision of circumstances that enable them to develop and to realize their powers. This aim strengthens the companion effect, since the affirmation of justice makes their activities, in a way, our own. By contrast, persons who act in ways that undercut their sense of justice may lose the enjoyment that comes from taking the complex activity of coordinating on fair terms as their own and from identifying with the diverse aspirations of others and the achievements that follow on those aspirations.

Although these considerations provide some grounds for congruence, they do not turn on the presence of maximin. To see whether maximin strengthens the case for congruence, we begin with its contribution at the minimum position. I will consider both the relative benefits of affirming the sense of justice and the costs of doing so.

On the side of benefits, embracing maximin involves a stronger attachment to the interests of others than does M_1–M_3 for reasons that I suggested in the discussions of reciprocity and the social foundations of self-respect. M_1, for example, rests on a willingness to improve one's own situation even if the result is a worsening of the situation of others who are less well-off to begin with. Neither the minimum requirement included in M_2 and M_3 nor the constraint on dispersion in M_3 changes the fact that maximin embodies a more complete affirmation of the interests of others. So maximin provides a firmer basis for the operations of the Aristotelian principle and the companion effect than the mixed conceptions. The stronger attachments reflected in maximin reduce alienation and dispose us "to appreciate the perfections of others" (523). The limited respect expressed in the other principles correspondingly limits the appreciation.

In addition, the respect expressed in maximin and the resources ensured by it help to ensure that the least well off are in a position to develop and to express their powers. So they are not offered the proposal that they find their (vicarious) enjoyment in advancing the aims of others. This aids in the operation of the companion effect, according to which our enjoyment of the activities of others is fostered by our own self-realization.

On the side of costs, there is no additional cost at the least advantaged position in affirming the sense of justice when maximin is added than there is when it is not part of the scheme. So there are added benefits, and no additional costs, and this implies that the contribution to congruence at the minimum by maximin is greater than the contribution by M_1–M_3.

What about those at higher positions? Why is it rational for them to find the enjoyments that come from a sense of justice preferable to the additional advantages they might derive from fewer constraints on the use of their current advantages to pursue their aspirations? Here again we should focus on the relative judgment: Is congruence more plausible under the two principles or under a mixed conception? In this case, there seems to be no clear advantage for maximin. The benefits of affirming it are greater for the same reasons that I mentioned in connection with the benefits at the minimum position. But the costs are greater as well, since the advantages at positions above the minimum under M_1–M_3 are almost certain to be greater than under maximin and are likely to be greatest under M_1. So the case for congruence above the minimum might be greater with M_1 than with maximin, though the balance of benefits and costs would presumably vary with circumstances. However, the combination of greater costs and a correspondingly weaker case for congruence is not deeply troubling. None of the alternatives has a stronger overall case for congruence, and the costs are not so high as to make it impossible to live a decent life while affirming the principles of justice. That is not true at the minimum position, and so it is not true at higher positions either—at least if the parties accept the democratic idea that standards of decency are not fixed by class background.

4. Conclusions

On balance, then, the considerations I have discussed support maximin and give it a natural place in the ideal of democratic association. To conclude, I want to consider two related objections to my general interpretation of arguments from the original position.

In presenting the case for maximin, I have focused on the notion of a well-ordered society in which all positions are acceptable. But this may obscure the role of the original position in the argument. Why consider the choice of principles from behind a veil of ignorance? Why not simply consider the conditions that are required for an arrangement to be acceptable at each position? Answering the former question requires an answer to the latter, since the parties in the original position must consider the acceptability of positions. But once we have an answer to the latter, the initial choice seems to be an "unnecessary shuffle" (32). We want to know what would be chosen in the original position *because* we want to know which arrangements (if any) are acceptable from each point of view. We can answer this question without proceeding through an initial choice situation. So isn't the original position pointless?

I do not think so. Proceeding via the original position focuses attention on the question, "Which principles (if any) are acceptable from each position?" It helps to bring out the ethical interest of this question and to get a clearer picture of how to answer it. We answer by attributing certain basic interests to citizens and by considering what people with those interests would rationally choose. Asking what would be chosen from behind the veil of ignorance brings focus and clarity by depriving people of the information that is irrelevant to the problem of acceptability and by providing a unified point of view from which that problem can be addressed. The original position is not *essential* to the argument for principles, since we can address the question of acceptability without introducing it at all. Still, this does not represent a serious objection to the original position, which is a device for solving a problem. Like most devices, it is not essential. Like other good devices, it is helpful. Like other good intellectual devices, it helps by clarifying.

But this response to the first objection suggests a second difficulty: treating the original position as a device for clarifying the problem of finding a social equilibrium for a well-ordered society may appear to deprive choice in the original position of its ethical interest. For the focus on social equilibrium might be thought to reduce the problem of justice to an issue of social stability and, in particular, to the issue of what conditions might people be brought to accept. But this criticism misses the point of the SEI. The SEI does not identify the problem of justice with the problem of social stability but with the problem of finding the conditions required for stability *in a well-ordered society.* Whatever ethical interest the generic problem of stability might have, the more specific issue of the stability of a well-ordered society does have ethical interest. Or at least it has as much interest as the question, "What principles of justice are appropriate for a democratic society of free and equal citizens?"

4

A MORE DEMOCRATIC LIBERALISM

What do we do when we find the truth? . . . When men
learned the Earth was round, did they allow their geographers
to continue to teach that it was flat?
. . .
If you would see the monuments of a society that has come to
consider the truths that Jesus Christ taught us as one among
an indefinite variety of moral codes by which to live, look
around you. Amen, and Happy Easter.

— PAT BUCHANAN, "Tolerance and Truth at Easter"

1. Social Unity and Moral Pluralism

When Peter Laslett published his first collection of essays on *Philosophy,
Politics and Society* in 1956, he reported that "for the moment, anyway,
political philosophy is dead."[1] Things have certainly changed since
then. Political philosophy is back, and its revival owes much to John
Rawls's A *Theory of Justice* (hereafter *Theory*).[2] Published more than
twenty years ago, *Theory* remains the starting point for contemporary
work on justice. This fact by itself is sufficient to make the appearance of

I am grateful to Frank Michelman and Michael Sandel for discussions of drafts of their re-
views of *Political Liberalism*, to John Rawls for countless discussions on the themes of his book
and for helpful comments on an earlier draft of this essay, and to participants in political theory seminars at Yale University and Wesleyan University for their suggestions. Epigraph
source: Pat Buchanan, "Tolerance and Truth at Easter," *Arizona Republic*, April 3, 1994, E5.
1. Peter Laslett, "Introduction," in Peter Laslett, ed., *Philosophy, Politics, and Society* (Oxford: Blackwell, 1956), vii.
2. John Rawls, A *Theory of Justice* (Cambridge, MA: Harvard University Press, 1971). [The
revised edition of A *Theory of Justice* includes a conversion table that links page numbers in
the 1971 edition with page numbers in the 1999 edition. See John Rawls, A *Theory of Justice*,
rev. ed. (Cambridge, MA: Harvard University Press, 1999), 517–519.]

Rawls's second book, *Political Liberalism* (hereafter *Liberalism*), an important event.[3]

But the intellectual importance of *Liberalism* reaches well beyond the biography of its author and the recent history of political philosophy. Rawls's book is a deep and original examination of a fundamental problem of modern politics. Modern societies are marked by manifest ethical, religious, and philosophical disagreements among citizens.[4] Moreover, the disagreements are of a special kind. Although citizens commonly regard the moral, religious, and philosophical views of others as *false*, they need not regard others as *unreasonable* for endorsing those views.[5] Because human reason appears not to converge on a single moral outlook, we seem to face "a plurality of reasonable yet incompatible comprehensive doctrines" (xvi). What are the implications of these doctrinal conflicts—this "fact of reasonable pluralism" (xvii)—for our understanding of the requirements of justice and the possibility of a just society?[6]

A. Democratic Toleration

Liberalism addresses this question against the background of the account of justice as fairness advanced in *Theory*. In *Theory*, Rawls proposed an ideal of a well-ordered, democratic society featuring consensus on a con-

---

3. This essay was originally published as a review of John Rawls's *Political Liberalism* (New York: Columbia University Press, 1993). References to that book are included parenthetically in the text. *Political Liberalism* is presented as a series of eight lectures, which descend in complex ways from earlier lectures and papers. The first five lectures are revisions of previously published articles, but the revisions are substantial even when—as with lectures 4 and 5—the titles have not been changed. Lecture 6 is a significantly modified version of material presented in public lectures but never before published. Lectures 7 and 8 were published previously and are reproduced without modification. See *Political Liberalism*, xii–xiv. Apart from lectures 7 and 8, then, it is a mistake to identify the views advanced in *Political Liberalism* with positions taken in earlier versions of the lectures.

4. I say "manifest" because I do not suppose that any society is morally or religiously homogeneous, however much its institutions may suppress the expression of differences by limiting expressive liberty, establishing compulsory forms of worship, or narrowly circumscribing associative liberty.

5. I will say more about the distinction between reasonable and unreasonable later. See section 4.C below. It will suffice here to note the familiar logical distinction between *is true* and *is reasonable*: inconsistent views cannot both be true, but they can both be reasonable.

6. Versions of this question are posed at xviii, xxv, 4, and 133. Rawls does not suppose that the fact of reasonable pluralism taken on its own leads us to a particular conception of justice. The problem of *Political Liberalism* is generated instead by an apparent tension between the fact of reasonable pluralism and the ideal of a well-ordered society featuring consensus on a conception of justice that articulates such fundamental political values as fairness, equality, and liberty.

ception of justice rooted in the value of fair cooperation among citizens as free and equal persons.[7] But *Theory*, Rawls now thinks, did not take the fact of reasonable pluralism seriously enough. The presentation suggested that justice as fairness depends on a *comprehensive liberal philosophy of life*—that only people who endorse a view of our nature and of the human good that emphasizes independence, choice, and self-mastery have good reason to endorse justice as fairness.[8]

Liberalism asks, then, whether justice as fairness can be freed from this dependence. Can views that disagree about moral fundamentals— some of which reject a comprehensive liberal philosophy of life— nevertheless agree on a political conception of justice rooted in "values of equal political and civil liberty; fair equality of opportunity; . . . economic reciprocity; [and] the social bases of mutual respect between citizens" (139)? Or does the fact of reasonable pluralism imply that we ought to give up on the idea of a consensus of justice, that democratic politics can never *be* more than a combination of individual calculation, group bargaining, and assertions of discrete collective identities—when democracy works well—and deceit, manipulation, and naked force—when democracy works badly?

In a world full of cruelty, depravity, and grief, we ought not to dismiss the virtues of a politics of group bargaining within a framework of rules that win general compliance—"a mere modus vivendi" (145). Still, *Liberalism* defends the possibility of doing better: of achieving a consensus on political justice under conditions of fundamental moral, religious, and philosophical disagreement.

The key to that possibility is that political values—for example, the value of fair cooperation among citizens on a footing of mutual respect— are extremely important values and can be acknowledged as such by conflicting moral conceptions, by views that disagree with one another about ultimate values and about the best way to live.[9] To be sure, those views will explain the importance of political values in very different terms:[10] for

---

7. Rawls, A *Theory of Justice*, 12–13.

8. On the idea of a comprehensive moral conception, see *Political Liberalism*, 13. For the concern that *Theory* endorses such a conception, see xvi–xvii.

9. See *Political Liberalism*, 139, 155–157, 168–169, 208–209, 217–219.

10. Some views may treat fairness itself as a fundamental value and not as an implication of some deeper moral value. See the "third view" at *Political Liberalism*, 145.

example, as rooted in autonomy,[11] or self-realization,[12] or human happiness properly understood,[13] or the appropriate response to life's challenges,[14] or the value of individuality,[15] or the equality of human beings as God's creatures.[16] These competing explanations of the political values will in turn manifest themselves in conflicting views about individual conduct and personal virtue.

Still, an affirmation of the importance of political values is not the unique property of a particular moral outlook. For this reason, the different moral views that flourish in a society governed by a conception of justice rooted in the ideal of fair cooperation on a footing of mutual respect may each have good and sufficient reason to support that conception as the correct account of justice and not simply as a suitable accommodation to conditions of disagreement. Citizens who endorse different moral axioms may still arrive at the same theorems about political justice, and some people may simply endorse a view of justice without resting that endorsement on a more comprehensive moral theory.[17]

In such a society, we have an "overlapping consensus" on a "political conception of justice."[18] Citizens achieve social unity because they all accept that conception and so agree to conduct the fundamentals of political argument on the shared ground that the conception makes available

---

11. See Immanuel Kant, *Metaphysical Elements of Justice*, trans. John Ladd (Indianapolis: Bobbs-Merrill, 1965); Joseph Raz, *The Morality of Freedom* (Oxford: Oxford University Press, 1986).

12. See T. H. Green, *Lectures on the Principles of Political Obligation* (Ann Arbor: Ann Arbor Paperbacks, 1967); T. H. Green, *Prolegomena to Ethics*, 5th ed., ed. A. C. Bradley (Oxford: Oxford University Press, 1906).

13. See John Stuart Mill, *Utilitarianism*, reprinted in *Utilitarianism, Liberty, and Representative Government*, ed. H. B. Acton (New York: E. P. Dutton, 1972); John Stuart Mill, *On Liberty*, reprinted in *Utilitarianism, Liberty, and Representative Government*.

14. See Ronald Dworkin, "Foundations of Liberal Equality," in Stephen Darwall, ed., *Equal Freedom: Selected Tanner Lectures on Human Values* (Ann Arbor: University of Michigan Press, 1995), 190–306.

15. See Stuart Hampshire, *Innocence and Experience* (Cambridge, MA: Harvard University Press, 1989), 114, 117–118, 124–136. Hampshire also explains the value of fair political process in terms of its role in preventing such great evils as "murder and the destruction of life, imprisonment, enslavement, starvation, poverty, physical pain and torture, homelessness, friendlessness" (90).

16. See John Locke, *Second Treatise*, in *Two Treatises of Government*, ed. Peter Laslett (Cambridge: Cambridge University Press, 1988), § 5.

17. This possibility plays an important role in *Political Liberalism*. See 155–156.

18. On overlapping consensus, see ibid., 132–172; on the idea of a political conception of justice, see ibid., 11–15, 174–175.

and to set aside for political purposes their deep, ultimate, and persistent disagreements about what we are like, what the world is like, and how best to face its demands.

This account of the combination of unity and pluralism rests on a new interpretation of the ideal of toleration—call it "democratic toleration"[19]—paralleling the new interpretation of the social contract advanced in *Theory*. In *Theory*, Rawls proposed "to generalize and carry to a higher order of abstraction the traditional theory of the social contract."[20] The combination of social unity and moral pluralism captured in *Liberalism*'s idea of overlapping consensus generalizes and carries to a higher order of abstraction the conventional idea of toleration.

Conventionally understood, toleration is a substantive political principle condemning the imposition of an authoritative form of religious worship or, in a more expansive version, an authoritative form of personal morality.[21] Aiming to provide a conception of toleration better suited to "the historical and social circumstances of a democratic society" (154), Rawls's political liberalism deepens the idea of toleration and "applies the principle of toleration to philosophy itself" (10, 154). That is, in addition to accepting the substantive requirement of toleration, *Liberalism* presents toleration as a condition on political justification, at least when the question concerns "constitutional essentials" and "basic questions of justice."[22] Given the plurality of incompatible yet reasonable views held by equal citizens in a democratic society, the ideal of fair cooperation recommends that we free the vocabulary and premises of political justification from dependence on any one view. Put otherwise, Rawls suggests that when we understand political power as "the power of free and equal citizens as a collective body" (136) and take account of the fact of reasonable pluralism, we will want to be sure that political argument on fundamentals proceeds on grounds that are acceptable to citizens generally, not in the terms provided by a particular philosophical or religious tradition (136–168, 216–218).

To be sure, it may be impossible to gain support for a conception of justice from all views. But perhaps support for the conception, and a

---

19. Rawls rejects perfectionism in the name of "democracy in judging each other's aims." Rawls, *A Theory of Justice*, 442.

20. Rawls, *A Theory of Justice*, viii; see also *Political Liberalism*, xv.

21. On the central role of religious toleration in understanding the value of toleration, see Susan Mendus, *Toleration and the Limits of Liberalism* (London: Macmillan, 1989), 6–8.

22. See *Political Liberalism*, 137, 227–230.

willingness to conduct public political argument in its terms, will come from the "reasonable comprehensive doctrines" (59) held by reasonable citizens: the views held by people who are concerned to cooperate on terms that others accept and who recognize that reason itself does not select a single comprehensive view.[23]

The central line of thought in *Liberalism,* then, is that we can achieve the good of consensus on justice without comprehensive moral agreement;[24] the absence of comprehensive agreement does not reduce politics to calculations of individual advantage, interest-group bargaining, or the self-affirmation of discrete collective identities. Instead, because political values are highly important values and are recognized as such within a wide range of moral conceptions, consensus on a conception of justice is possible under conditions of reasonable pluralism and must accommodate those conditions if it is to suit the equal citizens of a democratic society.

B. Reconciliation without Metaphysics

Rawls's project in *Liberalism* bears certain important similarities to Hegel's in his *Philosophy of Right,*[25] and it will be instructive to sketch both the commonalities and the differences between their projects.

In his political theory, Hegel aimed to reformulate a classical ideal of political society, which supposed that citizens share an understanding of justice and the human good,[26] in light of the post-Reformation idea of unbridgeable differences among citizens on fundamentals. How is it possible, Hegel asked, to achieve the good of shared commitments in the face of apparently ultimate differences in interest and outlook that are so much the focus of the energies of modern civil society? How, in Hegel's terms, can we give stable expression to both the universal and particular aspects of our nature?[27]

23. On reasonable comprehensive doctrines, see ibid., 58–66.

24. But see Alasdair MacIntyre, *After Virtue* (South Bend, IN: University of Notre Dame Press, 1981), 227–237.

25. G. W. F. Hegel, *Elements of the Philosophy of Right,* ed. Allen Wood, trans. H. B. Nisbet (Cambridge: Cambridge University Press, 1991).

26. For a statement of this aspect of the classical ideal of political society, see Aristotle, *Politics,* trans. Benjamin Jowett, in *The Complete Works of Aristotle,* vol. 2, ed. Jonathan Barnes (Princeton: Princeton University Press, 1984), 1280b23–1281a3.

27. On the role of the modern state in achieving this stable expression, see Hegel, *Philosophy of Right,* § 260.

Hegel and Rawls share broadly similar questions and both endorse the hopeful possibility of reconciling apparently competing demands of unity and difference. Their proposals about how to achieve that reconciliation differ profoundly, however, both in substance and in the insight about the reconciliation they expect philosophy to provide.[28]

Hegel located his answer within a generally anti-dualistic, logicometaphysical theory. His philosophical system revealed our nature as free beings,[29] showed how our differences are less fundamental than we are prephilosophically inclined to think, linked the expression of our free nature to the institutions of a state whose aim is the realization of the good—understood as the expression of our nature[30]—and showed how that expression and those institutions were the natural upshot of historical evolution.[31]

According to Rawls, evaluative theories are matters of reasonable disagreement, and for that reason we ought not to build a conception of political justice around the view of the good advanced within any one such theory. Moreover, the reconciliation of social unity and moral pluralism cannot proceed on the terrain of metaphysics. Because there are ultimate, reasonable disagreements about metaphysical doctrines, a *general* philosophical argument against dualisms, for example, cannot provide part of the case for overcoming the *specific* tension between pluralism and social unity.[32] Political philosophy, if it seeks to operate on the shared ground available to equal citizens in a pluralistic public, cannot rest on a metaphysical theory of our true nature, nor can it provide any assurances, grounded in such a theory, about the ultimate expression of that

---

28. For discussion of the idea of reconciliation in Hegel's political philosophy, see Michael O. Hardimon, *Hegel's Social Philosophy: The Project of Reconciliation* (Cambridge: Cambridge University Press, 1994).

29. Hegel, *Philosophy of Right*, § 4.

30. "[The good is] *realized freedom, the absolute and ultimate end of the world.*" Ibid., § 129.

31. G. W. F. Hegel, *The Philosophy of History*, trans. J. Sibree (New York: Dover Publications, 1956).

32. In an earlier version of some of the material published in *Political Liberalism*, Rawls indicated that "one of Hegel's aims was to overcome the many dualisms which he thought disfigured Kant's transcendental idealism," that Dewey "shared this emphasis throughout his work," and that "there are a number of affinities between justice as fairness and Dewey's moral theory which are explained by the common aim of overcoming the dualisms in Kant's doctrine." John Rawls, "Kantian Constructivism in Moral Theory," *Journal of Philosophy* 77, 9 (September 1980): 515–572. My point is not to deny this common aim. I want only to emphasize that the presentation of justice as fairness as a political conception implies that its resolution of the apparent tension between social unity and moral pluralism cannot draw on a general antidualistic metaphysical view.

nature in history.[33] Its aims must be less ambitious, focused on clarifying *how* social unity is possible under pluralistic conditions. Such clarification will not yield the assurances of unity associated with a historical theodicy;[34] at best it will lead to an understanding of why the hope for reconciliation is not unreasonable.

Once we understand *how* the stable combination of shared principles and conflicting faiths that defines an overlapping consensus is possible, then we can see—Rawls thinks—that it is reasonable to adhere to the ideal; the conditions of its possibility are not so demanding as to condemn it. In this way *Liberalism* offers a "defense of reasonable faith in the possibility of a just constitutional regime."[35] It argues for the reasonableness of that faith by revealing the commitments it requires as minimally demanding, emphasizing in particular that people within different moral and religious traditions can reasonably endorse those commitments. If *Liberalism* is right, then it is possible to combine fundamental moral pluralism—to take seriously one sort of *difference*—with consensus on a conception of justice suited to the equal citizens of a democratic society. But although philosophy can provide that service in a democratic society—that defense of reasonable faith—it can deliver no greater assurance of the rationality of what is actual.

C. Consensus? Really?

Those are the aims of *Liberalism*. They are likely to meet with skeptical response. The idea of combining disagreement on fundamentals with consensus on political principles suited to free and equal citizens may strike us as nice work if you can get it. In particular, it is natural to suspect that the demands of consensus are less minimal and the faith in its possibility correspondingly less reasonable than Rawls claims.

There are at least four reasons for skepticism about the ideal of consensus, and I will discuss them in detail in Part IV of this essay.[36] As back-

33. Later I will discuss some reasons for operating on shared grounds. *See* below, notes 114–116 and accompanying text.

34. History, Hegel says, is the "true theodicy." Hegel, *Philosophy of History*, 457.

35. *Political Liberalism*, 172; also 101. The idea of philosophy as a defense of reasonable faith derives from Kant. See 100–101, 172. On the background of Kant's idea of reasonable faith in Rousseau, see Dieter Henrich, *Aesthetic Judgment and the Moral Image of the World: Studies in Kant* (Stanford: Stanford University Press, 1992), 10–28.

36. See section 4 below. One basis of skepticism that I will not explore below endorses the possibility of combining political consensus and moral pluralism, but only if the political

ground for that discussion, I want first to explore more fully Rawls's new view, tracing the route from *Theory* to *Liberalism*—in Part II—and outlining the strategy of *Liberalism* itself—in Part III. Before getting to the route and the strategy, however, I want to enter a caveat.

D. A Different Book

Liberalism is a very abstract book, in ways that contrast sharply with *Theory*. Much of the excitement of *Theory* derived from its claim to argue from relatively weak, abstractly stated assumptions to powerful, controversial, substantive claims about justice. Here was an egalitarian and liberal account of justice, concerned both with the protection of basic civil and political liberties and with assuring a distribution of resources that would enable people to make fair use of those liberties, and supported by premises arguably much less controversial than its conclusions.[37]

Moreover, *Theory's* many polemical edges helped to sharpen its central claims. Utilitarianism had dominated the field of systematic moral and political philosophy, and *Theory aimed* to displace it.[38] In addition, *Theory* proposed an alternative to the ideal of natural liberty—sharp libertarian limits on the legitimate actions of the state—and to a liberal pluralism that would ensure fair process but would leave questions of substantive justice to bargaining in political and economic markets.[39] To be sure, Rawls devoted stretches of *Theory* to the nature of justification, rationality, and goodness. But the discussion of these matters was never longer—or shorter—than necessary, and one felt that the discussion was never very far from first-order issues of justice.

---

consensus is confined to questions of just procedure. I explore and criticize this view in Joshua Cohen, "Pluralism and Proceduralism," *Chicago-Kent Law Review* 69, 3 (1994): 589–618.

37. A central claim in *Theory* is that we will be led to surprising, egalitarian conclusions about the limits of legitimate socioeconomic inequality by reasoning from the same fundamental ideas—about the equality of moral persons and our basic interests—that support familiar and settled convictions about the injustice of religious intolerance and racial discrimination. See Rawls, *A Theory of Justice*, 19–20, 150–183. To make his case, Rawls gathers the less controversial claims and convictions together in the original position, thus requiring our reasoning about socioeconomic issues to conform to principles and ideas to which convictions about fairness and basic liberties already commit us. *See* Joshua Cohen, "Democratic Equality," *Ethics* 99, 4 (July 1989): 727–751 (reprinted as Chapter 3 in this volume).

38. Rawls, *A Theory of Justice*, vii–viii.

39. On natural liberty and liberal pluralism, see ibid., 65–75. For an argument against natural liberty and liberal pluralism, see Brian Barry, *Theories of Justice* (Berkeley: University of California Press, 1989), 217–234. I contrast liberal pluralism with Rawls's view in Cohen, "Pluralism and Proceduralism."

By contrast, Rawls's presentation of political liberalism puts substantive questions of justice aside. Here, Rawls does not focus on the content of justice but on whether justice as fairness can provide shared political ground given conflicting comprehensive moralities.

Moreover, *Liberalism* lacks the well-defined opponents of *Theory*. To be sure, Rawls contrasts the ideal of overlapping consensus on a political conception of justice with the communitarian aspiration to achieve social unity through a shared conception of human nature and the human good.[40] But communitarianism lacks the sharp definition of utilitarianism, libertarianism, or liberal pluralism, contributing to the relentlessly abstract character of Rawls's presentation.

Because it pays less attention to substantive issues of political justice and lacks such sharply defined opponents, *Liberalism* is unlikely to generate either the excitement of *Theory* or the same interdisciplinary ferment. But these are caveats, not criticisms. *Liberalism is* a book of very great depth and importance. In due course it will likely change the shape of political philosophy, sharpening political philosophy's autonomy by increasing its distance from moral philosophy, and perhaps will have similarly salutary effects on political argument itself.

2. *Liberalism: A Philosophy of Life?*

Liberalism, Rawls says, addresses "a serious problem internal to justice as fairness" (xv)—the view presented in *Theory*. In general terms, the problem arises from a lack of realism engendered by inattention to the fact of reasonable pluralism (xv-xviii). More particularly, the difficulty emerges in the account of stability advanced in Part Three of *Theory*. To locate the difficulty more precisely, and to see why it is so troubling, I will first sketch three main elements of *Theory*, then present an objection that many commentators have raised about the main line of argument in *Theory*, and finally restate that difficulty as a tension internal to justice as fairness.

A. Three Elements of Theory

Theory presents, first, an attractive ideal of a just society—a well-ordered, democratic society, featuring a consensus on norms of justice. The content of the consensus is given by two principles:

40. See *Political Liberalism*, 42–43, 146, 201.

First Principle: Each person has an equal right to a fully adequate scheme of equal basic liberties which is compatible with a similar scheme of liberties for all.

Second Principle: Social and economic inequalities are to satisfy two conditions. First, they must be attached to offices and positions open to all under conditions of fair equality of opportunity; and second, they must be to the greatest benefit of the least advantaged members of society.[41]

A society satisfying these principles achieves, Rawls proposes, some measure of "reconciliation of liberty and equality."[42] Suppose that the real value of the freedom guaranteed to a person by the protection of basic liberties is fixed by that person's command of resources, rather than by her position relative to others.[43] Then the two principles together require that a society "maximize the worth to the least advantaged of the complete scheme of equal liberty shared by all."[44] This requirement of maximizing the minimum worth of liberty, Rawls says, "defines the end of social justice."[45]

Second, Rawls offers a contractual defense of this egalitarian-liberal conception of justice. Carrying the social contract idea "to a higher order of abstraction" (xv), he argues that the two principles would be chosen in an initial situation of choice—the "original position"[46]—in which the parties are assumed not to know anything particular about themselves—about their position in the distribution of alienable resources, their position in the distribution of native endowments, and the determinate aims,

---

41. I take the formulation of these principles, first stated in *Theory*, from *Political Liberalism*, 291.

42. Rawls, *A Theory of Justice*, 204.

43. Rawls does not think that the worth of *political* liberty to a person is fixed by that person's absolute command of resources. Because the political process has "limited space," the value of political liberty also depends on relative position. See *Political Liberalism*, 328–329. For this reason, Rawls imposes a special requirement of the "fair value" of political liberty: roughly, that people in different social positions have equal chances to hold office and influence the political process. See *Political Liberalism*, 327–331, 356–363; Rawls, *A Theory of Justice*, 224–227. For a discussion of relative positions, see *A Theory of Justice*, 530–541.

44. Rawls, *A Theory of Justice*, 205.

45. Ibid.; in *Political Liberalism*, 326, Rawls says, less strongly, that maximizing the minimum worth of liberty "defines one of the central aims of political and social justice."

46. Rawls, *A Theory of Justice*, 17–22.

attachments, or views of the world that comprise their conception of the good.[47] Required to choose under conditions of severe ignorance, they are uncertain of the effects of their choice on their own lives. Concerned to assure that they can live with that choice wherever they end up, the parties would choose to provide themselves, Rawls argues, with the strong downside protection assured by the two principles.[48]

Third, Rawls proposes that the various constraints on knowledge imposed in the original position represent requirements that strike us, on reflection, as reasonable to impose on norms of justice or on their justification.[49] Concerns about fairness, for example, and a conception of individuals as equal moral persons with a conception of the good and the capacity for a sense of justice fuel these constraints.[50]

B. Original Position: A Liberal Philosophy of Life?

None of these three central elements of justice as fairness has won general acceptance.[51] But criticisms of Rawls's claims about the reasonableness of the conditions imposed in the original position have been especially sharp among moral and political philosophers. Although the details of the criticisms take many forms, the central objection to Rawls's construction is that the design of the original position presupposes a particular conception of the good. It does not, contrary to Rawls's claims, provide a reasonable device for addressing controversies about justice among people with different conceptions of the good, because it will only be found attractive by people drawn to a liberal philosophy of life—one that holds

47. Ibid., 136–142.

48. Ibid., 150–157, 175–183.

49. See ibid., 18, 587. For a complete list of passages in *Theory* that state the idea of the original position as expressing reasonable requirements on arguments for principles, see *Political Liberalism*, 25n28.

50. "If the original position is to yield agreements that are just, the parties must be fairly situated and treated equally as moral persons." Rawls, *A Theory of Justice*, 141; see also *Political Liberalism*, 23–27.

51. For criticisms of the principles themselves, see David Gauthier, *Morals by Agreement* (Oxford: Oxford University Press, 1986); Robert Nozick, *Anarchy, State, and Utopia* (New York: Basic Books, 1974); G. A. Cohen, "Incentives, Inequality, and Community," in G. B. Petersen, ed., *The Tanner Lectures on Human Values*, vol. 13 (Salt Lake City: University of Utah Press, 1992), 262–329. On the argument from the original position, see John C. Harsanyi, "Can the Maximin Principle Serve as a Basis for Morality? A Critique of John Rawls's Theory," *The American Political Science Review* 69, 2 (June 1975): 594–606.

that individual independence, choice, and self-mastery are the fundamental values that ought to govern our lives.

Critics have localized the offending bias in different places. Thomas Nagel criticized Rawls's assumption that all the parties in the original position want "primary goods"—in particular, income and wealth—as unfairly biased in favor of individualistic conceptions of the good.[52] Brian Barry objected to the individualism implicit in Rawls's contractual method of justification, which proceeds from individual judgments about what is best for me, all else equal, to judgments about how society ought to be arranged.[53] According to Michael Sandel, Rawls assumed a liberal philosophy of life when he required that we place our conceptions of the good behind a veil of ignorance.[54]

To see the force of these criticisms, consider Sandel's objection. Reasoning from behind the veil of ignorance requires that we evaluate norms of justice without reference to our own conception of the good. It is a puzzling idea. Why, and how, are we to reason about justice without drawing on our views about the proper conduct and ends of human life? If we hold the sincere conviction that a life of self-realization is a better life—if we think that such a life is *genuinely better*, not simply the life that we prefer—

---

52. See Thomas Nagel, "Rawls on Justice," *Philosophical Review* 83 (April 1973): 220–234. Rawls replies at *Political Liberalism*, 195–200.

53. Brian Barry, *The Liberal Theory of Justice* (Oxford: Oxford University Press, 1973), 116–127. For Barry's statement of the liberal philosophy of life, see 126–127.

54. Michael J. Sandel, *Liberalism and the Limits of Justice* (Cambridge: Cambridge University Press, 1982). Sandel sketches the liberal philosophy of life—a conception of "the deontological universe and the independent self that moves within it" (177). William Galston also criticizes Rawls for failing to acknowledge his reliance on a conception of the good. See William A. Galston, *Liberal Purposes: Goods, Virtues, and Diversity in the Liberal State* (Cambridge: Cambridge University Press, 1991), 118–162. Galston argues, however, that such reliance is no embarrassment. On the contrary, liberalism must openly avow its dependence on a view of the good, albeit a "deliberately thin" view, "a kind of minimal perfectionism" (177). Galston's view is puzzling. It is not controversial that some account of the good is required for an account of justice. See *Political Liberalism*, 173–211; Rawls, *A Theory of Justice*, 395–399. Moreover, Galston's account of the good is itself constrained by a concern "to provide a shared basis for public policy." Galston, *Liberal Purposes*, 178. This constraint suggests that Galston's account of the good may not be part of a comprehensive perfectionist conception but may instead be part of a political conception of the good in the sense defined by Rawls in *Political Liberalism*, 174–176. I say that Galston's account "may be" political because it is not clear what he means by a "shared basis of public policy" or how the concern to provide such a basis—as distinct from concerns within an account of the good—constrains the role of ideas of the good in his presentation of liberalism.

then what reason could there be for bracketing that conviction when we assess principles of justice?

One reason for such bracketing is that we cannot agree on terms of co-operation for a pluralistic society if the rationale for those terms premises a particular conception of the good. Peaceful cooperation requires agreement, and agreement requires that citizens put aside "the contingencies that *set them in opposition.*[55] But Rawls's reasons in *Theory* are not simply a matter of securing social peace. He argues instead that fairness to citizens as moral persons requires that we not rely on any particular conception of the good in justifying principles that all will have to live by. Instead, fairness demands that "[t]he arbitrariness of the world . . . be corrected for by adjusting the circumstances of the initial contractual situation."[56]

But why is it unfair to people as moral persons to treat them in accordance with principles of justice chosen on the basis of an account of the best life? Why correct for the "arbitrariness of the world" by abstracting from convictions about the best life? Why not correct for that arbitrariness by encouraging everyone to endorse the truth about the best life? To be sure, conceptions of the good sometimes set people in opposition; but why are such conceptions "contingencies"? According to Sandel's objection, Rawls's answer to these questions itself relies in the end on a particular account of the best life and a particular view of the person suited to that account. We will only take an interest in what is chosen behind the veil of ignorance if we deny that our fundamental aims and attachments are good indicators of who and what we are. Moreover, we will be drawn to that denial only if we regard ourselves as, at bottom, agents unencumbered by fundamental attachments to our actual ends, as essentially choosers of values rather than as carriers and renewers of the values of particular traditions and communities—only if we are attracted to the idea that our basic allegiances themselves are elements of the arbitrariness of the world and that the unchosen life is not worth leading.[57]

---

55. Rawls, A *Theory of Justice*, 137 (emphasis added).

56. Ibid., 141.

57. Sandel identifies two key assumptions in *Theory*: that we are essentially choosers—the priority of the self with respect to its ends—and that we are not essentially members of a community—"the priority of plurality over unity." Sandel, *Liberalism and the Limits*, 50–59. Notice that it is possible to deny the first proposition—thus affirming that our identity is fixed by our ends—without denying the second—that is, without affirming that we are essentially

This will do as a statement of comprehensive liberalism, and we can understand a theory of justice built on these foundations as presenting the political implications of such a liberal outlook. But, according to the criticisms, the original position's dependence on such specific commitments disqualifies it from serving as a shared or neutral basis for settling on principles of justice in a democratic society whose equal citizens disagree sharply about liberal ideals of autonomy and individuality.

Sandel goes further. He thinks that Rawls's implicit commitment to a conception of the self as an essentially unencumbered chooser of ends is not merely morally sectarian; it is also inconsistent with Rawls's avowed aim of avoiding obscure and controversial Kantian metaphysical commitments[58] and with our experience of both ourselves and our connections with our commitments.[59] In short, Sandel is concerned not simply to demonstrate Rawls's own reliance on a view of the good but also to undermine the liberal conception of justice by exploding the views of the good and the self on which it depends.[60] These further points are not, however, essential for our current purpose.

C. The Internal Problem: Congruence and Stability

Earlier, I mentioned Rawls's claim that *Liberalism* addresses a problem "internal" to justice as fairness.[61] Thus far, however, I have presented an objection to the original position that might be thought to operate externally. I propose now to show how claims about the objectionable dependence of the original position on a particular philosophy of life can be

---

members of a community. I might regard myself as standing in an essentially personal relationship with God and as bound by obligations arising from that relationship, or as a locus of artistic creativity, or as essentially a seeker of truth. In each case, I might treat my relations with others as instrumental for those deeper purposes, rejecting the ideal of community. To put the point in historical terms, both Hegel and Nietzsche rejected the conception of the self as essentially a chooser of ends. But, not to put too fine a point on it, they had very different views about community. For criticisms of the conception of the self as chooser, see Hegel, *Philosophy of Right*, §§ 15–20, 105–141; and Friedrich Nietzsche, *On the Genealogy of Morals*, ed. Walter Kaufmann, trans. Walter Kaufmann and R. J. Hollingdale (New York: Vintage Books, 1969), 44–46.

58. Sandel, *Liberalism and the Limits*, 94–95.

59. Ibid., 179.

60. The project of undermining liberalism by excavating and exploding its psychological and metaphysical commitments traces back to Hegel, *Philosophy of Right*. The most ambitious modern effort along these lines is Roberto M. Unger, *Knowledge and Politics* (New York: Free Press, 1975).

61. See the introduction to section 2 of this essay.

turned into the internal tension in justice as fairness—the problem in *Theory's* account of stability—that *Liberalism aims* to address.

In characterizing the ideal of a well-ordered society and presenting an account of its stability, Rawls makes essential use of the idea of normative consensus.[62] In a well-ordered society, everyone has a similar sense of justice, and in this respect a well-ordered society is homogeneous. Political argument appeals to this moral consensus."[63] Moreover, this shared sense of justice plays a "fundamental role" in ensuring that "the basic structure is stable with respect to justice."[64]

To be sure, some idea of agreement figures in any contractual theory of justice. But the "moral consensus" Rawls refers to is not simply an ex ante agreement on institutions and relations of authority of a kind associated with Hobbesian and Lockean social contracts.[65] Closer in this respect to Rousseau, Rawls supposes that citizens in a just political society share a conception of justice and that politics is openly guided by that conception.[66] Justice as fairness aims to specify the appropriate content for such a conception, the content of the general will for a society of free and equal persons.

This emphasis on the role of consensus in the ideal of a well-ordered society is understandable. A moral consensus on political fundamentals is a basic good for at least four reasons.

First, for any conception of justice, the existence of a moral consensus on it increases the likelihood that social order will stably conform to the conception.[67]

Second, a moral consensus promotes a variety of specific values of considerable importance. Assuming that norms of justice are not motivationally inert, consensus on them increases social trust and harmony, supports social peace, simplifies decision making, reduces monitoring and enforce-

---

62. The following discussion draws on Joshua Cohen, "Moral Pluralism and Political Consensus," in David Copp, Jean Hampton, and John Roemer, eds., *The Idea of Democracy* (Cambridge: Cambridge University Press, 1993), 270–291.

63. Rawls, *A Theory of Justice*, 263. On the role of consensus in the ideal of a well-ordered society, see 35 and 453–458.

64. Ibid., 458.

65. See Thomas Hobbes, *Leviathan*, ed. Richard Tuck (Cambridge: Cambridge University Press, 1991), 120–129; Locke, *Second Treatise*, 374–77, 395–400.

66. On the role of a shared conception in Rousseau, see Joshua Cohen, "Reflections on Rousseau: Autonomy and Democracy," *Philosophy and Public Affairs* 15, 3 (Summer 1986): 275–297.

67. See Rawls's "third general fact," in *Political Liberalism*, 38.

ment costs by encouraging a willingness to cooperate, and—if public debate and decisions reflect the consensus—reduces alienation from public choices because citizens embrace the norms and ideals that guide those choices.

Third, a consensus on norms of justice provides a way to reconcile the ideal of an association whose members are politically independent and self-governing with an acknowledgment of the central role of social and political arrangements in shaping the self-conceptions of citizens, constraining their actions, channeling their choices, and determining the outcomes of those choices.[68] When a consensus on norms and values underlies and explains collective decisions, citizens whose lives are governed by those decisions might nonetheless be said to be independent and self-governing. Each endorses the considerations that produce the decisions as genuinely moral reasons and affirms their implementation.[69]

Finally, under conditions of political consensus, citizens achieve a form of mutual respect. Each offers as reasons for a decision only considerations that others who are subject to political power take as reasons, and state power is exercised only within the bounds set by these reasons.[70] The force of this point as a basis for mutual respect is increased by recalling the distinction I noted earlier between a unanimous, ex ante agreement and an ex post consensus on norms of justice that frame political debate.[71] In a Hobbesian contract of subordination, everyone agrees to submit to a common agent, accepting the will and judgment of that agent as authoritative.[72] Nothing in the content of the agreement—nothing manifest in

---

68. See the discussion of full autonomy at 77–78. Rawls distinguishes there between endorsing full autonomy as a political value and affirming autonomy as a comprehensive moral value to be realized in all aspects of life and conduct. The concern to reconcile self-government with interdependence is central to Rousseau's project, although Rousseau's own presentation suggests that he thinks of self-government or moral liberty as a comprehensive moral value tied to an account of our true nature. On moral liberty, see Jean-Jacques Rousseau, *The Social Contract and Other Later Political Writings*, ed. and trans. Victor Gourevitch (Cambridge: Cambridge University Press, 1997), 49–50, 53–54. On our nature as free beings, see Jean-Jacques Rousseau, *Discourse on the Origin and the Foundations of Inequality among Men*, in *Rousseau: The Discourses and Other Early Political Writings*, ed. trans. Victor Gourevitch (Cambridge: Cambridge University Press, 1997), 140–141, 179.

69. We also need to add that everyone believes with good reason that the decisions express the shared norms and values.

70. See the discussion of legitimacy in *Political Liberalism*, 136–137, 216–219.

71. See notes 66–67 above, and accompanying text.

72. *See* Hobbes, *Leviathan*, 120–121.

political experience itself—directly expresses mutual respect.[73] With a political consensus, by contrast, the authorization of power proceeds in terms that all citizens accept ex post—in accordance with reasons that are shared and therefore accepted by all who are subject to the power. That does provide a basis for mutual respect.

Consensus, then, has its virtues. But not every consensus is attractive. Those attractions depend on the content of the consensus and on the conditions under which it is sustained. Suppose, for example, that a moral consensus is attractive because it provides a way to make self-government—or association on terms of mutual respect—consistent with the unavoidable chains of political connection (see the third and fourth reasons stated above). Then the consensus must be freely sustained and not simply a form of enforced homogeneity. A consensus is free only if it is arrived at under conditions that ensure the possibility of individual reflection and public deliberation—for example, conditions that protect expressive and associative liberties.

Here we arrive at the internal problem of *Liberalism*. Assurances of expressive and associative liberties—necessary if the consensus that defines a well-ordered society is to be free and attractive—are bound to be associated with moral, religious, and philosophical pluralism.[74] But can the value of substantive consensus on justice survive such pluralism? Let us say that a society is liberal only if it strongly protects expressive and associative liberties. Then, to restate the question: Can there be political consensus and social unity, given the inevitable pluralism of a liberal society?[75] Why, in particular, ought we to expect—as Rawls suggests—that the members of a well-ordered society regulated by Rawls's principles of justice will find the conditions imposed on the original position reasonable? According to the criticisms I referred to earlier, the original position assumes a liberal philosophy of life and presents the political extension of that philosophy.[76] If these criticisms are right, then the comprehensive views that

73. But see Rousseau, *The Social Contract*, 112. ("The instant the people is legitimately assembled as a sovereign body . . . the person of the last citizen is as sacred and inviolable as that of the first magistrate.")

74. See the "first general fact," in *Political Liberalism*, 36.

75. I do not mean to suggest that other societies are not pluralistic. See note 5 above.

76. See section 2.B of this essay. In his Tanner Lecture on "the foundations of liberal equality," Ronald Dworkin defends a version of liberalism on the grounds of its continuity with a more comprehensive liberal outlook on life. See Dworkin, "Foundations of Liberal Equality," 190–306.

some members of a just society find attractive will likely lead them to reject the original position.

The discussion of stability in Part Three of *Theory* suggests that the criticisms are right. Because it does, Rawls concludes that his account of the stability of a well-ordered society is in trouble: that it is "not consistent with the view as a whole" (xvi).

In Part Three, Rawls advances a two-stage case for the stability of a society regulated by his principles of justice.[77] The first stage focuses on the acquisition of a sense of justice—"an effective desire to apply and to act from the principles of justice [the two principles chosen in the original position] and so from the point of view of justice."[78] Rawls sketches how the members of a just society could be expected, through membership in a series of institutions—from family, to the associations of civil society, to citizenship in the state—to acquire an understanding of and an effective desire to act from a sense of justice to which Rawls's principles give content.[79]

The second stage shifts attention from the acquisition of a sense of justice to the *congruence* of that sense with a person's conception of the good. Here Rawls argues that the members of a just society would, with reason, regard the regulation of their conduct by their sense of justice—as given by the two principles—as itself good for them: that is, they would find their sense of justice *congruent* with their good, rather than regarding it as an unwelcome constraint on the pursuit of their good. If this claim about the good of a sense of justice is right, then we have an important force for stability in a just society.[80]

Moral pluralism causes troubles for this happy picture. Consider one of the arguments for congruence: "Acting justly is something we want to do as free and equal rational beings. The desire to act justly and the desire to express our nature as free moral persons turn out to specify what is practically speaking the same desire."[81] The claim that these desires have the same content rests on the argument from the original position. Or, as Rawls indicates elsewhere, the "sentiment of justice" is—for anyone who

---

77. Rawls presents the first part of the case in A *Theory of Justice*, 462–496, and the second part at 513–577.

78. Ibid., 567.

79. Ibid., 462–496. See also Hegel's theory of the formation of the will through the various spheres of ethical life—family, civil society, and state. Hegel, *Philosophy of Right*, §§ 142–329.

80. See Rawls, *A Theory of Justice*, 499, 501.

81. Ibid., 572 (citation omitted).

"understands and accepts the contract doctrine"—the very same desire as the desire to act on principles that would be chosen "in an initial situation which gives everyone equal representation as a moral person," and also the same as the desire "to act in accordance with principles that express men's nature as free and equal rational beings."[82] In the original position, we are represented as free moral persons, so to act from the principles chosen there is to express our nature as free and not to "give way to the contingencies and accidents of the world."[83]

Moreover, the argument from the original position not only selects principles of justice but also requires that those principles take priority in regulating our conduct. To express "our freedom from contingency and happenstance,"[84] then, we need more than a sense of justice given content by the principles chosen in the original position. We must also give priority to our sense of justice, assigning it an authoritative role in the regulation of conduct.

A central element in the case for congruence and stability, then, is that members of a well-ordered society will develop a conception of their nature as free beings, will regard the expression of that free nature in their own conduct as a fundamental good, and will understand—because of their "lucid grasp of the public conception of justice upon which their relations are founded"[85]—that such expression requires acting from the principles of justice that would be chosen in the original position, giving those principles a special regulative role.[86]

The case for the two principles, then, depends upon the case for stability; the case for stability depends in part upon the case for congruence; and the case for congruence depends upon an account of our "nature as free moral persons"[87] and the desire to express our nature as free.[88] But this line of dependence strongly suggests that the argument for congruence, and so

82. Ibid., 478.
83. Ibid., 575.
84. Ibid., 574.
85. Ibid., 572.
86. The condition of "full publicity," defined at 66–67, requires public availability of the conception of justice and the full rationale for it.
87. Rawls, A Theory of Justice, 572.
88. Rawls ties this argument to the Kantian interpretation of justice as fairness. See ibid. The argument is one of four he offers in support of congruence. It might be interpreted as an argument addressed to those who endorse a comprehensive Kantian view, rather than as one of four arguments that citizens generally will find persuasive. But Theory clearly offers it as the latter.

the case for stability, depends upon a set of moral commitments and self-understandings that some members of a well-ordered society will reasonably reject.[89]

For example, some citizens may think that their nature consists in the possession of various natural, human powers, that the human good consists in a perfection that fully realizes those powers, and that the requirements of morality set out the conditions for such perfection. Others may think of themselves as creatures of a God who imposes obligations that bind their moral freedom. Such citizens accept moralities that are, to use Kant's term, heteronomous. They, too, wish to express their nature and not to give way to the contingencies and accidents of the world. But it is unclear why they should find the original position a plausible way to specify the content of their expression. With Locke, they may suppose that their fundamental powers are the capacity to understand and to act from the Creator's requirements and that they express their nature by acting from those requirements.[90] To be sure, adherents of such a view might reject the imposition of a religious establishment and affirm the importance of the free exercise of religion. But they would do so because forced religious practice does not fulfill basic religious duties and so provides no route to salvation,[91] rather than because a regime of religious toleration expresses their "nature" as free moral persons. They do not acknowledge themselves to have such a nature.

Some people, then, may reject the characterization of our nature as free; they will be drawn neither to the reasonableness of the original position as a rendering of their nature, nor to acting from the principles selected there *because* such action expresses their nature.[92] Thus Rawls concludes that the conception of a well-ordered society presented in *Theory* "is

89. I have concentrated on the problem for congruence. The account of acquisition, however, faces a parallel difficulty. An account of the acquisition of a desire to act on principles must explain why that desire, which is not instrumental, does not reflect a strange affection for rules. In *Theory*, Rawls responds to this concern by explaining that moral principles can "engage our affections" in part because acting on them expresses our "nature as free and equal rational beings" (476). But this explanation leaves us with a gap in the account of acquisition in the case of those citizens who do not see their nature in such terms. In this connection, see *Political Liberalism*, 82–86 on principle-dependent and conception-dependent desires.

90. *See* Locke, *Second Treatise*, 310–311.

91. *See* John Locke, *A Letter Concerning Toleration*, ed. Patrick Romanell (New York: Prentice-Hall, 1955), 18–20.

92. They may, of course, be attracted to those principles and to the original position itself for other reasons. See below, notes 110–112 and accompanying text.

unrealistic . . . because it is inconsistent with realizing its own principles under the best of foreseeable conditions" (xvii). Under the best of foreseeable conditions, a society that satisfies the two principles will be a society in which some citizens reject the conception of our nature used in *Theory* to underwrite the original position and the account of congruence. "The account of the stability of a well-ordered society in Part III is therefore also unrealistic" (xvii).

How, then, is it possible to achieve consensus on a conception of justice suited to a democratic society of equal citizens and to reap the benefits of that consensus, given the pluralism of comprehensive moralities that inevitably marks such a society? More particularly, can the presentation and defense of a conception of justice for a democratic society be freed from the unacceptably narrow premises of a comprehensive moral liberalism? That is the question of political liberalism.

3. Political Liberalism

Rawls's answer to the question of political liberalism contains two parts. The idea of a political conception of justice plays a central role in the first part; the idea of an overlapping consensus is the key to the second.

A. A Political Conception of Justice

Given the plurality of comprehensive moralities, the claim that consensus is possible faces a threshold problem. A conception of justice can win general acceptance only if it can be suitably formulated. Its formulation must be understandable to citizens with competing views of the good and must not itself preclude acceptance by some citizens.[93] Some conceptions of justice would, however, on their face, be unacceptable to some citizens—for example, if the conceptions appeal to values that are not implicated in public institutions or that reasonable people might reject. Suppose an account of justice requires a distribution of resources that ensures equal pleasure, or suppose it mandates a distribution that enables each citizen to come equally close to achieving his aims. Both views face troubles because citizens reasonably disagree about the relative value of pleasure and of

---

93. This condition is necessary but not sufficient because a view that is formulated without reference to any comprehensive moral view may nevertheless be attractive only to those who hold a particular *view*. See below, notes 109–112 and accompanying text.

relative achievement. So these conceptions would be, on their face, unacceptable.[94]

Rawls calls a view that is suitably formulated a "political conception of justice" (11). Three features—each necessary if the conception is plausibly to provide the focus of agreement, given the fact of reasonable pluralism—define such a conception:[95] it must have limited scope, extending only to issues about the basic structure of society and not to norms of personal conduct or ideals of life; it must draw on ideas familiar to citizens from the political culture of a democracy, not on ideas belonging exclusively to particular traditions of moral thought that are not available to *all*; and it must be presented as freestanding, not as depending for formulation or justification on its roots in a comprehensive morality.[96] In short, a political conception of justice is formulated as autonomous from comprehensive conceptions of the good with respect to scope, content, and justification. Each of these three forms of autonomy should contribute to the possibility of its general acceptance.

To see how these kinds of autonomy help to address the problems about the original position and veil of ignorance I sketched earlier, consider the aspect of the political conception that Rawls refers to as a "political conception of the person" (18–20, 29–35, 48–54, 86–88). The original position isolates certain features of people as relevant to its problem of justice, setting aside other features as irrelevant—and so to be excluded by the veil of ignorance. The relevant features include certain basic moral powers: the capacities for a conception of the good—to form, pursue, and revise such a conception—and for a sense of justice.[97] The irrelevant features include gender, race, natural abilities, and determinate conceptions of the good.

As my earlier discussion of the original position indicates,[98] *Theory* was not entirely clear about the basis of this distinction between relevant and

---

94. For discussion and criticism of these two versions of equality of welfare, see Ronald Dworkin, "What Is Equality? Part 1: Equality of Welfare," *Philosophy and Public Affairs* 10, 3 (1981): 204–209, 220–224.

95. See *Political Liberalism*, 11–15.

96. A political conception is presented as freestanding in the way that logic or number theory is. A presentation of logical laws—for example, the law of excluded middle—proceeds without tying the laws to a theory of truth or issues in the theory of meaning; a presentation of number theory proceeds without reference to questions about the ontological status of numbers.

97. *Political Liberalism*, 18–20; Rawls, *A Theory of Justice*, 561.

98. See above, notes 79–93 and accompanying text.

irrelevant characteristics. This lack of clarity contributed to the impression that justice as fairness was the political expression of a comprehensive moral liberalism. Thus Rawls often referred to the *morally* relevant or irrelevant as if to say that the distinction derives from a comprehensive moral doctrine.[99] Sometimes he referred to the irrelevant characteristics as "contingencies," as though to suggest a metaphysical foundation for the distinction.[100] Sometimes—as I indicated in my discussion of congruence and stability[101]—he suggested that the distinction is rooted in an account of "our nature," permitting both metaphysical and moral interpretations.[102]

Liberalism draws the distinction between relevance and irrelevance in the same place: the power to form, pursue, and revise a conception of the good and the power to form and act from a sense of justice are relevant; and gender, race, natural abilities, and determinate conceptions of the good are irrelevant (29–35). But the point of the distinction, according to *Liberalism, is* to present a conception of the person that will play a role in a political conception of justice, and so *Liberalism* underscores that the conception of the person is itself political in each of the three ways noted earlier: scope, content, and justification. Thus *irrelevant* should not be understood absolutely, metaphysically, or in terms of a general moral view, but only as implying that a feature of a person is not important for the purposes of political argument—in particular, not important for political argument aimed at specifying the requirements of justice for a society in which members are understood as free and equal. *Contingent* ought similarly to be given a non-metaphysical rendering, as implying that a feature is not relevant to political argument.

99. For example, Rawls refers to the constraints in the original position as "conditions that are widely recognized as fitting to impose on the adoption of moral principles." Rawls, *A Theory of Justice,* 584. Similarly, the criticisms of natural liberty and liberal equality refer to social circumstances and natural assets as features that are "arbitrary from a moral point of view." *A Theory of Justice,* 72, 74–75.

100. I say "sometimes" because some passages in *A Theory of Justice* strongly suggest that apparently metaphysical notions should be interpreted morally. Take, for example, the following remark: "Our moral sentiments display an independence from the accidental circumstances of our world, *the meaning of this independence being given by the description of the original position and its Kantian interpretation.*" *A Theory of Justice,* 475 (emphasis added). To say that the description of the original position gives the meaning of independence is to say that independence is a matter of the irrelevance for moral purposes of certain features of the person rather than a matter of the metaphysical contingency of those features.

101. See above, notes 78–93 and accompanying text.

102. Rawls, *A Theory of Justice,* 251–257, 572.

We can, then, determine which features are "irrelevant, politically speaking, and hence [to be] placed behind the veil of ignorance" (79) by systematizing and extending reasonably familiar ideas about the justification of political arrangements in a democratic society. This basis is appropriate for the distinction given the question that justice as fairness sets out to resolve: "What is the most appropriate conception of justice for specifying the terms of social cooperation between citizens regarded as free and equal, and as normal and fully cooperating members of society over a complete life?" (20). The conception of citizens as free and equal represents a familiar element of the political culture of democratic societies. The problem is to determine more precisely what that political conception involves and to address a longstanding controversy about what account of justice is best suited to citizens as free and equal.[103]

Thus we look to settled ideals and convictions about basic democratic institutions, and to settled understandings about the justification of public norms in a democratic society, and then draw the relevant-irrelevant distinction by reference to the characteristics of persons that play a role in those ideas, convictions, and understandings. One may then call the irrelevant features "contingencies," but with no intention to affirm—or to deny—that an individual could exist without the feature in question, or to say—or to deny—anything about the importance of irrelevant features in other settings. They are simply unimportant for the purposes at hand, whatever their metaphysical standing and however important they may be for other purposes, including other ethical purposes.

To be more specific, arguments aimed at establishing that certain properties are contingent (irrelevant to the problem of political justification) and that others are aspects of our essential nature (important to that problem) proceed along at least two main lines. The first seeks to show that current ideals—for example, of fairness, religious toleration, and racial and sexual equality—and patterns of political argument—for example, on constitutional matters—treat certain facts as irrelevant. For instance, it is widely agreed that we ought to protect certain basic rights—expression, political participation, conscience, and equal treatment—without regard to social background, gender, or race. Furthermore, social class ought not to restrict opportunity. These are clear cases of unfairness. So in reasonably

---

103. See *Political Liberalism*, 20, 22, 26, 34–35.

settled understandings of justice, we treat facts about class, gender, and race as contingencies—matters that are irrelevant to argument about the justice of basic institutions.

Similarly, the constitutional treatment of religious and political ideals suggests the irrelevance of conceptions of the good to such argument. For example, conversion, sin, and religious laxity are not civil offenses. Whatever its implications for a person's self-conception, being "born again" has no civil consequences; being born again does not, for example, absolve a person of contractual obligations undertaken prior to that rebirth or give a person who is reborn on election day a right to a second vote. Furthermore, in the case of political ideals, endorsing the legitimacy of the political order is not—in principle, at least—a precondition for equal political rights, a point underscored by conventional hostility to regulating expression by virtue of its content and, more particularly, its viewpoint.[104]

A second strategy is to show that certain features of people are themselves so dependent on concededly irrelevant facts that to permit them to play a role in political justification would be tantamount to allowing the irrelevant facts to play a role. So they too should be treated as irrelevant. The development of abilities and talents, for example, seems closely linked to the social circumstances and aspirations that the entrenched forms of argument fix as contingencies. So talents and abilities ought to be treated as contingencies and not appealed to as fundamental reasons for differential advantages.

I would need to say much more about these matters in order to evaluate Rawls's distinction between relevant and irrelevant, and the associated political conception of the person. I have provided only an outline of the

---

104. I assume this hostility to be widely shared, even by people who do not think that content or viewpoint regulation is always impermissible. Justice Marshall provided a classic statement of the general concern about content regulation in *Police Department v. Mosley*, 408 U.S. 92, 95 (1972) ("Above all else, the First Amendment means that government has no power to restrict expression because of its message, its ideas, its subject matter, or its content.") On viewpoint discrimination, see *Texas v. Johnson*, 491 U.S. 397, 414 (1989). For discussion of content and viewpoint regulation, see John Hart Ely, "Flag Desecration: A Case Study in the Roles of Categorization and Balancing in First Amendment Analysis," *Harvard Law Review* 88 (1975): 1482–1508; T. M. Scanlon Jr., "Content Regulation Reconsidered," in Judith Lichtenberg, ed., *Democracy and the Mass Media* (Cambridge: Cambridge University Press, 1990), 331–354; Geoffrey R. Stone, "Content-Neutral Restrictions," *The University of Chicago Law Review* 54 (1987): 46–118; and Geoffrey R. Stone, "Restrictions of Speech Because of Its Content: The Peculiar Case of Subject-Matter Restrictions," *The University of Chicago Law Review* 46 (1978): 81–125.

rationale for the distinction. But its force—and limits—as a response to the original position's difficulties should now be clear.

According to the objection, the original position rests on a liberal philosophy of life that places especially great weight on the importance of choice and that sees the self as, in its fundamental nature, a chooser of its own ends. Rawls's claim that "the self is prior to the ends which are affirmed by it"[105] suggests a commitment to such a philosophy. But the political conception of the person offers a restrictive interpretation of this priority. It neither affirms nor denies that people could, as a metaphysical matter, exist without their aims as pure choosers of ends, as "Kantian transcendent or disembodied subject[s]" who are "shorn of empirically-identifiable characteristics";[106] or that citizens can *imagine* their own lives continuing with their final aims different from what they now *are*; or that they would actually *be* the same persons if their final aims were radically altered; or that, as an ethical matter, the aims of citizens are worth pursuing only if chosen by them. Instead, the political conception ties both the content of and the rationale for the alleged priority to the aims of a theory of justice for a democratic society and to the public availability of the idea of citizens as equals.

According to the political conception, citizens are prior to their ends in that no particular ends are mandatory from a public point of view, and citizens must be assured favorable conditions for reflecting on and revising their aims, should they wish. For example, obligations that a person has by virtue of her conception of the good do not have public standing *as obligations*. Moreover, civil standing does not alter with shifts in fundamental aims, no matter how much a person's self-conception is bound up with those aims. This is not to say, however, that all obligations are matters of self-legislation, or that fundamental values are a product of choice, or that they are only worth pursuing if they are such a product. The political conception of the person does not state a position on these matters.[107] That conception is simply a statement about how citizens should be represented for the purposes of political argument. For this reason, nothing in the very statement of the political conception of the person conflicts with

105. Rawls, A *Theory of Justice*, 560.

106. Sandel, *Liberalism and the Limits of Justice*, 95.

107. The political conception does not take a position in the way that statements of logical laws do not, on their face, take a position about the nature of meaning.

comprehensive moralities that are not organized around the ideal of autonomy or around the thought that we are, by our nature, free beings.

B. Overlapping Consensus

Suppose this enterprise of reinterpretation succeeds—that a liberal conception can be formulated as a freestanding political doctrine, facially independent of any comprehensive moral conceptions. Providing this formulation would help in securing social unity under conditions of moral pluralism. It would overcome the threshold problem that I disclosed earlier.[108] But it would not suffice to defeat the objections to or the associated internal troubles for Rawls's view.

The objection to the original position was not that its very statement reveals it to be part of a liberal philosophy of life but rather that citizens will be drawn to it—will find it a reasonable device for settling on principles of justice—only if they endorse such a philosophy. So, too, even if the formulation of a political conception is freed from objectionable sectarianism, it may still win support only from adherents to a single comprehensive doctrine or a narrow range of such doctrines. Consider an analogy: logical laws can be formulated in a freestanding way, independent of controversies in the theory of meaning. Still, certain logical laws—such as the law of excluded middle—will arguably be found compelling only by people who hold particular views in the theory of meaning—for example, that we can understand the meaning of statements whose truth or falsity transcends our recognitional capacities.[109]

Take the claim that people with different conceptions of the good have the capacity to choose and revise their conception, as well as a fundamental interest in circumstances that enable them to revise it should they wish. This claim is an element of the political conception of the person, and it is one of the aspects of the person known behind the veil of ignorance. In presenting a political conception of the person, Rawls shows that endorsing this claim does not *consist in* believing that reflectively held convictions are uniquely worthy of our full allegiance or that we are essentially choosers of ends rather than servants of God; by formulating the political conception of the person as a freestanding view, he shows that

---

108. See above, notes 94–95 and accompanying text.
109. See Michael Dummett, *The Logical Basis of Metaphysics* (London: Duckworth, 1991), 184–199.

that conception does not imply any particular nonpolitical view of the person, for the content of the political conception is very different from the content of any such view. Nevertheless, it may be true that we only have good reason to accept the political conception and the associated account of justice if we endorse a comprehensive liberal philosophy of life.

Therefore, we may be misled when Rawls says that "accepting the political conception does not *presuppose* accepting any particular comprehensive . . . doctrine; rather, the political conception *presents itself as* a reasonable conception for the basic structure alone" (175; emphasis added). Even if the conception *presents itself* as political, accepting it may still *presuppose* accepting a comprehensive view if a single view provides the only reasons for accepting the political conception.

Here, then, we need the idea of an overlapping consensus: the idea that all people can—for the different reasons provided by their own reasonable comprehensive moral views—think that the same conception of justice is correct and not merely an accommodation required to ensure a stable peace under conditions of moral pluralism. Rawls imagines, for example, an overlapping consensus composed of four views, each of which is reasonable and each of which provides a rationale for political liberalism: one rooted in a Kantian morality of autonomy, another in utilitarianism, and a third in a religious conception that endorses free faith, while the fourth treats political liberalism as one part of a pluralistic ethical view—a part that needs to be adjusted to the other parts, although it is not derived from them.

Consider, for example, the political conception of citizens as free. How might these four views endorse the idea that citizens are free as a shared basis for political argument? One aspect of political liberalism—captured in the veil of ignorance—is that citizens have the capacity to revise their aims and an interest in favorable conditions for such revision should they wish to pursue it, but that for the purposes of an account of justice the determinate aims of citizens are irrelevant. The Kantian view accepts this aspect of political liberalism because the Kantian conceives of the reflective choice of ends as a feature of an autonomous life and holds that the protection of citizens who wish to pursue such choice is required by respect for their dignity as autonomous. The utilitarian might endorse the interest in revising aims as fundamental because true happiness—whether consisting of pleasurable feelings or the satisfaction of rational desires—

depends on the possibility for such revision.[110] The conception of free faith also endorses this interest because of its connections with the appropriate fulfillment of religious obligations: that such fulfillment must reflect genuine "inward persuasion of the mind."[111] In short, each view accepts, for its own reasons, a conception of persons and their basic interests that provides shared ground in political argument.

But an overlapping consensus on a conception of justice cannot be sustained simply by the existence of points of agreement, for points of disagreement among reasonable views are bound also to exist. Each view implies that the others are a mixture of truths and falsehoods. Why, then, should citizens who endorse a particular moral view—who believe it to be true—not hold that political power ought to be used to advance the values of that view?[112] Why should they endorse as correct a view of justice that is confined to shared ground and accept that public discussion must provide justification according to that view? Three considerations explain this restraint.[113]

1. It is worth emphasizing again that citizens who hold competing comprehensive views may nevertheless agree that the values incorporated within the political conception are important values and that the norms and principles included in it provide genuine reasons. From within each comprehensive view, the political conception states nothing but the truth, even if not the whole truth. As my example about the interest in favorable conditions for revising aims indicates, adherents to different moral conceptions do not think that the political conception reflects a compromise required to ensure a stable peace. Instead they believe that the conception expresses a correct account of basic political interests.

2. In accepting as correct a conception of justice that does not include the whole truth, by their lights, citizens acknowledge both the reasonable-

110. See, e.g., Mill, *On Liberty.* 116–117. Similar considerations would support a case for the interest within a view emphasizing self-realization.

111. Locke, *Letter Concerning Toleration*, 18.

112. It might be said that holding a moral view is a matter of having pro-attitudes rather than beliefs that are apt to be true or false. For a sketch of the difficulties in sustaining this position, see Paul Horwich, "Gibbard's Theory of Norms," *Philosophy and Public Affairs* 22, 1 (Winter 1993): 67–78 (book review). But see Michael Smith, "Why Expressivists about Value Should Love Minimalism about Truth," *Analysis* 54, 1 (January 1994): 1–12; and the reply by Horwich in Paul Horwich, "The Essence of Expressivism," *Analysis* 54, 1 (January 1994): 19–20.

113. Rawls mentions the first two considerations in *Political Liberalism*, 127–128 (referring to Cohen, "Moral Pluralism and Political Consensus").

ness of at least some of the views that conflict with their own and the un-reasonableness of imposing arrangements whose justification depends on aspects of their own view that others reasonably reject.

The Kantian, for example, rejects the utilitarian conception of the good as the satisfaction of rational desires, but he can understand the utilitarian view as an application of theoretical and practical reason, appreciate the considerations that lead to that view, and see how its endorsement is com-patible with a willingness to cooperate on terms that others can accept. So the Kantian's endorsement of a political conception that contains only part of the truth—that takes political autonomy rather than moral au-tonomy as a fundamental value in political argument[114]—is not simply a compromise required by the existence of other views. Instead, the Kan-tian thinks it would be wrong to impose institutions and policies justified by a political conception that is rejected by others who are themselves fully reasonable.

3. As the second point suggests, the key to the possibility of overlapping consensus is that a conception of justice articulates values of great impor-tance and that the existence of a shared political conception itself consti-tutes an important good. I suggested a case for these claims in my earlier remarks about the good of consensus on a conception of justice.[115] Sup-pose that case is correct and that the political consensus does articulate important values. Suppose, too, that different, conflicting comprehensive moral conceptions agree on a conception of justice. Then adherents to those moral conceptions will be able to say—each from her own standpoint—that it is normally best to uphold institutions satisfying the conception of justice, even when policies selected by the institutions are inconsistent with her particular moral conception. These conflicting moral views will also agree that it is normally best to conduct public discussion about political fundamentals in terms of the values and principles of the political concep-tion rather than to appeal to a particular comprehensive moral view that others reasonably reject.

Much here rests on "normally." Views that form an overlapping con-sensus will rarely, if ever, hold that political values are ultimate. For that reason, there may well be occasions when a comprehensive moral view supports the conclusion that the stakes are too high and that political

---

114. See note 69 above.
115. See above, notes 67–74 and accompanying text.

values must give way. Adherents to such a view may be optimistic and see deep disagreement as an occasion for a high-stakes effort to persuade others to drop their ultimate convictions; more likely, however, they will think that the time for debate has ended. Because political values are not widely regarded as ultimate values, this kind of breakdown is always possible. To that extent the bases of civic unity are fragile: such fragility is the inevitable result of the pluralism of comprehensive moralities.

Despite this fragility, one can hope that civic breakdown will not occur. More immediately, the existence of cases in which it does occur, together with the fact that we all have more to say than we are prepared to say in politics, does not imply that consensus is impossible or unattractive, or that operating on the shared ground of a political conception of justice is merely a compromise dictated by circumstance.

4. Consensus?

I said earlier that the idea of consensus is likely to elicit a skeptical response,[116] and I want now to explore some of the sources of that skepticism. I will consider four objections to the idea of an overlapping consensus.[117] Because I find the idea of consensus attractive, I will present replies to each of the objections. The four objections form a natural sequence, beginning from the thought that it is simply naive to expect consensus in a large-scale political society. The second and third objections present different variants of a common concern: that the case for consensus reveals that it can be achieved only through an objectionable exclusion of views that fall outside the consensus. The fourth objection accepts the possibility of consensus but argues that an overlapping consensus truncates political argument; by effectively taking comprehensive moral views as given, overlapping consensus forestalls the deeper agreement that might emerge from a more vigilant political criticism.

A. Hopelessly Naive

Consider the depth and extent of disagreement on any important political issue: from abortion and taxes to health care reform and trade policy.

---

116. See Cohen, "Pluralism and Proceduralism."

117. The first objection I will consider overlaps with the fourth objection discussed by Rawls, *Political Liberalism*, 158–158, although my reply differs from Rawls's in important details. The other three objections I will discuss differ from those Rawls considers in *Political Liberalism*, 145–158.

Against this background of disagreement the idea of consensus may strike us as hopelessly naive. This objection gains added force from Rawls's rejection of the possibility of comprehensive moral agreement. If we are prepared to exclude convergence on morality quite generally—to affirm the fact of reasonable pluralism as a "permanent feature of the public culture of democracy" (36)—why should we find agreement on a political conception of justice plausible?

It will not suffice to say that political agreement is more plausible than comprehensive moral agreement because matters of political justice are a proper subset of moral issues, and agreement on a proper subset is more likely than agreement on the wider set itself. Issues about abortion are a subset of the moral, but I think most of us would be nearly as surprised by consensus on the morality of abortion as by consensus about morality in general. Moreover, it is not enough simply to point to the *possibility* of agreement on a political conception of justice among people who have different comprehensive views. That possibility is established by the coherence of the idea of an overlapping consensus. But the coherence of that idea does not suffice to show that it is any more realistic than agreement on comprehensive moral views, which is also possible.

To answer these doubts, we need a *mechanism*—a social or political process that might produce convergence on political values but that does not similarly generate consensus on comprehensive moral values. The right place to look for such a mechanism is at the level of shared institutions, as they might plausibly play an educative role with respect to political ideas but not with respect to comprehensive moral conceptions.[118] Before explaining this role, however, I need to make two background points.

First, it is worth emphasizing that we are concerned with agreement on conceptions of justice, not with a convergence of interests. Of course, if people are moved principally by interests, then the absence of such convergence may imply that agreement on justice is not a matter of great moment. Still, the immediate issue is convergence on justice—which, after all, seems less hopeless than an absence of conflicts of interest.

---

118. This distinction is implicit, I believe, in Rawls's remarks on the "wide role" of a political conception "as educator." When a political conception is fully public, citizens "are presented with a way of regarding themselves [as free and equal] that otherwise they would most likely never be able to entertain." *Political Liberalism*, 71.

Second, the agreement on justice will be limited in various ways; it will not extend to all judgments of policy or even to all fundamentals that might possibly arise. In overlapping consensus, agreement on procedures and basic protections—in Rawls's terms, on constitutional essentials and matters of basic justice—suffices to make the remaining disagreements less important or less immediate.

Even with these two points of clarification, it may still seem unrealistic to expect agreement on matters of basic justice, given persisting differences in moral outlook. But perhaps we can address this concern about realism if we keep in mind the institutional aspect of the acquisition of political ideas and values. Although it is implausible to expect agreement on a conception of justice to result from a convergence of practical reasoning conducted within different, independent moral traditions, it is not so implausible to expect such agreement to emerge from the acquisition of ideas and principles embodied in shared institutions.[119] As I indicated in the earlier discussion of stability, Rawls's views about the development of moral-political understandings are deeply institutional.[120] The acquisition of conceptions of justice proceeds via participation in institutions of various kinds—families, associations, the state. The formation of moral-political ideas and sensibilities also proceeds less by reasoning or explicit instruction—which may be important in the formation of comprehensive moral views—than by mastering ideas and principles that are expressed in and serve to interpret these institutions. The underlying idea—which traces to Rousseauean and Hegelian theories of will formation—is that people living within institutions and a political culture shaped by certain ideas and principles are likely to come to understand those ideas and principles and to develop some attachment to them.[121]

---

119. I do not mean to deny that convergence of independent traditions is a possibility; my point is that an account of political consensus should not depend on it. Bernard Williams has argued that if there were moral consensus it could not be explained by the (perspective-independent) truth of the moral beliefs on which different traditions converged. See Bernard Williams, *Ethics and the Limits of Philosophy* (Cambridge, MA: Harvard University Press, 1985), 132–155. Rawls's account of the possibility of consensus on a conception of justice does not require that the truth of the conception explains the agreement on it.

120. See *Political Liberalism*, 158–168; Rawls, *A Theory of Justice*, 462–479.

121. See Hegel, *Philosophy of Right*, §§ 142–329. On institutional forms and the acquisition of self-conceptions, see John Stuart Mill, *Representative Government*, in *Utilitarianism, Liberty, and Representative Government*, 171, 185–202; Karl Marx, *The German Ideology*, in *The Marx-Engels Reader*, 2nd ed., ed. Robert C. Tucker, trans. S. Ryazanskaya (New York: Norton, 1978), 146–200.

Take, for example, an aspect of the political conception of the person—the (political) idea that citizens are equals in possessing to a sufficient extent the capacity for a conception of the good and for a sense of justice. This idea is manifest in various ways in the practices and traditions of interpretation and public discussion associated with citizenship in a democracy: for example, equality before the law, or equal civil and political rights. Moreover, a stable democratic political process, in which individuals and parties seek to win support for their projects from other citizens, puts some pressure on views to endorse the idea of citizens as equals.[122] We can understand how citizens quite generally might acquire an understanding of one another as moral equals by holding the position of citizen and living in a political culture in which ideas of equality associated with that position play a central role in political discourse.[123]

The different comprehensive views that accept this political understanding of equality will have different ways of fitting it into their broader conceptions. Some will accept political equality as following from their more fundamental moral or religious convictions; others will accept political equality as an important, non-derivative value. But what keeps the expectation of general agreement from being hopelessly naive is the plausible thought that citizens who grow up within a reasonably stable democracy will find this (self-)conception familiar and attractive: the political ideas "expressed" in common, public institutions and appealed to in the culture to justify those institutions will shape citizens' moral-political education.

Of course, the acquisition of moral ideas does not proceed exclusively through institutions. So citizens will need to find or to make a place within their comprehensive views for the political ideas and self-conceptions they acquire through institutions: to find a way to combine, for example, a conception of human beings as servants of God bound by natural duties with a political conception of citizens as free, equal, and self-governing. Many views—religious, moral, philosophical—have sufficient internal flexibility or openness to make such accommodations possible.[124] But because political values are a subset of moral values, we have no reason to

---

122. For further discussion, see Cohen, "Pluralism and Proceduralism."

123. Consider in this connection the virtually unanimous popular endorsement of political equality and equality of opportunity indicated in Herbert McClosky and John Zaller, *The American Ethos: Public Attitudes toward Capitalism and Democracy* (Cambridge, MA: Harvard University Press, 1984), 74 (table 3-5), 83 (table 3-9).

124. See *Political Liberalism*, 159–161.

expect the accommodation of shared political values to produce a more comprehensive agreement that extends to moral values generally; no institutional mechanism in a democratic society imposes pressure to overcome fundamental differences among moral, religious, and philosophical traditions. The pressure of the shared institutions in forging political agreement ends even as considerable disagreement remains.

To be sure, this explanation provides only the barest sketch of a reply to the objection about realism, but it makes an essential point that is commonly overlooked when political philosophy is understood simply as applied moral philosophy. Political ideas are institutionalized in a democratic society in ways that comprehensive moral—or religious or philosophical—ideas are not. More precisely, comprehensive ideas are institutionalized—if at all—in more particular social associations that are not shared: different churches, for example, advance different comprehensive views. So citizens acquire conflicting comprehensive views through such associations. Political ideas, by contrast, are acquired in part through shared associations. So an account of how consensus might emerge on a political conception of justice among citizens living in a political society can draw upon resources unavailable to an account of a more comprehensive moral consensus. Of course no political mechanism can guarantee agreement: the development of an overlapping consensus requires, as I mentioned, that separate traditions are each able to accommodate the political values within their view, and nothing guarantees that they are able to do so. But we are not looking for a guarantee;[125] we only need a mechanism that might plausibly produce convergence of political values even under conditions of moral pluralism.

Finally, given the institutional explanation, it is not surprising that the political consensus is itself limited, being principally a matter of agreement on basic political values—such as fairness, equality of citizens, and liberty, for example—rather than an agreement on a definite conception of justice. For no definite conception—no specific interpretation and balancing of the basic political values—is institutionally expressed in the way that the basic values themselves are. Of course there may be an optimal way to articulate and combine those values, and then the underlying agreement may recommend a specific conception.[126] But that is a matter for further

---

125. Recall the contrast I drew earlier between Hegel and Rawls in section 1.B.

126. The claim that there is such an optimal way provides the basis of Rawls's argument for justice as fairness. See *Political Liberalism*, 9.

argument—for political philosophy. It is not a conclusion that is manifest from the values themselves or from their institutional articulation.

B. Unattractively Explained

Let us suppose that this explanation of the difference between the expectations of political and comprehensive moral consensus can be sustained. Then, a second objection seems natural: that the institutional explanation limits the attractiveness of the consensus it explains. An attractive explanation would see political consensus as emerging from a convergence of argument within conflicting moral and religious traditions, or perhaps from unconstrained practical discourse among adherents of separate traditions.[127] In either case, political consensus would reflect the operation of reason, driving separate moral positions to common political conclusions.

By contrast, the explanation I have just sketched traces the emergence and reproduction of political consensus to shared background institutions. Through these institutions, citizens acquire moral-political ideas—including ideas of person and society. Moreover, the role of the institutions is crucial, because the content of a political conception for a democratic society does not rely only on practical reason; rather, it draws also on "political conceptions of society and person"—in particular, the idea of citizens "regarded as free and equal in virtue of their possessing the two moral powers to the requisite degree."[128] Thus the political conception of justice expresses an ideal of political deliberation and justification in a democratic society, not a more generic conception of justification through reason.[129] So it is especially implausible to think that the political conception might arise simply from the work of practical reason within and among traditions. Precisely this implausibility, however, may make an overlapping consensus seem less a result of free reflection than a product of the institutional constraints under which political argument proceeds.

127. I believe that Stuart Hampshire attributes such a view to Rawls when he suggests that Rawls endorses a "myth of reason" with roots in the Platonic conception of the soul. Hampshire neglects the institutional explanation of consensus. See Stuart Hampshire, "Liberalism: The New Twist," *New York Review of Books*, August 12, 1993, 43.

128. *Political Liberalism*, 109; also xx, 107–110.

129. See also Joshua Cohen, "Deliberation and Democratic Legitimacy," in Alan Hamlin and Philip Pettit, eds., *The Good Polity: Normative Analysis of the State* (Oxford: Blackwell, 1989), 17–34. I emphasize there (esp. 22–23) that a conception of reasons suited to the ideal of deliberative democracy reflects an ideal of free deliberation among equals.

This criticism rests on an exaggerated distinction between institutional constraint and free reflection. Recall the background assumptions: the deliberative liberties are in place—and have a fair value—and the society features a range of comprehensive views, which provide intellectual and practical elaborations of different moral, religious, and philosophical traditions. Suppose now that as a consequence of democratic institutions and the position of equal citizen within these institutions, the members of such a society acquire a shared understanding of the equality of moral persons. Suppose, too, that citizens adjust their comprehensive views—if they have them—to accommodate this shared understanding. For example, they adjust their conceptions of flourishing and true happiness to the many directions in which citizens develop and pursue their native abilities; they adjust their conception of the conditions required for salvation to accord with the circumstances of a political society that includes citizens of different faiths; and they adjust their views of the "nature" and "proper conduct" of men and women to take account of the equality of men and women as moral persons. Under these conditions, we face strong pressure to regard the acquisition of shared ideas and the adjustment of comprehensive views as a matter of learning rather than mere inculcation via institutional constraint: how, we may ask, does the inculcation work, given a background of deliberative liberties with a fair value? Why are the shared ideas that emerge resilient in the face of challenge?

Of course, we can only presume learning. Someone may be able to show how the agreement reflects power, limited information, confusion and weakness born of moral cacophony, or a deep disparity between the apparent logic of institutions and their real operation. But the presumption is significant and imposes a serious burden on those who would treat the agreement merely as a product of inculcation and constraint.

Consider again the political conception of the person: in particular, the idea of the equality of citizens as rooted in their possession of a capacity both for a sense of justice and for a conception of the good. Assume that people brought up in a just, democratic society find this conception compelling, and that this is so whether their comprehensive views are secular—perfectionist, utilitarian, Kantian—or religious.[130] Suppose further that

---

130. To be sure, important historical strands of these views have rejected the political conception of equality. But we have already rejected the idea that the political conception must emerge from the separate elaboration of competing traditions.

considerations within their own comprehensive views support the conception of citizens as moral equals. But suppose also that citizens reflect on the fact that their traditions would likely have evolved differently under different institutional conditions; had their traditions not been subjected to these particular institutions, the traditions would not now provide the resources to support the political conception. If, for example, these same citizens had been raised in a more hierarchical society, their conceptions of flourishing, salvation, and gender might not be so egalitarian. How, they might ask, could the fact that a conception of justice is rooted in the political conception of the person give any special weight to the conception of justice, given the historically contingent attractiveness of the conception of the person?

The problem with this objection is that it neglects the content of the institutional conditions under which the political conception of the person emerges. Recall that we are assuming that the deliberative liberties of citizens are secure and that citizens have a fair chance to exercise those liberties. Though the political conception of the person does not arise through reasoning that proceeds outside an institutional setting, it must successfully withstand pressures arising from the institutionalization of deliberation itself, from freedom of expression and association, and from a fair distribution of resources.[131] The attractions of the political conception of the person, then, are assumed to survive criticisms that might be directed against it. If they do survive, then how could the mere fact that people would find other views attractive under different circumstances provide a reason for rejecting the views that they do hold? The fact that citizens' views are in part institutionally explained should not lead us to think that an allegiance to them is merely a product of political circumstance rather than free reflection, given the specificity of the institutions and their role in protecting public deliberation.

C. Objectionably Exclusionary

The third objection begins from the observation that the difficulty of achieving consensus depends on the range of positions among which agreement is sought. As this range narrows, the likelihood of agreement increases. But at the same time, concern intensifies that this narrowing

---

131. On institutionalizing deliberation, see Cohen, "Deliberation and Democratic Legitimacy," 26–32.

requires arbitrary and exclusionary restrictions on the set of relevant alternatives. Such restrictions would of course diminish the interest of the agreement.

Let us bring this observation a little closer to the ground: Rawls tells us that an adequate conception of justice must be able to win the support of "reasonable citizens who affirm reasonable comprehensive doctrines."[132] Other views likely exist and ought not to be suppressed: "That there are doctrines that reject one or more democratic freedoms is itself a permanent fact of life" (64n19). But the fact that certain doctrines do not accept the political conception of justice as the correct account—the fact that they do not compose part of the overlapping consensus—raises no troubles, Rawls claims, for the justification of the political conception. If a political conception is rejected by unreasonable comprehensive views, the legitimacy of the exercise of power through institutions justified by that conception is not undermined. Reasonable comprehensive doctrines "are the doctrines that reasonable citizens affirm and that political liberalism must address" (36).

The difficulty should now be clear: although confining the range of relevant conceptions to reasonable views increases the likelihood of agreement, it also prompts concern that the label *unreasonable* will be used to exclude views arbitrarily—simply to ensure agreement or to silence dissent. We may state the objection as follows: If *unreasonable* simply amounts in the end to an abstract abbreviation for "disagrees with the dominant political conception of justice," then of course all reasonable views will support the political conception. But then the idea that an adequate conception must win the support of reasonable citizens who affirm reasonable doctrines will be of uncertain interest. If, however, *reasonable* is defined independently from acceptance of the political conception—say, in terms of a willingness to entertain and respond to objections—then reasonable citizens will likely affirm reasonable views that reject the political conception.

To respond, I should first note that even if acceptance of a particular political conception of justice in part *constituted* "reasonableness," the idea of an overlapping consensus would still be of interest. Given the fact of reasonable pluralism, a political conception that could be supported on

132. *Political Liberalism*, 36; see also Cohen, "Moral Pluralism and Political Consensus," 281–285.

the basis of premises provided by a variety of conflicting comprehensive moral conceptions would still be desirable. Because such conceptions would be reasonable in part because of their support for the political conception, we could not construe support from competing reasonable conceptions as providing an entirely independent check on the acceptability of the conception of justice. Still, this constitutive interpretation of *reasonable* would permit us to make a case for the thesis that consensus on a political conception of justice is compatible with moral pluralism—that it does not require agreement on a comprehensive conception of the good.

Although *reasonable person is* a normative notion, the constitutive interpretation of *reasonable* is not right. Instead, persons count as reasonable only if they are concerned to live on terms that are acceptable to others who share that same concern (48–54). In addition, they must acknowledge the "burdens of judgment": the conditions that cause disagreement among persons who affirm the importance of cooperating on terms that others can accept—that is, among persons who are reasonable in the first sense (54–56). Thus reasonableness is defined abstractly and not—as with constitutive interpretation—in terms of the acceptance of a particular political conception. It more or less directly follows from these two features of reasonableness, however, that reasonable citizens will endorse certain basic liberties (58–61): how else could they show that they wish to live according to principles that they can justify to others, given disagreements with others that reflect the burdens of judgment?

But doesn't this characterization of *reasonable* show that the restriction of the overlapping consensus to reasonable views endorsed by reasonable citizens is arbitrarily exclusionary? Perhaps the arbitrariness is not as transparent as the constitutive interpretation suggests. Still, the restriction may seem to provide license to define away dissenting views as unreasonable and to exclude them from public discussion, while celebrating public consensus among the reasonable. Three points suggest otherwise.

First, we need to distinguish between tolerating a view and ensuring that it forms part of the overlapping consensus. It is no crime to be unreasonable—to favor institutions and policies that cannot be justified to others—or to express an unreasonable view, nor does the endorsement of such a view have any bearing on basic rights.[133] The basis for such rights as

---

133. Rawls says: "That there are views that reject one or more of the democratic freedoms is itself a permanent fact of life, or seems so. This gives us the practical task of containing them—

expression and association is independent of the content of one's views. Insofar as unreasonable views are "excluded," then, that exclusion is of a special kind.

Second, it is a mistake to suppose that, as a general matter, dissenting views turn out unreasonable according to the account provided earlier. Consider, for example, dissident movements on the left in the recent history of this country. Why would anyone think that anti-intervention movements, or movements for civil rights, racial equality, women's equality, economic justice, and gay and lesbian rights, are or were unreasonable? All these movements appeal, as a general matter, to political values in the democratic tradition. They struggle against the injustice of circumstances in which life chances are fixed by race, class, gender, or sexual orientation. Critics of these movements may disagree with the ways they have articulated democratic values, but we expect reasonable people to disagree.[134]

As an example of a view that *is* at least in part unreasonable, Rawls mentions—plausibly, I think—the position that would deny to a woman "a duly qualified right to decide whether or not to end her pregnancy during the first trimester."[135] The case for the unreasonableness of this denial proceeds implicitly in two steps. First, Rawls supposes that any reasonable view will endorse and seek to accommodate three political values as relevant to addressing the issue of reproductive choice: "the due respect for human life, the ordered reproduction of political society over time . . . and finally the equality of women as equal citizens" (243n32). Second, he

---

like war and disease—so that they do not overturn political justice." *Political Liberalism*, 64n19. This remark does not imply that we may do whatever we judge appropriate for containing objectionable views any more than we can fight a disease by simply quarantining people who are sick. On tolerating the intolerant, see Rawls, *A Theory of Justice*, 216–221; on the right of subversive advocacy, see *Political Liberalism*, 340–356.

134. Consider, to take just one example, proposals to regulate pornography in order to ensure sexual equality. See, for example, Catharine MacKinnon, *Only Words* (Cambridge, MA: Harvard University Press, 1993). These proposals appeal to political values. They do not reject the value of liberty generally, or freedom of expression in particular. Instead, they offer a particular way to combine freedom of expression and equality. Although I do not agree with these proposals, it is simply wrong to argue that they reject the value of freedom of expression or that the arguments for them rely on a particular comprehensive view. *See* Joshua Cohen, "Freedom of Expression," *Philosophy and Public Affairs* 22, 3 (Summer 1993): 207–263; Joshua Cohen, "Freedom, Equality, Pornography," in Austin Sarat and Thomas R. Kearns, eds., *Justice and Injustice in Law and Legal Theory* (Ann Arbor: University of Michigan Press, 1996), 99–137.

135. *Political Liberalism*, 243n32. This right is much weaker than the right upheld in *Roe v. Wade*, 410 U.S. 113 (1973), which is not confined to the first trimester.

claims that any "reasonable balance" of these values will support the "duly qualified right" (243n32). To deny the right is either to deny, at the first step, that the equality of women is an important political value, or to claim, at the second step, that one of the other values—say, the due respect for human life—overrides the value of the equality of women, even if we confine our attention to the early stages of pregnancy.

Assume that the case for denying the right accepts the equality of women and is based on the value of due respect for human life. What prevents someone who accepts the three values from rejecting the duly qualified right as inconsistent with the due respect for human life? The problem is that people reasonably disagree about the precise content of the value of "due respect for human life." Given the complexities of the question of the status of the fetus, the conscientious rejection by many citizens of the claim that due respect for human life requires that we treat the fetus as a human person in the first trimester, the weight of the equality of women as a political value, and the importance of justification to others when such weighty values are at stake, how could it be reasonable to urge the state to endorse and to enforce the view that due respect for human life bars first-trimester abortions? Someone who rejects first-trimester abortions may reply that when it comes to preventing the murder of innocent babies, being right is more important than being reasonable. But that reply concedes the point about reasonableness, which is the only issue I am now addressing.

Coming now to the third point about the exclusionary character of the notion of reasonableness: it is not arbitrary to worry only about ensuring support from the reasonable conceptions endorsed by reasonable citizens and therefore to exclude unreasonable views from an overlapping consensus. Such views do not aim to find terms that can be justified to others, and to that extent they deny the values of self-government and cooperation on terms of mutual respect. Moreover, one of the reasons for seeking common ground among conflicting views in the first place—for rejecting the appeal to the truth of our own view—is that we regard it as unreasonable to impose political power on others in the name of values that they reasonably reject—even if those values are correct. So the rationale for an overlapping consensus commits us to regarding views unconcerned with common ground as unreasonable. To permit those views to shape the content of a conception of justice is to permit the content of justice to be determined by the power of those views to make themselves heard. But no attractive conception can be built around such an accommodation to power.

D. Overly Accommodating

The final line of criticism I wish to explore accepts the ideal of political consensus but urges that an overlapping consensus is too limited. There are several variants of this concern, but I will focus here on one that takes Rawls's idea of public reason as its immediate target (212–254).

According to the idea of public reason, we should set aside comprehensive conceptions of the good in certain political settings—when discussing constitutional essentials and matters of basic justice (227–230)—and conduct political argument on the shared ground provided by political values. The criticism I have in mind rejects these limits of public reason because the constraints they impose on political deliberation prevent us from achieving a deeper level of political agreement than the idea of an overlapping consensus promises.[136]

To be sure, Rawls describes several exceptions to the requirement of respecting the limits of public reason—several cases in which it is permissible to appeal to a wider range of moral values than those within a political conception of justice (247–252). But limits remain. None of the exceptions mentioned in *Liberalism*—and none added in a recent essay modifying *Liberalism*'s account of public reason[137]—would permit citizens, in the nor-

---

136. "[Liberalism] forgets the possibility that when politics goes well, we can know a good in common that we cannot know alone." Sandel, *Liberalism and the Limits*, 183. See also the illuminating remarks by Seyla Benhabib on the limits of liberal and discursive models of the public space in Seyla Benhabib, "Models of Public Space: Hannah Arendt, the Liberal Tradition and Juergen Habermas," in *Situating the Self* (New York: Routledge, 1992), 89–120. Benhabib explores feminist criticisms of "overly rigid boundaries . . . between matters of justice and those of the good life, public interests versus private needs, privately held values and publicly shared norms" (111). In the end, however, I am not sure how far her own view differs from Rawls's. Here I will note just one reason. Benhabib uses the term *political discourse* in a very expansive way (see 104). So her concern to open up public, political discourse to more comprehensive views—both matters of justice and those of the good life—reflects her idea that such discourse "can be realized in the social and cultural spheres as well." *Political discourse* covers debates in "cultural journals" about sexual and racial stereotyping, for example. As I explain in the text (see below, text accompanying note 140), Rawls uses the terms *political* and *public* more narrowly. So he agrees that the limits of public reason do not apply to political discourse, understood in such a capacious way. See *Political Liberalism*, 214–215.

137. *See* John Rawls, "The Idea of Public Reason: Further Considerations" (January 3, 1994) (unpublished manuscript, on file with author). [This was a draft of the essay that Rawls published as "The Idea of Public Reason Revisited," *The University of Chicago Law Review* 64, 3 (Summer 1997): 765–807.]

mal course of political argument, to bring the comprehensive views of others to the surface for the purpose of criticizing those views and the political implications that flow from them. Nor does the Rawlsian view encourage or require citizens to express their comprehensive conceptions in the course of political debate with a view to opening those conceptions up to the challenge of public discourse. The account of public reason may seem, then, to undervalue the importance of forms of *critical discourse* that do not respect the distinction between moral and political argument and as a result to truncate politics and practical reason. This tendency might seem objectionable for two reasons.

First, actual conceptions of the good may reflect traditions of injustice. A consensus that assumes such conceptions without challenging them—putting them behind a veil of ignorance, at the basis of an overlapping consensus, or off the political agenda—is for that reason less compelling as an account of ideal justice. According to the objection, if we wish to link justice and consensus, we need a consensus that emerges from unconstrained discussion, in which we may call on people to articulate their comprehensive conception of the good, which others may then challenge.

Second, constricting the arena of public discussion—limiting its scope to what can now be shared—perhaps excludes constructive possibilities of consensus and community that might emerge from challenging received moral traditions. Opening up the public arena by dropping the limits of public reason allows deeper challenges to existing conceptions of the good, thus permitting a more expansive consensus to emerge, if only as an ideal of reason.

To clarify the point of the objection, it may help to distinguish two conceptions of the aim of critical discourse. On one view, the point is to expose unreflective assumptions, thereby freeing ourselves from illusions and a false sense of coherence and necessity. This first understanding neither expects nor hopes that such a critique will generate a new and deeper consensus in which all previous views are understood as partial versions of the truth.[138] According to an alternative conception, critique serves as an instrument of reasonable consensus. Instead of taking differences as fundamental

---

138. In the legal academy, Duncan Kennedy is the great exponent of this first form of critique. See Duncan Kennedy, *Sexy Dressing, Etc.* (Cambridge, MA: Harvard University Press, 1993).

and given, it invites a more searching public debate about hidden interests, suppressed alternatives, and moral disagreements with an eye to transcending current conflicts.

Here I am concerned only with the second line of thought: with the rejection of the limits of public reason in the name of possibilities of more comprehensive agreement and a corresponding rejection of overlapping consensus for its relaxed accommodation of de facto conceptions of the good. There are two responses.

First, as a matter of clarification: to affirm the limits of public reason is not to deny the importance of a more comprehensive critical discourse, in which conceptions of the good—even if reasonable—are subject to challenge, unmasking, irony, and ridicule. Protection of freedom of expression always permits such discourse, and in some settings—even political settings—it may be entirely appropriate as a way to clarify views, to change minds, and perhaps to establish deeper mutual understanding.

The question is whether comprehensive critical discourse is appropriate[139] in deliberative settings that are concerned with establishing the basic terms of political cooperation in a democratic society and sanctioning the exercise of power to enforce those terms. The idea of the limits of public reason is that "political values alone are to settle such fundamental questions *as*: who has the right to vote, or what religions are to be tolerated, or who is to be assured fair equality of opportunity, or to hold property" (214). Whatever the benefits of more comprehensive critical discourse in such settings, there is likely to be a cost. Critical discourse is likely to impede cooperation on terms of mutual respect, particularly when the views at issue are acknowledged—as I am supposing they are—to be both fundamental and reasonable. But "many if not most political questions do not concern those fundamental matters" (214). Accordingly, the case for limits on argument in the conduct of debate about issues such as trade policy is correspondingly weaker.

Second, given reasonable disagreements, the basis for expecting that a more comprehensive critical discourse will lead to a deeper consensus is unclear, which implies that the benefits are also unclear. It appears that "difference" is a fundamental fact, as fundamental as our commonalities.

---

139. The issue is not whether critical discourse ought to be legally permissible. The legal right must be established because of the requirement of equal basic liberties. See *Political Liberalism*, 337.

People disagree deeply, and political reason appears insufficient to resolve these differences. Putting aside comprehensive metaphysical theories according to which we all are the manifestations of spirit, or religious views accessible through faith, what reason could there be for denying that there are such rationally irresolvable disagreements? Everything points to the permanence of moral disagreement, and nothing points against it: there is the *fact* of disagreement and the absence of any apparent tendency to comprehensive convergence; we have no *theory* of the operations of practical reason that would lead us to expect convergence on comprehensive moralities; and there is no *mechanism* of the kind I sketched earlier in the case of political values[140] that might produce agreement on comprehensive views.

One might argue that differences are not so deep because adherents of comprehensive moral conceptions believe their conceptions to be true and think they can withstand rational criticism. This observation suggests a fundamental common interest—in the truth, in living according to the best conception, or in living according to a view that can stand up to rational criticism—that lies deeper than any of our substantive disagreements about which conception is in fact true or best and therefore ought to guide conduct.

The availability of such abstract characterizations of common interests that underlie moral disagreements is of considerable importance and may help to secure mutual understanding and respect. It may be important for me to view people who believe that the best life is a life that comports with God's prescriptions as having the same abstract, fundamental interest as I do—an interest in knowing what is true and in living the best life— even if I cannot imagine myself believing what they believe or conducting myself as they do. We all know how complex evaluative questions are, and we can understand how people conscientiously aiming at the same target might end up in very different places.

Finding deep commonalities of interest within moral differences is, then, a significant value. Nevertheless, the availability of such common ground gives us no reason for expecting a more substantial convergence on comprehensive moralities. The interests are too abstract to provide a basis for such an expectation. People with conflicting religious convictions

140. *See* above, notes 120–126 and accompanying text.

might acknowledge one another as sharing an abstract common interest in believing the truth and in conforming their conduct to their understanding of the truth. This point of agreement might, in turn, be important in ensuring mutual respect among people with conflicting religious convictions. It provides minimal leverage, however, in resolving religious disagreement, and thus very little reason for expecting people's religious convictions to converge. Why should comprehensive moralities be any different?

5. Democratic Toleration and Liberal Universalism

Early in this essay, I described *Political Liberalism as* a deep and original book. I want to conclude by returning to the sources of that depth and originality, indicating their continuity with *Theory*.

There is of course no originality in the thought that people with different views of life can live together in a political society, and there is some evidence—relatively little, unfortunately—that toleration is a practical possibility. But the defense of toleration, when it does not appeal principally to the very great practical advantages of toleration, commonly proceeds in an "exclusivist" way. What I mean is that the defense of the claim that a political society ought to permit different outlooks on life to flourish within it commonly proceeds from the perspective of one of those outlooks.[141]

John Locke's defense of religious toleration, for example, seems to depend for its force on a Protestant view of salvation.[142] Or consider John Stuart Mill's endorsement of individuality in *On Liberty*, his powerful defense of a society featuring "different experiments of living."[143] In the course of that defense, Mill urges that "it may be better to be a John Knox than of an Alcibiades, but it is better to be a Pericles than either."[144] Presumably Mill thought that at least some experiments in living would proceed more in the tradition of Alcibiades and Knox than of Pericles. The non-Periclean experiments should certainly be tolerated; Mill sum-

---

141. There are some exceptions. See, for example, Bruce A. Ackerman, *Social Justice in the Liberal State* (New Haven: Yale University Press, 1981). Ackerman emphasizes (355–359) the independence of political argument from moral argument and also the many routes to liberal political arguments. But his discussion of "four of the main highways to the liberal state" (359–369) suggests that his liberalism is a partially comprehensive doctrine. I am indebted to John Rawls for a discussion of this issue.

142. *See* Locke, *Letter Concerning Toleration*, 17–20.

143. Mill, *On Liberty*, 115.

144. Ibid., 120.

marizes their toleration in his "harm principle."[145] His reasons for such toleration, however, reflect the Periclean perspective; they draw on a conception of human excellence with roots in the "Greek ideal of self-development."[146] Mill reveals the depth of these roots when he urges that "developed human beings are of some use to the undeveloped" and that "those who do not desire liberty, and would not avail themselves of it" may nevertheless be won to the cause of liberty because they might "in some intelligible manner [be] rewarded for allowing other people to make use of it without hindrance."[147]

Rawls proposes something different, which I referred to earlier as "democratic toleration." By requiring toleration as a condition for acceptable public justification, he aims to free the defense of diverse experiments of living from the outlook of one such experiment. More broadly speaking, Rawls wishes to free the democratic ideal of a shared arena of public deliberation among equal citizens from dependence on the particular ethical outlook of any subset of the public. Whether he succeeds in this enterprise is another matter, although I find the case compelling for reasons I have already presented. The point I wish to stress here is that in advancing a democratic conception of toleration, Rawls presents a sustained response to an important line of criticism of classical liberal ideas of citizen, person, reason, and public. According to the criticism, the superficial and abstract universalism of these ideas masks a much deeper parochialism. Rawls's conception of an overlapping consensus on a political conception of justice suggests a way to present those ideals as genuinely shared ground.

To be sure, liberal political thought has always been self-consciously universalistic, speaking in the name of all human beings, and urging the protection of the rights and interests of all, regardless of race, class, gender, religion, or any other of the particularisms that distinguish and divide us. But critics of liberalism have vigilantly revealed the hidden (and not-so-hidden) exclusions—of, for example, class, race, and gender—that

145. Ibid., 72–73, 114, 132, 149–150.
146. Ibid., 120. For interesting suggestions about the connections of this feature of Mill's view with his affection for colonialism, see Bhikhu Parekh, "Superior People: The Narrowness of Liberalism from Mill to Rawls," *Times Literary Supplement* (London), February 25, 1994, 11.
147. Mill, *On Liberty*, 122. For example, the undeveloped "might possibly learn something" from the developed.

compromise liberalism's defining promise: its capacity to say "all" without quite meaning it.[148] Some critics have argued that its promise is essentially compromised. For them, liberal universalism is unavoidably exclusive; its fundamental categories, such as citizen, person, public, and rights, cannot be extended to include all people without losing their definition. These critics argue, for example, that the idea of a public sphere takes shape from its opposition to a private sphere and that the distinction between public and private stands in the way of the equality of women;[149] or that the abstractions that define liberal universalism require that we neglect the more concrete differences—such as class and natural endowment—that shape actual lives.[150]

Liberals, of course, deny that the project of liberal universalism is hopelessly compromised and that abstraction is the enemy of equality and inclusion. But denial is one thing; it is quite another to make a constructive case that liberalism can deliver more fully on the universalistic promise of its classical proponents and to abandon key elements of liberalism to ensure that delivery.

Consider in this light Rawls's project in *Theory* and *Liberalism*. *Theory* took seriously the egalitarian critique of liberalism: the charge that the defense of liberty is a defense of the privileges of people with the wealth or status needed to make effective use of their liberty. In response, Rawls moved the idea of the social contract to a higher order of abstraction, presenting it as an agreement among free and equal persons, not among property owners, or among men, or among individuals with definite con-

148. For representative examples of such criticisms in the case of Lockean liberalism, see C. B. MacPherson, *The Political Theory of Possessive Individualism* (Oxford: Oxford University Press, 1962); Carole Pateman, "Feminist Critiques of the Public/Private Dichotomy," in *The Disorder of Women* (Stanford: Stanford University Press, 1989), 118; Joshua Cohen, "Structure, Choice, and Legitimacy: Locke's Theory of the State," *Philosophy and Public Affairs* 15, 4 (Autumn 1986): 301–324 (reprinted as Chapter 2 in this volume); and Uday S. Mehta, "Liberal Strategies of Exclusion," *Politics and Society* 18, 4 (1990): 427–454.

149. *See* Benhabib, "Models of Public Space," 107–113; Catharine A. MacKinnon, *Toward a Feminist Theory of the State* (Cambridge, MA: Harvard University Press, 1989), 157–170; Pateman, "Feminist Critiques," 119–124; Nancy Fraser, "Rethinking the Public Sphere: A Contribution to the Critique of Actually Existing Democracy," in Craig Calhoun ed., *Habermas and the Public Sphere* (Cambridge, MA: MIT Press, 1992), 109–142.

150. *See* Karl Marx, "Critique of the Gotha Program," in *The Marx-Engels Reader*, 2nd ed., ed. Robert C. Tucker, trans. S. Ryazanskaya (New York: Norton, 1978), 525, 530–531; Karl Marx, "On the Jewish Question," in *The Marx-Engels Reader*, 26. For discussion of this issue as it arises in the context of distributive ethics, see Amartya Sen, *Inequality Reexamined* (Cambridge, MA: Harvard University Press, 1992).

ceptions of their own advantage.[151] Through this abstract reinterpretation of the social contract, Rawls made a compelling case for the view that the best version of liberalism is more egalitarian and inclusive than had traditionally been thought. In short, Rawls gave us a more genuinely *universalistic* liberalism, committed to "democratic equality"[152] and less susceptible to charges of class exclusion.

Although *Liberalism* is not so concerned with the class question, it, too, aims at a more genuinely universalistic liberalism. Generalizing and deepening the ideal of toleration—by carrying it to a higher order of abstraction—Rawls offers a democratic liberalism less susceptible to charges of moral parochialism, sectarianism, and elitism and more suited to "the historical and social circumstances of a democratic society" (154). By "apply[ing] the principles of toleration to philosophy itself," political liberalism leaves it "to citizens themselves to settle the questions of religion, philosophy, and morals in accordance with views they freely affirm" (154).

Here we come to the heart of Rawls's work and the basis of his permanent contribution to political philosophy: he offers us a new version of democratic liberalism, marked by a commitment to liberalism's universalistic promise and a willingness to pursue that commitment by transforming those aspects of liberal thought that are condemned by its own high aspirations.

Consider the common ground of *Theory* and *Liberalism* from a different angle. In his Gettysburg Address, Lincoln said that the United States was "conceived in Liberty, and dedicated to the proposition that all men are created equal," and he wondered whether a political society with such abstract devotions could "long endure."[153] Perhaps such a society would be unable to make good on the promise of liberty and equality; perhaps dedication to an idea and a proposition would provide too thin a basis for stable social unity.

Theory and *Liberalism* are the product of a life's engagement with these concerns. *Theory* gives us an account of what the promise of liberty and equality demands and a measure of how far we are from keeping that

151. On the Lockean contract as an agreement among property owners, see Cohen, "Structure, Choice, and Legitimacy," 149.

152. "Democratic equality" is Rawls's term for the conception of fair distribution that includes the difference principle. See Rawls, A *Theory of Justice*, 75–83; Cohen, "Democratic Equality," 727–731.

153. Abraham Lincoln, "Gettysburg Address," November 19, 1863.

promise. *Liberalism* offers hope and a warning: the hope that we can achieve social unity in a democracy through shared commitment to abstract principles and the warning that any political bonds thicker than these would, by excluding some citizens, represent yet another failure to endure.[154]

154. For an example of thicker bonds, see the quotation from Pat Buchanan that begins this essay.

5

FOR A DEMOCRATIC SOCIETY

1. Justice as Fairness

John Rawls's A *Theory of Justice* tells us what justice requires, what a just society should look like, and how justice fits into the overall good of the members of a just society. But it does not tell us much about the politics of a just society: about the processes of public argument, political mobilization, electoral competition, organized movements, legislative decision-making, or administration comprised within the politics of a modern democracy. Indeed, neither the term "democracy" nor any of its cognates has an entry in the index to A *Theory of Justice*.[1] The only traditional problem of democracy that receives much sustained attention is the basis of majority rule, which is itself addressed principally in the context of a normative model of legislative decisions, with an uncertain relation to actual legislative processes.[2] This relative inattention to democracy—to politics more generally—may leave the impression that Rawls's theory of justice in some way denigrates democracy, perhaps subordinating it to a conception of justice that is defended through philosophical reasoning and is to be implemented by judges and administrators insulated from politics.[3]

I wish to thank Samuel Freeman for his nearly infinite patience, Tim Scanlon for puzzling with me on and off for several years about what Rawls meant in saying that his theory of justice is "for a democratic society," Oliver Gerstenberg for his comments on an earlier draft, and students in my political philosophy seminar during the spring of 2000 for their comments and questions about earlier versions of this material.

1. Unlike *Justice as Fairness: A Restatement*, ed. Erin Kelly (Cambridge, MA: Harvard University Press, 2001), which has many entries under "democracy," "democratic regime," and "democratic society." The same is true for "citizen," which is not in the index to A *Theory of Justice*, but many references to the term appear in *Justice as Fairness* (hereafter *JF*).

2. A *Theory of Justice*, rev. ed. (Cambridge, MA: Harvard University Press, 1999), 313–318. Hereafter, all references to A *Theory of Justice* will be included parenthetically in the text and will refer to the revised edition.

3. I associate this important objection with, among others, Michael Walzer, Sheldon Wolin, Benjamin Barber, and Bonnie Honig. But I also hear it, in more intuitive form, from

So it comes as something of a surprise when Rawls says, in the Preface to the first edition of A *Theory of Justice*, that his conception of justice as fairness "constitutes the most appropriate moral basis *for a democratic society*."[4] To be sure, the idea that justice as fairness has a particularly intimate democratic connection is prominent from the 1980 *Dewey Lectures* forward.[5] And in the Preface to the revised edition of A *Theory of Justice* (dated 1990), Rawls says that the "ideas and aims" of justice as fairness are "those of a philosophical conception *for a constitutional democracy*" (emphasis added) which, he hopes, "will seem reasonable and useful, even if not fully convincing, to a wide range of thoughtful political opinions and thereby express an essential part of the common core of the democratic tradition" (xi). But while the idea of democracy (more precisely, as we will see, a family of ideas of democracy) is increasingly in evidence in Rawls's work after A *Theory of Justice*, it plays an important role there as well, and in discussing Rawls's conception of democracy, I will not give much attention to the shifts in emphasis or to the broader shifts in outlook from A *Theory of Justice* to *Political Liberalism*.[6] Though justice as fairness is not a theory of democracy, and says little about the processes of democratic politics, it is a contribution to democratic thought. It argues that a democratic political regime is itself a requirement of justice—and not simply for instrumental reasons. Moreover, the fundamental aim of the conception of justice as fairness is to present principles that provide the most reasonable norms for guiding the political judgments of members of a democratic society in exercising their responsibilities as citizens.

---

students and colleagues in political science, and have tried to respond here to the intuitive concern rather than to its theoretical articulation.

4. A *Theory of Justice* (Cambridge, MA: Harvard University Press, 1971), xviii (emphasis added).

5. In *Collected Papers*, ed. Samuel Freeman (Cambridge, MA: Harvard University Press, 1999), 303–358, esp. 305–307 (hereafter *CP*).

6. *Political Liberalism* (New York: Columbia University Press, 1996). Hereafter, references will be included parenthetically in the text, with *PL*. For discussion of the shifts in outlook, see Joshua Cohen, "A More Democratic Liberalism," *Michigan Law Review* 92, 6 (May 1994): 1503–1546 (reprinted as Chapter 4 in this volume). Of all the early commentators on A *Theory of Justice*, H. L. A. Hart seems to have best understood the democratic background of the work. Although Hart overstates the importance of an ideal of active participation, he rightly emphasizes the central role in Rawls's view of a conception of democracy. See "Rawls on Liberty and Its Priority," in *Reading Rawls*, ed. Norman Daniels (Stanford: Stanford University Press, 1989), 252.

What, then, does Rawls mean when he says that justice as fairness is "for a democratic society"? How precisely does Rawls fit justice and democracy together?

I begin (in section 2) by explaining three ways in which justice as fairness is a conception for a democratic society. The three ways are connected to three ideas of democracy: a *democratic political regime,* which means a political arrangement with rights of participation, elections, and surrounding rights of association and expression designed to make participation informed and effective; *a democratic society,* which means a society whose members are understood in the political culture as free and equal persons; and *deliberative democracy,* which means a political society in which fundamental political argument appeals to reasons suited to co-operation among free and equal persons, and the authorization to exercise collective power traces to such argument. Justice as fairness is "for a democratic society," then, first because it assigns to individuals an equal right to participate, and thus requires a democratic regime as a matter of basic justice. Second, it is addressed to a society of equals and its principles are shaped in their content by that public understanding. Finally, it is intended to guide the political reasoning and judgment of the members of a democratic society in their exercise of their political rights.

In section 3 I discuss a few central elements of the conception of political democracy in justice as fairness, exploring in particular why political liberties are basic liberties and how the account of political liberties provides a non-instrumental rationale for a democratic regime.

Finally, in section 4, I engage more directly with the complaint that justice as fairness, though presented as a conception "for a democracy," inappropriately subordinates democracy—more particularly, the value of political autonomy—to a substantive conception of justice: that the requirements of justice narrow the scope of political debate in ways that deprive democracy of much of its significance. After responding to several variants of the criticism, I suggest that it points to an important limitation on the conception of democracy in A *Theory of Justice.* In brief, Rawls is insufficiently attentive there to political disagreement. The fact of disagreement among citizens in a democracy—fostered in part by the organization of mass democratic politics as a competition for political power between candidates and parties—need not lead us to the familiar conception of democracy as nothing more than a struggle to advance interests and partisan ideals by winning political power through elections. But once we acknowledge that disagreement about justice is a permanent feature of democratic societies, then we need to draw a crisper distinction between politics even in an idealized modern democracy and the idealized moral argument that Rawls relies on in A *Theory of Justice*.[7]

Before discussing the three interpretations of the claim that justice as fairness is "for a democratic society," I want to make three background points about focus and terminology.

1. As to focus, I will not address the issues of relativism that may be suggested by the phrase "for a democratic society." Thus it might be said that, in telling us what justice requires in a democratic society, Rawls suggests that the content of justice is always determined relative to a society's political culture. So we could ask what the most reasonable conception of justice is for a democracy, for an aristocracy, or for a community with a shared religious outlook, but not simply ask, What does justice require? Suffice it to say here that no such conclusion follows. In asking what the most reasonable conception of justice is for a democratic society, we answer a question of considerable importance: we address a disagreement among people who all accept an understanding of persons as equals, but who dispute the implications of that understanding. In answering this question, we need not also decide whether the understanding of persons as equals is a compelling cultural assumption, or the most reasonable way to regard people, or a truth of religion or morality.

2. I will use the term "justice as fairness" to name a conception of justice that comprises both principles of justice, and an account of how those principles are to be justified.

The first principle of justice says that each person is to have an equal right to the most extensive total system of equal basic liberties compatible with a similar system of liberties for others. This principle requires stringent protections for liberty of thought and conscience; political liberties (rights of participation); liberty of association; liberty and integrity of the person; and rights and liberties associated with the rule of law. The protection of political liberties under the first principle is expressed in the *principle of participation*, according to which "all citizens are to have an equal right to take part in, and determine the outcome of constitutional processes that establish the laws with which they are to comply" (p. 194).

N.B

---

7. Rawls appears to endorse this view in the final edition of *Political Liberalism* but without developing the implications for the ideal of democracy. See *PL*, xlviii–xlix.

Moreover, political liberty is to be assured a *fair value:* chances to hold office and exercise political influence are to be independent of socioeconomic position (197–199; *PL*, 327–329).

The second principle—a principle of *democratic equality*—states that socioeconomic inequalities are to be arranged so that they meet two conditions: they are to be attached to offices and positions open to all under conditions of *fair equality of opportunity*, which means that people who are equally talented and motivated are to have equal chances to attain desirable positions, so far as this is consistent with maintaining equal basic liberties; and, according to the *difference principle*, the inequalities attaching to those positions are to operate to the greatest benefit of the least advantaged.

Moreover, the first principle has priority over the second. This "priority of liberty" means that justifications for limiting a basic liberty must show how the proposed limit would contribute to strengthening the system of liberties. To better protect religious liberty, then, it is permissible to limit political liberty by restricting the scope of majority rule and establishing a basic right to liberty of conscience: one liberty is restricted in order to better protect another basic liberty. But it is impermissible to restrict political liberty in order to improve the material conditions of the least advantaged: for example, it is not permissible to restrict the voting rights of the better off in order to improve the economic circumstances of the less well-off.

As to the justification of principles: in A *Theory of Justice*, Rawls sought, as he says, to revive the social contract tradition by carrying the idea of the social contract to a "higher order of abstraction" (xviii). Underlying the contract is the fundamental idea of a well-ordered society of persons understood as free and equal, who cooperate on fair terms as specified by a conception of justice. According to justice as fairness, principles of justice are requirements of fair cooperation among free and equal persons: the social contract of justice as fairness is framed to present such principles.[8] The contract mediates between the abstract ideal of fair cooperation among free and equal persons and substantive principles of justice: it presents the content implicit in that—as we will see—democratic ideal.

8. I emphasize: not simply principles of fair cooperation among individuals with conflicting interests and values but fair cooperation among persons understood as free and equal. See *TJ*, 11–13. In *JF* (7), this characterization of persons as free and equal is connected to a "democratic conception of justice" founded of how citizens are conceived in a democratic society.

More particularly, the contract is made by rational individuals reasoning about how best to advance their interests under conditions of extreme ignorance. And the most reasonable principles of justice for a society of free and equal persons are "the principles that free and rational persons concerned to further their own interests would accept in an initial situation of equality as defining the fundamental terms of their association" (10). But the fundamental idea is that principles of justice present requirements of fair cooperation among free and equal persons. The agreement by rational individuals concerned to advance their own interests under constraints of ignorance models that fundamental idea and expresses its content. Thus the fact that certain considerations are irrelevant in an argument about which principles of justice characterize fair conditions of cooperation among free and equal persons is modeled by assuming that those persons are ignorant of the irrelevant conditions: we model irrelevance through ignorance (or restrictions on reasons through limits on information). But the social contract idea models an idea about which considerations are irrelevant in arguments for fair principles for free and equal persons that is given before the construction of the original position.[9]

3. Justice as fairness is a *substantive*, not simply a *procedural*, conception of justice.[10] The substance—procedure distinction is not settled, and for the purposes of discussion here, I will stipulate the content of the distinction. In particular, justice as fairness is a substantive conception of justice in that it comprises standards of justice for assessing not only processes of collective decision-making but also the outcomes of those processes. For example, a just basic structure must protect basic personal liberties, in-

---

9. It is worth noting that the relevant-irrelevant distinction does not lead us, without further argument, to the idea of justification via prudential-rational choice under ignorance. We could do without a contract altogether and simply assess principles by reflecting on which conception of justice is best supported by the balance of relevant considerations. But even if we model the problem of deliberation among alternative conceptions of justice as a problem of agreement under ignorance, we could simply think of the parties as reasoning under ignorance about irrelevant considerations. But not all ethical norms are irrelevant. So, for example, it is not intuitively irrelevant in assessing a principle of justice that it would permit people to benefit from undeserved assets; awareness of this principle, then, is not excluded simply by the assumption that parties are ignorant about irrelevant considerations. Modeling irrelevance through ignorance does not, then, lead to the original position model of rational choice under ignorance but is fully compatible with a model of ethical reasoning in the initial situation. See Rawls's remarks on "ethical variations of the initial situation" (512).

10. Joshua Cohen, "Pluralism and Proceduralism," *Chicago-Kent Law Review* 69 (1994): 589–618.

cluding liberty of conscience. Decisions to restrict those liberties are unjust, even if they are made through a democratic process. In assessing the
justice of the basic structure, the principles of justice instruct us to consider directly whether the arrangements protect basic liberties, not simply
whether abridgements of those liberties were enacted through a democratic process.[11] A proceduralist, in contrast, rejects standards of justice
other than requirements of democratic procedure: the proceduralist says
that no norms are binding on a democratic process other than those that
emerge through that process. So the democratic proceduralist says that
justice requires democratic process, and (perhaps) that any outcome of an
open democratic process is just.

Virtually all leading theories of justice—whether utilitarian, libertarian, or egalitarian—are substantive, according to the account I have just
stipulated. Variants of democratic proceduralism are more commonly advanced as theories of political legitimacy (as justifications for the exercise
of authority), or as statements of a sufficient condition for political obligation, or as interpretations of the American constitution, rather than as
theories of justice. So it might be said that democratic etiology suffices to
make a regulation legitimate law, or to impose obligations to obey, or that
the main aim of the Constitution is to ensure democratic procedures of
lawmaking. In any case, justice as fairness affirms that judgments of justice are independent of judgments about such etiology. That justice as
fairness is substantive will play a large role in the later discussion about
whether justice as fairness subordinates democracy to justice.

2. Justice and Democracy

Rawls's conception of justice as fairness connects ideas of democracy and
justice in three ways. The *content* of the most reasonable conception of
justice requires a democratic political system; the *foundation* of the principles lies in the idea of a democratic society, understood as a society of
equals, and the content of the principles expresses that idea; and the *role*
of the principles is to guide the judgments of members of a democratic
society by presenting fundamental norms of public political argument

---

11. For the sake of simplicity of statement, I am assuming here that we can identify the
"democraticness" of the process independent of its protections of all basic liberties. Elsewhere
I suggest some difficulties for this view. See "Democracy and Liberty," in Jon Elster, ed., *Deliberative Democracy* (Cambridge: Cambridge University Press, 1998), 185–231.

suited to their standing as equals (that is, as members of a democratic society). I will consider these in turn.

Content: Constitutional Democracy

Justice as fairness is "for a democracy," in the first place, because the principles of justice require a democratic political regime. Those principles support a democratic constitution, with a representative legislature, universal political rights (including freedom of speech, assembly, and association), and regular elections in which parties that advance different views of the public good compete for office (195–196). Such a constitution establishes a political procedure that is just inasmuch as it satisfies the principle of participation (part of the first principle) and that is "imperfect" with respect to advancing other requirements of justice: "the constitution satisfies the principles of justice and is best calculated to lead to just and effective legislation" (173).

The principle of participation states that "all citizens are to have an equal right to take part in, and determine the outcome of constitutional processes that establish the laws with which they are to comply" (194). It signifies that political liberty is among the basic liberties whose equal assignment to all members is required as a matter of justice. But justice as fairness, as a substantive and not simply procedural conception of justice, also requires protections for nonpolitical liberties, fair equality of opportunity, and a fair distribution (as determined by the difference principle). Rawls's idea is that the nonpolitical liberties will be, in some way, entrenched in a constitution (perhaps in a bill of rights) along with the political liberties, and not up for consideration in normal politics: "The first principle of equal liberty is the primary standard for the constitutional convention. Its main requirements are that the fundamental liberties of the person and liberty of conscience and freedom of thought be protected and that the political process as a whole be a just procedure" (174–175).

The other requirements of justice provide standards for just legislation, and this leads to the idea that a constitution presents a case of *imperfect procedural justice*. Through its substantive principles, justice as fairness provides the basis for assessing legislation, and political institutions established by the constitution must be designed in part with an eye to generating legislation that gets the right answers—for example, legislation that ensures fair opportunity and promotes the interests of the least well-off group. And within institutions so designed, the legislative process itself must be expressly directed, in the first instance, to ensuring justice, as defined by principles set out in advance, and not simply serve as a forum for fair bargaining among organized social interests. But because the standards of justice are independent of the legislative process, and because there is no assurance that the process will meet the standards—even if the participants conscientiously aim to meet it—we have *imperfect procedural justice*: an independent standard, and no assurance that the process will yield the right results (74–75, 173). When it comes to constitutions, "The best attainable scheme is one of imperfect procedural justice. Nevertheless some schemes have a greater tendency than others to result in unjust laws." So we are to "select from among the procedural arrangements that are both just [as procedures] and feasible those which are most likely to lead to a just and effective legal order" (173). More precisely, our judgments about the justice of constitutions are to reflect our assessments of what would (or could) be chosen at a hypothetical "constitutional stage" after the principles of justice are on hand and with fuller knowledge than in the original position about the historical circumstances of the society to which the principles are being applied—its resources, level of economic development, and political culture (172–173). Thus a constitution is just if and only if it is the constitution that would be chosen—or one of the constitutions that could be chosen—by delegates to a constitutional convention who aim to apply the principles of justice in light of the relevant facts about their society.

In selecting a democratic constitution, then, we need to look in two directions: to the justice of political process and to the justice of outcomes that issue from that process. Justice of process is defined by the rights and liberties included in the first principle; justice of outcomes is assessed by reference to the second principle. In assessing the justice of constitutions, these two directions of consideration converge upon constitutional democracy. The case for political democracy is founded in the first instance on the contents of the first principle—both the principle of participation and the requirement of a process that protects other basic liberties. The second principle reinforces the case for political democracy, at least if we suppose that greater equality of political power means a smaller likelihood of class legislation.

But it would be wrong to suppose that the second principle only has that reinforcing role. Democracy comes in many forms, and the second principle might play a more affirmative role in deciding which form of constitutional democracy to adopt. Thus, consider Arend Lijphart's distinction between consensual and majoritarian (Westminster-style) forms of democracy. The idea of consensual democracy is that laws should have the support of broad coalitions, including each of the major groups in the society. So consensual forms are characterized by multiparty arrangements (typically founded on proportional representation) with executive power sharing among the parties, cooperation between the legislative and executive branches, and coordinated representation of interests; in addition, consensual systems have strong federalism, judicial review, relatively rigid constitutions, strong bicameralism, and independent central banks.[12] Majoritarian democracies differ on each of these institutional dimensions. According to Lijphart, these differences in forms of democratic political arrangement are economically and socially consequential: consensual democracies show higher rates of political representation for women, reduced economic inequality, and stronger welfare states.[13]

I do not wish to assess the evidence for these findings, or whether the consequences Lijphart considers are precisely the right ones for evaluating forms of democracy within justice as fairness, or whether the consensual-majoritarian distinction itself is entirely compelling. Lijphart's view is sufficiently clear and plausible to serve an illustration. Thus, suppose consensual and majoritarian arrangements are both capable of ensuring basic personal and political liberties and that both perform reasonably well at achieving such democratic values as responsiveness, effectiveness, and accountability.[14] Then we might select a more consensual form of democracy (that is, judge that it would be selected in an ideal constitutional convention) because it appears to be more suited to advancing the requirements of fair equality and the difference principle that fall under the sec-

---

12. See Arend Lijphart, *Patterns of Democracy: Government Forms and Performance in Thirty-Six Countries* (New Haven: Yale University Press, 1999).

13. See ibid., chap. 16.

14. Dahl argues that different kinds of democratic arrangement will perform differently with respect to these "democratic values" and that none is perfect "from a democratic point of view." This claim underscores the reasonableness of using considerations of economic and social fairness as a basis for assessing constitutions. See Robert A. Dahl, *On Democracy* (New Haven: Yale University Press, 1998), chaps. 10–11.

ond principle. Making this decision requires believing, as Lijphart does, that the correlation of consensualist institutions and more just outcomes is not spurious: that, for example, consensualism and justice are not both products of a solidaristic culture. Moreover, it must be the case that if participants in the constitutional convention believe that adopting consensual democracy would produce a more solidaristic political culture, and that greater solidarity would in turn enable a society to achieve greater benefits for the least advantaged at a smaller cost in inequality, then those participants would choose consensualism. That is, participants in the constitutional stage must not suppose that they are bound to treat the existing political ethos as a parameter and to pick the constitution that best fits that ethos. They treat the political culture as a fact, not as a binding constraint.[15]

When substantive norms of justice—for example, considerations of distributive fairness—are deployed in assessing types of democratic arrangement, one of two impressions may emerge: first, that the rationale for democracy itself is instrumental. But in the case of justice as fairness, that impression is misguided. While the appropriate form of democracy may be partly determined by judgments about how best to advance substantive justice, the rationale for democracy itself lies in the requirements of the first principle of justice. Second, it might be argued that building substantive standards of justice into the design of democratic arrangements represents an objectionable constraint on the scope of democratic self-government. I will come back to this objection in section 4.

Foundation: Democratic Society

"Democratic" is sometimes used, as in the previous paragraphs, to characterize a form of government. But it is also used to describe a type of society, characterized by conditions of equality. When Tocqueville discusses the democratic revolution in his *Democracy in America* and the replacement of an aristocratic by a democratic society, he has in mind a transformation of the social hierarchy characteristic of feudalism into equality of condition and not the emergence of elected government with widespread suffrage rights. In his review of *Democracy in America*, Mill states:

15. For discussion see my "Taking People as They Are?" *Philosophy and Public Affairs* 30, 4 (2001): 363–386.

> By Democracy, M. de Tocqueville does not, in general, mean any particular form of government. He can conceive a Democracy under an absolute monarch. . . . By Democracy M. de Tocqueville understands equality of conditions, the absence of all aristocracy, whether constituted by political privileges, or by superiority in individual importance and social power. It is towards Democracy in this sense, towards equality between man and man, that he conceives society to be irresistibly travelling.[16]

Whether a democratic society will be complemented by democratic government—or instead by a centralized despotism—is, for Tocqueville, an open question.

In A *Theory of Justice*, Rawls uses "democratic" in this second way, as describing a kind of society rather than a political regime when he says, for example, that his two principles of justice express the underlying "democratic conception of society as a system of cooperation among equal persons" (336). Elsewhere, he tells us that the principles of justice express an idea of "democracy in judging each other's aims," meaning that members of a just society do not—"for the purposes of justice"—assess the "relative value of one another's way of life" (388). And when he refers to his interpretation of the second principle of justice as "democratic equality," he also (as I explain on pp. 194–196) appears to be using "democratic" to describe a society of equals. Two ideas are essential in the characterization of a society as democratic (as a society of equals): first, each member is understood to be entitled to be treated with the same respect (and therefore is to have the same basic rights), regardless of social position; in contrast, an aristocratic society requires equal respect (and equal rights) within social ranks, but differential respect (and rights) across ranks.[17] Second, the basis of equality lies, in particular, in the capacity for a sense

---

16. See John Stuart Mill, "M. de Tocqueville on Democracy in America," in *John Stuart Mill on Politics and Society*, ed. Geraint L. Williams (Glasgow: Fontana/Collins, 1976), 191.

17. See *CP*, 116. Tocqueville's own description of the democratic revolution focuses as much on the emergence of greater equality of conditions—social mobility, dispersion of land, spread of education, and associated sentiments and feelings—as on a conception of equality of respect and rights. See, for example, the sweeping summary of French social and political history in *Democracy in America*, trans. and ed. Harvey C. Mansfield and Delba Winthrop (Chicago: University of Chicago Press, 2000), 3–6. For Rawls, an understanding of the lack of social fixity—an abandonment of the "belief in a fixed natural order sanctioning a hierarchical society"—is "part of the background of the theory of justice" (480).

of justice: we owe equal justice to those who have a minimally sufficient capacity to understand the requirements of mutually beneficial and fair cooperation, grasp their rationale, and follow them in their conduct. So the basis of equality does not lie in a capacity for self-regulation, or in a generic moral capacity, but specifically in the capacity to understand requirements of justice that provide the fundamental standards of public life. And a democratic society is a society of equals, whose members are regarded, in the political culture, as having that capacity.

These two uses of the term "democratic"—to describe a form of society, and a form of political regime—are not founded on mere equivocation. The link, in brief, lies in the fact that a democratic political arrangement expresses, in the design of the highest level of political authority, the idea that the members of the society are equal persons. The connections between a democratic society and democratic regime run in both directions.

Thus, once we have the institutions of political democracy, it is natural to regard the members as equal persons, with a claim to equal concern and respect when issues of justice arise, that is, natural to endorse the democratic conception of society. It is natural inasmuch as the conception of members as equal persons, entitled to equal concern and respect in matters of justice, is itself suggested by the practices associated with a democratic regime. For those practices entitle individuals—irrespective of class position or place in the distribution of natural assets—to bring their interests and their judgments of justice to bear on authoritative collective decisions. Thus Rawls describes the principle that "none should benefit from certain undeserved contingencies with deep and long-lasting effects, such as class origin and natural abilities, except in ways that help others" as a "democratic conception." And this conception is "implicit in the basic structure" of a society that satisfies the first principle and a requirement of fair equality of opportunity.[18]

At the same time, once the members of society are regarded as equal moral persons—once we reject the idea of a fixed aristocratic hierarchy of unequal worth and entitlement where "each person is believed to have his allotted station in the natural order of things" (479)—it is natural to conclude that there ought to be widespread suffrage and elected government under conditions of political contestation, with protections of the relevant

18. See "Reply to Alexander and Musgrave," in CP 246.

liberties.[19] For the extension of political (and other) liberties expresses the respect owed to persons as equals in their possession of a basic capacity for a sense of justice (and thus supports self-respect, a matter to which I return later). Thus in his account of the priority of liberty, Rawls contrasts a society in which mutual respect is secured by establishing the rights associated with equal citizenship from a caste or feudal society in which respect is associated with occupying an allotted social station. And he claims that "when the belief in a fixed natural order sanctioning a hierarchical society is abandoned . . . a tendency is set up in the direction of the two principals in serial order. The effective protection of the equal liberties becomes increasingly of first importance in support of self-respect and this affirms the precedence of the first principle" (480). So the emergence of a society that is democratic in Tocqueville's sense fosters the emergence of a political democracy with the basic liberties of citizenship secured for all adult members—fosters, at least in this sense: that it provides a forceful rationale for a democratic regime.

One way in which the idea of a democratic society plays a role in justice as fairness is connected to the original position. Rawls presents the justification for the two principles in terms of a rational choice of individuals under constraints of ignorance. But as I noted earlier, the fundamental idea is that certain considerations are not relevant in arguments about principles of justice. And the relevant-irrelevant distinction embodied in the original position draws on the idea of persons as equals that helps to define a democratic society. The constraints on arguments that are captured by the veil of ignorance are not founded on the concept of morality or the concept of justice but on the democratic conception of persons as free and equal. So the model of justification associated with justice as fairness—unanimous agreement in the original position—expresses a form of normative reflection suited to a democratic society.

Consider, too, how justice as fairness's second principle of justice—comprising fair equality of opportunity and the difference principle—represents an idea of "democratic equality" (65–73). Let's start with the requirement of fair equality, which condemns inequalities of life chances that owe to differences in social class background. To see the rationale for it, begin with the intuitive and relatively uncontroversial idea that no one

---

19. See Dahl, *On Democracy*, 10, on the "logic of equality."

should be excluded arbitrarily from attaining a socially desirable position to which special benefits attach (or arbitrarily have their chances of attaining that position reduced). How are we to interpret the notion of an arbitrary exclusion or reduction of chances? In a society with equal political rights, differences of class background are understood as arbitrary, irrelevant differences. If they are irrelevant to a person's standing in the sovereign arena of collective decision-making, how could they be relevant to opportunities elsewhere?

N.B.

In the case of the difference principle, we begin from the controversy about the legitimate extent and sources of inequality, fueled in particular by the apparent tension between equal standing as citizens with equal political and personal rights and unequal economic standing. We look for guidance in addressing that controversy. And we try to resolve (or at least reduce) the controversy by drawing out certain ideals that might be regarded as implicit in—by providing the best justification for—democratic institutions and practices and the position of equal citizen within those institutions. Those institutions include the rule of law, the ideal of equality before the law, mass democracy with universal rights of suffrage, individual rights of expression, association and assembly, public education, the separation of church and state, and the universal vulnerability to such burdens as taxation. We arrive in particular at the ideal of a society that treats members as equal moral persons, irrespective of differences of class background and natural endowment; that ideal provides a strong rationale for the equal liberties of citizens. It seems plausible then to use this democratic idea of persons—in effect, the idea that in matters subject to collective decision, differences of class background and natural endowment are not relevant—as a basis for addressing the problem of distributive justice. Whether that idea leads us precisely to the difference principle is another matter, but it seems clear that it leads to some form of egalitarian correction of market distributions, as those distributions do reflect the distribution of natural assets.

To see the force of this strategy of argument, contrast it with a more familiar way of defending social and economic norms on the basis of the idea of democracy. Thus Dahl distinguishes conditions "integral to democratic process" from conditions that are "external but necessary for democratic process."[20] Rights of political speech, for example, are integral to

20. Robert Dahl, *Democracy and Its Critics* (New Haven: Yale University Press, 1989), 167.

democracy: the failure to provide those rights directly condemns a regime as undemocratic. Limits on socioeconomic inequality are arguably essential but external. With too much economic inequality, citizens are unlikely to have the equal chances for political influence that is an aspect of democratic process. So while the distribution of income and wealth is not itself a feature of the political process, it influences the extent to which that process conforms to democratic principles. Rawls's extension of democratic ideas to guide judgment about distributive justice is different from (though of course not at all inconsistent with) this political-sociological exploration of external but essential conditions. The idea of democratic equality is to use the most compelling justification of democracy to provide guidance for our judgment about issues other than democratic process, not to work out the conditions that are needed to support a stable and fair democratic process. Thus, where the democratic theorist might say that great inequalities undermine fair democratic process, the Rawlsian says that inequalities in conflict with the difference principle are unjust "in a society that already affirms the other parts of the two principles" because the difference principle "extend[s] to the regulation of these [socioeconomic] inequalities the democratic conception already implicit in the basic structure."[21]

Deliberative Democracy

The principles of justice are intended for the use of citizens in a democracy. This third point about justice and democracy is tied to the practical role of political philosophy. Generally speaking, one of the essential roles of political philosophy is to provide practical guidance: "guidance where guidance is needed" (18).[22] Now in a democracy, final political authority lies in the hands of equal citizens. The principles of justice, then, are intended to guide the judgment of citizens—who, as a group, are the ultimate authority in a democracy—on fundamental constitutional questions and on issues of basic justice, and set out the terms of public debate on such matters. Disagreement about fair distribution, for example, is a fundamental feature of modern democratic politics, and the second principle is intended to provide guidance for the judgment of citizens on issues of fair distribution.

21. Rawls, "Reply," in *CP*, 246.
22. Rawls distinguishes four roles of political philosophy, practical guidance being the first, in *JF*, 1–5.

Lying behind this conception of the intended practical role of the principles is a deliberative conception of democratic politics. To clarify, let's distinguish four conceptions of democracy, each of which offers an account of the point and purpose of the rights of participation, association, and expression; regular elections; accountability; parties; and public debate that we associate with modern democracy. A first view, commonly called "minimalist," is that democracy is a method for peacefully taming the competitive struggle for power (between elites)—in particular, struggle for control over the state—that defines political life in any society. In a democracy, electoral competition between parties replaces factional intrigue and dynastic struggle as the way to determine who controls the power to punish and to extract resources.[23]

A second, less minimalist conception emphasizes that democracy is not simply a matter of electoral competition, but comprises broad citizen rights to associate, participate, and express (perhaps through organized groups) interests and opinions—conditions that provide a free and fair background for elections. In this "aggregative" conception of democracy, the underlying democratic idea is to ensure that the exercise of power reflects a fair summation of the interests of citizens: that it gives equal consideration to the interests of each.[24]

A third view is that the arrangements of democracy enable a people—a distinct collective agent, with shared history and sentiments—to govern itself by expressing in law and policy the shared commitments that unify it. Though this conception may suggest a plebiscitary form of democracy, it might be argued instead that open discussion is needed to explore how best to advance those shared commitments and to choose governors on the basis of their announced programs.[25]

23. See Joseph Schumpeter, *Capitalism, Socialism, and Democracy* (New York: Harper & Brothers, 1942), chap. 22; Adam Przeworski, "Minimalist Conception of Democracy: A Defense," in Ian Shapiro and Casiano Hacker-Cordon, eds., *Democracy's Value* (Cambridge: Cambridge University Press, 1999), 23–55.

24. See Dahl, *Democracy and Its Critics.* The literature on democratic transitions often vacillates between Schumpeter's minimalist view and Dahl's more demanding and less-narrowly electoralist account. For discussion, see Larry Diamond, *Developing Democracy: Toward Consolidation* (Baltimore: Johns Hopkins University Press, 1999), 7–15.

25. A view of this kind is sometimes associated with Rousseau. The general will and the laws issuing from it are understood to be rooted in prior communal attachments, perhaps shaped initially by a legislator-founder, and subsequently sustained through public rituals. For the attribution to Rousseau, and endorsement of the idea that substantive homogeneity and

The fourth view—a deliberative conception of democracy—emphasizes the importance of public debate about law and policy but is skeptical about the existence or importance of a shared culture and sentiments in framing public debate.[26] Instead this conception emphasizes the idea that citizens in a democracy are to defend fundamental laws and policies, and thus the exercise of their collective power, by reference to reasons (say, reasons of the common good), perhaps as expressed in a conception of justice; moreover, the content of the relevant reasons (say, the content of the conception of the common good) must be suited to the fact that citizens are equals.[27] The essential point is that, in this fourth conception, public political argument aimed at authorizing the exercise of collective power is an exercise of the common reason of citizens—more particularly, a form of moral argument, framed by reasons, whose content is suited to the idea of a democratic society (a society of equals). Thus a political opinion is deemed such not simply by its topic (that it is about institutions, laws and policies) but by its content; it "concerns what advances the good of the body politic as a whole and invokes some criterion for the just division of social advantages" (229).

Though Rawls says little in A *Theory of Justice* about democratic process, he seems there to endorse some variant of a deliberative conception (199–200, 313–318). In justice as fairness, the justice of laws is defined by reference to an idealized legislative process, in which representatives aim to enact just laws (173–174). Rawls does not explain precisely how this idealized legislative process, which is part of the theory of justice, is connected to an actual legislative process in a just society. But it is clear that actual

associated solidarities underlie democracy, see Carl Schmitt, *The Crisis of Parliamentary Democracy*, trans. Ellen Kennedy (Cambridge, MA: MIT Press, 1985), esp. 14–15.

26. The literature on deliberative democracy emerges in the mid-1980s, so the terminology is not found in A *Theory of Justice*. But in my own initial paper on deliberative democracy (written in 1987), I indicated that Rawls had many of the ideas of the deliberative conception, though I was skeptical about how well they fit with the background theory of justice as fairness. See "Deliberation and Democratic Legitimacy," in Alan Hamlin and Philip Petit, eds., *The Good Polity: Normative Analysis of the State* (Oxford: Basil Blackwell, 1989), 17–34. Rawls discusses the idea of deliberative democracy in "The Ideal of Public Reason Revisited," in *CP*, esp. 579–581. For an illuminating exploration of the whole terrain, see Samuel Freeman, "Deliberative Democracy: A Sympathetic Comment," *Philosophy and Public Affairs* 29, 4 (Fall 2000): 371–418.

27. On the importance of connecting the content of the reasons used in public argument with the democratic idea of persons as free and equal, see Cohen, "Democracy and Liberty"; Rawls, "Reply to Habermas," in *PL*, 430–431; Freeman, "Deliberative Democracy," 402–404.

political processes will not adopt just laws, as defined by the ideal process, unless citizens, representatives, and officials aim to enact just laws (317), and, as in the ideal process, jointly explore how best to achieve that aim (315). Thus representatives "represent their constituents in a substantive sense; they must seek first to pass just and effective legislation, since this is a citizen's first interest in government" (199–200). Citizens, in turn, judge their representatives in the first instance by reference to principles of justice, and only secondarily by how well those representatives represent other interests than the basic interest in assuring justice. It is an important part of the account of how people acquire an understanding of justice as fairness is that "principles of justice apply to the role of citizen held by all, since everyone, and not only those in public life, is meant to have political views concerning the common good" (413). In presenting justice as fairness, then, Rawls supposes that he is addressing himself to citizens who hold political opinions (ideas of justice and the common good); acknowledge that they, along with officials and parties, have the deliberative responsibility of presenting public arguments at least about fundamental laws and policies by reference to such opinions; and are uncertain about whether their actual views are the most reasonable political opinions. Recognizing their responsibility, they are looking for guidance on how best to understand justice and the common good in a society of equals (17–18).

In *A Theory of Justice*, Rawls assumes this view of democratic politics as an arena of argument, rather than a tamed competition for power, fair aggregation of interests, or expression of shared cultural commitments. And he supposes that his task is to articulate the most reasonable view of justice for citizens and officials to use in their political deliberations—a conception of justice that is for a democracy in that it is intended to guide the judgments of citizens in exercising their deliberative responsibility. While it is common for readers to think that Rawls neglects "politics" in presenting justice as fairness, I suspect that at least part of what fuels the complaint is disagreement with the plausibility of this "reason-giving" picture of politics. If you believe that reasoning from principles could play a substantial role in an attractive form of modern democratic politics, then Rawls's presentation and defense of principles is likely to strike you as engaged with the fundamentals of democratic politics. But if you embrace a more conventional minimalist or aggregative view of democracy, then it is likely to strike you as addressed to political morality rather than real politics.

Now Rawls ties this conception of political deliberation to the idea of a well-ordered society in which there is a consensus on principles of political morality, and deliberation takes place among people who share that conception. While members of a well-ordered society have diverse conceptions of the good, they share an understanding of justice, given by the two principles: In a well-ordered society, "Political argument appeals to this moral consensus" (232). But the idea of political deliberation does not depend on this demanding ideal of consensus. And in his political liberalism, Rawls embraces the deliberative conception of democratic politics while also accepting that even under the best circumstances we can reasonably hope for, members of a democratic society will disagree with one another about what justice requires.

But even when Rawls describes political deliberation without a shared conception of justice—when, in *Theory* and in *Political Liberalism*, he imagines citizens endorsing different political conceptions of justice and political parties not acting as "mere interest groups" but instead advancing "some conception of the public good" (195)—he still supposes that politics is, in the first instance, a matter of deliberation: of citizens and representatives defending laws and policies by reference to reasons drawn from a conception of justice that they might reasonably expect others to endorse. Putting the expectation of consensus to the side does not make the need for a conception of justice that is, in this third sense, for a democracy any less pressing.

This conception of politics as an arena of argument may strike some as overly idealized and as underestimating the strategic and competitive side of politics. I cannot address this issue here. Suffice to say that justice as fairness is a conception for a democratic society in part because it is offered as a practical guide for citizens who, as ultimate political authority, are assumed to rely in their political judgments on a conception of justice, to be uncertain about what the best conception is, and to take an interest in defending their views by reference to the most reasonable conception for a society of equals.

3. Democratic Government

I said earlier that Rawls's first principle of justice includes a principle of participation, which states that "all citizens are to have an equal right to take part in, and determine the outcome of constitutional processes that establish the laws with which they are to comply" (194). Ensuring this equal right almost certainly requires some form of democratic process of collective choice. So in justice as fairness, the rationale for democracy is not exclusively instrumental. The case for democracy is based, in part, directly on the content of the first principle, and not simply on a judgment made at the constitutional stage about how best to protect personal liberty or advance other requirements of justice. Why, then, are the political liberties so fundamental?

In his discussion of the priority of liberty, Rawls suggests two lines of argument that might be used to identify basic liberties and argue for their priority. The first line of argument turns on the content of certain "fundamental aims" that are commonly ingredient in determinate conceptions of the good; the second turns on our "highest order interests" associated with our moral powers as citizens (475–476).[28]

Consider first the argument from fundamental aims. Suppose we are deciding between a conception of justice that assures stringent protection for liberty of conscience and one that does not. The argument from fundamental aims defends the former on the basis of considerations about the contents of the conceptions of the good, and surrounding moral and religious convictions, that we know people commonly to endorse.

Suppose I consider a choice between a conception of justice that does not guarantee liberty of conscience and freedom of worship to all and a conception that does. If I choose one that does not, then whether or not I receive protection will depend on whether I am in the religious majority or religious minority. If I choose one that does, then I am protected either way. Now reasoning under the veil of ignorance, I have no basis for assigning a likelihood to *my* being in the group whose liberties would be protected rather than in the group whose liberties would be suppressed.

28. The passage that distinguishes these lines of argument was added in the revised edition, and was written in 1975 (xi); it anticipates points that are made more fully in "The Basic Liberties and Their Priority" (1982), which is presented as Lecture 8 of *Political Liberalism*. In the discussion that follows, I draw on "Basic Liberties," which argues more fully and explicitly than elsewhere that political liberty is among the basic liberties, and indicates, as I suggest in the text, that the strategy of argument cannot simply be a generalization of the argument for liberty of conscience. Still, I think that the two main points—that the capacity or "moral power" for a sense of justice is the basis of equality, and that treating political liberty as a basic liberty expresses an essential form of respect—are presented in sections 77 and 82 of the 1971 edition. Moreover, I think that paragraph 4 of section 82 of the 1971 edition suggests the distinction of strategies of argument that I make in the text. So, once more, I will present the argument without worrying over issues about shifts in position.

But liberty of conscience is required for me to keep the commitments assigned to me by religious or moral convictions, assuming I have such. Thus, if I have a religious outlook, then I will understand that the view assigns to me as adherent certain basic obligations such as the proper day and manner of worship. And having religious liberties will be required for the fulfillment of those obligations. To be sure I don't know if I have a religious outlook, but I might have one, or I might have a more secular moral outlook that also assigns me fundamental obligations. And that suffices to make liberty of conscience a fundamental primary good and provide a compelling reason for choosing the conception of justice that ensures its protection.

The crucial point is that I am aware that I may well hold a religious or moral view that in effect says to me: "these are your basic obligations." The idea that the obligations are fundamental does not depend on my way of endorsing the view (say the intensity or enthusiasm of my endorsement); it is part of the content of the view itself and thus among the things I believe when I believe the view. Believing a religious view, say, is a matter of believing that I have (for the reasons stated by the view) a set of supreme obligations (say, the obligations are assigned by God as supreme lawgiver). So once I believe it, treating it as basic is not optional because believing it includes believing the parts that say or imply that it is basic. And the fact that the fundamental aims are "non-negotiable" (*PL*, 311) is not a psychological thesis but is part of the content of the religious, philosophical, or moral outlook one may find oneself endorsing: "An individual recognizing religious or moral obligations regards them as binding absolutely" (182) because of the content of religious and moral convictions, not the person's attitude towards them. For this reason, "even granting (what may be questioned) that it is more probable than not that one will turn out to belong to the majority (if a majority exists), to gamble [by choosing a principle that does not ensure equal liberty of conscience] . . . would show that one did not take one's religious or moral convictions seriously" (181). And that is so even if the gamble brings some other sort of other benefit. Consider choosing a conception of justice that does not assign priority to liberty of conscience, but allows a person's religious liberties to be restricted if that person is compensated with material resources. To make that choice, one would have to accept that "all human interests are commensurable" (*PL*, 312). But the person who believes the religious or moral view rejects commensurability because the view itself denies that all goods are commensurable.

So if we choose a conception of justice that does not ensure liberty of conscience, we may find ourselves unable to keep the agreement, because it may require that we violate what we judge to be fundamental commitments and obligations. We cannot, therefore, make a good faith agreement to a conception that does not ensure liberty of conscience.

I have stated the argument from within the original position. But the crucial thesis is that liberty of conscience has special importance, which is not an argument made within the original position: that importance is simply given to the parties. For the rest, we can take the argument about rational choice under ignorance and restate it as an argument about the balance of acceptable reasons, once we acknowledge the background concern to find principles of fair cooperation suited to free and equal persons. What the argument brings out is that we can only endorse a public conception of justice that does not provide equal liberty of conscience if we are prepared to let *someone* be subject to conditions to which we would not be prepared to subject ourselves: only if we are prepared to have someone be subjected to conditions that we would reasonably regard ourselves as having compelling reasons to reject. This is an unreasonable failure to treat others as equals, and can be seen as such directly.

Rawls says that this reasoning for equal liberty of conscience can be "generalized to apply to other freedoms, though not always with the same force" (181). The other freedoms he has in mind include the political liberties. But he leaves unexplained how precisely this reasoning about fundamental aims generalizes. What are the properties that do carry over from this liberty to other cases? Nor does he explain what limits the force of the generalization.[29]

To extend the argument, we need some way to distinguish certain interests as especially important, in the way that religious and moral views present interests in fulfilling their own fundamental requirements as of special importance. But the case for including political liberties among the

---

29. The same observation can be made about the argument in Rawls's 1963 paper on "Constitutional Liberty and the Concept of Justice," in *CP*, 73–95. He begins by enumerating a variety of basic liberties, including political liberty, then focuses exclusively on liberty of the person and liberty of conscience and offers a version of the "fundamental aims" argument sketched above (see esp. *CP*, 86–88). The paper includes no discussion of how the argument for liberty of conscience, which turns on the idea that religious views impose obligations that are "binding absolutely," might be extended to other basic liberties.

basic liberties cannot turn on the Aristotelian idea that human beings have a political nature (are political animals): that they realize their true good by exercising their sense of justice and participating in making the collective decisions that are binding on them. Appeal to that idea would violate the requirement that the case for a basic liberty not appeal to a particular view of the best human life. For the same reason, it cannot turn on the Rousseauean or Kantian idea that autonomy is the supreme good and that we achieve a form of autonomy (call it "public autonomy") when we have equal political liberties.

The proposal, then, is to found the importance of the interests not on a person's basic aims, but on an idea about basic moral powers—in particular, the capacity for a sense of justice. There are three elements of this idea as it figures in the case for political liberty as a basic liberty.

First, as to the content of the idea: citizens understood themselves and one another as having two basic powers: (1) the capacity for a sense of justice, understood as the capacity to form and to act on a conception of fair terms of social cooperation and (2) the capacity for a conception of the good, understood as comprising the capacity to powers of reasoning ("deliberative reason") to form, revise, and actively pursue a system of ends and values. Here, I focus only on the first moral power.

Second, as to the basis of this conception of the moral powers: the official view of *A Theory of Justice* (see *PL*, xlv) is that this conception is part of a moral doctrine, and presents an account of what it is to be a moral agent, with the capacity to act on moral principles, to constrain the pursuit of those aims by reference to those requirements, and to achieve moral worth by having a settled disposition to act on those requirements. A second account—suggested in *A Theory of Justice* and then more fully developed subsequently—says that the basis for the conception of the person, with the two moral powers, is that it articulates the way that we, as members of a democratic society, understand one another when we are considering matters of political and social justice.

So citizens, on this view, regard one another as free and equal persons in virtue of their possession of these powers. Citizens regard one another equals in matters of social and political justice, not in that we have an equal right to have our interests (well-being) taken into account, or in being of equal intrinsic worth—much less, in having the same natural endowments or interests—but in that we have, to a sufficient degree, the capacity to understand principles of justice, to offer reasons to others in support of them, and to assess the basic institutions within which we live and that shape our aims and identity in light of those principles.

Third, as to the role of the conception of the person and the moral powers, the development of these powers is connected to the good of persons as free and equal members of a democratic society. How this is so, and what precisely the connection is, needs to be explained, and I will come back to it later. Here I want only to emphasize that the conception of ourselves as free and equal in virtue of the possession of the two moral powers shapes our understanding of our good and of what is needed to achieve it. The underlying idea, modeled in the original position, is that we are to reason about justice by reference to the good (the advantage) of individuals, conceived as free and equal members of a democratic society who possess the two moral powers, and whose status as such members is founded on their possession of those powers. The claim is not that the liberties are fundamental to advancing human interests, under all conditions (though that may be so), but that they are essential to advancing the good of citizens, understood as free and equal persons.

This important idea is not clearly stated in A *Theory of Justice*—which originally presented the interest in the liberties (and in other primary goods) in terms of what it is rational for individuals to want to pursue their ends without an idea of the person in the background. Thus Rawls said that primary goods, including personal and political liberties "are things it is rational to want whatever else one wants. Thus given human nature, wanting them is part of being rational" (223). So the idea seemed to be that, whatever our ends are, we will need the primary goods, including the liberties, in a special place of prominence. Constrained to advance those interests rationally under the veil of ignorance, we get the two principles of justice.

In the revised version of *Theory*, the presentation of primary goods generally—and of the liberties in particular—is modified. Thus the account of primary goods generally, and of the liberties in particular, is now said to "depend on a moral conception of the person that embodies a certain ideal. . . . Primary goods are now characterized as what persons need in their status as free and equal citizens, and as normal and fully cooperating members of society over a complete life" (xiii).[30]

---

30. In *JF*, Rawls offers this change in the account of primary goods to illustrate one of the main kinds of change in the presentation of justice as fairness. The revised account links the

With those three points as background, we come back now to the political liberties. The central idea is that the argument that political liberty is a basic liberty is tied to the account of the moral powers and the conditions required for their development and expression. The argument is complicated, and I want here to focus on just one piece of it, which connects self-respect with the political liberties, which are understood as favorable conditions for exercising the capacity for a sense of justice.[31]

Thus self-respect is a fundamental good because it is typically a precondition for the pursuit of our aims (386). Furthermore, because self-respect is so important to a person's good, the social basis of self-respect— essentially, respect from others—is also a crucial good.[32] But to appreciate what is required for others to show us respect (and thus required to support self-respect), it is important to understand how people regard one another, namely, as free and equal moral persons who are free and equal by virtue of their possession of the two moral powers. In particular, we regard one another as equals in that we regard one another as having, inter alia, the capacity for a sense of justice: we take "the two moral powers as the necessary and sufficient condition for being counted a full and equal member of society in questions of political justice" (PL, 302). Having the capacity for a sense of justice—the capacity to understand and act on fair terms of cooperation—is a fundamental basis of equal status. We regard one another as equals in part because we regard one another as having the capacity to assess the justice of the society: to make reasonable judgments about the rights we should have and about a fair distribution of benefits and burdens. So my self-respect is founded in part on my sense of myself as an equal member, who shares responsibility for making the fundamental judgments, with final authority, about social and political is-

---

primary goods "with the political and normative conception of citizens as free and equal persons" (xvi).

31. The argument is developed most explicitly in Rawls, "Basic Liberties," 318–319, although it is also suggested in A Theory of Justice, 155–156, 205–206, 476–478.

32. For reasons that have to do with the construction of the original position in terms of rational choice under ignorance, Rawls formulates his argument in terms of the good of a person and not in terms of the respect to which a person is entitled. But it is worth noting that the argument for the right to political liberties could be stated in terms of the respect to which persons are entitled in virtue of their possessing the capacity for a sense of justice and not in terms of the contribution of respect from others to self-respect and the contribution of self-respect to a person's own good.

sues. When others respect me as an equal, they confirm my sense of my own value. But since the possession of the moral power to form and exercise a sense of justice is the basis of equality, they show that respect by acknowledging and protecting my right to bring my sense of justice to bear on public affairs. And among the conditions required for doing so are the political liberties.

Intuitively, then, the idea is that others show respect for me by expressing their willingness to share responsibility on equal terms for making judgments of justice that provide supreme guidance for collective political life—not simply by recognizing me as an equal in some way, or attributing to me some equal rights regardless of the content of those rights, but as an equal with respect to making the final authoritative judgments about collective affairs. Rawls says: "The basis for self-respect in a just society is not . . . one's income share but the publicly affirmed distribution of fundamental rights and liberties. And this distribution being equal, everyone has a similar and secure status when they meet to conduct the common affairs of the wider society. No one is inclined to look beyond the constitutional affirmation of equality for further political ways of securing his status" (477). The reason that "no one is inclined to look"—or perhaps, does not have good reason to look—is that political equality is understood as equal standing *with respect to making authoritative collective decisions* in light of principles of justice, and ensuring equality with respect to making judgments about these fundamental matters is an especially compelling expression of respect.

Thus "taking part in political life does not make the individual master of himself, but rather gives him an equal voice along with others in settling how basic social conditions are to be arranged" (205). Moreover, because of that equal voice, "everyone has a similar and secure status when they meet to conduct the common affairs of the wider society" (477). "By publicly affirming the basic liberties citizens in a well-ordered society express their mutual respect for one another as reasonable and trustworthy, as well as their recognition of the worth all citizens attach to their way of life" (PL, 319). Note that the same importance cannot be attributed to an assurance of equality with respect to other rights. Other rights—to liberty of conscience, or personal property, or privacy—do not have the same connection with the development and exercise of the sense of justice (the basis of equality), nor is there the same showing of respect in acknowledging a right to sovereignty over one's own affairs as there is in acknowledging that right as well as a right to an equal share of sovereignty in determining the conduct of common affairs.[33]

On this account of the nature and basis of the political liberties, the political liberties are not exclusively "protective"; that is, their importance to the subject of political rights is not exhausted by their role in protecting other rights or advancing our interests: "the effect of self-government where equal political rights have their fair value is to enhance the self-esteem and the sense of political competence of the average citizen. His awareness of his own worth developed in the smaller associations of his community is confirmed in the constitution of the whole society" (205). Because of what they enable us to do—namely, bring our sense of justice to bear on the basic structure and fundamental policies—being assured a right to the political liberties affirms our equal standing as sovereign judges, and thereby promotes the fundamental good of self-respect.

Moreover, the case for the importance of the political liberties is not founded on a view about the importance of the exercise of those liberties in the best human life. Instead it is founded on the following ideas:

- A person's having self-respect plays an important role in that person's achieving his or her ends
- Being respected by others as an equal is important to achieving self-respect.
- The capacity for a sense of justice lies at the basis of our claim to be treated as an equal in matters of justice.

The right to political liberties acknowledges our possession of that moral capacity and enables us to develop and exercise it. What is essential

33. Jeremy Waldron makes a case for democratic participation by arguing that the respect that we show to individuals by extending participation rights to them—including the right to participate in debate about the resolution of conflicts of rights—is "continuous with the respect that rights as such invoke." Waldron thinks that "rights as such" express respect for a person's capacity for moral deliberation; thus, extending a right to participate expresses this respect by entitling the right-bearer to bring that moral capacity to bear on matters of common concern. The failure to extend the right is "insulting" because it treats the person's views (and thus the person himself) as of lesser importance. See *Law and Disagreement* (Oxford: Oxford University Press, 1999), chap. 11. The line of argument I have attributed to Rawls assigns a more specific moral power to individuals (capacity to cooperate on fair terms), and suggests a more intimate connection between our moral powers and the right to participate. By extending the right to participate we do not simply provide another venue for moral deliberation, but, more specifically, ensure that persons can bring their sense of justice to bear on the arena in which issues of justice are under consideration.

is not so much the good that flows to us from the exercise of the liberties as the affirmation of our equality that comes from acknowledging our right to the political liberties. Martin Luther King Jr. said that the "great glory of American democracy is the right to protest for right"—that citizens are not simply *able* to advance their *interests,* but have the *right* to bring their *sense of justice* to bear on matters of common concern.

4. Too Little Democracy

Justice as fairness, then, requires a democratic form of government in which the authorization to exercise political power comes from fair processes of collective choice.[34] This conception expresses a democratic idea of society (a society of equals), and it is meant to guide the judgment and public argument of members of a democratic polity, who are assumed to have a sense of justice and to rely on that sense of justice as the supreme standard for public conduct. Though democracy figures in Rawls's view in these three fundamental ways, it might nevertheless be argued that the idea of democracy does not figure with sufficient prominence in justice as fairness and that Rawls assigns an unacceptable priority of justice to democracy.

This concern about the relative importance of justice and democracy, while important, defies easy specification. One way to state the concern is to say that justice as fairness subordinates actual democratic politics, including the debate that surrounds it, to the results of an agreement *made by rational agents reasoning under ignorance.* But this formulation, with its emphasis on rational choice under ignorance, does not strike me as the best way to express the fundamental concern. Thus, suppose we adopt what Rawls calls "an ethical variation of the initial situation," according to which justice is determined by hypothetical agreement; however, the parties are not assumed to be rational agents aiming to secure their own good, but reasonable persons defending principles by direct appeal to political values—say, values of reciprocity, fairness, and cooperation on terms of mutual respect (512). Still, the objection might be raised that this subordinates actual democratic debate to a hypothetical agreement—although an agreement among reasonable persons, not simply rational agents. But even this reformulated objection, with its emphasis on the actual-hypothetical

---

34. I have been helped by many conversations with Joshua Flaherty about the issues here.

distinction, does not get at the heart of the concern. Thus consider the view that justice is not determined by hypothetical agreement but by balancing a set of reasons that we find intuitively forceful or by appeal to God's law. These, too, might be found objectionable even with the appeal to hypothetical agreement removed completely.

That's because the real concern about the subordination of democracy is that justice as fairness understands actual democratic politics, and the debate surrounding it, to be guided and restricted by substantive principles that we arrive at through reasoning that can be conducted independently of open public argument between and among citizens. The point is that justice as fairness assigns too large a role to an exercise of philosophical reason and too small a role to public-political argument in fixing the fundamental political norms in a democracy. Even in the ideal constitutional and legislative stages, where a just constitution and just laws are determined, principles of justice are set out in advance, and the problem of political life might be seen as the application of those prior principles, whose content is fixed prior to argument between and among citizens. Actual democratic politics—as distinct from idealized constitution- and lawmaking—is even more constrained in that political judgments are supposed to be guided by beliefs about the judgments of the ideal constitution makers and lawmakers. Thus Habermas puts the intuitive objection with considerable force and clarity when he says that citizens

> cannot reignite the radical democratic embers of the original position in the civic life of their society, for from their perspective all of the *essential* discourses of legitimation have already taken place within the theory; and they find the results of the theory already sedimented in their constitution. Because the citizens cannot conceive of the constitution as a *project*, the public use of reason does not actually have the significance of a present exercise of political autonomy but merely promotes the nonviolent *preservation of political stability*.[35]

So justice as fairness conceives of democratic political life as ideally guided by substantive principles of justice set out in advance—principles that are said to articulate the (democratic) idea of society as a scheme of

---

35. Jürgen Habermas, "Reconciliation through the Public Use of Reason: Remarks on John Rawls's Political Liberalism," *Journal of Philosophy* 92 (March 1995): 128.

fair cooperation among free and equal persons. But why is this an objection? To be sure, a democratic politics founded on (disciplined by? informed by? guided by?) principles might be less exciting than a more creative, contestative, agonistic, open-ended, edgy, ironic, transformative, everything-up-for-grabs political arena. But while no one wishes for insufferably dull politics, the importance of excitement in political life—unlike stock car racing, slam poetry contests, and bungee jumping—is controversial. In any case, we need some way to clarify precisely what the criticism is once we move away from the idea that it is fundamentally about prudential rationality regulating reasonableness, or the grays of hypothetical agreement regulating life's greens.

The idea that a substantive philosophical theory of justice decides too much in advance of real public argument and claims a kind of authority over actual debate might, then, be understood in at least three ways.

- The point might be that because the conception of justice offers "an independent standard of the desired outcome" (174)—a standard of justice that is independent from the decisions arrived at even through an idealized process of democratic collective decision-making—it threatens to *subordinate* those decisions to the judgments of a court, or some other "guardian-like" agent that operates independently from the participation and judgments of citizens. Call this the problem of *institutional subordination*: assigning priority to justice may lead to support for undemocratic arrangements as a better way to achieve justice.

- Alternatively, settling fundamental questions in advance might be interpreted not as inviting political guardianship but as *denigrating* the importance of public argument and political participation. Political life would consist not in making the basic judgments and choices about how to live our collective life—about the fundamental rules that govern us—but in implementing a conception of justice that is already fixed. Politics would not involve any real exercise of autonomy, of self-legislation, through an actual choice of basic ideals and arrangements, or a creative act of initiation (of a kind that Hannah Arendt celebrates, and that is characteristic of a new constitutional founding) but would simply determine how best to preserve existing arrangements. Thus Habermas' remark that "the public use of reason does not actually have the significance of a present exercise of political autonomy but merely promotes the nonviolent *preservation of political stability.*" Let's call this the problem of *denigration:* with justice fixed prior to and independently of democratic practice, democratic self-government and politics quite generally are left with the task of implementing first principles rather than specifying their content.

- Or it might be interpreted as claiming that a substantive, philosophical conception of justice is founded on a mistrust of citizens, who need to have their judgments confined by strictures set out in advance. But this mistrust, and the associated effort to cabin judgment, is not only ill-founded but incompatible with a basic idea of the theory: that citizens are equals and are entitled to equal political rights in virtue of having a capacity to live together on mutually acceptable terms. If they are capable of reasoning with others and cooperating on terms of mutual respect, it might be said, then why do they need to have their judgment guided by substantive principles fixed in advance?

If the first two concerns can be addressed, then the suspicion about an underlying mistrust has less force. So I focus here on the complaints about subordination and denigration, both of which express the idea that justice as fairness does not give sufficient weight to the value of political autonomy—that it fails to give self-government its due by depriving people of the authority to decide collectively on the fundamental principles that govern them. Eventually, I will want to embrace a version of the claim that justice as fairness, as presented in A *Theory of Justice,* lacks an adequate account of democracy—not, however, because it endorses a substantive conception of justice but because it lacks a plausible account of political disagreement.

Institutional Subordination

The first concern is that a substantive conception of justice, laid out in advance of democratic practice through rational argument, may lead to a preference for an alternative to democracy in which expert judgment—guided by principles of justice and a knowledge of the relevant facts—determines how best to implement the requirements of justice. If justice is truly what matters most—"the first virtue of social institutions" (3), as Rawls famously says—then perhaps we ought to hand the authority to promote justice to its most reliable institutional proponent. To be sure, the most reliable proponent may be a democratic political arrangement in which citizens and representatives, animated by a sense of justice, discern the demands of justice through public deliberation and debate the constitutional and legislative implications of those demands.[36] But surely democratic decisions may turn out to be unjust: that is the result of acknowledging a political-procedure-independent standard of substantive justice, which makes the issues of constitution and legislation both matters of imperfect procedural justice. No procedure can ensure just results.

That a democracy can make unjust decisions does not of course imply that some alternative to democracy is preferable. After all, no procedure is perfect with respect to justice; judges make mistakes—sometimes large, costly, and hard-to-undo mistakes. Consider an ideal legislative process, in which legislators aim to achieve just laws and make their legislative decisions according to principles of justice on which all agree. Even then, limits on knowledge and failures of reasoning and judgment may lead to unjust regulations (316–317). The same point applies, a fortiori, to any actual (nonideal) political process whether legislative or judicial (at least some constitutional courts operate by simple majority rule). "We are to decide between constitutional arrangements according to how likely it is that they will yield just and effective legislation. A democrat is one who believes that a democratic constitution best meets this criterion." A democrat need not take the silly position that democracy ensures justice. When unjust laws are passed, "there is no reason why a democrat may not oppose the public will by suitable forms of noncompliance, or even as a government official try to circumvent it. . . . One does not cease to be a democrat unless one thinks that some other form of government would be better and one's efforts are directed to this end" (261).

These observations are strengthened by the fact that a just constitution must, in the first instance, satisfy the requirements of the principle of equal basic liberties, including the principle of participation. Again, "all citizens are to have an equal right to take part in, and determine the outcome of constitutional processes that establish the laws with which they are to comply" (194). So a constitution with rights of participation is itself

---

36. For some suggestive remarks about why a deliberative democracy would be the ideal way to implement substantive norms of justice, see Brian Barry, *Justice as Impartiality* (Oxford: Oxford University Press, 1996), sec. 16.

a requirement of justice. Because democracy cannot permissibly be restricted to achieve greater economic justice, the only requirements of substantive justice that would provide a case for guardianship are the other requirements of the first principle; that is, the requirement of protecting the nonpolitical liberties.[37] I will come back to this later. For now, it suffices to say that the case for institutional subordination is limited by the priority of liberty.

But suppose we agree that a person is a democrat just in case he or she thinks democracy is best from the point of view of justice. Perhaps he thinks that in part because democratic government is more likely than alternatives to yield just and effective legislation. Democrats, thus understood, do not favor replacing democracy with something else. They might endorse Churchill's estimate that democracy is the worst possible form of government, except for all the others. But a democrat, in the sense now under consideration, might also think that we have an *obligation* to comply with collective decisions, even democratic ones, only when those decisions are just. Let's call such a person a *minimal democrat*. Thus minimal democrats are *democrats* because they do not favor replacing democracy with something else, but they are *minimal* because they do not think that democratic etiology provides any reason to comply with regulations judged to be substantively unjust.

But justice as fairness does not lead to such minimalism. Keep in mind that the choice of a democratic constitution reflects a judgment about how best to meet the requirements of the principle of participation as well as the other requirements of justice. Suppose we judge that a democratic constitution of a certain kind best meets those demands. That it satisfies the principle of participation will be one important part of the case for that conclusion: the case for a democratic constitution is not founded simply on the claim that it helps to promote just legislation. And suppose we recognize that majority rule is an element of a democratic constitution because decisions with support from a majority, made within a democratic constitution and assumed to be animated by a concern with justice, are more likely to advance justice. Now add that we have a natural duty to support and uphold just institutions, in particular, a natural duty "to comply with and do our share in just institutions" (293)—natural

37. Though it is permissible, as I noted earlier, to use the second principle in selecting among forms of democracy. See pp. 189–191 of this chapter.

because it binds us irrespective of any voluntary acts on our part. Because a democratic constitution is just and some form of majority rule is an essential part of a democratic constitution, we have a duty to comply with laws that issue from majority judgments within democratic arrangements, even when we judge those laws to be infected by some injustice (311). It is, after all, unreasonable to expect only just laws to issue from any political process. When it comes to reasons for compliance, then, as distinct from justice itself, democracy has a certain priority. More precisely, given the justness of a democratic constitution, and the natural duty to comply with just institutions, democratic etiology does make a difference to the case for compliance with laws, even when we judge them to be unjust.

Let's return now to the point I made earlier: that justice requires some form of democratic constitution, and that the only considerations of sufficient weight to justify restrictions on democratic process are provided by the other liberties covered by the first principle, say, religious liberties. So justice as fairness is compatible with a system of judicial review of legislation. Not, to be sure, with review that implements the second principle of justice but with review of legislation to ensure the satisfaction of the first principle, that is, the appropriate protection of basic liberties. But such review, it might be said, invites judicial guardianship over the people.[38]

This concern about democracy and judicial review raises a large set of important questions that I can only touch on here. For current purposes, four points are essential.

---

38. Concerns about judicial guardianship, and skepticism about the U.S. Supreme Court as a guarantor of rights have been persistent themes in Robert Dahl's work. See Dahl, "Decision-Making in a Democracy: The Supreme Court as a National Policy-Maker," *Journal of Public Law* 6 (1957): 279–295; *Democracy and Its Critics*, chap. 13; *On Democracy*, 121. For illuminating recent discussion, see Ronald Dworkin, *Freedom's Law: The Moral Reading of the American Constitution* (Cambridge, MA: Harvard University Press, 1996), 1–38; Robert Post, *Constitutional Domains: Democracy, Community, and Management* (Cambridge, MA: Harvard University Press, 1995); Frank Michelman, *Brennan and Democracy* (Princeton: Princeton University Press, 1999); Waldron, *Law and Disagreement*, section III; Cass Sunstein, *One Case at a Time: Judicial Minimalism on the Supreme Court* (Cambridge, MA: Harvard University Press, 1999). A full discussion would require attention to the very different practices in different legal systems that are grouped together as "judicial review." For discussion of the uncertain democratic status of the specifically "common-law" style of American judicial review, see Antonin Scalia, *A Matter of Interpretation: Federal Courts and the Law* (Princeton: Princeton University Press, 1997).

1. Though justice as fairness is compatible with judicial review, its core ideas do not require protection of basic liberties through an unelected court's review of national legislation to test its constitutionality (*PL*, 234–235).[39] Indeed, it is hard to see how any serious theory of justice—least of all a theory that assumes that citizens in a democracy have and are animated by a sense of justice—could issue without considerable additional empirical argument in an institutional conclusion of this kind.[40]

To be sure, justice requires the protection of basic personal and political liberties. But those liberties could in principle be suitably protected by a democratic process in which citizens and elected representatives endorse principles of justice and act with self-restraint within the bounds set by those principles.[41] Some citizens may think that a supreme court should have the role of protecting rights because they think that the political process is unlikely to serve as an appropriate "forum of principle," in which considerations of justice are given due attention. They might observe that the normal responsibility of the political process is not to operate as such a forum and perhaps note that politics in settled democracies continues to be organized to a large extent by competing parties with interests in winning election, not in vindicating principles. And they might urge that a court is well-suited to serve as an "exemplar of public reason" (*PL*, 235) that educates citizens and legislators about constitutional principles and thus improves the quality of public debate in part because it is not a party to conventional political bargaining and is not organized by competing political organizations.

But the issue is clearly empirical, and the fundamentals of justice as fairness do not force that conclusion. Indeed, the idea that citizens have a sense of justice and are entitled to basic political liberties as a way to bring

---

39. For explanation of the "national legislation" qualification, see Dahl, *On Democracy*, 121.

40. Unfortunately, the empirics of judicial review are poorly understood. The same can said for virtually every major institution of modern constitutional democracies. For discussion of this point, see Joshua Cohen and Archon Fung, "Introduction," in Joshua Cohen and Archon Fung, eds., *Constitutionalism, Democracy, and State Power: Promise and Performance*, 4 vols. (Brookfield, VT: Edward Elgar, 1996).

41. For discussion, see Waldron, *Law and Disagreement*, esp. part 3. Dworkin believes that if a court decides correctly to overturn legislation that impairs democratic self-government, then the fact that the decision was made by a court imposes no "moral cost"—in particular, no reduced democraticness follows. But he also thinks that judgments about which institutions are best suited to preserving a democratic arrangement are broadly empirical matters. See Dworkin, *Freedom's Law*, 32–35.

that sense of justice to bear on collective decisions suggests that normal politics could, in principle at least, work as a forum of principle. Whether or not majorities abuse their power depends in part—and perhaps ultimately (PL, 237)—on the substance and strength of their convictions in political morality and not simply on the presence of institutional constraints on their power.

Of course, if the political traditions of a country assign a supreme court with powers of judicial review a special role in protecting liberties, then citizens may become accustomed to it and assume a division of deliberative labor. Democratic politics, they may suppose, is about interest bargaining, whereas the responsibility of courts is to ensure that such bargaining stays within the bounds of a just constitutional frame. Citizens need not be indifferent to the justice of the constitutional frame; indeed it will be hard for a court to play its role if citizens are indifferent: "Liberty lies in the hands of men and women; when it dies there, no constitution, no law, no court can save it. . . . While it lies there it needs no constitution, no law, no court to save it."[42] Still, citizens might accept a division of deliberative labor and regard the protection of the constitution as typically the work of a special body—perhaps a constitutional court. And once that conception of the division of labor becomes deeply rooted in the political culture, it may be difficult to ensure the protections of basic liberties through normal political processes.[43] But once again, judgments about the best way to protect basic liberties are not a basic feature of justice as fairness with its commitment to the idea that there are substantive requirements of a just, democratic constitution beyond those of fair political process. Majoritarian and constitutional democrats may well agree on what justice requires but disagree on the kinds of institutions that best serve justice.

2. Judicial protections of rights might be justified not only by reference to nonpolitical liberties that fall under the first principle (say, liberty of conscience) but also by reference to the principle of participation itself. Just as liberty of conscience may not be suitably protected even by a fair democratic process, so, too, rights of political participation may not be so

---

42. Learned Hand, *The Spirit of Liberty* (New York: Knopf, 1952), 190.

43. For a forceful statement of the concern, see Henry Steele Commager, *Majority Rule and Minority Rights* (New York: Peter Smith, 1943), 73. I am grateful to Daniel Munro for this reference.

protected. Indeed, one of the major justifications for judicial review is that such review is, in John Hart Ely's phrase, "representation-reinforcing": it works to prevent majorities from eroding democratic process itself by depriving people of rights to participate, or to speak freely about political issues, or have their interests duly considered in collective decision-making. Indeed constitutional provisions that assign rights to individuals might, as Alexander Meikeljohn argued, best be understood as conferring powers on citizens that enable them to participate as equals in a fair democratic process—best understood, that is, as provisions that establish or constitute popular sovereignty rather than as protections of individuals from government.[44] So if judicial review is, in some circumstances, the best way to protect individual rights, it need not be seen as reflecting any hostility to democracy, or willingness to assign it an objectionably subordinate position, but might rather as founded on a commitment to it, at least insofar as the rights that are protected are connected to the ideal of democratic process.[45]

3. Justice as fairness, with the principle of participation as part of the first principle of justice, does appear to support, not implausibly, a preference, all else equal, for protecting basic liberties covered by the first principle through political rather than judicial means. Thus judicial review does impose a restriction of the scope of decisions governed by majority rule processes, and for this reason imposes a restriction on the extent of political liberty (200). If majority rule processes *can* afford adequate protection of political and personal liberties, then justice recommends this political method of protection.[46] If majority rule processes do not provide adequate protection, then justice requires restrictions on majoritarian process, though not a perfectly generalized restriction on democracy—only a restriction when it comes to the protection of basic rights from normal political process. It is hard to see how any reasonable, democratic political

---

44. Alexander Meikeljohn, "The First Amendment Is an Absolute," in *The Supreme Court Review: 1961* (Chicago: University of Chicago Press, 1961), 245–266.

45. To which it should be added that the range of liberties that are suitably connected to an ideal of democratic process is itself a disputed question. Some argue that basic personal liberties are essential to democracy, properly understood. See Dworkin, *Freedom's Law*, 25–26, and Cohen, "Democracy and Liberty."

46. This observation applies straightforwardly to the view in *A Theory of Justice*, which says that any restriction on the scope of majority rule is a restriction of political liberty and therefore requires special justification. But it also applies to the position in "Basic Liberties," which emphasizes the idea of a "fully adequate scheme of basic liberties" (secs. 8, 9).

view could find regulations that require religious uniformity unobjection-
able simply because they win the support of the majority in a fair political
contest.

4. You might suppose that the commitment to a substantive conception
of justice with nonpolitical liberties in the first principle must, in at least
some circumstances, lead to a subordination of democracy to guardian
judges. After all, suppose that the people—acting as sovereign through a
constitutional amendment process and not simply through normal majoritarian means—seek to amend the constitution and deny religious liberty to some group. It might be thought that justice as fairness holds that
it would be permissible for a court to override this judgment, whereas a
view that assigned democracy and popular authority a more fundamental
role would reject this preemption of popular authority. Justice as fairness
would almost certainly reject the amendment as unjust. But the institutional implications are much less clear. Perhaps the right thing to say is
not that the Court is authorized by the Constitution to reject the Amendment, but that when the people make such a decision the constitution has
broken down: that two of its fundamental elements—assuring popular
authority and assuring liberty of conscience—are at war, and that there is
no correct answer within the Constitution (*PL*, 239).[47]

Denigration

Consider now the second interpretation of the idea that justice as fairness
improperly subordinates democracy to a philosophical conception of justice. This second interpretation, recall, claims that justice as fairness denigrates the importance of public argument and political participation: that
it subordinates citizens to philosophers. For it says that political life consists not in making the basic judgments and choices about how to live our
collective life, and what the rules are that we will be required to comply
with, but in implementing a conception of justice whose content is fixed
in advance by philosophical reasoning. So in the ideal society of justice
as fairness, politics would not, the objection says, involve any real exercise of
political autonomy. We are politically autonomous when we give ourselves
our basic ideals and arrangements. The great moments of political autonomy

47. Rawls's discussion on this issue at PL 238–239 draws on Samuel Freeman, "Original
Meaning, Democratic Interpretation, and the Constitution," *Philosophy and Public Affairs*
21 (Winter 1992): 41f.

are the moments of real constitution-making. But in the ideal society of justice as fairness, politics would be simply a matter of determining how best to preserve existing arrangements (assumed to be just) and of applying principles determined through an exercise of reason. "The idea of right and just constitutions and basic laws is always ascertained by the most reasonable political conception of justice and not by the result of an actual political process" (PL, 233).

1. A first response is simply to observe that if this objection comes from a *democratic proceduralist*, then it is deeply misleading. According to the democratic proceduralist, justice requires fair democratic process, but imposes no further constraints on outcomes than that they issue from that process. But the requirement of fair democratic process itself imposes constraints on politics. Thus, suppose that we say that outcomes are justified if and only if they can be traced to a fair democratic process. And suppose now that the result of such a process is a series of laws that, if enacted, would unambiguously eliminate fair democratic process by depriving some group of people of its participation rights or by punishing the advocacy of dissenting political views. Suppose, in short, that democracy, as understood by the democratic proceduralist, kills democracy.

Democratic proceduralists might respond in either of two ways. First, they might object to the regulations and insist that the fundamentals of the fair democratic process be maintained. But a democratic proceduralist who responds this way acknowledges that some norms—those associated with fair democratic procedure—are fixed prior to actual democratic politics. Even the proceduralist, should he or she follow this first track, invokes a standard independent of the outcomes of democratic process that can be used to rebuke and revoke the results of that process. So the problem cannot be the bare fact of setting such conditions.

Certainly Dahl's democratic proceduralism is of this kind.[48] It is not a majoritarian theory of justice or of legitimacy, according to which justice or legitimacy is determined by the judgments of the majority, but holds instead that justice requires the equal consideration of interests, and that equal consideration demands a fair, democratic process. But if that process produces laws that are incompatible with equal consideration, then the results are unjust and fair process should be preserved.

48. See Dahl, *Democracy and Its Critics*.

The second line of response is for the democratic proceduralist to argue that the decision to undermine democracy is legitimate because of its own fair, democratic etiology. If so, it is hard to see how the democratic proceduralist can object to a substantive account of justice on grounds of its denigration of the importance of democracy or political autonomy inasmuch as the proceduralist himself is committed to preserving democracy and political autonomy themselves only if they have the de facto support of a majority.

2. Suppose the democratic proceduralist responds along the first track, and thus permits constraints on political decisions when those decisions would undermine democratic process but rejects any other substantive constraints. Then we need to ask about the basis for this distinction, the rationale for drawing such a sharp procedure-substance distinction. One rationale might be to emphasize the importance of the value of collective self-regulation: the fundamental idea that the only legitimate source of law is the collective judgments of the people, imposing laws on itself. But appeal to the value of collective self-regulation will not support the intended procedure-substance distinction for reasons suggested in the *fundamental aims* argument for basic liberties.[49]

To see why, consider the importance assigned by equal citizens to basic religious and moral requirements. Given that importance, how could there be *collective* authorization of a regulation that restricts basic religious liberty—authorization by the people as a collectivity of equal members—or collective authorization of a constitutional permission to adopt such regulation? To be sure, a majority, concerned with its group interests, might authorize such a regulation. But that observation simply forces restatement of the question: How could there be collective authorization of an arrangement that empowers a majority to adopt such a regulation? Suppose we interpret the idea of collective authorization as requiring that regulations be backed by appropriate reasons, which is a fundamental notion in a deliberative conception of democracy. And suppose we say that appropriate reasons are those that (very roughly) we can reasonably expect to be acknowledged as acceptable by those to whom the regulations apply (equal members of the political society). Then, no collective authorization

49. See my "Procedure and Substance in Deliberative Democracy," in Seyla Benhabib, ed., *Democracy and Difference: Changing Boundaries of the Political* (Princeton, NJ: Princeton University Press, 1996), 95–119, and my "Democracy and Liberty."

of such a regulation is possible, because the reasons are bound to be rejected as of insufficient weight given the importance of religious and other moral requirements within the views of those who endorse them[50] If this is right, then the idea of collective self-regulation carries substantive as well as procedural commitments.[51]

So the argument for drawing a procedure-substance distinction of a kind that only allows constraints on democratic decisions if those constraints can be seen as required to preserve fair democratic process cannot appeal to the value of collective self-regulation—to the principle that a people can be subject to laws if and only if it imposes those laws on itself. For that idea, plausibly understood, does not support democratic proceduralism, but a more substantive conception of democracy and political right.

3. The denigration objection suggests that the content of justice is "already fixed"—that it is given prior to political argument—and that politics simply implements prior principles and ensures the stability of just arrangements settled in advance. But this complaint is misleading, in at least two ways. In the first place, suppose we interpret "fixed in advance" to mean that, prior to actual politics, citizens have a clear grasp of the requirements of justice and of the rationale for those requirements. The problem with the objection, thus interpreted, is that Rawls presents us with an account of moral learning—about the acquisition of principles of justice—which says that we come to understand the requirements of justice in part by holding the position of equal citizen and by participating in political argument in a society of equals. In particular, we acquire a morality of principles—a direct commitment to principles of justice, and desire to be a just person—after first acquiring a morality of association, where the relevant association is the political society comprising equal citizens.

> The morality of association quite naturally leads up to a knowledge of the standards of justice. In a well-ordered society anyway not only do those standards define the public conception of justice, but citizens who take an interest in political affairs, and

---

50. While the burdened group may be especially keen to raise the objection that the burden is inappropriate, others have equally good reason to raise it.

51. See my "Democracy and Liberty." For Rawls's doubts about the substance/procedure distinction, see "Reply to Habermas," 421–433.

those holding legislative and judicial and other similar offices, are constantly required to apply and to interpret them. They often have to take up the point of view of others, not simply with the aim of working out what they will want and probably do, but for the purpose of striking a reasonable balance between competing claims and for adjusting the various subordinate ideals of the morality of association. To put the principles of justice into practice requires that we adopt the standpoints defined by the four-stage sequence. . . . Eventually one achieves a mastery of these principles and understands the values which they secure and the way in which they are to everyone's advantage. (414)

Thus one natural interpretation of the idea that principles of justice are given in advance and simply implemented through the political participation makes the claim simply false. Politics is understood as in part a process of learning through which the principles and the political values of equality and liberty they articulate are acquired and mastered.

But these observations and suggestions about the acquisition of principles of justice may actually serve to underscore the force of a second interpretation of the objection. Thus it might be said that, while the principles are mastered in part through political association, their content is given in advance. The content of the principles and the basic structure that satisfies them are given to us, and our role as citizens is simply to internalize the content and preserve the basic structure intact. But our political autonomy is limited by the fact that the content of the principles and corresponding basic structure are given in advance, and not actually chosen by us.

4. The objection just stated seems flawed, for two reasons. First, let us suppose—with Rawls—that the institutions of constitutional democracy are just, and let us suppose too that those institutions already exist. Still, their persistence is not guaranteed, but requires the work of the current generation. Their reproduction depends on us. Now suppose we reproduce the institutions of constitutional democracy—by complying with the requirements they set on us and supporting them in other ways—because we believe that those institutions are just. Then in at least one sense, we are fully politically autonomous: we give ourselves the institutions that govern us, not, to be sure, by creating those institutions but by sustaining them in light of our own judgments of political morality. Once more, it is worth noting that parallel with the way this issue arises for a democratic

proceduralist. Assume that fair democratic procedures already exist. Then citizens cannot choose their own institutions, but they can preserve them for good reasons. So if there is a limit on political autonomy (and I am not sure why there is), it applies with equal force for both views: the substantive view of justice and the democratic proceduralist conception. If there is a limit, it comes from circumstances and not from the content of the view of justice—not, in particular, from its being a substantive conception of justice.

Still it might be said that, while the institutions persist because we sustain them, in light of our commitment to principles of justice, and to that extent the institutions are not simply given to us, the principles themselves are given to us. Their content is fixed by a philosophical theory and more particularly by their being chosen in a hypothetical original position. But suppose now we accept for the sake of argument both that the principles would be chosen in the original position and that the original position represents a natural way to capture an idea that we already embrace of constraints on arguments for principles of justice *for a democratic society*. Then why should the availability of a good argument for the principles—a compelling case, let us assume, for the conclusion that they are the best articulation of the relevant considerations and restrictions on arguments— lead us to think that our political autonomy is compromised when we act on them? To be sure, we do not give the principles to ourselves in the sense of making the principles up, endorsing them through an act of radical, ungrounded choice, or discovering them for the first time. But the principles are founded on a view of persons as free and equal, and that view is expressed in democratic practices.

Suppose, then, that we follow the argument for the substantive principles and understand the reasons for endorsing them—in particular, that they articulate the idea of a fair system of cooperation among free and equal persons. Then why do we face any restriction on autonomy when we follow the principles? We understand the reasons for the principles, accept them in light of those reasons, and reproduce the institutions because we accept the principles. How could the possibility of presenting the argument as a matter of what people who are free and equal would choose under hypothetical conditions suggest limits on political autonomy once we see the hypothetical choice argument simply as a way to express conditions on arguments for principles addressed to persons thus understood? It is not as though actual persons are being constrained by hypothetical decisions; instead actual persons are being guided by their own reflective views about reasonable conditions on principles of justice, which are then worked up into an argument for principles through the original position. My autonomy is not restricted, as a general rule, if I act on conclusions that I understand to follow from premises I accept (my autonomy is not limited if I use Bayes's Theorem as a constraint on my degrees of belief given that I accept axioms of probability theory). Of course, the principles may not be well-supported, but that is a different order of objection. If they are well supported, then concerns about restrictions on political autonomy have uncertain force.

These observations leave vast issues about self-government unresolved. In particular, how can a person, even in a well-ordered society with consensus on substantive principles of justice, be politically autonomous when he or she believes that the laws in force (even elements of the constitution) are not justified by principles on which there is broad agreement, and which express democratic ideas of equality? But this question emerges with equal force for a proceduralist view of democracy or justice, because there will always be disagreements both about laws and about whether the actual form of democracy in place is the form best suited to ensuring self-government. Moreover, the adherent to the substantive principles can argue that an open democratic process that subjects decision makers to the "full blast of sundry opinions and interest articulations in the society" helps to give us confidence that the laws in force (including the constitution) are among those that could have been adopted in an idealized constitutional or legislative setting.[52] Once more, the absence of actual choice seems not to denigrate democratic self-government.

5. Finally, the denigration objection supposes that justice as fairness reduces political decision-making to the implementation of principles given in advance. But this complaint is misguided. To be sure, justice as fairness includes principles of justice that are meant to guide the political judgments of citizens, and in this respect it has a different ambition from democratic proceduralism. Democratic proceduralism presents an account of legitimate collective decision-making, but does not itself offer any guidance for the judgments of citizens acting within that framework. They may be guided by individual or group interests, or (presumably) by moral

52. See Michelman, *Brennan and Democracy*, esp. 57–60.

or religious views, but nothing in democratic proceduralism corresponds to the conception of democratic equality in justice as fairness.

But the availability of substantive principles of justice does not eliminate political disagreement or the need for political debate and judgment, even if we assume that all citizens embrace the same substantive principles. For example, in applying the difference principle, citizens must already have decided how much to save, and the just savings principle does not dictate a particular savings rate. So disagreements about the extent of obligations to future generations are bound to emerge and inform debates about the requirements of intragenerational justice as given by the difference principle. Moreover, many political issues do not raise questions of justice as understood within justice as fairness (for example, lots of issues about environmental protection do not). And when issues of justice are not in view, there are no prior principles to implement, and we have a politics of interests and values.

Furthermore, the application of the principles of justice themselves calls for judgment, for example, about the kind of constitution that best ensures the protection of political and personal liberties, about whether a proposed law infringes too deeply on a fundamental liberty, or about when efforts to ensure fair equality of opportunity have gone to far. Consider current debate in the United States about campaign finance. Translated into the terms of justice as fairness, the disagreement is about whether and how to restrict a liberty protected by the first principle—the right to political speech—to ensure the fair value for political liberty which is also required by the first principle. Adherents of justice as fairness may disagree about the proper balance,[53] as they disagree about every major substantive political question that has been debated over the past generation in the United States, including abortion, affirmative action, tax reform, campaign finance, health care, educational choice and finance, market regulation, and welfare reform. Justice as fairness does not foreclose argument on these issues but proposes terms on which they are to be debated.[54]

---

53. Though they are almost certain to reject the idea presented in *Buckley v. Valeo* that it is impermissible to restrict the quantity of speech to ensure fair political equality. For discussion, see Rawls, "Basic Liberties," 356–363; Joshua Cohen, "Money, Politics, Political Equality," in Alex Byrne, Robert Stalnaker, and Ralph Wedgwood, eds., *Facts and Values* (Cambridge, MA: MIT Press, 2001), 47–80.

54. Amy Gutmann and Dennis Thompson make the essential point that even agreement on Rawls-like principles of justice leaves considerable room for political disagreement and

In this respect, justice as fairness is like every other plausible theory of justice: Millians argue about whether the harm principle permits regulations of pornography and hate speech, and libertarian democrats argue about which kinds of education are, to a sufficiently high degree, public goods to warrant tax support.[55] The availability of principles to guide judgment does not eliminate the need for judgment, and therefore does not eliminate the disagreements that result when there are (as there often are) conscientious differences of political judgment among people who embrace the same fundamental principles. Nor does reasonable disagreement among sincere adherents show any failure of principles, or reveal their vacuousness. Instead it shows how political principles always operate: they provide a shared, public terrain of reasoning, that enables mutually respecting parties to explore their disagreements. Neither apparent nor actual indeterminacies imply nihilism.

But . . .

Still, the well-ordered society of justice as fairness is missing something that we associate with democratic politics.[56] And this absence owes, I believe, to the assumption that in the well-ordered society of justice as fairness everyone endorses the same conception of justice. "The original position is so characterized that unanimity is possible. . . . Moreover, the same will hold for the considered judgments of citizens of a well-ordered society effectively regulated by the principles of justice. Everyone has a similar sense of justice and in this respect a well-ordered society is homogeneous. Political argument appeals to this moral consensus" (232). As Rousseau might say, the political society Rawls contemplates in A *Theory of Justice* has a determinate general will, whose content is given by the principles of justice. Even in *Political Liberalism*, where pluralism about

---

that a substantive account of justice will inevitably (and properly) leave much work for a deliberative democratic process that brings the principles to bear on laws and policy. Moreover, as the campaign finance case illustrates, participants in that process will disagree on more than matters of nonevaluative fact. See *Democracy and Disagreement* (Cambridge, MA: Harvard University Press, 1996), 34–37. Gutmann and Thompson misstate Rawls's own response, but they are right that Rawls says little about political argument in the ideal society of justice as fairness.

55. For the basics, see Friedrich Hayek, *The Constitution of Liberty* (Chicago: University of Chicago Press, 1960), 376–394; Milton Friedman, *Capitalism and Freedom* (Chicago: University of Chicago Press, 1982), 85–98.

56. Rawls acknowledges this concern with particular force in the introduction to the paperback edition of *Political Liberalism*, xxxviii, xlviii–l.

moral, religious, and philosophical doctrines is taken to be a fundamental feature of a democratic society, Rawls seemed to be holding out the prospect of a consensus on a (political) conception of justice among adherents of different comprehensive outlooks (*PL*, 35). I say "seemed" because the Introduction to the final edition emphasizes that democracies include a plurality of reasonable liberal political conceptions of justice, as well as a plurality of comprehensive doctrines and that social unity and stability cannot be achieved, as a practical matter, through agreement on any specific conception of justice.[57]

Because a well-ordered society is homogeneous in its understanding of justice, democratic politics excludes argument over fundamentals—excludes not by banning such argument (nothing absurd is being said), but by idealizing it away. Thus, suppose we say, with Rawls, that "it is a political convention of a democratic society to appeal to the common interest" (280). The difference principle gives one specification of the content of this convention, one particular account of when inequalities work to the common advantage: "Since it is impossible to maximize with respect to more than one point of view, it is natural, given the ethos of a democratic society, to single out that of the least advantaged and to further their long-term prospects" (280–281). Let's suppose that this account is right. Still, citizens, representatives, and parties can, consistent with endorsing the fundamentals of a democratic constitution, embrace alternative views about how best to understand that convention. If we endorse justice as fairness, we are bound to think that their reasoning is flawed. Nevertheless, other views—for example, "mixed" conceptions of justice that set an acceptable minimum, but do not require maximizing the minimum—are not simply unreasonable (309–310). We can expect such alternatives to flourish in a democratic society and to "compete with one another" (*PL*, xlviii). Thus Rawls says that the competing political parties in a constitutional democracy "must advance some conception of the public good" (195). But in a well-functioning democracy, we expect different parties to advance different conceptions, and not simply different policies animated by a single outlook. We want to see justice enacted, and hope that all the major parties are committed to upholding a just constitution. Still, organized debate between competing parties on competing ideas of justice both expresses disagreements among citizens and en-

57. See *Political Liberalism*, xlviii–l.

ables them to fulfill their deliberative responsibilities by presenting reasonable alternatives.[58] Such debate seems to be part of a well-functioning democracy and not a sign of democratic failing.

If we ask what the roots of the problem are in the assumption of unanimity on a conception of justice in a well-ordered society, it is instructive to note what Rawls says in defense of this assumption. Thus, immediately after the passage in which he says that "political argument appeals to this moral consensus," he wonders whether this "assumption of unanimity" is founded on a specifically idealist political philosophy. Rejecting that claim, he notes that the utilitarian philosophies of Hume and Smith, and not simply the idealist views of Kant and Hegel, include the suggestion that "there exists some appropriate perspective from which unanimity on moral questions may be hoped for, at least among rational persons with relevantly similar and sufficient information" (233). And he goes on to say that "the idea of unanimity among rational persons is implicit *throughout the tradition of moral philosophy*" (emphasis added). The ideal of political unanimity on a conception of justice is appropriate, then, because moral thought typically brings with it an expectation of unanimity, at least under idealized conditions of reflection.

But politics and morality are different: moral thought is concerned in part with what *I* should do in a world in which other people do not see eye to eye with me, but democratic politics is concerned with what *we* should do when we do not see eye to eye with one another. As Rawls has argued in *Political Liberalism,* we cannot reasonably demand or even expect a single moral philosophy or doctrine to be embraced by citizens in a democratic society even if we think that some specific view would be endorsed by all under idealized conditions. So it is a mistake to defend the plausibility of an assumption of political unanimity by pointing to the role of expectations of unanimity within moral thought. And once we give up on the expectation of moral unanimity in a democracy, we should also give up on the expectation of political unanimity. It is unreasonable to expect all members to accept the same conception of justice and arguably a virtue of democratic politics that they disagree.

58. For discussion, see Committee on Political Parties of the American Political Science Association, "Toward a More Responsible Two-Party System," *American Political Science Review* 44 (September 1950), Supplement: 1–96; Charles Beitz, *Political Equality* (Princeton: Princeton University Press, 1989), 114–116, 180–185.

Justice as fairness may be the most reasonable conception of justice for a democratic society. But we cannot expect the most reasonable democratic society to be founded on an agreement about justice. So how might the most reasonable conception of justice be achieved in the most reasonable form of democracy? That question remains open.

6

KNOWLEDGE, MORALITY, AND HOPE:
THE SOCIAL THOUGHT OF NOAM CHOMSKY

WITH JOEL ROGERS

In his first published essay on politics, Noam Chomsky announced his conviction that "it is the responsibility of intellectuals to speak the truth and to expose lies."[1] Acting on that conviction, Chomsky has long supplemented his work in linguistics with writing on contemporary political affairs, focusing principally on the politics of the Middle East, the moral acceptability of U.S. foreign policy, and the role of American mass media and intellectuals in disguising and rationalizing that policy.[2] By contrast with his work in linguistics, which is principally theoretical, Chomsky's political writings in the main address more straightforwardly factual questions. As he emphasizes, these can be settled without special methods or training, and their significance can be appreciated through the application of common-sense norms and beliefs (for example, that aggression is wrong, concentrated power is dangerous, and citizens have greater responsibility for the policies of their own country than for those of other states), as aided by "a bit of open-mindedness, normal intelligence, and healthy skepticism."[3]

The characteristic focus, intensity, and hopefulness of Chomsky's political writings, however, reflect a set of more fundamental views about human nature, justice, and social order that are not simple matters of fact. This essay explores these more fundamental ideas, the central elements

We would like to thank Robin Blackburn, Robert Brenner, Edward Herman, Paul Horwich, and Carlos Otero for their comments on an earlier draft of this essay.

1. "The Responsibility of Intellectuals" (1967), in Noam Chomsky, *American Power and the New Mandarins: Historical and Political Essays* (New York: Vintage, 1969), 325. References to Chomsky's work that appear in the footnotes are intended only to support the claims we make about his views, not to provide an exhaustive inventory of relevant passages.

2. Chomsky also, of course, has long engaged in more direct forms of political activism, including civil disobedience.

3. *Language and Responsibility* (New York: Pantheon, 1977), 3.

in Chomsky's social thought. We begin (in section 1) by sketching the relevant features of Chomsky's conception of human nature. We then examine his libertarian social ideals (section 2), and views on social stability and social evolution (section 3), both of which are animated by this conception of our nature.

To anticipate what follows, we take Chomsky's social views to be marked by four key claims: (1) human beings have a "moral nature" and a fundamental interest in autonomy; (2) these basic features of our nature support a libertarian socialist social ideal; (3) the interest in autonomy and the moral nature of human beings help to explain certain important features of actual social systems, including for example the use of deception and force to sustain unjust conditions, as well as their historical evolution; and (4) these same features of human nature provide reasons for hope that the terms of social order will improve from a moral point of view. Thus stated, these four claims are clearly neither concrete nor precise. But neither are they vacuous. They provide what we take to be a distinctive, optimistic perspective on human beings and human possibilities. The exposition that follows aims principally at a sympathetic clarification of this perspective. Although our discussion is often critical, the criticisms themselves are intended to clarify Chomsky's views and to underscore deeper points of agreement with them.

Before turning to that discussion, however, a cautionary remark about the character and self-conception of Chomsky's work in this area is in order. Most important, Chomsky does not have a theory of society or justice, in the sense of a clearly elaborated and defended set of fundamental principles. In fact, he believes that significant progress in ethical and social inquiry requires a systematic theory of human nature, something that does not now (and may never) exist,[4] and that in the absence of such a theory, social and ethical thought must rely on relatively speculative and imprecise ideas ("guesses, hopes, expectations"[5]). Moreover, Chomsky denies any originality for his social and ethical views, identifying himself as a merely "derivative fellow traveller"[6] in the anarchist and libertarian socialist traditions.

4. Chomsky's own work in linguistics may be understood as a contribution to the development of such a theory, but he would be the first to assert its distance from a complete and systematic account.

5. *Language and Politics*, ed. Carlos P. Otero (Montreal: Black Rose, 1988), 756.

6. "The Relevance of Anarcho-Syndicalism," in *Radical Priorities*, ed. Carlos P. Otero (Montreal: Black Rose, 1981), 247.

Finally, and no doubt in part owing to his conviction that his social and ethical views are neither systematically developed nor original, Chomsky presents those views in an occasional and sketchy fashion. Almost always announced as speculative, and often advanced only in response to promptings from interviewers, their presentation commonly takes the form of quotation from and endorsement of certain views of other thinkers (for example, Rousseau, Kant, Humboldt, and Marx).[7] Apart from creating natural difficulties for any attempt at systematic summary, the character of Chomsky's presentation underscores the need for caution in reading more into, or expecting more of, his work in this area than he invites. We hope that we have heeded our own warning in what follows.

1. What Can We Know? Rationalism Romanticized

As already noted, Chomsky believes that a substantive conception of human nature must play a central role in both the ethical assessment of social arrangements and in the explanation of their operation. By a "conception of human nature" he means an account of the biological endowment of the human species, and in particular the aspects of that endowment that figure in the development of human cognitive systems—aspects that are common to all human beings (excepting those suffering from pathologies) and perhaps unique to the human species. At its core, Chomsky's own conception of human nature draws together a romantic emphasis on the distinctive human capacity for creative expression and a rationalist contention that there is an intrinsic and determinate structure to the human mind.[8] In his work, these romantic and rationalist strands are joined through the contention that the intrinsic structure of mind provides a framework of principles that underwrites the possibility of the relevant forms of creative activity, while at the same time limiting the attainable forms of human expression.[9]

---

7. See, for example, "Language and Freedom" (1970) and "Notes on Anarchism" (1973), in *For Reasons of State* (New York: New Press, 1973); and "The Relevance of Anarcho-Syndicalism."

8. On the background in rationalism and romanticism, see *Cartesian Linguistics* (New York: Harper & Row, 1966); "Language and Freedom," 402–403; *Language and Mind* (New York: Harcourt Brace, 1972), 76–77.

9. In the case of language, Chomsky's idea was to secure the connection between creativity and rules—to show what enables us, as Humboldt put it, to "make infinite use of finite means"—by incorporating recursive rules into a representation of the grammatical knowledge of ordinary speakers. For discussion of the role of recursive rules in solving Humboldt's problem, see *Aspects of the Theory of Syntax* (Cambridge, MA: MIT Press, 1965), 8; *Language and*

This conception of human nature is most fully developed in Chomsky's linguistic theory, which emphasizes both the creativity exhibited by normal human language use and the modularity of the human language faculty.[10] According to Chomsky, the "fundamental fact about the normal use of language"[11] is its "creative aspect." Human beings have the capacity for a potentially unbounded novelty in the production of utterances that are appropriate to their circumstances but that are not controlled by immediate stimuli (though they are commonly prompted by such stimuli). The linguistic knowledge expressed in such creativity is acquired by virtually all human beings in a relatively short period of time and in the face of unstructured and impoverished inputs from the environment. Given this "poverty of the stimulus," Chomsky argues that language acquisition can plausibly be explained only on the assumption that human nature includes a language "module"—an innate system of language-specific principles, or "universal grammar."

Chomsky's more general remarks about human nature are fueled by the speculation that these ideas about creativity and modularity in the domain of language might have more general application, and that the theory of language might suggest a paradigm for a more general account of

---

Politics, 146, and the striking remark: "I think that the ideal situation would have been to have someone in 1940 who was steeped in rationalist and romantic literary and aesthetic theory and also happened to know modern mathematics."

10. The discussion that follows draws on various remarks that Chomsky makes about the connections between his views about language, human nature and politics. For a representative sample, see *Cartesian Linguistics*, 24–26, 91–93; "Language and Freedom"; "Equality: Language Development, Human Intelligence, and Social Organization," in *The Chomsky Reader*, ed. James Peck (New York: Pantheon, 1987), 195–199; *Language and Problems of Knowledge: The Managua Lectures* (Cambridge, MA: MIT Press, 1988), chap. 5; *Language and Politics*, 143–148, 240–246, 318, 385–387, 402–403, 468–469, 566–567, 593–594, 696–697, 755–756. In these passages Chomsky does not separate, as we do, issues of modularity and creativity in considering the relevance of the understanding of human language for a more general theory of human nature. But the passages listed above suggest the relevance of both, and they are, so far as we understand, independent. Thus the existence of a visual module employing a rigidity principle in the interpretation of visual experience does not imply anything about the creative use of visual perception (whatever that might mean). And the absence of a module in a particular domain is consistent, at least in principle, with creativity since the latter might reflect general features of human reason (as Descartes seems to have thought). Finally, the relevance (such as it is) of the study of human language to a more general theory of human nature is not affected, so far as we understand, by the shift from a conception of language in terms of rule systems to Chomsky's more recent "principle-and-parameters" view. For discussion of the shift in the account of language, see *Knowledge of Language: Its Nature, Origin, and Use* (New York: Praeger, 1986); *Language and Problems of Knowledge*.

11. *Aspects of the Theory of Syntax*, 57.

our nature. Thus he notes that "at some very deep and abstract level some sort of common-core conception of human nature and the human drive for freedom and the right to be free of external coercion and control" of the kind that figures "in a relatively clear and precise way in my work on language and thought" also "animates my social and political concerns."[12]

To understand how the ideas featured in the linguistic theory might be extended to provide a broader account of human nature, consider first the modularity hypothesis. In areas other than language—for instance, vision, scientific reasoning, aesthetic and moral judgment—human beings might be thought to attain complex and determinate cognitive systems in the face of relatively impoverished data, thus suggesting the presence of modules governing cognitive development in these other domains as well. For example, human beings appear to have a moral nature. That is, there appears to be a natural human tendency to interpret human interaction in moral terms—to display a concern about the justifiability of actions in light of their effects on the well-being of others. That concern is manifest in, among other things, complex systems of moral judgment that are deployed in response both to actual problems and to the hypothetical cases of moral philosophy; furthermore, these systems appear to go well beyond anything that might plausibly be found in the "impoverished and indeterminate" data available to a child who receives moral instruction.[13] The hypothesis of moral modularity would explain the acquisition of a system of moral understanding in part in terms of a set of intrinsic features of mind that are specific to morality. A characterization of the moral module would of course need to be consistent with the variety of moral systems, but it would also impose limits on possible human moralities. Thus features of it might help to explain certain formal properties that are allegedly displayed in systems of moral understanding (for example, why moral conceptions are either deontological or teleological, or why moral norms feature elements of symmetry, generality, and impartiality) and/or certain substantive features that seem to be common in moral systems (for example, prohibitions against killing innocents, wantonly imposing pain, or enslaving members of the community).[14]

12. *Language and Politics,* 696–697.
13. *Language and Problems of Knowledge,* 153.
14. Orlando Patterson emphasizes that slaves are characteristically represented as outsiders to the community that enslaves them, as "natally alienated." See his *Slavery and Social Death* (Cambridge, MA: Harvard University Press, 1982), chap. 2.

Consider next a natural generalization of the creative aspect of language use. Here the thought would be that, by underwriting the acquisition of a variety of complex cognitive systems, our nature enables us to engage in creative activities that deploy those systems. Thus creativity would be a feature not just of language use but of moral judgment, common-sense understanding, and the use of that understanding in productive work, artistic activity, and scientific achievement. Of course, a human potential for creativity might be joined with a desire for habit and repetition and a hatred or dread of novelty. But Chomsky's contention is that, associated with the intrinsic possibilities for human creativity and underscoring their relevance for ethics and social explanation, there exists an innate propensity to pursue the forms of creative expression for which our nature suits us. Borrowing a phrase from Bakunin, Chomsky sometimes refers to this as an "instinct for freedom."[15] Elsewhere he suggests that we have not merely an instinct toward but also a need for such free activity, and that the failure to accommodate that need results in individual and social pathologies.[16]

Taking the remarks about instinct and need together, Chomsky appears to endorse the view, associated with Aristotle, that human beings enjoy the exercise of their natural powers, with enjoyment perhaps scaled in part to the complexity of the activity in which those powers are engaged, and that we enjoy as well the exercise by others of their powers, at least when we have the opportunity to engage in like activities ourselves.[17]

Certain features of this view strike us as significant and plausible. Much historical sociology testifies to the claim that there is a fundamental human interest in free activity (alongside other interests in some level of material comfort and in being treated with respect by others) and that human beings have a moral nature in the sense just described.[18] It is, for example,

15. *Language and Problems of Knowledge*, 155.

16. For example, "Language and Freedom," 405.

17. On enjoying the activities of others, see "Equality: Language Development, Human Intelligence, and Social Organization," 198–199. For discussions of the "Aristotelian principle" and its connection with the value of community, see John Rawls, *A Theory of Justice* (Cambridge, MA: Harvard University Press, 1971), 424–433, 523–525 (the background in Humboldt is noted on 525n4).

18. For discussion of these features and their relevance to historical sociology, see Barrington Moore, *Injustice: The Social Bases of Obedience and Revolt* (White Plains, NY: M. E. Sharpe, 1978); Roberto Unger, *Politics: A Work in Constructive Social Theory, Part I: False Necessity* (Cambridge: Cambridge University Press, 1987); Joshua Cohen, "The Arc of the

not implausible to explain the destruction of slavery, the development of religious pluralism, and the evolution of democratic ideals and their (admittedly highly imperfect) expression in social and political arrangements, in part, by recourse to these basic features of human beings. It is less clear, however, that these matters are illuminated by considerations of modularity and creativity drawn from the theory of language. It may be the case, for example, that human beings have a moral nature but lack a specifically moral module. What underlies our acquisition of moral systems might instead be, as Kant supposed, intrinsic features of human reason as such. On this account, the construction of moral systems would not involve the deployment of principles specific to a moral faculty, but rather the application of a "pure reason" to matters of human action.[19] This might be sufficient to account for moral competence—for the complexity and determinateness of human moralities, and the capacity to respond to novel cases in ways that transcend specific instruction—even if the parallel contention about the acquisition of linguistic knowledge is not at all plausible. We do not wish to defend this alternative perspective, but only to stress that the important contention that human beings have a moral nature does not depend for its plausibility on the assumption of a moral module.

Similarly, reflection on the creative aspect of language use does not seem to help in understanding human aspirations to self-directed activity—the fact that "people really want to control their own affairs . . . [and] don't want to be pushed around, ordered, oppressed, etc."[20] What is central to linguistic creativity is the capacity for unbounded novelty. But what matters to people in their aspirations to self-direction—to form conceptions of a decent life and to act on those conceptions—appears not to depend on the prospect of novelty of expression. For example, even if one were persuaded that one's artistic, craft or intellectual activities would issue in nothing novel, one's interest in pursuing that activity free of external control, without being "pushed around," would be likely to remain undiminished.

In sum, we agree with Chomsky's claims about our moral nature and "instinct for freedom," but we are less persuaded by the suggestions about

---

Moral Universe," *Philosophy and Public Affairs* 26, 2 (Spring 1997): 91–134 (reprinted as Chapter 1 in this volume).

19. Immanuel Kant, *Critique of Practical Reason*, in Immanuel Kant, *Practical Philosophy*, trans. and ed. Mary J. Gregor (Cambridge: Cambridge University Press, 1996), Book 1, Part One.

20. *Language and Politics*, 756.

how these features of human nature might be understood on the model of the theory of language. Reflecting this conclusion, our references in what follows to Chomsky's "conception of human nature" will be confined to the fundamental points of agreement.

2. What Ought We to Do?

Chomsky's normative views, and in particular his account of a good society, are set against the background of his conception of human nature and the conception of an instinct for freedom that lies at its heart. In outline, Chomsky takes freedom to be the supreme human good, and he endorses the libertarian principle that the evaluation of social arrangements should proceed by considering whether those arrangements impose tighter limits on human activity than are necessary, given existing material and cultural constraints.[21] This, of course, is not an especially determinate view. Embracing the supreme value of freedom, and endorsing the principle that unnecessary constraints on it should be eliminated, does not settle issues about the appropriate treatment of time trade-offs (for example, the relative importance of freedom for present and future generations) or distributional issues (in particular, whether it is legitimate to trade the freedom of some for the freedom of others). Still, the conception is not empty. According to Chomsky, indeed, it supports a particular ideal for human beings operating under the material and cultural constraints of modern industrial societies—namely, socialist anarchism. The best known of his ethical-political views, Chomsky's anarchism is worth exploring at length.

It may be useful here to distinguish two conceptions of anarchism, each of which figures in Chomsky's work. In the first, anarchism is represented not as a substantive "doctrine" but as a "historical tendency," a "permanent strand of human history."[22] Reflecting the human aspiration to freedom, this tendency underlies the emphasis on freedom as the supreme value in assessing social forms and encourages skepticism about familiar contentions of the "necessity" of social arrangements constraining freedom. To endorse anarchism in this sense is straightforward enough; it

21. See "Notes on Anarchism," 404; "Equality: Language Development, Human Intelligence, and Social Organization," 195; *Language and Politics*, 147.
22. "Interview" (with James Peck), in *The Chomsky Reader*, 29; also "Notes on Anarchism," 371.

amounts to endorsing a critical standpoint in social thought and action, rooted in a concern to eliminate unnecessary constraints on human freedom.

The second sense in which Chomsky (more tentatively) invokes anarchism is less straightforward. Here anarchism does appear as a substantive, libertarian socialist, ideal of social order. Chomsky's anarchism is socialist in that it endorses the social ownership of the means of production, a form of ownership permitting the extension of democratic procedures to economic decisions both in individual workplaces and across the economy as a whole. What that means in detail is not explored at any length in his writings, but the essential principle is clear enough. The content of the more specifically anarchist aspect of his views, however, is less clear.

The basic idea of anarchism is that social cooperation can and should proceed without a state. But the content of that idea depends on the underlying conception of the state and its offending aspects—what is to be eliminated—and this has no single interpretation within the anarchist tradition. To locate Chomsky's views, it may help to begin by distinguishing three aspects of states that an anarchist might seek to eliminate—that states exercise coercive power at all, that they claim a legitimate monopoly on the exercise of coercive power, and that they specialize in the exercise of coercive power.[23] Corresponding to these three aspects of states are three distinct visions of social order, each of which has a claim to capture the basic anarchist ideal of state-free cooperation.

Conceptions of the State and Social Order

The first conception is a coercion-free system. In such an order there is no state, in that socially organized coercion does not exist at all and is in fact unnecessary, since the members willingly comply with rules and standards that are publicly announced.[24] Chomsky's endorsement of anarchism seems not to depend on the thesis that a coercion-free system is possible. For example, he often cites the 1936 Spanish anarchist experiments as exemplary of anarchist practice, but they were hardly free of co-

23. Our discussion of Chomsky's anarchism has been greatly aided by Michael Taylor, *Community, Anarchy, and Liberty* (Cambridge: Cambridge University Press, 1982).
24. Alexander Berkman, for example, asserts that "Anarchism teaches that we can live in a society where there is no compulsion of any kind." See *What Is Communist Anarchism?* (New York: Dover, 1972), 182.

ercion.[25] Furthermore, although he assumes that an anarchist order will reflect and further a "spiritual transformation" of human beings, registered in much greater self-confidence and voluntary cooperation among them,[26] he seems to agree that it would be unreasonable to expect complete civic consciousness and a fully harmonious coordination of interests in a social order that operates on the scale of a modern society.[27] Thus he notes the likelihood that (in part because of popular empowerment) "factions, conflicts, differences of interest and ideas and opinion" will be expressed throughout a libertarian socialist society.[28] Especially given his recognition of such a high degree of disagreement and conflict, it seems safe to assume that Chomsky recognizes as well the need for the continued existence of some agencies with powers of enforcement—if only to assure those who were willing to comply that others would not take advantage of their compliance.

A second possibility, then, is a dispersed-coercion system. Recognizing the need for powers of enforcement, but concerned about the dangers of a concentration of power,[29] the anarchist might identify the ideal of statelessness with a condition in which no single institution successfully claims a legitimate monopoly on the use of force. Instead, enforcement powers would be dispersed across a set of institutions, each of which would nevertheless be specifically political—that is, defined chiefly by its administrative and enforcement powers. One example of a dispersed-coercion system might be an order governed by a variety of administrative agencies, each with its own enforcement capability. Another would be a territory featuring a variety of specifically protective associations, each providing security for certain people in the territory, but none with a monopoly on

---

25. "Objectivity and Liberal Scholarship," in *American Power and the New Mandarins*, 72–124.

26. "The Relevance of Anarcho-Syndicalism," 260.

27. Drawing on a range of anthropological and historical studies, Michael Taylor argues that virtually all anarchist communities have relied on some scheme of social controls (threats and offers of sanction) to ensure compliance and not simply on socialization and education. See Taylor, *Community, Anarchy, and Liberty*, 39, 76ff.

28. "The Relevance of Anarcho-Syndicalism," 250.

29. Chomsky commonly emphasizes a general concern about concentrated power, suggesting that the nineteenth-century libertarians focused on concentrations of power in the State and Church, while twentieth-century libertarians (especially socialist anarchists) have extended such concerns to the concentration of economic power. See, for example, ibid., 248; *Language and Politics*, 301, 744.

powers of enforcement.[30] But this view also fails to capture the core of Chomsky's anarchism. To see why, let us contrast it with a third interpretation of the ideal of state-free cooperation.

This third possibility is a system with dispersed coercive powers but in which those powers, and all other traditionally political powers of collective decision-making and administration, are dispersed over institutions that do not specialize in the performance of political functions. Rather, on this conception, which we take to be Chomsky's own, political powers are exercised by institutions that also, and perhaps chiefly, perform other (for example, productive, associative) functions. Here, the "statelessness" of society is achieved neither by the abolition of coercion (the coercion-free system), nor by the multiplication of its authoritative dispensers (the dispersed-coercion system), but by the transcendence of the traditional division of labor in governance between specialized political institutions that rule and the rest of a society subject to their rule.

Several elements of Chomsky's view underscore the importance of the elimination of specialized political institutions, the distinguishing feature of this third interpretation of anarchism. Thus he supports political representation, but imagines representation to be based on such "organic groups" as workplace or community associations, and to feature a "rather minimal" delegation of powers.[31] He sees the need for administration, but thinks that it ought to be a rotating "part-time job" performed only "by people who at all times continue to be participants in their own direct activity" (that is, who act in other capacities as well).[32] And although he does not think that political parties could legitimately be banned in an anarchist order, he does think that if parties, or any other specialized organizations with an exclusive devotion to political affairs, were "felt to be necessary," then "the anarchist organization of society will have failed."[33]

Within this conception, for example, workers' councils and their representatives might have responsibility for economic planning and for the elaboration and enforcement of rules governing workplace relations (such as rules on occupational safety and health). Tasks traditionally assigned to

---

30. See, for example, the discussion of the possibilities of providing protection within a state of nature in Robert Nozick, *Anarchy, State, and Utopia* (New York: Basic Books, 1974), 12–17.
31. "The Relevance of Anarcho-Syndicalism," 249.
32. Ibid., 251.
33. Ibid., 250.

local governments (the maintenance of local order, sanitation, primary education, and the like) would devolve to neighborhood associations composed of citizens active in other affairs; regional and national tasks of government would be handled through recallable representatives of such groups; national defense would be assured through citizen militias; and so on. What is essential is that all traditional functions of government would be discharged by groups whose members also engaged in non-governing activities.

How plausible is this conception? Anarchist views are typically criticized for resting on implausible accounts of human motivation, for being inattentive to the ways that decentralization can exacerbate political and material inequalities, and for ignoring the attractions and requirements of economic efficiency. Chomsky's conception avoids at least the most obvious versions of these objections. As noted earlier, for example, he appears to reject accounts of human motivation that would deny the persistence of conflict and disagreement under anarchy. He endorses the idea of a framework of basic rights, and reasonably encompassing arrangements for making collective decisions and administering those decisions, and in these ways addresses some concerns about the pathologies of decentralization. And, responding to concerns about economic efficiency, he stresses that his view does not imply primitive communitarian economic production (the denial of all economies of scale and specialization), and indeed welcomes technological development and increased productivity, which contributes to free social cooperation by limiting the need for human toil. In fact, he thinks that anarchism really comes into its own as a social ideal only with a high level of development of the productive forces of society.

The Weaknesses of Chomsky's Anarchism

We, however, are less convinced than Chomsky of the attractions of anarchism, for three reasons. First, we are simply not persuaded that policies of, for example, economic coordination, environmental protection, and public health are most efficiently made in the absence of specialized bodies, devoted to formulating policy alternatives and to assessing the likely consequences of their implementation. Assuming conditions of large-scale social interdependence, there are likely to be problematic third-party effects or "externalities" in each of these areas (for example, a significant degree of pollution, affecting large populations, resulting from the actions of individuals and enterprises).

Such externalities, and the complex problems of policy planning and evaluation they pose, are not solely attributable to "the irrational nature of [present] institutions"[34] and the incentives to selfish behavior that they generate. In some important measure, they are intrinsic to social interdependence itself. If only because of problems of imperfect information, they can be expected to appear in an interdependent and technologically advanced society even under the most favorable of motivational conditions (for example, perfect altruism). Given the persistence of externalities and their attendant complexities, however, we doubt that any reordering of social institutions, however welcome, will simplify public policies to the point that reasonably efficient governance can become simply a "part-time job."[35]

Second, we would expect tensions between the proposed dispersion of political responsibility and the effective exercise of that responsibility. Underlying this concern is our assumption that actions needed to enforce the terms of order would be costly; that is, both detecting violations and sanctioning violators would generate costs for enforcers. For reasons familiar from the theory of public goods, the coexistence of dispersed benefits (those accruing to citizens in general from enforcement of the terms of the order) and concentrated costs (incurred by those who engage in enforcement) presents a situation ripe for "free-riding," and a concomitant failure to provide appropriate levels of enforcement.

Such problems are, it should be said, much less pervasive in smaller-scale associations. Reduction of scale almost certainly makes violations more apparent, thus reducing the cost of their detection. And since association norms can be invoked in a process of informal sanctioning, this is also likely to reduce the cost of imposing sanctions, including sanction of those who decline to sanction others. But we are assuming a fairly large and complex association. Here, we believe, the problem of providing incentives to enforce the terms of the order has real bite. And here, a natural solution to the enforcement incentive problem is to establish specialized agencies for administration and enforcement. The specialization of agencies eases the task of providing incentives to enforcement, since those who work in them can be held accountable for their failures (for instance, by being removed from their positions). And it greatly simplifies the problem

34. Ibid., 250.
35. Ibid., 251.

of monitoring enforcement performance, since the division of political labor enables citizens and their representatives to focus their inquiry on particular institutions and individuals.

Third, we doubt whether the proposed anarchist order would encourage the motivations necessary to its stability, in particular whether it would encourage the formation of a sense of justice comprehensive enough to include all members of the order. We noted earlier that Chomsky supposes that an anarchist order will encourage a "spiritual transformation" of human beings. But it remains unclear how the sort of anarchism he endorses would elicit motivations of the required kind. In particular, we assume that a stable democratic socialist scheme must ensure continuing relative equality among the participants in the order. It might be the case, for example, that considerable portions of the surplus generated in some enterprises would be used to benefit those in others. But how is a concern to preserve such equality of condition to be encouraged among citizens, assuming (what seems obvious) that it could not be counted on to emerge spontaneously?

Presumably the idea is that citizens acquire a sense of justice and a willingness to act on that sense through the normal course of their maturation. But if organic groups, based in particular workplaces or neighborhoods, provide the basis of political cooperation, then it would seem natural that the principal allegiance of citizens would be to those organic groups. And if that were true, then a sense of justice supporting the distributive measures required to maintain the order would not be likely to form. One of the virtues of less organic and more "alienated" political forms that are abstracted from everyday life—political parties, territorially defined representative bodies, and specialized organizations for making and enforcing collective decisions—is that they plausibly encourage the members of society to regard one another as equal citizens, deserving of justice whatever the particulars of their aspirations, class situation, or group affiliations. It seems likely that some such more cosmopolitan sense of citizenship, encouraged by less organic forms of political association, is necessary to provide the motivation needed to sustain the egalitarian background required of a genuinely democratic society.

Of course it may be that the establishment of specialized political bodies to address these problems would engender a concentration of power, and that such a concentration would produce greater threats to human freedom than those resulting from the absence of specialized political arrangements. This is, clearly, an empirical issue, and one about which we can only hope someday to have data. In the absence of more compelling evidence than we now have, however, Chomsky's anarchism seems to stand on relatively shaky grounds. This limits its appeal even to those who share his commitment to eliminating unnecessary constraints on human beings, and in particular constraints deriving from economic inequality.

3. What, If Anything, May We Hope For?

Setting these particular criticisms aside, Chomsky's account of human nature and the social conditions appropriate to its full expression naturally suggest two questions about contemporary societies. First, why are present social arrangements and the distribution of basic material resources and political power they provide so distant from the arrangements and distribution appropriate to human nature?[36] Second, given the distance between the actual and ideal, what reason is there for maintaining even the hope that current arrangements will come to approximate this ideal more closely? In this final section, we consider these questions in turn.

At least at an abstract level, Chomsky's answer to the first question is clear. Once an unjust order exists, those benefiting from it have both an interest in maintaining it and, by virtue of their social advantages, the power to do so. Maintenance is of course not in the interest of those who do not benefit from the order. So, dominant groups must use their power against subordinate ones to ensure the latter's consent or acquiescence to the unjust scheme. The basic mechanisms for achieving this are force and fraud. Either those who do not benefit must, in effect, be frightened and beaten into submission, or they must be distracted from their real interests and deliberately confused about the way the world works.

More particularly, Chomsky believes that the relative importance of force and fraud to social reproduction depends on the specific scheme of unjust distribution in place. Fascist orders and Stalinist "socialism" are marked by the denial of liberties of expression, association, and participation. Thus, while they feature well-developed propaganda systems, they rely primarily on force to suppress the natural aspiration to freedom. Capitalist democracies, by contrast, provide at least formal rights of expression, association, and participation. While they feature considerable use of

36. Chomsky indicates that this question arises naturally, given his views on human nature. See *Deterring Democracy* (London: Verso, 1991), 397.

force, the availability of channels of expression and association increases the importance of what people think, and fraud accordingly plays a more central role in preserving order.[37] In capitalist democracy, the real "enemy" of governing elites, their "ultimate target," is the human mind itself.[38] The preservation of unjust advantage requires thought control, the deliberate "manufacture of consent."[39]

In elaborating these themes, Chomsky has focused principally on the role of the mass media in capitalist democracies, and then almost exclusively on the case of the media in the United States—a case marked, in comparative terms, by an apparently paradoxical combination of extreme media servility and minimal state control of those media.[40] These writings, some authored jointly with Edward Herman, present a "propaganda model" of the media's operation—not, it may be stressed, of its effects on consciousness or behavior (see the discussion on p. 250)—with two component parts.[41]

The Propaganda Model

The first component is the contention that the principal propagators of ideas in capitalist democracies (again, and throughout, particularly in the United States) advance ideas that conform to elite interests. More specifically, the range of positions featured in the media, the issues that receive emphasis, the timing of stories, the sources that are treated as respectable, and the interpretation of the role of the media itself, are all "highly functional for established power and responsive to the needs of the government and major power groups."[42]

37. See 'Manufacturing Consent,' in *The Chomsky Reader*, 131–132; *Deterring Democracy*, chap. 12.

38. *Turning the Tide: U.S. Intervention in Central America and the Struggle for Peace* (Boston: South End Press, 1985), 234–236.

39. The term, taken from Walter Lippmann's *Public Opinion* (London: Allen and Unwin, 1932), provides the title for Edward Herman and Noam Chomsky, *Manufacturing Consent: The Political Economy of the Mass Media* (New York: Pantheon, 1988).

40. See, for example, *On Power and Ideology: The Managua Lectures* (Cambridge, MA: MIT Press, 1987), which notes that the United States is near the "libertarian end in the spectrum of existing societies" (114) but that debate proceeds "within very narrow limits" (124).

41. Herman and Chomsky, in *Manufacturing Consent*, use the term "propaganda model" to refer just to the first of the two components discussed in the text. For reasons of terminological convenience we use the term to cover a wider range of Chomsky's views about the media. We do not assume, however, that Herman embraces all aspects of the propaganda model as it is characterized here.

42. Herman and Chomsky, *Manufacturing Consent*, xv.

The second component of the model is an account of the mechanisms of social power, and the particular organization of the media, that explain this "highly functional" pattern. Here, in an account of why the media operates as it does, general propositions about the organization of capitalist democracies are fused with specific contentions about the role of four broad groups of social actors within such systems.

At the top are various interconnected elites, predominantly business elites (including those who own the media) and government elites (often the same as the former).[43] These actors, or at least important segments of them, appear to be relatively "free of illusion," a freedom explained by the fact that a clear understanding of the world is essential to maintaining their privileged positions within it. ("The propaganda may be what it is, but dominant elites must have a clearer understanding among themselves.")[44] Thus capitalists need to know how the world works in order to compete successfully, and state managers need to know in order to serve the interests of business. Understanding their own interests and what is needed to advance them, and recognizing that their interests are commonly opposed to the interests of the rest of the population, the elites sow illusion outside their ranks.[45] In this connection, it should be noted that Chomsky thinks that "most people are not liars,"[46] and that a low tolerance for cognitive dissonance leads most propagators of falsehood to self-deception; they tend to say what they believe, having first come to believe what they say. But Chomsky seems to except at least certain crucial elements

43. The account of the five filters advanced in Herman and Chomsky is basically a refined version of the conception of elite interests sketched here (though we have abstracted from their fifth filter, namely anti-communism). Thus in *Manufacturing Consent*, they discuss the way that news is filtered through (1) the "important common interests [that owners of major media share] with other major corporations, banks, and government" (14); (2) the need of the media to sell an audience to advertisers who are interested in "audiences with buying power" (16); (3) the dependence of media on government and corporate sources of information (19); and (4) the requirement of sensitivity to "flak" produced by "individuals or groups with substantial resources" (26). The basic, "guided market" model of explanation is that the power to fix what gets said is held by individuals and groups who have substantial resources, who have a reasonably good understanding of their interests, and who seek to ensure that what is said conforms to those interests.

44. "Interview," 45.

45. In emphasizing that this policy is deliberately pursued, we do not mean to suggest that there is a conspiracy—that elites explicitly coordinate in the pursuit of a common interest in deception. On the other hand, the explanation is not a classical invisible hand explanation, since the pattern of distortion is the result of deliberate acts of distortion by individuals.

46. "Interview," 39.

of elites from this generalization, since he holds that they both know the truth and regularly deceive others about it.[47] Given his assumptions about normal people, such behavior, which on his view was, for example, characteristic of the "stunning lunatics and liars" who prosecuted the U.S. effort in the Vietnam War, must be termed "pathological."[48]

A second group is composed of journalists and the "secular priesthood" of (primarily) academic experts.[49] Members of this class typically attain their positions by propagating views that serve elite interests. But, displaying the normal human intolerance of conscious deception, they commonly come to believe what they say.[50]

A third group of actors is composed of the educated and politically active middle classes. They provide the "primary targets"[51] for propaganda, since elites recognize that they could and would do enormous harm to existing arrangements of authority if told the truth. That they could do such harm is a function of their resources and political activism. That they would is a function of the fact that, as Chomsky puts it, "most people are not gangsters."[52] He believes, and believes clear-minded elites believe, that the middle class would not support immoral U.S. policies if it knew the truth about them, which is why elites seek "to prevent any knowledge or understanding" of those policies.[53]

A fourth group is composed of the politically immobilized lower classes. Members of this group benefit least from the operation of the system and thus might be thought to pose the greatest threat to its continuance. But

47. For example, in one interview Chomsky claims, "The more intelligent people are just lying, but the less intelligent believe it." See *Language and Politics*, 713.

48. "The Backroom Boys," in *For Reasons of State*, 3. Chomsky borrows the "lunatics" phrase from then New York Times reporter Gloria Emerson.

49. Although Chomsky's earliest political essays focused on the "secular priesthood," the emphasis in his writing shifted in the late 1970s to the role of the mass media in the manufacture of consent. At least part of the explanation may lie in the role that academic experts on Latin American politics played in opposing U.S. policy in Central America in the 1980s. See, for example, the discussion of the report by the Latin American Studies Association in the 1984 Nicaraguan election, in Herman and Chomsky, *Manufacturing Consent*, chap. 3. For note of the relative unimportance of such opposition, however, see *Deterring Democracy*, 105n24.

50. Chomsky often emphasizes that illusions about the operation of the world are most pronounced among such "experts." See, for example, "Interview," 43.

51. *Necessary Illusions: Thought Control in Democratic Societies* (Boston: South End Press, 1989), 47.

52. *Language and Politics*, 373.

53. "Interview," 48–49.

their lack of resources and difficulties with collective action ("They are not part of the system; they just watch")[54] in fact make them less threatening than the middle classes; they are as a consequence only a secondary target of the propaganda machine. Moreover, although members of this group are less highly "educated," and thus less indoctrinated,[55] than other elements in the population, they are effectively discouraged from political activity by such distractions as spectator sports, lifestyle preoccupations, and "religious fanaticism of an almost Khomeinist variety."[56] Often profoundly alienated from the operation of the system, and thus susceptible to the attractions of "charismatic figures who promise to lead them out of their problems and to attack either the powerful or some other bogeyman, the Jews or the homosexuals, or the communists, or whoever is identified as responsible for their troubles,"[57] they typically "can be satisfied, it is hoped, with diversions and a regular dose of patriotic propaganda, and fulminations against assorted enemies."[58]

As these last observations may suggest, Chomsky does not study the secondary target or popular culture in any detail. His work concentrates instead on the "dominant intellectual culture and the values that guide it"[59]—the interactions among the first three groups just noted. To summarize, his claim is that the functional pattern of media propagation of ideas conforming to elite interests (the first component of the propaganda model) reflects a relatively conscious policy of deception pursued by elites, who act with the willing, if unwitting, support of intellectuals and journalists, and who are concerned to forestall the emergence of opposition to their power that would likely arise from a (middle class) population that knew the truth about their immoral aims and actions. Before assessing the force of this conception, two clarifications of its aims may be helpful.

First, and as emphasized above, the propaganda model is offered as an account of the operation of the major media, not of its effects. The model in itself neither states nor implies that ideological conformity in the target group(s) is actually produced by propaganda, or that ideological conformity is the principal cause of obedient behavior, or even that ideological

54. *Language and Politics*, 685.
55. Ibid., 765.
56. Ibid., 602.
57. Ibid., 765.
58. *Necessary Illusions*, 47–48.
59. *The Culture of Terrorism* (Boston: South End, 1988), 3, and note 3.

conformity exists. So the propaganda model would not be falsified if it were established that propaganda was unsuccessful in generating false beliefs, or that it was irrelevant to the production of consent, or that consent was produced by means other than illusion (such as self-interest or cynicism).[60] Nevertheless, the propaganda model is advanced in aid of understanding the actual manufacture of consent in capitalist democracies, and not simply as an account of the functioning of major media in them. Its interest and importance thus do depend on there being some real and significant effects of propaganda on social action,[61] and Chomsky in fact holds the view that propaganda efforts are successful in generating both illusion and consent.[62]

Second, it is no objection to the propaganda model to observe that the distortions featured in the major media are not complete fairy tales, utterly at odds with the facts. On the contrary, attention to the model's underlying mechanisms would suggest that distortions will be more often a matter of framing and emphasis than simple fabrication.[63] As already noted, for example, governing elites need to understand the world. But since they in part rely on the major media for information about the world, this imposes some truth constraints on reporting in those media (constraints more severe than those exerted on more "yellow" or "tabloid" journalism).[64]

An Overstated Case?

Even with these qualifications noted, however, our assessment of the propaganda model is mixed. Chomsky presents reams of evidence for the model, most of it addressed to the first of its two components—that media representations are highly functional for elite interests. With copious documentation, he effectively makes the case that the bulk of information

---

60. *Necessary Illusions*, 148–149.

61. Chomsky himself states that he decided to focus his political writings on the operation of "ideological institutions" for two reasons. The first was a "judgment of importance," the second a matter of personal circumstances and abilities. And he says that considerations of the second kind would have been sufficient to lead him to concentrate on the ways in which schools, universities and media "serve to indoctrinate and control." *Language and Politics*, 372. But saying this is perfectly consistent with what we state in the text.

62. See, for example, *On Power and Ideology*, 128; *Necessary Illusions*, 148.

63. Herman and Chomsky, *Manufacturing Consent*, xiv–xv.

64. *Necessary Illusions*, 151.

provided by the major media is extremely and systematically biased toward the maintenance of existing arrangements of power and advantage; that departures from orthodoxy, particularly among those who threaten to reach a more than miniscule audience, are deliberately sanctioned; and, above all, that debate about U.S. foreign policy commonly proceeds within a set of presuppositions about the role of the United States in the world that are quite distorted but rarely even noted, much less disputed. With all this we are in agreement.

The first Gulf War, for example, provided an advanced display of all these phenomena. Information supplied to the press was sharply restricted by American diplomatic and military personnel, while the restrictions themselves were barely noted or challenged. Accordingly, press "coverage" of events, particularly in the United States, consisted largely of canned human-interest stories, military briefings, and pool reports from sites selected by military authorities. Information unfavorable to the official U.S. position—on, for example, the details of Iraqi peace initiatives before the war, or the destruction of Iraq during the war—was generally dismissed or not reported at all. Even the slightest departures from orthodoxy—for example, the fact that the Cable News Network actually offered reports from inside Iraq on war damage—were objects of high-ranking political attack. And the most preposterous and cynical statements of public officials—for example, George Bush's repeated declaration that "America stands where it always has, against aggression, against those who would use force to replace the rule of law"—were repeated and amplified without critical comment.[65]

All in all, then, this was an almost laboratory-perfect demonstration of manipulation of and by the media.

Nonetheless, Chomsky's view of the media and the manufacture of consent seems overstated in three ways. First, the claim that business people and state managers are in the main relatively "free of illusion" seems overdrawn, at least when that claim is offered (as Chomsky usually offers it) without substantial qualification. There is of course ample reason to believe that business and state elites are on the whole better informed about their interests than ordinary citizens, since they have more resources to acquire

65. For Chomsky's own criticisms of media coverage of events leading up to the Gulf war, see *Deterring Democracy*, chap. 6.

information, and, as a rule, greater incentives to ensure its accuracy. But they are not immune to "ordinary" failures of human understanding (such as shortsightedness, excessive attention to the status quo), evidence of which is legion in the ranks of business and the state. Nor, critically, are they immune to the distortions of ideology, which not uncommonly grips elites with at least the force that it grips other citizens.

On the latter point, Chomsky himself provides evidence for a more complex picture in his essay on the "Backroom Boys" who administered the American war on Vietnam.[66] The history he discusses there suggests that during and immediately after World War II, U.S. policymakers did operate with a relatively clear understanding of their interests, the requisite elements of a world order that would conform to those interests, and the content of the ideology needed to provide popular support for their imperial designs. Once the terms of the postwar world were set in place, however, political and economic elites themselves accepted the terms of postwar ideology and clung to that ideology even when it no longer served their material interests. In particular, we find that by the 1960s, "other and more irrational considerations (than the economic interests of U.S. capital) may have come to predominate" in the prosecution of U.S. policy in Southeast Asia,[67] as United States policy-makers were "caught up" and "trapped" by the "fantasies" they had earlier devised as illusions for the public.[68] The lesson to be drawn from this example is, we think, straightforward. During some periods—for example, the ascendant period of a new world power—elites may be relatively free of illusion about their interests. During others, however, they may be much less so. But at no time does it seem warranted to assume that elite understanding, however clear about the short term, extends much beyond that.

Second, and closely related, the model's claim that elite-generated ideologies are always "highly functional" for elite interests seems exag-

---

66. "The Backroom Boys," in *For Reasons of State*.

67. Ibid., 66. See also Chomsky's remarks about the "persistence of . . . astonishing illusions" among presidential advisors and the existence of "historical fantasies at high levels of decision-making"—"absurdities that must be taken seriously, given the vast resources of terror in the hands of those whose decisions are guided (or justified) by them." See ibid., 165n193, and the references there to *American Power and the New Mandarins*.

68. "The Backroom Boys," 54.

gerated. The "Backroom Boys" example just given indicates otherwise; there, elites were not only trapped by illusions dysfunctional for their interests but were, as a consequence, propagating such illusions. How often and how significantly dysfunctional conduct is produced by such illusion (or by other mechanisms) is, of course, an empirical issue beyond the scope of this discussion. It seems plausible, however, to think that such investigation would yield other examples of elite propagation of ideologies that are not "highly functional." In the area of foreign policy, for example, the conviction that world "order" must be supplied chiefly by the United States—a notion that postwar elites did their best to encourage among the general population—now arguably inhibits rational elite response to a range of military and economic concerns occasioned by political transformation in Eastern Europe, turmoil in the Soviet Union, and abiding economic challenge from Western Europe and Japan.

Consider, for example, the Gulf War's effective definition of "collective security" in the new world order as the raising of foreign subsidies to pay for American military force. This might seem a perfectly rational U.S. elite response to problems of military management after the decline of American hegemony. Crudely put, if a nation is less competitive in machine tools than in bombers, it makes sense for it to "trade" in bombers. Collectively underwritten but American-led, such an arrangement might help stabilize the U.S. comparative advantage in military power by defraying its costs, while offering continued U.S. influence in the world disproportionate to its economic power.

It might. Or it might not. The underwriting project could get bogged down in ways that military threats themselves could not overcome. Celebration of the comparative advantages of American military power might lead to the neglect of other sources of power. First World needs for the submission of the Third World (against which force is most readily applied) might simply diminish, leading to a decline in the demand for American military forces. And even if none of these things happened, the choice of the bomb trade may simply not be the best, or even close to the second-best, strategy for maintaining U.S. dominance. It might after all be the case that more constructive uses of U.S. resources—to educate its children or train its workforce, clean its environment or nationalize its health-care system, rebuild its material infrastructure or invest more in basic research—would benefit American elites substantially more than adoption of the mercenary route. At the very least, this question seems open.[69]

Third, we think Chomsky exaggerates the importance of the media's informational bias in explaining consent and stability in capitalist democracies. In entering this objection, we must note that a word of caution is in order. As noted earlier, commitment to the propaganda model itself does not imply commitment to the view that the media's informational bias is the fundamental source of ideological conformity, nor that ideological conformity is the fundamental source of consent (at least for the target groups). Nevertheless, Chomsky's writings do suggest, at least as a general matter, commitment to both of these claims.[70] So it seems worthwhile to register our objection to the claim about the importance of ideology in producing consent.[71] Since, however, this is not a claim to which Chomsky is committed by the propaganda model, and is not a claim he makes explicitly in his work, we use the name "Chomsky*" in the following paragraph to underscore our uncertainty about attributing these views to him.

Ideology and Consent

The source of our objection to Chomsky*'s emphasis on the importance of ideology in producing consent is simple. Chomsky* uses the term "ideology" in a pejorative sense; the term denotes a system of false beliefs about the world, popular action in accord with which is favorable to the realization of dominant interests.[72] In our view, however, such false beliefs ("false consciousness") play a less central role in explaining consent than

69. Adding further openness, or doubt, is the fact that American elites are divided, and what is functional for one elite group may not be functional for others. One consequence of this is that the predictive power of the propaganda model is diminished. Different popular ideologies may be equally functional for elites in general, but not for elites in particular. In these circumstances the model does not tell us which ideology will reign.

70. Chomsky does discuss several other sources of consent, agreeing for example with our view (presented in chapter 3 of Joshua Cohen and Joel Rogers, *On Democracy* (New York: Penguin, 1983) that consent reflects the fact that the operation of capitalist democracies tends to channel political action into the pursuit of interests in short-term material gain and to enable individuals to satisfy those interests. See, for example, *Turning the Tide*, 233–234. This, however, is consistent with the claims we attribute to him in the text, which concern the fundamental sources of ideological conformity and consent.

71. That most people, we think, take Chomsky to be making a claim of this sort provides another motivation for engaging it.

72. For a careful discussion of this and other senses of ideology, see Raymond Geuss, *The Idea of Critical Theory* (Cambridge: Cambridge University Press, 1981).

Chomsky* suggests. Even individuals who know the ugly truth may consent for reasons of, for example, material self-interest, cynicism, fatigue, or simple lack of concern, and much evidence suggests that many do consent for some combination of these reasons. Survey data in the United States (the country that has been the primary focus for Chomsky's political writings) regularly confirm a very widespread (exceeding the bounds of the "secondary target") public conviction that public officials are corrupt, that the country is run in an undemocratic fashion, and that many public policies are immoral.[73] But this confirmation is provided in a context of profound political stability. This suggests that something other than illusion and ignorance is producing that stability.

An expansion on this suggestion may be used to conclude our discussion of the propaganda model. Consider the case of capitalist democracy, the social system in which, on Chomsky's view, propaganda plays the greatest role in producing stability. There, instead of explaining the generation of consent chiefly by reference to ideological mechanisms, one might rely on two, arguably more central, features of that system. First, the private control of investment featured in a capitalist democracy subordinates the interests of workers to those of capitalists (without profits there is no investment, and without investment no jobs) and thus leads workers to restrain their demands on employers and the state. It also tends to focus those demands on material gain, a concern that can be in some measure satisfied within the system. Second, the characteristic inequalities of resources between capitalists and workers systematically favor the former as collective actors, providing further obstacles to organized opposition and further bases for worker consent to the system.[74]

Assuming that such an account seems generally plausible (an assumption that we do not propose to defend here), it has an additional attraction in this discussion, namely that one can accept it as consistent with endorsing our first two criticisms of the propaganda model and embracing that model's most central claims about media bias and the narrowness of debate. That is, once explanatory emphasis has been shifted onto nonideological sources of consent, there is no difficulty in granting that elites are

73. Chomsky is aware of this. See, for example, *Turning the Tide*, 240–245. Although he takes it (properly in our view) as a basis for hope in achieving a better political system, he does not explore the limits it suggests to his own account of the stability of that system.

74. For such an account, see Cohen and Rogers, *On Democracy*, chap. 3.

often confused and that ideologies are not always highly functional for elite interests. At the same time, the view does not exclude ideology as a possible source of consent, let alone exclude the media as a source of its propagation. Indeed, by softening some of the claims made for the importance of propaganda, while admitting the central insights of the propaganda model, such an account of consent seems to us a natural way to highlight the force of Chomsky's work in this area.

Expanding the Domain of Freedom

We come, finally, to Chomsky's views on social evolution, and the second question posed at the outset of this section. Why should one think that existing societies, structured in ways so hostile to the exercise of human freedom, might change in a direction more in keeping with that essential human capacity? Our discussion of Chomsky's view of social order (even admitting the amendments to that view we have suggested) underscores the force of this question, for it may suggest that he sees dominant groups as in some sense invincible. In light of that discussion, it is easy to see why he believes that the "struggle for freedom and social justice" is "unending, often grim,"[75] and why political actors face "temptations of disillusionment . . . many failures and only limited successes."[76] But it may be more difficult to understand why he also thinks the struggle against oppression is "never hopeless,"[77] or to understand the grounds for his "hope that our world can be transformed to 'a world in which the creative spirit is alive, in which life is an adventure full of hope and joy, based rather upon the impulse to construct than upon the desire to retain what we possess or to seize what is possessed by others.'"[78]

In Chomsky's view, the source of hope lies in human nature itself. He speculates that constraints on human freedom that are not "required for survival in the particular state of history" will tend to be sloughed off, as a result of the moral nature of human beings, the "instinct for freedom," and the "continual efforts to overcome authoritarian structures and to expand the domain of freedom" that result from that instinct.[79] Put otherwise,

---

75. "Language and Freedom," 406.
76. *Turning the Tide*, 253.
77. "Language and Freedom," 406; *Deterring Democracy*, 64.
78. *Problems of Knowledge and Freedom: The Russell Lectures* (New York: Pantheon, 1971), 110–11. Chomsky is here quoting Bertrand Russell.
79. *Language and Politics*, 469.

systems that impose unnecessary constraints on natural tendencies to human expression will, by that very fact, face intrinsic sources of instability. The significance of these destabilizing pressures for reform will of course depend on a range of factors relevant to political mobilization—including the number of people who feel the constraints of existing order, the capacities for and willingness to pay the costs of collective action on the part of those who do, the willingness of dominant groups to repress or murder their own populations, the power of foreign states to thwart mass action, and the strategic choices of opponents of oppressive regimes. Still, such pressures are present, and their presence suggests a weak evolutionary tendency toward societies more accommodating of human freedom.

Illustrating these claims about basic human nature and the pressures it exerts on unjust arrangements, Chomsky suggests, for example, that the "propaganda system" in the United States—its tremendous power and durability notwithstanding—is "extremely unstable because of the reliance on lies. Any system that is based on lying and deceit is inherently unstable."[80] The thought that underpins this view is that lying about U.S. policies (or disguising them in other ways, for example through covert action) is necessitated by the decency of the population, who if confronted with the truth would resist those policies. And elsewhere, in arguing (correctly, we believe) against the familiar "expert" view that the American public has recently shifted profoundly to the right on social and foreign-policy questions, he notes the continuing dissent of the population from many of the more brutal aspects of recent U.S. policy, "despite all the brainwashing and indoctrination and so on."[81] Here again, such resilient decency, and the threat it poses to indecent institutions and policies, derive from our moral nature and our fundamental aspiration to freedom.

More broadly, Chomsky rejects the currently fashionable neo-Nietzschean view that the history of the world is merely a history of change, in which old forms of domination are simply replaced by new ones, without significant progress in meeting such fundamental human interests as the interest in freedom.[82] A "child of the Enlightenment,"[83] Chomsky finds

80. "Interview," 49.
81. *Language and Politics*, 735; *Deterring Democracy*, 173.
82. See, for example, Chomsky's summary of his disagreements with Foucault, in *Language and Responsibility*, 80.
83. *Language and Politics*, 773.

instead that human history, at least at some moments, exhibits "detectable progress in the guarantee of fundamental human rights, difficult as it may be to pronounce such words in the century that has given us Hitler and Stalin, agonizingly slow as the process may be."[84] Such progress reflects "continual efforts to overcome authoritarian structures and to expand the domain of freedom." And those efforts, in turn, "probably (reflect) instinctual patterns that are just part of our moral nature."[85]

To us, Chomsky's "optimistic view"[86] seems highly plausible. As noted earlier, a fundamental human interest in autonomy and capacity for moral judgment appear to have played a significant role in many historical achievements in the cause of human freedom (for example, the abolition of slavery, the extension of religious and political toleration). Despite the murderousness of the twentieth century, such aspirations and capacities have clearly been operative in many of the great political struggles of the recent past—from Third World efforts to break free of colonial bondage, to the civil rights movement in the United States, the worldwide movement for women's liberation, or the revolution against Stalinism in Eastern Europe. And whatever the political doldrums of the present, there is every reason to think that those aspirations and capacities are operative now.

Chomsky has disavowed a "faith" in any project or tradition, including a faith in reason itself.[87] But his weak evolutionary theory suggests a "reasonable faith"[88] in human beings that works in support of hope about social advance.[89] Although the evidence about people is not decisive, nothing that we know about human nature is inconsistent with the contention that aspirations to freedom and decency are fundamental features of that nature; and nothing that we know about social order defeats the hope that the pursuit of these aspirations will produce significant improvement in human circumstances. The fact that such hopefulness is consistent with

84. *Necessary Illusions*, 355.
85. *Language and Politics*, 469.
86. *Language and Problems of Knowledge*, 154.
87. "Interview," 48.
88. The term comes from Kant, who held that it is reasonable, on moral grounds, to have faith that God exists, that the will is free, and that the soul is immortal. See Immanuel Kant, *Critique of Practical Reason*, Part I, Book 2.
89. And, recently, he appears to acknowledge as much. See *Deterring Democracy*, 397–401.

the evidence enables children of the Enlightenment to be optimists of the will, without condemning themselves to being irrationalists of the intellect. It is Chomsky's insistence on this point, his commitment to both reason and moral hope, that we take to be his signal contribution to social thought.

7

REFLECTIONS ON HABERMAS ON DEMOCRACY

1. Radical Democracy

Jürgen Habermas is a radical democrat.[1] The source of that self-designation is that his conception of democracy—what he calls "discursive democracy"—is founded on the abstract ideal of "a self-organizing community of free and equal citizens," coordinating their collective affairs through their common reason (7). In this essay, I discuss three large questions about this radical-democratic ideal of collective self-regulation:

1. What is the role of private autonomy in a radical-democratic view?
2. What role does reason play in collective self-regulation?
3. What relevance might a radical-democratic outlook have for contemporary democracies?

I will address these questions by considering Habermas' answers and then presenting alternative responses to them. The alternatives are also radical-democratic in inspiration, but they draw on a richer set of normative-political ideas than Habermas wants to rely on and are more ambitious in their hopes for democratic practice. Before providing an initial sketch of Habermas' answers and my alternatives, I will make a few general comments on the philosophical background of Habermas' view.

I am grateful to Oliver Gerstenberg and Kenneth Baynes for discussion of the material in section 2, to Sebastiano Maffettone for making available a draft of his essay on "Liberalism and Its Critique," and to Leonardo Avritzer and Joshua Flaherty for extensive discussion of many themes in this essay. I presented earlier versions at a Political Theory Workshop at Nuffield College, Oxford, and to the McGill University Philosophy Department. I also wish to thank Jürgen Habermas for comments on an earlier draft. My broader intellectual debt to Habermas should be clear from virtually everything I have written. I am pleased to have this occasion for expressing that debt.

1. Jürgen Habermas, *Between Facts and Norms: Contributions to a Discourse Theory of Law and Democracy*, trans. William Rehg (Cambridge, MA: MIT Press, 1996), xlii–xliii. References to *Between Facts and Norms* are included parenthetically in the text, as page numbers.

Habermas offers two lines of argument in support of his radical-democratic ideal of discursive democracy. In brief, he claims that it is both rooted in reason and practically relevant to contemporary political societies. First, then, Habermas locates the bases of democracy in a general, "post-metaphysical" theory of human reason, which he presents in the theory of communicative action, and of argumentation as the reflective form of such action. The intuitive idea is that democracy, through its basic constitution, institutionalizes practices of free, open-ended, reflective reasoning about common affairs, and tames and guides the exercise of coercive power by reference to those practices. To be sure, democracy does not guarantee the subordination of sovereign will and the coercive power it guides to the force of the better argument—what *could* guarantee that practical reason guides political power?—but it establishes conditions favorable to such subordination. Moreover, the promise to subordinate political will to practical reason is a justifying ideal underlying democratic practice. By requiring a more complete subordination of political will to practices of reasoning, then, we hold democracy to its own internal standards.

Second, Habermas aims to show how "the old promise" of a community of free and equal members, guiding their collective conduct through their common reason, can be redeemed if it is "reconceived under the conditions of complex societies" (7). He offers such redemption by elaborating the content of the democratic ideal—he describes the rights that citizens must assign to one another—and showing how it can serve as a practical guide once it is reinterpreted in light of modern conditions of social and political complexity, including a market economy and an administrative bureaucracy.

I will say very little about the philosophical bases of democracy in the communicative account of reason and concentrate instead on the content of Habermas' conception of democracy and its implications. I steer clear of the wider philosophical framework—Habermas' postmetaphysical theory of human reason, communicative action, and argumentation—because I think that political argument should not be made to depend on, or be presented as dependent on, a philosophical theory about the nature of reason. Philosophical theories about the nature and competence of reason do not provide the common ground for equal citizens that is desirable in public argument in a democracy. An appeal to *reason* cannot help us "get behind" the plurality of competing moral, political, religious, metaphysical outlooks, because the nature and competence of reason is one matter on which such outlooks disagree. Thus a postmetaphysical conception of reason, which ties the account of reason to the presuppositions of argumentation, will not find favor with a natural law theorist who believes that reason delivers substantial metaphysical truths and insights about the best human life.

Instead, I accept (with Rawls) the *relative autonomy of political reason*. Political reason is autonomous in that it can and should proceed in articulating a conception of democracy without relying on an encompassing philosophy of life or claiming to resolve the controversies among them, including controversies about the nature and competence of reason. It is only relatively autonomous because autonomous political argument needs to make sense in light of the diverse and conflicting encompassing philosophies that (at least some) citizens endorse: Citizens must judge, from within those separate philosophies, that autonomous political argument is appropriate and accept, as a public matter, that the diversity of such philosophies recommends an autonomous political reason. Political reason, we might say, lacks *public foundations*, because there is no single, publicly authoritative basis for its principles and modes of argument. But it may well have a plurality of nonpublic foundations, different for different citizens.

For these reasons, I will put to the side claims about the connections between democracy and the nature and competence of reason and focus instead on the substance of Habermas' radical account of democracy. That account takes its fundamental orientation, I said, from the idea of a self-organizing community of free and equal citizens.[2] Radically understood, democracy is not simply a matter of selecting among competing elites (through regular elections), nor simply a matter of ensuring, through such selection, a protected framework of private liberties, founded on antecedent liberal commitments. Instead, democracy is a form of self-rule

2. For this reason, Habermas understands his view as having important affinities with anarchist and socialist ideas, once the "normative core" of those ideas is properly understood. That's because he supposes (correctly, I think) that the normative core is provided by the ideal of a free association among equals, guiding the exercise of their collective power through their common reason. See Jürgen Habermas, "Discourse Ethics: Notes on a Program of Philosophical Justification," in *Moral Consciousness and Communicative Action*, trans. C. Lenhardt and S. Weber Nicholsen (Cambridge, MA: MIT Press, 1992), 43–115; and "Further Reflections on the Public Sphere," in *Habermas and the Public Sphere*, ed. Craig Calhoun (Cambridge, MA: MIT Press, 1993), 421–461.

and requires that the legitimate exercise of political power trace to the free communication of citizens, expressed through law. For the radical democrat, the fundamental fact of political sociology is not the distinction between a decision-making elite and others subject to the decisions of that elite, and the consequent need to organize the exercise of power by that elite, but the horizontal, communicative relation among equal citizens; democracy establishes a framework for that relation and makes the exercise of collective power sensitive to it.

Such a conception of democracy has two components. First, one must describe the *content* of the abstract conception: What, more precisely, is it for a political society to be a self-organizing community of free and equal citizens, and for the exercise of collective power to trace to the free communication of citizens? Assume as background that the conception is addressed to a pluralistic society, whose members embrace competing philosophies of life; a reflective culture, that self-consciously embraces a distinction between the fact that a practice is socially accepted and the legitimacy of the practice (between facticity and validity); a society whose complexity, size, and pluralism preclude social coordination through communication alone, as distinct from market exchange and administrative power; and a society whose members engage in strategic action (25). What could popular self-organization and self-government possibly amount to under these conditions? How could free communication among citizens play a regulative role in the political life of such a society? Perhaps under these conditions the ideal of a self-organizing community of free and equal citizens loses its capacity to guide social and political arrangements. The first task, then, is to address this concern: to show "how a radically democratic republic might even be conceived today."[3]

Second, one needs to consider whether such a society is *possible*. Here we take the content of the normative ideal—say, of Habermas' discourse model of democracy—that is developed on the social-political assumptions just noted, which include no unfavorable assumptions about power and human motivation. And we ask: Can this ideal be realized, given the realities of contemporary power and human motivation? Or do sociological and psychological realism imply that we must reduce our normative expectations, and adopt a more minimalist understanding of democracy,

3. See Jürgen Habermas, "Popular Sovereignty as Procedure," in *Between Facts and Norms*, 463–490, esp. 471.

according to which democracy is a system of competitive elections in which citizens chose who will rule, rather than in any more substantial sense a system of self-rule?

Of the three questions that I mentioned earlier and propose to discuss in this essay, two fall under the problem of content, the third under the problem of possibility.

(1) In section 2 I discuss the first question, the role of rights of private autonomy in a democratic constitution. The place of such rights in a radical democratic view is uncertain. One might think that a radical democrat, concerned with the self-rule of citizens, would make the protection of personal liberties dependent on how the people choose to exercise their collective power. But a radical-democratic view that cannot provide personal liberties with a secure basis will seem, to that extent, unreasonable. In response to this concern, Habermas argues that rights of private and public autonomy (rights of participation) are equally fundamental (co-original): Indeed, each is required to explain one another. More particularly, both kinds of rights of autonomy are founded on the conjunction of the rule of law and the discourse principle—a requirement of impartiality that provides the basis for judgments of the legitimacy of law.

Although I agree with Habermas' conclusion, I find the argument for it unpersuasive, and I outline an alternative view that shares radical-democratic inspiration but founds rights of private autonomy on ideas of deliberative justification and reasonable pluralism, both devised for democratic conditions. My alternative strategy of argument makes richer normative assumptions than Habermas does: reasonable pluralism instead of mere legality, deliberation among persons understood as free and equal rather than the impartiality required by the discourse principle. But I think such richer assumptions are necessary, and also defensible, if our aim is to articulate a conception of democracy and not to found that conception on a general philosophical theory of reason and action.

(2) In section 3 I consider a pair of related questions about the role of reason in the collective self-regulation we associate with democracy. First, why should a radical democrat insist on reason: Assuming mass participation, why is it important for democracy to be deliberative? And second, once we decide to insist on a requirement that law be reasonable (rooted in practices of argumentation), why is it important for deliberation to be democratic? Assuming reasonable outcomes, why insist on mass participation?

To explore Habermas' answers to this pair of questions, I sketch his "two-track" discourse model of democratic process. Democracy, thus conceived, comprises both an informal track of free public communication, founded on the dispersed associations of civil society, and a formal track of deliberative decision-making by conventional political institutions that are responsive to the informal discussion of the first track. Working together, the two tracks suggest a way to combine mass participation, through the informal public arena, with competent and reasonable political decisions, through deliberation in formal politics. By displacing the principal locus of participation from formal politics to the informal public sphere, Habermas suggests a way that the public can come into politics without requiring small-scale states or large, long meetings.

The answers to the questions about democracy and deliberation that Habermas proposes on the basis of this model are suggestive, but once more I think that conceptions of deliberative justification and reasonable pluralism, both suited to democratic conditions, provide more compelling responses.

(3) In section 4 I discuss the practical relevance of the radical democratic ideal to the exercise of power in a modern political society (the possibility problem). If Habermas' two-track scheme is to describe a way to join mass participation through the informal public sphere with competent and reasonable formal decision-making, then it must be possible for associations in the opinion-forming public sphere to exercise autonomous influence on politics. Otherwise radical democracy dissolves into a scheme in which open-ended debate among citizens proceeds in splendid isolation from the exercise of political power.

Habermas makes a case for the possibility of such autonomous influence, and his case has some force. Understood as an account of democracy in its most compelling form, however, I think it is unnecessarily restrictive. To sharpen the point, I contrast Habermas' model of discursive democracy with a more institutionalized version of radical democracy, based on an idea of "directly-deliberative polyarchy" that Charles Sabel and I have presented elsewhere.[4] This conception ties practices of deliberation more closely to the exercise of collective power than does Habermas' model of separate tracks.

4. See Joshua Cohen and Charles Sabel, "Directly-Deliberative Polyarchy," *European Law Journal* 3, 4 (1997): 313–342.

This is a very full plate, and I cannot hope to discuss any of these issues in detail. Instead, my aim is to provoke further debate about certain fundamental elements of Habermas' statement of the radical democratic outlook. I share the fundamentals of that outlook, but I think that some of its elements can be presented in more compelling ways. In general terms, Habermas' account is insufficiently explicit about the normative substance of radical democracy, in part because he seeks to found it on a general theory of human reason rather than the political values associated with democracy, and, in turn, insufficiently ambitious in specifying possible institutional ideals that are suggested by radical democracy.

2. Co-originality and Private Autonomy

2.1. According to Habermas, political philosophy has always misconceived the relationship between civic autonomy, and the equal political liberties associated with it, and private autonomy, and the equal personal liberties associated with it: "Thus far no one has succeeded in satisfactorily reconciling private and public autonomy at a fundamental conceptual level," as is "evident" if we consider the tensions between ideas of "human rights and popular sovereignty in social-contract theory" (84).

Liberalism, in Habermas' stylization, defends public autonomy in terms of its capacity to protect private autonomy, thus turning democracy into an instrument for the protection of private liberties: Democracy is the systematic deprivation of basic personal liberties. Republicanism makes the protection of private autonomy contingent on democratic collective decisions, thus rendering liberty dependent on popular judgments about the best means for achieving collective aims or on the collective commitments contingently embraced by a particular community. Stuck between these two options, "political philosophy has never really been able to strike a balance between popular sovereignty and human rights, or between the freedom of the ancients and the freedom of the moderns."[5]

Habermas rejects the idea that either public or private autonomy is more basic: The requirement of ensuring private autonomy cannot legitimately be imposed on a people, but a legitimate legal order cannot fail to protect private autonomy. Instead, he argues that civic and private auton-

---

5. See Jürgen Habermas, "On the Internal Relation between the Rule of Law and Democracy," in *The Inclusion of the Other*, trans. C. Cronin and P. De Greiff (Cambridge, MA: MIT Press, 1998), 258.

omy are co-original—equally fundamental: "The universal right to equal liberties may neither be imposed as a moral right that merely sets an external constraint on the sovereign legislator, nor be instrumentalized as a functional prerequisite for the legislator's aims" (104). In Habermas' own explanation of co-originality, each form of autonomy is required to explain the other; they are, as it were, co-originating, as well as co-original. But the claim about co-origination is best understood as a theory about why the two forms of autonomy are co-original and not as identical to the thesis of co-originality itself.[6]

More particularly, the notion of co-originality implies the following: A democratic process of legitimate lawmaking must ensure a variety of equal liberties to citizens, including both communicative-participatory liberties and personal liberties. Providing both is constitutive of a process of legitimate lawmaking. So, for example, just as a process of legitimate lawmaking cannot ensure rights of political participation, association, and expression only for some, it cannot establish a system of legal rights in which the rights of conscience, privacy, or bodily integrity required for personal independence in pursuing a "private conception of the good" are available only to some citizens. Even though the specific rights of private autonomy

---

6. Thus Rawls agrees that both forms of autonomy are equally fundamental but argues for this conclusion by connecting each to a fundamental aspect of the moral powers of citizens, rather than by showing that each in some way required by the other. See John Rawls, "Reply to Habermas," *Journal of Philosophy* 92 (1995): 132–180; and Rawls, *The Basic Liberties and Their Priority: The Tanner Lectures on Human Values*, ed. Sterling M. McMurrin (Salt Lake City: University of Utah Press, 1987), esp. secs. 5, 6. Ronald Dworkin, too, endorses the idea that both forms of autonomy are equally fundamental, arguing that (roughly) democracy fosters freedom only if the subjects of the laws can also regard themselves as its authors. But to regard themselves as its authors, they must identify with the political community and understand themselves as its "moral members." And they can understand themselves as *moral* members only if they preserve *independent* judgment about the values that will govern their own individual lives and about the quality of the community's decisions. Personal liberties are, in turn, required for this requisite independence. See *Freedom's Law* (Cambridge, MA: Harvard University Press, 1996), 19–26, esp. 25–26. Dworkin's account seems close to at least part of what Habermas identifies as the intuitive idea behind his account of the "mutually presupposing" character of public and private autonomy: "That . . . citizens can make adequate use of their public autonomy only if, on the basis of their equally protected private autonomy, they are sufficiently *independent*." See Habermas, "On the Internal Relation," 261 (emphasis added). Still, Rawls and Dworkin present explicitly normative treatments of the importance of such individual independence, whereas Habermas' theory aims to derive the requirement of independence and associated rights of private autonomy from the need to institutionalize popular sovereignty and democratic process through law. My own discussion is also explicitly normative and draws on the idea of respect for those who hold views that are "reasonable, politically speaking." See below, section 3.

that receive protection are not given by the principle itself, but need to be specified through a democratic process, liberties of both kinds are constitutive of a process of legitimate lawmaking.

The argument for this conclusion proceeds (schematically) as follows.[7]

Step 1. Begin with the fact of law: that coordination and regulation under modern conditions proceed through law. This is a basic fact of modern social life, following from the "functional requirements of a complex society," with a considerable degree of decentralized decision-making.

Step 2. The rule of law leads to a scheme of minimal personal liberty. Two aspects of the rule of law lead to this result. First, law is "Janus-faced": Law is a distinctive form of social coordination in that it permits individuals to choose whether to comply for strategic or normative reasons—from fear of sanctions or from respect for the law's legitimacy—thus assigning "latitude to act according to personal preferences." By leaving reasons for compliance open to choice, and by rejecting the idea that individuals can be held accountable for their reasons for compliance, legal regulation establishes a minimal order of liberty, the liberty not to give an account of reasons for conduct: "Private autonomy extends as far as the legal subject does *not* have to give others an account or give publicly acceptable reasons for her action plans" (120).

Moreover, it is a feature of a legal order that individuals are at liberty to act as they wish unless the law prohibits it: "Modern law as a whole implements the principle that whatever is not explicitly prohibited is permitted."[8] That is, individuals are to be free specifically from coercive collective power unless it is used to enforce valid law.

I do not propose to focus on these claims about what is ingredient in the rule of law as such, although I do want to draw attention to two limitations of the scheme of liberty that follows from the rule of law. First, the claim is not that legality as such—the very existence of a legal code—gives us a requirement of equality or a principle of equal subjective liberties, according to which each person is entitled to the same liberties as others. Instead, the existence of a legal code implies only that some individuals have some rights of private autonomy. Furthermore, the rights of private

---

7. I am not confident that I have the argument right. I draw particularly on discussions in Habermas, *Between Facts and Norms*, and "On the Internal Relation." I also have benefitted from discussions with Joshua Flaherty, Kenneth Baynes, and Oliver Gerstenberg.

8. See Habermas, "On the Internal Relation," 256.

autonomy that emerge from the principle that whatever is not prohibited is permitted are very weak in that there are no limits on what might be prohibited, or for what reasons.

Step 3. Next, moving from legality as such to legitimate law, we introduce a principle of legitimacy: The discourse principle, an interpretation of the idea of impartiality, according to which practical norms, whether legal or moral, are *legitimate* if and only if all possibly affected persons could agree to them as participants in rational discourses (107). This Principle explicates the claim to justifiability or rightness characteristic of the Janus-faced law as such, one face of which looks to legitimacy.

I say that "we introduce" this principle, but the claim is that the discourse principle explicates the claims to normative validity characteristic of the (Janus-faced) law as such. If that is right, then the discourse principle is law's own implicit standard of validity, and any implications that follow from applying the discourse principle to the legal medium are implicit elements of legality as such (although the connection between legality and those implications is not analytic).

Step 4. A legal code, which must establish some system of rights, can be approved by all affected parties (approved by them through rational discourses) only if that code assigns equal liberties to each person, which strengthens the assurance of personal autonomy; for only if the code incorporates this equal liberty principle can the addressees of the legal code also regard themselves as its authors:

> Norms appearing in the form of law entitle actors to exercise their rights or liberties. However, one cannot determine which of these laws are legitimate simply by looking at the *form* of individual rights. Only by bringing in the discourse principle can one show that *each person* is owed a right to the greatest possible measure of *equal* liberties that are mutually compatible. (123)

The precise argument for this claim about how the discourse principle (the requirement of impartiality) leads to equal liberties is not entirely clear, although the basic idea is familiar, at least since Hobbes's derivation of the second law of nature: Assuming that individuals are legitimately concerned to protect their own fundamental interests, we cannot expect universal agreement on the code unless it provides equal protection of personal liberty. Thus, if law as such implies a minimal order of liberty, legitimate law requires a stronger scheme of rights to liberty.

Step 5. To apply the discourse principle to law—using it to judge the acceptability of legal regulations—requires that law be available as a medium for collective regulation. But citizens can only apply the discourse principle to law if that same legal order already ensures their rights of public autonomy: That is, they can only judge whether those affected could consent after reasoned consideration if they have rights to reflect, to communicate, to associate, and to bring their judgments to bear on proposed regulation. So, we get a requirement of democracy, as the way in which the discourse principle is brought to bear on evaluating proposed laws.

Public autonomy, then, requires private autonomy because public autonomy requires a legal order, which order is legitimate only if it ensures equal liberties; and private requires public, because the legal regulation of private autonomy is legitimate only if it emerges from a discursive process that ensures political rights. Thus we have co-originality.

The equal liberty principle that comes with legitimate law only gives us the requirement that there be some system of equal liberties for all; it does not give determinate content to that system. In particular, specifically liberal rights—to conscience, bodily integrity, privacy, property, and so forth—do not emerge simply from the requirement that the legal code be specified through a process that satisfies the discourse principle but emerge instead (if they do) from the actual exercise of civic autonomy under particular historical conditions: basic rights "must be *interpreted* and *given concrete shape* by a political legislature in response to changing circumstances" (125). Such exercise—democratic process—"saturates" (ibid.) the otherwise abstract principle of equal subjective liberties and gives us a system of rights that can be understood as embodying the equal liberty principle. But, as comparative and historical reflection on constitutional democracies suggests, there may be many such systems.

So there is an important difference in status between specifically liberal rights (to conscience, and personal privacy) and the abstract principle of equal subjective liberties. Satisfying the equal liberty principle by establishing some determinate system of equal liberties is required for actual decision-making to be discursively democratic: Antecedent to any actual exercise of public autonomy, we can say that the system of rights adopted through democratic discourse, whatever its precise content, must ensure equal liberties. If it does not, then collective decision-making would not count as an application of the discourse principle to the law—just as the system of collective decision-making would not count as an application of the discourse principle to the law if it failed to ensure the political liberties necessary for public autonomy. In contrast, the specification of the concrete liberties—say, the liberal liberties—essentially involves actual discourse: The conjunction of legality and discourse simply does not yield a determinate system of private liberties, only the requirement that some system of equal private liberties for each must be adopted.

The argument for the constitutive status of the equal liberty principle is based, so to speak, on the theorist's or reflective person's own application of the discourse principle; put otherwise, it is based on hypothetical discourse rather than actual discourse. This, I believe, is the force of the idea that "private autonomy" is "at first abstractly posited" (121). We, as theorists or reflective citizens thinking about constitutional issues, ask what system of rights is normatively justified: What rights must citizens "accord one another if they want to legitimately regulate their common life by means of positive law" (82)? To answer this question, we ask what kind of system can be impartially justified; and we approach this issue by asking what system the addressees of the law could agree to under idealized conditions. We then argue, by appeal to the discourse principle, that they (or we) could only agree, with reason, to a system of equal liberties for all. Of course we may bring this argument to actual discourse. But the argument we would make is an argument about what idealized discourse would deliver, together with an argument to the effect that idealized discourse reconstructs our understandings of normative validity.

In contrast, the specification of the concrete liberties—say, the liberal liberties—essentially involves actual discourse through a democratic process. The conjunction of legality and discourse simply does not yield a determinate system of private liberties, but only the requirement that some system of equal private liberties for each must be adopted: "Specificity results inasmuch as the external perspective taken initially by the theorist is, in the course of elaboration, internalized in the system of rights" (122). So we know from the argument at Step 4 that if actual political decision-making does not yield a constitution that meets the equal liberty principle, then that decision-making is not suitably discursive: The argument at Step 4 shows that satisfying the equal liberty principle is constitutive of actual discursiveness. To underscore, I am not claiming that actual decision-making is discursive only if citizens already operate within a legal order that satisfies that principle of equal liberty, but that actual decision-making is discursive—an application of the discourse principle (as implicitly understood or explicitly articulated) only if participants endorse the equal liberty principle.

2.2. I am in general sympathy with this line of thought—with the idea that both forms of liberty are equally fundamental, the associated claim that personal liberties are constitutive of a process of legitimate lawmaking, and the idea that this constitutive role flows from the requirement (expressed in the requirement of discursive justification) that the addressees of the law must be able to see themselves as its authors.

Still, I have three concerns about (perhaps objections to) this line of argument: I am not sure why the legal form itself plays an essential role in the argument; I do not find the equal liberty principle itself compelling, as distinct from a principle that assigns special importance to basic or fundamental liberties; and—the point I propose to concentrate on here—I do not see how the discourse principle gives us equal liberties. The problem is that the discourse principle, which states, again, that practical norms are *legitimate* if and only if all possibly affected persons could agree to them as participants in rational discourses, appears to rely on a highly generic account of reasons—not an account restricted to political argument in a democracy of equal members. But with no restriction on what can count as a reason, and with the full panoply of pragmatic, ethical, and moral reasons in play in the relevant forms of discourse, it would seem that anything could come from discourse. If all we need is that all possibly affected persons could agree to them as participants in rational discourses, and there are no constraints on acceptable reasons, then what constrains the "discursive equilibrium" in the way that Habermas proposes?

2.3. Let me suggest, then, an alternative argument for the constitutive role of nonpolitical liberties, based on two central ideas: the idea of reasonable pluralism and a deliberative conception of political justification, framed by the fundamental democratic idea of citizens as free and equal.[9] Although these assumptions appear to be normatively more substantive than the notions of impartiality and Janus-faced legality that Habermas officially relies on, I do not think they (or similarly richer normative ideas) can be avoided in a successful case for liberties (and co-originality). I begin with the fact of reasonable pluralism: The fact that there are distinct

9. The discussion that follows draws on Joshua Cohen, "Democracy and Liberty," in Jon Elster, ed., *Deliberative Democracy* (Cambridge: Cambridge University Press, 1998), 185–231.

and incompatible philosophies of life to which people, who are reasonable politically speaking, are drawn under favorable conditions for the exercise of practical reason. By a *philosophy of life—what* Rawls calls a "comprehensive doctrine"—I mean an all-embracing view, religious or secular in foundation, liberal or traditionalist in substance, that includes an account of all ethical values and, crucially, provides a general guide to conduct, individual as well as collective. People are *reasonable, politically speaking,* only if they are concerned to live with others on terms that those others, understood as free and equal, can also reasonably accept: only if they accept what Rawls calls the "criterion of reciprocity."[10]

I say "reasonable, politically speaking," because the relevant notion of reasonableness is suited to political questions. Generically speaking, a reasonable person is someone who gives due attention to the considerations that bear on an issue—and who acts in light of that attention. So the notion of being reasonable, politically speaking, is a matter of giving due attention *to the facts about the political relation of citizens in a democracy*: the fact that political power is the collective power of citizens, understood as equals. The fact of reasonable pluralism, then, is that conscientious, good-faith efforts in the exercise of practical reason, by politically reasonable people (thus understood), do not converge on a particular philosophy of life—that such philosophies are matters on which (politically) reasonable people disagree.

A deliberative conception of democracy puts public reasoning at the center of political justification. According to the deliberative interpretation of democracy, then, democracy is a system of social and political arrangements that institutionally ties the exercise of collective power to free reasoning among equals. This conception of justification through public reasoning—the core of the deliberative democratic ideal—can be represented in an idealized procedure of political deliberation, constructed to capture the notions of free, equal, and reason that figure in the deliberative democratic ideal. The point of the idealized procedure is to provide a model characterization of free reasoning among equals, which can in turn serve as a model for arrangements of collective decision-making that are to establish a framework of free reasoning among equals. Using the model, we can work out the content of the deliberative democratic

10. See John Rawls, "The Idea of Public Reason Revisited," in *Collected Papers* (Cambridge, MA: Harvard University Press, 1999), 578.

ideal by considering features of public reasoning in the idealized case, and then aiming to build those features into institutions.

Thus, in an ideal deliberative procedure, participants are and regard one another as *free*: recognizing the fact of reasonable pluralism, the defining condition of participation or a test of the acceptability of arguments in support of the exercise of political power. To represent participants as free is not to say that their philosophy of life is, morally or metaphysically speaking, a matter of choice. To someone who has a religious view and takes God's laws as the touchstone of morality, for example, believing the view is a matter of believing what is true and acting on it a matter of fulfilling obligations that are not self-legislated and are perhaps more fundamental than political obligations. But politically speaking, citizens are free in that it is open to them to accept or reject such views without loss of status.

Moreover, participants regard one another as formally and substantively *equal*. They are formally equal in that the rules regulating the ideal procedure do not single out individuals for special advantage or disadvantage. Instead, everyone with deliberative capacities—which is to say, more or less all human beings—has and is recognized as having equal standing at each of the stages of the deliberative process. Each, that is, can propose issues for the agenda, propose solutions to the issues on the agenda, offer reasons in support of or in criticism of proposed solutions. And each has an equal voice in the decision. The participants are substantively equal in that the existing distribution of power and resources does not shape their chances to contribute to deliberation.

In addition, they are *reasonable* in that they aim to defend and criticize institutions and programs in terms of considerations that others, as free and equal, have *reason to accept*, given the fact of reasonable pluralism and on the assumption that those others are themselves reasonable.

2.4. Which considerations count as reasons? Generically speaking a reason is a consideration that counts in favor of something: in particular, a belief, or an action. That is not meant to be illuminating analysis of the concept of a reason: I doubt that illuminating analysis is available, or that it would be helpful in answering our question. What is needed is not an account of what a reason is but of which considerations count as reasons. And the answer to this question depends on context. Whether considerations count in favor in the relevant way depends on the setting in which they are advanced. Applying this point to the issue at hand: A suitable account of which considerations count as reasons for the purposes of an account of democratic deliberation will not take the form of a generic account of what a reason is, but rather a statement of which considerations count in favor of proposals within a deliberative setting suited to the case of free association among equals, understood to include an acknowledgment of reasonable pluralism. This background is reflected in the kinds of reasons that will be acceptable: meaning, as always, acceptable to individuals as free and equal citizens.

I have specified the relevant deliberative setting as one in which people are understood as free, equal, and politically reasonable, and as having conflicting, reasonable philosophies of life. Under these conditions—within the idealized deliberative setting that captures them—it will not do simply to advance considerations that one takes to be true or compelling. For such considerations may well be rejected by others who are themselves reasonable—in being prepared to live with others on terms that are acceptable to those others, given their different comprehensive views—and endorse conflicting comprehensive views. One needs instead to find reasons that are compelling to others, where those others are regarded as (and regard themselves as) equals with conflicting reasonable commitments. Considerations that do not meet these tests will be rejected in the idealized setting and so do not count as acceptable or sufficient political reasons. Let us say then that a consideration is an acceptable political reason just in case it has the support of the different comprehensive views endorsed by reasonable citizens.

2.5. These observations about reasonable pluralism, and the role of background understandings of citizens as free, equal, and reasonable in constraining the set of political reasons—thus giving content to democracy's public reason—play an important role in understanding the essential role of nonpolitical liberties within the account of democracy.

First, people hold some of their commitments—for example, religious commitments—on faith, and those commitments impose what they take to be overriding obligations. Such commitments are not, as such, unreasonable. To be sure, faith transcends reason, even as "reason" is understood within the tradition to which the commitments belong. Still, beliefs held on faith—perhaps beliefs in what are understood to be revealed truths—are not as such unreasonable. But such beliefs can reasonably be rejected by others, who rely on the darkness of an unconverted heart. So they cannot serve to justify legislation. And the fact that they cannot will impose pressure for personal liberties—say, religious, expressive, and moral liberty.

Second, acceptable considerations will have different weights in political justification. And the weight will depend on the nature of the regulated conduct, in particular the weight of the reasons that support the conduct. Take considerations of public order, for example. They provide acceptable reasons for regulating conduct. Different views have different ways of explaining the value of public order: utilitarians will found it on considerations of aggregate happiness, Kantians on the social preconditions of autonomous conduct, others on the intrinsic value of human life and human sociability. Moreover, people are bound to disagree about what public order requires. But it will not be acceptable to suppose that, as a general matter, the value of public order transcends all other political values. Except perhaps in the most extreme circumstances, for example, a state may not impose a blanket prohibition on alcohol consumption—including consumption in religious services—in the name of public order. The reasons that support such consumption include considerations of religious obligation— more generally, considerations of fundamental obligation, which are normally overriding—that will provide a suitable basis for rejecting a justification cast in terms of the value of public order, except in the most extreme conditions. To be sure, not all citizens acknowledge the obligations in question. But even those who do not can see the weightiness of those reasons, within the outlooks of other politically reasonable citizens.

As these two observations indicate, pressure for liberty comes from at least two sources. The pluralism of philosophies of life among politically reasonable citizens leads to the rejection of some bases of restriction as politically weightless; other bases of restriction will not be weightless, but they will be insufficient to outweigh the reasons that can be acknowledged, consistent with reasonable pluralism, as commending or commanding conduct. Taking these two considerations together, we have the basis for a strong case for religious, moral, and nonpolitical expressive liberties. Conduct in these areas is supported by strong (perhaps compelling) reasons, as when religious exercise is a matter of obligation according to a person's reasonable religious outlook. Moreover, standard reasons for restriction—religious and sectarian moral reasons—will often be weightless.

Given this deliberative rationale for personal liberties, we can see why their protection would be constitutive of democracy, and how, therefore, we get co-originality. For imposing regulations in the name of reasons that are either weightless or of insufficient force to override reasonable demands is a violation of the fundamental democratic idea that the authorization to exercise state power must arise from the *collective decisions* of the equal members of a society who are governed by that power—that it must be supported by reasons that can be shared by the set of politically reasonable citizens over whom power is exercised. Decisions to regulate are not suitably collective, for the addressees of the regulations cannot all be included in their collective authorization.

3. Discursive Democracy

3.1. Habermas' conception of discursive democracy provides an idealized, normative account of democratic process. Set within a constitutional order that protects personal and political liberties, discursive democracy ties together two elements or "tracks" of a process of collective decision-making: the informal discussion of issues in an unorganized, "wild," decentered (not centrally coordinated) public sphere that does not make authoritative collective decisions, and a more formal political process, including elections and legislative decision-making, as well as the conduct of agencies and courts. In the formal process, candidates and elected legislators deliberate about issues, make authoritative decisions by translating the opinions formed in the informal sphere into legal regulations, and monitor the execution of those decisions by administrative bodies. Whereas discourse in the public sphere is open-ended, the decision-making procedures are subject to conditions of deliberative-democratic legitimacy: for example, that decisions are to be founded on reasons; that the processes are to be open and fair; that they are to be free of coercion; and that results are to be determined by the better argument (305–306).

This discursive model of democratic process appears to be founded on a hypothesis about the connection between idealized discourse and actual democratic decision-making (understood as proceeding along both tracks). The central idea is that "democratic procedures should produce rational outcomes"—where rational outcomes are those that would emerge from idealized discourse. Suppose, then, that we think of collective decision-making as a form of problem solving: "The production of legitimate law through deliberative politics represents a problem-solving procedure that needs and assimilates knowledge in order to program the regulation of conflicts and the pursuit of collective goals" (318). Then, a discursively democratic process of decision-making provides grounds for expecting reasonable solutions to problems:

> The democratic procedure is institutionalized in discourses and bargaining processes (assumed to be fair) by employing forms of communication that promise that all outcomes reached in conformity with the procedure are reasonable. . . . Deliberative politics acquires its legitimating force from the discursive structure of an opinion- and will-formation that can fulfill its socially integrative function only because citizens expects its results to have a reasonable quality. (304, 296)

More generally,

> democratic procedure makes it possible for issues and contributions, information and reasons to float freely; it secures a discursive character for political will-formation; and it thereby secures that fallibilist assumption that results issuing from proper procedure are more or less reasonable. (448)

In achieving such reasonable results, the two tracks of deliberative politics play distinct roles, which correspond to different stages in an idealized process of problem solving. Informal communication in the public sphere provides a close-to-the-ground and unregulated arena for detecting new problems, bringing them to public view in a nonspecialized language, and suggesting ways to address those problems. Because information is not controlled and communication is unrestricted, "new problem situations can be perceived more sensitively" (308). Thus "the communicative structures of the public sphere constitute a far-flung network of sensors that react to the pressure of society-wide problems and stimulate influential opinions" (300). It is founded on a network of associations that "specialize . . in discovering issues relevant for all society, contributing possible solutions to problems, interpreting values, producing good reasons, and invalidating others" (485).

Formal political processes—elections, legislatures, agencies, and courts—provide the second stage in an idealized problem-solving system. They provide institutionally regulated ways to assess ideas: to deliberate about better proposals under fair conditions, evaluate alternative solutions, and make authoritative decisions after due consideration. So on the second, institutional track we have a disciplined testing through reason of proposals that emerge from open-ended public discussion:

> The operative meaning of these regulations consists less in discovering and identifying problems than in dealing with them; it has less to do with becoming sensitive to new ways of looking at problems than with justifying the selection of a problem making and the choice among competing proposals for solving it. The publics of parliamentary bodies are structured predominantly as a *context of justification*. These bodies rely not only on the administration's preparatory work and further processing but also on the *context of discovery* provided by a procedurally unregulated public sphere that is borne by the general public of citizens. (307)

Thus the case for the two-track process is founded on the claim that it will generate rational outcomes. And that claim is based on the interplay in discursive democracy between an open-ended exploration of problems and possible solutions, which "influences the premises of judgment and decision-making in the political system,"[11] and a disciplined, rational assessment of proposed solutions. This interplay between discovery and justification supports the presumption that the results will conform to idealized, discursive problem solving. Because the two phases of reasoning in the actual process conform to idealized reasoning, the actual process will generate results like those that idealized discourse would generate:

> Thus the normative expectation of rational outcomes is grounded ultimately in the interplay between institutionally structured political will-formation and spontaneous, unsubverted circuits of communication in a public sphere that is not programmed to reach decisions and thus is not organized.[12]

Thus Habermas interprets popular sovereignty procedurally, as the possible influence on authoritative political decisions of public discourses in an autonomous communicative network, rather than as the direct control of legislation by a determinate and coherent popular will. The two-track

11. See Habermas, "Popular Sovereignty as Procedure," 486–487.
12. Ibid., 485.

idea thus identifies a way to make the authorship of the terms and conditions of political association by free, equal, reasonable citizens compatible with the modern organization of social and political power.[13] Think of the achievement this way: Habermas has shown that the pluralist critique of sovereignty and of a state-centered conception of politics, and associated insights about the importance of social organization in modern democracy (about the social bases of democratic governance), can be freed from the pluralists' own theory of politics as bargaining between and among groups that represent well-defined interests. Those insights can be wedded instead to a conception of politics in which reasoning about the basic terms of association plays a central role. But the marriage requires the idea of the informal, discursive public sphere, in which all can freely participate, and which has the capacity to influence opinion through argument and thereby shape the agenda of formal politics. This strikes me as a fundamental contribution to democratic thought: a remarkable reconception, with redemptive promise.

3.2. So much for Habermas' view. Now I come to the pair of questions I identified earlier: Why should democracy be deliberative? And why should deliberation be democratic?

First, then, why is it important for democracy to be deliberative? Why should collective decision-making involve the giving of reasons of suitable kinds, rather than simply a fair aggregation of citizen interests? One rationale, already suggested, arises from concerns about the impartial justifiability of (or, as Habermas puts it, the rationality of) outcomes: the concern captured in Habermas' discourse principle. Suppose we have a hypothetical test of validity: Outcomes are justified only if they could be accepted by people who give suitable weight to the reasonable objections of others, assuming those others to be free and equal. Deliberative democracy, then, may seem a natural way to achieve such impartially justified outcomes. For it is a form of democracy that aims to mirror hypothetical conditions of good information, attentiveness to reasons, and regard for others as equals by requiring, in particular, that the exercise of power be justified by appeal to considerations that others acknowledge as reasons, and assuming a shared commitment to such justification. Bargaining un-

13. See Jürgen Habermas, "Three Normative Models of Democracy," in *The Inclusion of the Other*, 251, on popular sovereignty as consisting in "interactions between legally institutionalized will-formation and culturally mobilized publics."

der fair background conditions may also produce rational outcomes, but deliberation generates a stronger presumption because it requires attentiveness to reasons.

Rawls suggests this thought about the relationship between a hypothetical-contractual notion of justice and actual political decision-making when he remarks that his principle of participation—requiring fair political equality—transfers the requirement of equal standing that defines the original position into the design of the constitution of a political society: we have an effective political procedure that "mirrors" the "fair representation of persons in the original position."[14] Deliberative democracy might be seen as giving this idea of connecting contractual and actual a "Scanlonian" twist. Scanlon's contractualism presents an idealized model of moral reasoning rather suggesting that rational choice under conditions of ignorance can provide a substitute for such reasoning.[15] Correspondingly, then, instead of merely transferring a requirement of equal standing or fair representation, deliberative democracy institutionalizes the concern for justifiability to others from their standpoint that defines Scanlon's ideal contractualism, moving that concern from the contractual to the actual, and applying it to the special case of binding collective choice.

Brian Barry has a very illuminating discussion of this idea.[16] He considers what he calls the "circumstances of impartiality": the social-political conditions that "approximate those of a Scanlonian original position." Borrowing this term, then, we might think of deliberative democracy as an essential part of the circumstances of impartiality. The idea is that if we wish to realize impartial justice—say, to satisfy Habermas' discourse principle—then we must embrace in our actual collective decision-making a commitment to mutual reason-giving (and institutional conditions that express and sustain that commitment) of a kind that approximates the idealized practice of mutual reason-giving that determines the requirements of justice.

Put simply, impartial justice must, arguably, be aimed at in order to be achieved; and here, "aiming" at it means approximating its procedures. If

14. See John Rawls, *Political Liberalism* (New York: Columbia University Press, 1993), 330.
15. See Thomas M. Scanlon, *What We Owe to Each Other* (Cambridge, MA: Harvard University Press, 1998), chap. 5.
16. See Brian Barry, *Justice as Impartiality* (Oxford: Oxford University Press, 1995), sec. 16, p. 100.

the requirements of justice are fixed by a kind of impartial reasoning under hypothetical conditions, then, even if we do not know what would be agreed to, we will, arguably, only achieve the requirements of justice— the outcomes that could or would be agreed to—if we make collective decisions using our best actual approximations to impartial reasoning. We cannot simply trust the achievement of justice to the pursuit of interests even under ideally fair conditions, for those fair conditions themselves are likely to erode without a commitment to democratically deliberative decision-making.

I think this argument has much to be said for it, and it seems to be Habermas' idea about the relationship between the standard of justification stated in the discourse principle and deliberative-democratic practice:

> The democratic procedure is institutionalized in discourses and bargaining processes (assumed to be fair) by employing forms of communication that promise that all outcomes reached in conformity with the procedure are reasonable. . . . Deliberative politics acquires its legitimating force from the discursive structure of an opinion- and will-formation that can fulfill its socially integrative function only because citizens expect its results to have a reasonable quality. (304; see also 296, 448)

They have such expectation because actual decision-making, under the conditions of the discursive model, approximates (in ways noted earlier) idealized deliberation. Still, the case for the importance of deliberation need not proceed solely in terms of the requirements on a system of collective decision-making that is to match the results that would be achieved were decision-making to be ideally deliberative. The virtues of the deliberative view are also more intrinsic, and are allied closely with its conception of binding collective choice, in particular with the role in that conception of the idea of reasons acceptable to others whose conduct is governed by those choices, and who themselves have reasonable views. By emphasizing the importance of reasons acceptable to all citizens, the deliberative view expresses an especially compelling picture of the possible relations among people within a democratic order; moreover, it states a forceful ideal of political legitimacy for a democracy. I take up these two points in turn.

First, the deliberative conception offers a forceful rendering of the fundamental democratic idea—the idea that decisions about the exercise of state power are *collective*. It requires that we offer considerations that others whose conduct will be governed by the decisions, and who are understood to be free, equal, and reasonable, can accept, not simply that we count their interests, while keeping our fingers crossed that those interests are out-weighed. The idea of popular authorization is reflected not only in the processes of decision-making but in the form—and as we have seen, the content—of political reason itself.

This point about the attractions of the deliberative interpretation of collective decisions can be stated in terms of ideas of *political autonomy* and *political community*. If a political community is a group of people sharing a comprehensive moral or religious view, or a substantive national identity defined in terms of such a view, then reasonable pluralism ruins the possibility of political community. But an alternative conception of political community connects the deliberative view to the value of community. To see how, notice first that by requiring justification on terms acceptable to others, deliberative democracy provides for a form of political autonomy. Without denying the coercive aspects of common political life, it requires that all who are governed by collective decisions—who are expected to govern their own conduct by those decisions—must find the political values that provide the *bases* of those decisions acceptable, even when they disagree with the details of the decision.

Through this assurance of political autonomy, deliberative democracy achieves one important element of the ideal of community. This is not because collective decisions crystallize a shared ethical outlook that informs all social life generally, nor because the collective good takes precedence over liberties of members. Rather, deliberative democracy is connected to political community because the requirement of providing reasons for the exercise of political power that are compelling to those who are governed by it itself expresses the full and equal membership of all in the sovereign body responsible for authorizing the exercise of that power and establishes the common reason and will of that body.

Second, the deliberative conception of democracy also presents an account of when decisions made in a democracy are politically legitimate and how to shape institutions and forms of argument so as to make legitimate decisions.

Generally speaking, we have a strong case for political legitimacy when the exercise of political power has sufficient justification. But, as a conceptual matter, a person can believe that the exercise of power is well justified—

therefore legitimate—while also acknowledging that others over whom it is exercised reject the justification. As a conceptual matter, legitimacy does not require that the relevant justification be acknowledged as such by those who are subject to the legitimate power: there need be no justification *to* them. But the background of democracy—the idea of citizens as free and equal—and the fact of reasonable pluralism are important in characterizing a more limited conception of justification: because of these conditions, the relevant justification must be addressed to citizens, by which I mean that its terms must be acknowledged as suitable by those subject to political power. Given that citizens have equal standing and are understood as free, and given the fact of reasonable pluralism, we have an especially strong showing of legitimacy when the exercise of state power is supported by considerations acknowledged as reasons by the different views endorsed by reasonable citizens, who are understood as equals: no other account of reasons is suited for this case. The deliberative conception articulates an account of political legitimacy suited to democratic conditions, and through the ideal deliberative procedure, it aims to specify the content of those conditions.

3.3. Having considered why democracy should be deliberative, I turn now to the second question: Why should deliberation be democratic? Assume, *arguendo*, that the discourse principle can only be satisfied by deliberative decision-making. Still, we need to ask why deliberative political decision-making needs to be democratic—to satisfy the principle of political equality, with its guarantees of universal political rights. The mere fact that the outcomes are to match those that could be accepted by all under idealized conditions does not seem to lead to this conclusion: not, anyway, without further argument. It might be argued that an ideal deliberative procedure is best institutionalized by ensuring well-conducted political debate among elites, which enables citizens to make informed choices among them and the alternatives they represent. Why does a deliberative view such as Habermas' require equal political liberties? How does it connect to concerns about participation and political equality? Why, in short, does the discourse principle become the democratic principle, once it assumes legal shape?

I am not sure that I understand Habermas' answer to this question. In at least one place, he notes that his view has a "dogmatic core" in its commitment to an "idea of autonomy according to which human beings act as free subjects only insofar as they obey just those laws they give themselves in accordance with insights they have acquired intersubjectively."[17] A different line of thought, that does not depend on this normative understanding of autonomy, runs parallel to the argument about why democracy needs to be deliberative. Here the idea would be that the best way to determine what would be agreed to by all in idealized discourse is to see what is actually agreed to in actual democratic discourse, in which all have a right to participate. All we need to get this result is to add a non- normative assumption about personal autonomy, for example, the thesis that individuals are the best judges and most vigilant defenders of the interests and concerns that they would have in idealized deliberation: "Nothing better prevents others from perspectivally distorting one's own interests than actual participation. It is in this pragmatic sense that the individual is the last court of appeal for judging what is in his best interest."[18] A third argument is that equal political liberties are required because that is what applying the discourse principle implies: no democracy, no rational approval in idealized discourse (127).

Here, again, I think the first two points have some force, but that the bridge between an idealized account of political justification and actual democracy could be strengthened—and freed from a philosophy of life that assumes the supreme value of autonomy and from the empirical assumption of autonomy—by developing the third. And that means presenting a more explicit account of the nature of idealized justification and the kinds of reasons suited to it, given the background ideas of reasonable pluralism and members as free and equal. In particular, three considerations are important in an account of why deliberation should be democratic.

First, if we assume the equal liberty principle (or some analog to it, requiring personal liberties), the deliberative view can appeal to traditional *instrumental* reasons in support of institutions that ensure equal political rights. In particular, such rights provide the means for protecting other basic rights—for example, those that are protected under the equal liberty principle. Although such instrumental reasons are not the sole basis for equal political rights, part of the case for them turns on their protective role.

A second consideration turns on the issue of acceptable reasons. Consider conventional, historical justifications for exclusions from or inequalities of political rights. Those justifications—whether of formal exclusion or unequally weighted votes—have typically been based on considerations about

17. See Habermas, *Between Facts and Norms*, 446.
18. See Habermas, "Discourse Ethics," 67.

racial, gender, ethnic, or religious differences. But such considerations will not provide acceptable reasons in public deliberation, given the background conception of members as free and equal, and so arrangements of collective decision-making cannot be justified by reference to them.

The third consideration is analogous to a central point that figured in the case for private liberties. A characteristic feature of different philosophies of life is that they each give us strong reasons for seeking to shape our political-social environment: for exercising responsible judgment about the proper conduct of collective life. The theories underlying those reasons cover a wide range: Aristotelian views about the central role of civic engagement in a flourishing human life; Rousseauean claims about the connection between realizing the personal autonomy that is essential to human nature and political participation in a democratic polity; and views, founded on religious convictions, about the commanding personal responsibility to ensure social justice and the corresponding personal sin of failing in that responsibility. Common ground among these competing, reasonable philosophies is that citizens sometimes have substantial, sometimes compelling reasons for addressing public affairs and, therefore, a fundamental interest in favorable conditions for forming judgments about the proper directions of policy, and acting on their judgments.

The failure to acknowledge the weight of those reasons for the agent and to acknowledge the claims to political opportunities that emerge from them reflects a failure to respect the background idea of citizens as equals. We acknowledge the weight of these reasons in part by embracing equal rights of participation.

3.4. In my remarks about both personal liberty and democracy, I have been emphasizing in effect that we need to build into the actual process of political decision-making the conclusions of idealized, hypothetical deliberation, where the idealizations arguably articulate and organize ordinary understandings of acceptable political argument, under democratic conditions. Habermas might object that I am not giving suitable weight to actual deliberation. He says: "The justification of norms and commands requires that a real discourse be carried out and this cannot occur . . . in the form of a hypothetical process of argumentation occurring in the individual mind."[19]

19. Ibid., 68.

Here, I want in part to agree. It is not sufficient for political justification that outcomes be rationalizable—that the deliberative process issue in decisions for which appropriate reasons could be cited, and that it be left to another institution, say, a court, to determine whether that condition is met. Outcomes in a deliberative democracy are to be arrived at through discussion in which reasons of the appropriate kind are given by participants. Four considerations support the importance of actual deliberation:

1. Although deliberative justifiability itself is important, it must—as the Barry–Habermas argument about the circumstances of impartiality suggests—be aimed at to be achieved; that is, it will not in general be true that results achieved through a process of exchange or bargaining (under fair conditions), or outcomes that reflect a balance of power, will be defensible by reasons of an appropriate kind. So requiring actual deliberation helps to establish a presumption that results can be defended through reasons and thus a presumptive legitimacy for outcomes of collective decision-making.

2. Offering reasons to others expresses respect for them as equal members of a deliberative body. So actual deliberation plausibly helps to foster mutual respect, which in turn encourages citizens to confine the exercise of power as the deliberative idea requires. No similar result can be expected if we assign the job of assessing the justifiability of outcomes to a separate institution.

3. Actual deliberation is a way to acquire and master fundamental political principles and their rationale by drawing on those principles and having to defend them in open argument. The fact that the principles can be defended in hypothetical discourse of course does not suffice for their understanding or motivational impact.

4. In actual reason-giving, citizens are required to defend proposals by reference to considerations that others acknowledge as reasons and not simply by reference to their own interests. To the extent that such public reasoning shapes preferences, conflicts over policy will be reduced, as will inclinations to strategically misrepresent circumstances. A crucial point here is that the extent of preference diversity is not fixed, not given prior to political deliberation. Not that the *aim* of such deliberation is to change citizen preferences by reducing their diversity: The aim is to make collective decisions. Still, one thought behind a deliberative conception is that public *reasoning* itself can

help to reduce the diversity of politically relevant preferences because such preferences are shaped and even formed in the process of public reasoning itself. And if public reasoning does help to reduce that diversity, then it mitigates tendencies to distortion even in strategic communication.

So actual deliberation is important. But an account of democracy as the source of legitimate law must give some account of what the relevant democratic background is, such that deliberation under democratic conditions, thus specified, results in legitimate law. And we cannot simply say that the correct specification of those legitimacy-establishing conditions is itself to be the product of actual democratic deliberation, because we need an account of the conditions that make deliberation democratic and that make democracy deliberative. To be sure, the account of those conditions may receive support from actual deliberation, as citizens master its principles and the reasons for them; indeed, if they do not achieve such mastery and understanding, if the ideal is not actualized in the reflective political thought of citizens, there may well be problems about democratic stability. So actual deliberation can (perhaps must) renew the constitutive conditions of a democratic process of legitimate lawmaking. But it cannot bear the full weight of specifying those conditions.

4. Problem of Possibility

4.1. Finally, I come to Habermas' answer to the question of how radical democracy is possible.[20] Given the realities of social and political power, how is the abstract ideal of "a self-organizing community of free and equal citizens," coordinating their collective affairs through their common reason, of practical relevance? Habermas' answer draws on the two-track discursive model.

The two-track model indicates how (communicative) power might flow from citizens, reasoning in a dispersed network, through a deliberative legislature, to administration. But this flow from dispersed publics to administrative implementation is threatened by the control, perhaps manipulation, of formal and informal public discussion by organized social power and political agencies (including parties and interest groups) with

20. This section draws substantially from Cohen and Sabel, "Directly-Deliberative Polyarchy."

interests and modes of argument fixed independently from the concerns and opinions of freely communicating citizens. The possibility of the proper flow, in turn, is founded on the capacity of associations in the informal, unspecialized public sphere autonomously to identify issues and concerns, including "encompassing social problems" (365), that lie outside the agenda of formal politics, bring those issues and concerns to wider public attention, propose solutions to them, and, by moving public opinion, influence the operations of the formal political system.

The key is "autonomously" (375, 484). The discovery, articulation, and exploration of concerns, as well as the formulation on new understandings of reasonable practice, must not itself be subject to the initiation or subsequent control of organized political or social powers, with their specialized interests, routines, and vocabularies. Only when initiative and subsequent organized influence on legislative and administrative power come from outside institutionalized, routinized power—only if it breaks free from the "unofficial circulation of this unlegitimated power" (328)—can we say that the flow of power moves from equal citizens, through law, to administration (380). And if it can, then democracy is possible, despite the realities of organized social and administrative power.

The requirement of outside initiative strikes me as ill-conceived: Lots of political movements are initially provoked by developments internal to conventional institutions and actors—for example, by competition between and among elites who mobilize popular support with the expectation that that mobilization can be controlled—even though the subsequent evolution of those movements proceeds independently; when it comes to popular movements, genesis is not identity. But this is largely a matter of detail—although it does underscore the difficulties of giving empirical content to the relevant notion of "autonomy."

My larger concern with Habermas' answer to the possibility problem begins from the observation that this answer is, as Frank Michelman has put it, "a dispiriting meltdown of popular sovereignty."[21] On Habermas' account, radical democracy is possible largely because of the sporadic bursts of energy by social movements that, in their role as dispersed sensors, detect popular concerns that are off the public agenda, suggest novel

21. See Frank Michelman, "Democracy and Positive Liberty," *Boston Review* 21 (1996): 3–8.

solutions to them, and perhaps influence legislation (and ultimately administration). To demonstrate that possibility, it suffices to show that *"under certain circumstances* civil society can acquire influence in the public sphere, have an effect on the parliamentary complex, . . . and compel the political system to switch over to the official circulation of power"(373). And to make this case, it suffices to show that "in a perceived crisis situation, the actors in civil society . . . can assume a surprisingly active and momentous role" (380).

In saying that this conclusion is—to use Michelman's word—dispiriting, I do not disparage at all the "momentous role" of the social movements— for example, feminist and environmental—that Habermas here has in mind (381). But the argument does make democracy, as reconceived, foreign to the settled institutional routines of a modern polity. Except for the exceptional conditions in which associations break free from the institutionalized circuit of power, so to speak, the system rules: a reconception with limited redemptive force.[22]

Before we continue further, a qualification is in order. The conclusions we should draw from Habermas' account of democratic possibility—how dispiriting we should find it—depend on which of two purposes we assign to the argument. On one construction, the aim is simply to show that the "old-fashioned," radical-democratic ideal of a self-governing association of free and equal citizens—authors of the laws, not merely their addressees— still can connect to modern politics, thus turning back realist arguments for less demanding accounts of democracy. Interpreted this way, the argument succeeds, even if Habermas is only able to point to occasional disruptions of the normal routines of institutionalized power. The disruptions suffice as proof of possibility.

Suppose instead that the purpose of the two-track model, with its sharp distinction between free-floating discourse in a network of autonomous associations and institutional decision-making and exercise of power, is to identify democracy's most attractive possibilities. Then the view strikes me as less compelling. Perhaps because he is principally concerned with the issue of possibility, Habermas thinks it suffices to make the case for

22. In this respect, Habermas' view bears some resemblance to Bruce Ackerman's account of dualist democracy, with its distinction between normal and constitutional politics. See Bruce Ackerman, *We, The People: Foundations* (Cambridge, MA: Harvard University Press, 1991).

autonomous influence flowing from the periphery, under conditions of crisis. But once that case is on hand, we can ask whether there are other forms of citizen participation that would more fully achieve the radical democratic promise. Those forms would need to meet three conditions: They must permit and encourage inputs that reflect experiences and concerns that may not occupy the current agenda (sensors, rooted in local experience and information); they must provide disciplined assessment of proposals through deliberation that encompasses fundamental political values; and (here we go beyond Habermas' emphasis on social movements in periods of crisis), they must also provide more institutionalized, regularized occasions for citizen participation in collective decision-making (and perhaps, by so doing, improve the quality of discourse in the "informal public sphere"). In brief, they must be autonomous, deliberative, and institutional.

4.2. Sabel and I have recently suggested some ideas along these lines,[23] captured in the idea of a *directly-deliberative polyarchy*. The fundamental idea is to institutionalize direct problem solving by citizens and not simply to foster informal citizen discussion with promises of possible influence on the formal political arena. In directly-deliberative polyarchy, collective decisions are made through public deliberation in arenas open to citizens who use public services, or who are otherwise regulated by public decisions. But in deciding, those citizens must examine their own choices in the light of the relevant deliberations and experiences of others facing similar problems in comparable jurisdictions or subdivisions of government. Ideally, then, directly-deliberative polyarchy combines the advantages of local learning and self-government with the advantages (and discipline) of wider social learning and heightened political accountability that result when the outcomes of many concurrent experiments are pooled to permit public scrutiny of the effectiveness of strategies and leaders.

This conception is suggested by a range of political experiments, and reflection on how their separate energies might be combined.[24] Consider,

---

23. See Cohen and Sabel, "Directly-Deliberative Polyarchy."
24. For discussions of such experiments, see Tracey Meares and Dan Kahan, *Urgent Times*, ed. Joshua Cohen and Joel Rogers (Boston: Beacon Press, 1999); Daniel Luria and Joel Rogers, *Metro Futures*, ed. Joshua Cohen and Joel Rogers (Boston: Beacon Press, 1999); Deborah Meier, *Schooling a Democracy*, ed. Joshua Cohen and Joel Rogers (Boston: Beacon Press, 2000); and Charles Sabel, Archon Fung, and Brad Karkkainen, *Environmental Democracy*, ed. Joshua Cohen and Joel Rogers (Boston: Beacon Press, 2000).

for example, community policing: a strategy for enhancing public security that features a return of police officers to particular beats, regular discussions between them and organized bodies in the communities they are policing, and regular coordination between those bodies and agencies providing other services that bear on controlling crime. Or consider forms of school decentralization that—although they shrinking school size and permit parents to choose schools—also replace close controls by central bureaucracies with governance mechanisms in which teachers and parents play a central role. Or consider arrangements for local and regional economic development that include strong components of training and service provision and whose governance includes local community interests, service providers, representatives of more encompassing organizations, as well as local representatives of regional or national government.

These new arrangements are not conventionally public because, in solving problems, they operate autonomously from the dictates of legislatures or public agencies; they are not conventionally private in that they do exercise problem-solving powers, and their governance works through discussion among citizens rather than the assignment of ownership rights. Moreover, they are attractive because they appear to foster two fundamental democratic values—deliberation and direct citizen participation—while potentially offering advantages as problem solvers that programs conceived within the limits of conventional representative democracies do not.

Stated without much detail or nuance, the fundamental idea comprises the following three elements:

1. Local problem solving through directly-deliberative participation, which is well-suited to bringing the relevant local knowledge and values to bear in making decisions. Direct participation helps because participants can be assumed to have relevant information about the local contours of the problem and can relatively easily detect both deception by others and unintended consequences of past decisions. Deliberative participation helps because it encourages both the expression of differences in outlook and the provision of information more generally. The respect expressed through the mutual reason-giving that defines deliberation reinforces a commitment to such conversational norms as sincerity and to solving problems, rather than to strategic angling for advantage (perhaps by

providing misleading information). Furthermore, if preferences over outcomes themselves are shaped and even formed by discussion, and mutual reason-giving reduces disagreements among such preferences, then being truthful will also be good strategy.

2. An institutionalization of links among local units designed to address the narrowness commonly associated with localism—in particular, an institutionalization that requires separate deliberative units to consider their own proposals against benchmarks provided by other units. Because practical reasoning requires a search for best solutions, decision-makers need to explore alternatives to current practice. A natural place to look for promising alternatives—including alternatives previously unimagined in the local setting—is in the experience of units facing analogous problems. Thus alongside directly-deliberative decision-making we need deliberative coordination: deliberation among units of decision-making directed both to learning jointly from their several experiences and improving the institutional possibilities for such learning. Extending deliberation across units allows each group to see its viewpoints and proposals in light of alternatives articulated by the others: in effect, it ensures that the exercise of practical reason is both disciplined and imaginative.

3. Responsibility for ensuring that deliberation within and among units meets these conditions, vested ultimately in authorizing and monitoring agencies—legislatures, agencies, and courts. In contrast to the conventional "division of deliberative labor," this responsibility, under conditions of directly-deliberative polyarchy, is to be discharged by ensuring that the relevant decision-making bodies act deliberatively, not—so far as possible—by substituting for their decisions.

As this observation indicates (and as the term "polyarchy" is meant to signal), directly-deliberative polyarchy assumes the continued presence of the legislatures, courts, executives, and administrative agencies, controlled by officials chosen through free and fair elections, in which virtually all adults have rights to suffrage, office-holding, association, and expression, and face alternative, legally protected sources of information. Although the operation of these institutions and arrangements changes, they remain and continue to serve some of the political values with which they are conventionally associated: peaceful transitions of power, restraints on unbridled power, fair chances for effective influence over authoritative collective decisions, and opportunities to develop informed preferences.

The shift in the locus of problem solving, however, changes the operations and expectations of basic political institutions. Consider the role of legislatures. Directly-deliberative polyarchy is animated by a recognition of the limits on the capacity of legislatures to solve problems—either on their own or by delegating tasks to administrative agencies—despite the importance of solutions. The role of the legislature in directly-deliberative polyarchy is to empower and facilitate problem solving through directly-deliberative arenas operating in closer proximity than the legislature to the problem. More particularly, the idea is for legislatures to declare areas of policy (education, community safety, environmental health) as open to directly-deliberative polyarchic action; state general goals for policy in the area; assist potential deliberative arenas in organizing to achieve those goals; make resources available to deliberative problem-solving bodies that meet basic requirements on membership and benchmarking; and review at regular intervals the assignments of resources and responsibility.

This changed role for legislatures does not exclude national solutions through legislative enactment when uniform solutions are preferable (because of limited diversity among sites) or when externalities overwhelm local problem solving. Instead, the availability of alternative methods of problem solving imposes on legislatures a greater burden in justifying their own direct efforts: They must explicitly make the case that the benefits of those efforts suffice to overcome the advantages of direct-deliberative solutions.[25] Administrative agencies, in turn, provide the infrastructure for information exchange between and among units—the exchange required for bench-marking and continuous improvement. Instead of seeking to solve problems, the agencies see their task as reducing the costs of information faced by different problem solvers: helping them to determine which deliberative bodies are similarly situated, what projects those bodies are pursuing, and what modifications of those projects might be needed under local conditions.

25. For related discussions of federalism, see Stephen Gardbaum, "Rethinking Constitutional Federalism," *Texas Law Review* 74 (1996): 795–838, and the account of the "commandeering problem" in Michael Dorf and Charles Sabel, "Constitution of Democratic Experimentalism," *Columbia Law Review* 98, 2 (1998): 267–473.

4.3. This is the barest sketch of the idea of directly-deliberative polyarchy, but I hope it is clear even from the sketch that it offers a different redemptive project than we find in Habermas' response to the problem of possibility.

Here, I want to emphasize two points of difference, both focused on the conception of the public sphere. First, in directly-deliberative democracy (and, by extension, directly-deliberative polyarchy) the public arena is *organizationally dispersed* in that public opinion crystallizes not only in reference to the national legislature but also in the work of the local school governance committee, the community policing beat organization, and their analogs in areas such as the provision of services to firms or to distressed families. Nevertheless, the pieces of this dispersed public sphere are connected by the requirements of reason-giving, in particular the demand to respect basic constitutional values; the need for explicit comparison with other units that are themselves conducting similar comparisons; and a wider public debate informed by such comparisons and focused on national projects. In short, we do have a public sphere in directly-deliberative polyarchy: both because citizens participate in solving problems and because of the deliberative, reason-giving terms of that participation.

Second, and more fundamentally, the public arena is the place where practicality in the form of problem solving meets political principle in the form of deliberation through reason giving among free and equal citizens. In directly-deliberative polyarchy, with direct problem solving by groups of affected citizens, public deliberation cuts across the distinction between reflection on political purposes and efforts to address problems in light of those purposes. This marriage of principle and problem solving might have the effect of sharpening discussion in the informal public sphere; more immediately, it promises an effectiveness to public engagement that is absent from Habermas' account.

For Habermas, discussion within the "communicatively fluid" public sphere comprises all manner of topic and question and is guided by experiential concerns to which citizens themselves are attentive. So the dispersed network of communication that constitutes the public comes as close as can reasonably be hoped to a free community of equals, autonomously debating the terms of their collective life—as close as can be hoped, if we take as an assumption that the principal political, problem-solving institutions remain fixed in design and conception, and that citizens are to discuss encompassing political directions, and not solve problems. Inevitably, then, the capacity of the public's contributions to subsequently steer the state remain an open question. The freer the communication within the public, the greater clarification it can attain. But even the most radical extension and deepening of the public sphere will be of limited consequence precisely because the technical demands, to which administration, parliament, and party must respond, limit the direction that might issue from a more encompassing, unrestricted discussion among citizens: "Communicative power cannot supply a substitute for the systematic inner logic of public bureaucracies. Rather, it achieves an impact on this logic in a siege-like manner."[26] In the end, radical democracy on this conception serves more as a series of reminders—that human communication need not be narrowly technical, that unsolved problems remain outside the purview of conventional institutions—and a source of new ideas in periods of crisis, than a program to redirect the ensemble of institutions to ensure a controlling role for the communicative power of free and equal citizens. I see no compelling reason for that self-limitation: We should not confuse a proof of possibility with a redemption of promise.

26. See Jürgen Habermas, "Further Reflections on the Public Sphere," and "Popular Sovereignty as Procedure," 486.

8

A MATTER OF DEMOLITION?
SUSAN OKIN ON JUSTICE AND GENDER

Susan Okin and I last spoke in December 2003. We had an electronic
conversation, and it ended badly. Susan was angry with me, as I was
with her. She thought I was abusing power; I thought she was past stub-
born. Faced with rapidly diminishing returns to further communication,
I suggested that we renew our discussion when we could get back on a
more constructive footing. Susan did not respond. I interpreted the absence of response as an endorsement of the hopeful prospect of constructive future discussion. But that was it. A friendship of more than fifteen
years ended in a disturbing silence.

I take some consolation and comfort, then, from the fact that Susan
Okin left us with a substantial body of writing. Her writing makes it possible to continue a conversation with her, at least in an attenuated sense of
conversation, and at least about some common intellectual interests. Susan's voice—I am thinking of "voice" in that capacious sense that comprises both written and spoken words, both substance and intonation—
remains vivid for me, sufficiently vivid that I am able to continue to learn
from her, trying in imagination to occupy her sensibility, to see things as
she might have seen them, and to let those ways of seeing exercise the kind
of intellectual pressure on me that they did during the course of her life.

In that spirit, I would like to pick up a conversation that Susan Okin and
I had more than a dozen years ago. I had just published a long review of
Justice, Gender, and the Family.[1] The review, while generally very favorable,

I presented earlier drafts of this essay at the February 2005 Stanford conference in memory
of Susan Okin and at Stanford Law School. I am grateful for comments and suggestions from
Corey Brettschneider, Barbara Fried, Joseph Grundfest, Robert Reich, Deborah Rhode, and
Debra Satz.

1. See Joshua Cohen, "Okin on Justice, Gender, and Family," *Canadian Journal of Philosophy* 22, 2 (June 1992): 263–286.

also made some criticisms. After it appeared, I received a letter from Susan.[2] She was appreciative of the extended discussion, grateful for the praise, and prepared to acknowledge the force of one criticism. I had argued that two parts of her view were in some tension. The first, expressed in her analysis of "vulnerability by marriage,"[3] focused on the ways that gender inequalities in labor markets and families are mutually reinforcing parts of a single system. Simplifying a complicated terrain, the "dual-system" idea was that labor market inequalities make it rational for women to spend more time on family concerns, while gendered expectations about domesticity make it rational for women to devote less time and effort to the labor market. The second, a central theme running through *Justice, Gender, and the Family*, as well as through Okin's first book, *Women in Western Political Thought*,[4] identified domestic inequality as the "linchpin" in the gender system.[5] The dual-system analysis of mutual reinforcement, however, undermined the force of identifying domestic inequality as the linchpin—not because labor market inequality was really the linchpin, but because the system of mutually reinforcing disadvantage did not have or need a linchpin. In response, Okin agreed that the linchpin thesis may not have been doing any work.

But several of my criticisms struck her as misguided. She sketched some reasons; I was not convinced. But we never really explored the issues. That is what I would like to do here—with reduced confidence in my earlier convictions, but also with a little less preoccupation about who was right and who was wrong. Okin's central theme was that women and men are moral equals and that our normative political thought has not taken this point on board. My main concern is to appreciate more fully the ways in which that central theme shifts the terrain of political argument.

I will discuss the three points on which Okin expressed disquiet or disagreement with what I had written. Each point concerns an issue that loomed large in Susan Okin's work: the feminist method, the relationship between family and polity, and the public-private distinction.

---

2. I am reconstructing the letter from memory, but I am pretty confident that I have it more or less right.

3. *Justice, Gender, and the Family* (New York: Basic Books, 1989), chap. 7 (hereafter *JGF*).

4. Susan Moller Okin, *Women in Western Political Thought* (Princeton: Princeton University Press, 1979) (hereafter *WWPT*).

5. See, for example, *JGF*, 6.

1. Feminist Method

Susan Okin was not much interested in "method" (I share her limited enthusiasm for the subject). If she had a method, it was pretty straightforward. The idea was to consider a political-philosophical outlook, add to it the elementary feminist thesis—that women are "full human beings to whom a theory of social justice must apply"[6]—and then see whether the resulting combination combusts.

Okin believed that this method had some striking results. She thought that the elementary feminist thesis created troubles for an easy reconciliation of feminist and multiculturalist commitments by undermining a range of otherwise plausible-seeming proposals for group rights.[7] In *Justice, Gender, and the Family* she argued that some contemporary conceptions of justice—including libertarianism and some forms of communitarian theory—are "completely demolished"[8] when confronted with the moral equality of men and women expressed in the elementary feminist thesis. Now, if a conception of justice simply denied that women and men were moral equals, then the demolition born of that confrontation would be straightforward. But Okin had something else in mind, something deeper, more complicated, and addressed to views that do not reject the abstract principle that men and women are moral equals. Her reflections on libertarianism illustrate the point.

Okin's criticisms of libertarianism focus on Robert Nozick's possessive libertarianism.[9] I call it "possessive" because it assigned the notion of ownership a fundamental role in political argument, and it was founded in particular on the premise that persons are full proprietors of them-

---

6. Ibid., 23.

7. Joshua Cohen, Matthew Howard, and Martha Nussbaum, eds., *Is Multiculturalism Bad for Women?* (Princeton: Princeton University Press, 1999).

8. *JGF*, 23.

9. Robert Nozick, *Anarchy, State, and Utopia* (New York: Basic Books, 1974). Okin mentions that libertarianism "takes to extremes" the classical liberal ideas of Locke and Constant (*JGF*, 74); moreover, within the libertarian family, she distinguishes varieties that focus on property rights (Nozick and Ayn Rand) from other forms of libertarianism (*JGF*, 87–88). It is not clear, then, how and to what extent her criticisms of Nozick's possessive libertarianism were meant to generalize. For a forceful discussion and, I think, convincing discussion of the sharp distinction between classical liberalism and libertarianism, see Samuel Freeman, "Illiberal Libertarians: Why Libertarianism Is Not a Liberal View," *Philosophy and Public Affairs* 30, 2 (Spring 2001): 105–151.

selves: self-owners.[10] This view has been subjected to wide-ranging criticism, but Okin's objection was original. She claimed that, if one adds the elementary feminist thesis—that women are "full human beings to whom a theory of social justice must apply"—to possessive libertarianism, then possessive libertarianism degenerates into matriarchy and incoherence. To see how, consider a reconstruction of Okin's argument against Nozick:[11]

1. Each person fully owns him- or herself (libertarian premise 1).
2. A person's making something from materials that the person fully owns confers full ownership of the thing on the person who made it (libertarian premise 2).
3. I am a person (assumption).
4. I fully own myself (from 1, 3).
5. My mother is a person, within the meaning of premises 1 and 2 (applying the elementary feminist thesis).
6. My mother made me from materials that she fully owned (assumption).
7. My mother fully owns me (from 2, 5, 6).
8. But two people cannot fully own the same thing (definition of full ownership).
9. My mother does not own me (from 4, 8).
10. I do not own myself (from 7, 8).

Three points about this argument. First, to make it valid, a few details would need to be cleaned up, but it is close enough. Second, arguing over 6, although legitimate, will not help anyone.[12] Third, the argument does not, as Okin claims, give us "a bizarre combination of matriarchy and slavery": whereas 7 is matriarchy, we also have 9, which denies matriarchy. But never mind matriarchy. The view does look pretty incoherent, in fact, flat inconsistent. Moreover, the inconsistency does not arise because pos-

10. See Nozick, *Anarchy, State, and Utopia*, 171–172. I believe that G. A. Cohen was the first to identify the idea of self-ownership as the root idea in Nozick's libertarianism. See his *Self-Ownership, Freedom, and Equality* (Cambridge: Cambridge University Press, 1995), esp. chaps. 3, 6.

11. Here, I expand on the discussion in Cohen, "Okin on Justice, Gender, and Family," 274–275.

12. As Barbara Fried has reminded me, the assumption that birth mothers own genetic material is both obscure and highly controversial.

sessive libertarianism denies the elementary feminist thesis, but because possessive libertarianism accepts it.

The crucial idea in the argument is that possessive libertarianism is committed to 1 and 2. If we accept those moral premises, the only way to avoid inconsistency is to overlook 5. I say "overlook" because a possessive libertarian would not want to deny 5. Nozick in particular was simply not thinking about it: not thinking, in particular, that premises 1 and 2 apply to women, some of whom bear children. So we have a more or less perfect rendering of Okin's point: some theories are completely demolished—deriving an inconsistency from basic premises is a demolition job—once we attend to the commonly unattended but elementary feminist thesis.

The example is striking, but the obvious possessive libertarian reply is that the argument simply shows the need to restrict premise 2, which I will call the "modified Pottery Barn principle." The Pottery Barn principle says "you break it, you own it"; the modified Pottery Barn principle expressed in 2 says "you make it, you own it." The possessive libertarian, then, can call on a restricted version of the modified Pottery Barn principle, which says "you make it, you own it, except if you have made a person." Moreover, that restriction is well motivated. After all, the possessive libertarian story is that people own what they make with what they own *because* they own themselves: whatever the force of that "because," that is the theory. So self-ownership—expressed in the first libertarian premise—is the core idea: the modified Pottery Barn principle is not an independent principle but derived from the core idea. So we need to restrict the modified Pottery Barn principle so that it does not yield the ownership of other people; but that restriction is motivated by the basic self-ownership axiom. Put otherwise and more simply: only the restricted form of the modified Pottery Barn principle plausibly follows from the principle that people own themselves.

That is a slightly more elaborate version of what I said in my review, and it still strikes me as correct. I do not see that we have a demolition. So what might have bothered Susan Okin?

There are two possibilities.

Okin might have thought, first, that the possessive libertarian response almost facetiously exemplifies the very problem that she had labored so hard to expose. After all, doesn't it essentially say that the modified Pottery Barn principle applies to everyone, except women? Haven't we landed in the world of *Geduldig v. Aiello*, which denied that there was sex discrimination in a regulation that covered lots of medical disabilities but excluded pregnancy from its coverage?[13]

Not really. The response simply says that persons cannot be owned unless they are sold by themselves: that is the basic moral idea. Self-ownership supports the modified Pottery Barn principle only when it is thus qualified. Women and men own everything else that they make with what they own. But it is misguided to claim to own someone else who has the *very same claim to self-ownership that provides the basis of your claim to own that person*, unless the person has sold him- or herself to you (a sale that Nozick takes to be morally acceptable).

But a second and more forceful response is waiting in the wings. This second response does not rest everything on alleged troubles for the self-ownership principle generated by the childbearing experience of some women but treats that experience as the opening wedge in a broader argument about the moral significance of human relationships and the difficulty of using the category of ownership to capture the moral importance of those relationships. Consider me at age three. I was a person—a little person, but a person all the same. Still, I guess that I did not yet fully own myself. I could not make binding contracts, for example, or sell myself or parts of me. But my mother did not fully own me either: some sorts of treatment of me, even by her, were ruled out by my moral status. So, for example, on Nozick's view, it would have been fine for my mother, as full proprietor of her own person, to sell her eyes (fine, as in, had she contracted to do so, the contract would have been morally binding and the state ought to have enforced it). But it would have been wrong, impermissible, for her to sell my eyes. And that would have been wrong not because I owned myself and grabbing my eyes would have been a theft predicated on a trespass: as I said, at age three, I did not own myself, and no one else owned me either. So we need to say something about the moral relations between persons that cannot be fully explained by reference to the idea of self-ownership and the exercise of moral powers founded on self-ownership.[14]

---

13. *Geduldig v. Aiello*, 417 U.S. 484 (1974).

14. Of course, there are lots of powers that parents have over children: not to extract their eyes, but to require a safe medical procedure on their eyes. And there are large areas of reasonable controversy about the range of those powers. Moreover, some of the powers of parents will of course coincide with the powers that an owner would have (as some powers of an employer coincide with the more much expansive powers of a slaveowner). But the powers will not be as extensive as those that a Nozickian self-owner has over him- or herself. And once we agree that

And let's not stop here: it is not only that my mother should not have been peddling my eyes, or any other parts of me. She also owed me something more positive, say, appropriate care and concern, with attention to my health and, perhaps, as Locke supposed, some education.[15] Then, too, we might suppose that I owed something to my mother (and still do): some duty of respect, perhaps gratitude, maybe concern and support. But suppose I do owe something, in virtue of the concern and benefit conferred on me, the continuity of care over a long period, and not simply by virtue of the conferral of life (so the point applies to adopted children as well). Then we have a wider family of nonconsensual obligations, of nurturance and education, that cannot be explained in terms of self-ownership.

So we seem to have some kinds of moral relations, and it seems right to say that the relations bear on what we owe to one another (not only on what the humanly attractive qualities are). If one accepts that, then one agrees that we cannot fully account for the moral relations between and among persons by reference to considerations of self-ownership and the exercise of rights associated therewith. John Locke knew that. His natural law framework is founded on an overarching obligation to preserve humankind and provides a basis for obligations between parents and at least their biological offspring that cannot be accounted for in terms of the moral facts about equal freedom and consent that explain the obligations—in particular, the political obligations—owed to one another by free and equal adults.

The easy libertarian response is that these observations do not give us a demolition, but only show the need for an extension, that is, for supplementing the possessive libertarian's moral notions with an additional set of moral principles suited to the terrain of childbearing and childrearing. So the libertarian might say: "OK, I need to add something. I will get to that later. But what you say bears only on what I have not discussed. It has no bearing on my principal subject, which is the political morality of relations between and among adults." But maybe that response is not quite right. Maybe it is too quick.

---

the powers will be less extensive, we will make no headway in thinking about the proper range by using the idea of ownership as a basis for our reflections. On this last point, see Barbara Fried, "Left-Libertarianism: A Review Essay," *Philosophy and Public Affairs* 32, 1 (Winter 2004): 70–84.

15. John Locke, *Second Treatise*, ed. Peter Laslett (Cambridge: Cambridge University Press, 1988), para. 56.

To see why it might be too quick, consider two nonconsensual theories that are sometimes used to account for a range of social and political obligations: a theory based on the duty of fair play and a theory of "associative obligations." The first says, roughly, that when other people constrain their conduct to contribute to a cooperative activity, and that cooperative activity confers essential benefits on me (not simply any benefits at all, but those that are crucial to my having a minimally decent life), I have a duty to reciprocate by accepting corresponding constraints on my activity, even if I have not requested that the benefits be conferred nor volunteered to do a share of the work of providing them.

The second theory says, very roughly, that when I am a member of an association, and the other members of the association treat me with appropriate concern and respect, then I have an obligation to comply with the norms associated with my position or role in the association.[16] Ronald Dworkin advances this "associative theory" to account for a range of obligations, including—but not limited to—political obligations.

My concern here is not to argue the merits of these theories, understood in particular as accounts of political obligation. Suffice to say that they share the idea that political obligation is not founded on consent— more broadly, not voluntarily undertaken. The essential point here is that the plausibility of these views, as accounts of political obligation, depends on there being *some* relatively uncontroversial cases of nonvoluntary obligations that apply differently to different people. In particular, the plausibility of each theory—especially the associative—is enhanced by the case of familial obligations. But with these nonvoluntarist theories of obligation available—supported by, inter alia, the familial case and then extended to the political—the possessive libertarian now needs a more complicated story. Either the possessive libertarian needs to explain familial obligations—including the more positive obligations of nurturance and education—in terms of self-ownership (or the potential for such), or to explain why the fairness theory or the associative theory, which plausibly account for *some* obligations (namely, the familial), do not extend to the wider range of social and political obligations as well. The easy argument that familial obligations are simply a separate concern is too quick: there is a need to address the issue more directly.

16. See Ronald Dworkin, *Law's Empire* (Cambridge, MA: Harvard University Press, 1986), 195–202.

The possessive libertarian may have a good answer; he or she will certainly have something to say, and that something will likely include a crisp distinction between family and polity, an emphasis on the distinctiveness of political obligations, and an effort to cabin the nonconsensual. So we do not have a demolition: that was a mistake.

But philosophy does not work by demolition, and positions that can be dispatched so completely and so quickly were not worth the attention in the first place. Philosophy works in part by drawing attention to phenomena that people are overlooking and thereby shifting burdens of argument. But on this point about shifting burdens, I now think that Okin had an important point. I now see in retrospect that my proposed libertarian qualification of the modified Pottery Barn principle—that it does not apply to persons—was correct but superficial. The possessive libertarian can respond exactly as I suggested, but the libertarian cannot stop there: he or she now owes an account of nonconsensual familial obligations and then also an account of how to restrict the moral notions used to account for nonconsensual, particularistic, familial obligations so that they do not spread to a wider terrain of social and political obligations.

Whether that can be done is another matter: I will leave it to clever libertarians. But when one overlooks the elementary feminist thesis, one is less likely even to see the need to take this task on. And that is at least a version of Susan Okin's point.

2. Beyond Justice

A second point of disagreement that emerged in our communication after my review appeared is more complex, both as to its substance and as to the nature of the disagreement. But like the first, it began with my skepticism about a proposed demolition.

Susan Okin criticized a variety of views—Michael Sandel's in particular—for putting the family "beyond justice." It is not at all clear what it means to say (or therefore to deny) that the family is an arena beyond justice, any more than it was clear what Marx meant when he said that communist society lay beyond the "narrow horizon of bourgeois right."[17] It seemed clear to me (and still does) that there were interpretations of the idea of the family as an arena beyond justice that give romantic cover to abuse and privilege,

17. Karl Marx, "Critique of the Gotha Program," in *The Marx-Engels Reader*, 2nd ed., ed. Robert Tucker (New York: Norton, 1978), 531.

but also that there are interpretations that express something important about forms of human connection. And I supposed (as I still do) that some of the disagreement could be dispelled by fixing the interpretation.

Sandel seemed to think that if we say that principles of justice apply to the family then we are supposing something about, so to speak, the culture of family: that the members would openly and expressly aim to resolve their disagreements by explicit reference to, for example, Rawls's principles of justice. To say that the principles apply is to say that they are to enter in a fully explicit way into the domestic ethos. Thus we have the relevance of Sandel's claim that this appeal to abstract principles would only happen in a far-from-ideal family, ridden by conflict, whose members were not acting out of affection for one another but would only "dutifully if sullenly abide by the two principles of justice."[18] Whereas Sandel's point focused on Rawlsian principles, the force of the observation (like Marx's) seems to apply to other conceptions of justice as well: the point is about the (alleged) deficiencies of a social world in which people find it natural to make explicit appeals to abstract principles, to ideas about rights and about what we owe to each other. The point is about the form of justice and not only its content.

Okin, in contrast, seemed to be saying that, if one puts the family beyond justice, one is not making a point about how families are to make decisions about their own organization and allocation of resources but is instead denying that principles of justice have any bearing at all on our thought about the family. One is claiming that those principles do not, for example, provide appropriate standards for the framework of law and public policy within which families are set.

But if this interpretation is right, then they are talking past each other, and Okin is unnecessarily exaggerating the disagreement between the "beyond justice" view and her own emphasis on the priority of justice. I thought her view could be strengthened by accommodating what was plausible in the beyond-justice conception. My strategy of accommodation was to distinguish two deliberative standpoints, each associated with distinct norms, attitudes, and understandings: the standpoint of a citizen reflecting on the implications of domestic arrangements for issues of justice, and the standpoint of a person as a member of a family, who is thinking

18. Michael Sandel, *Liberalism and the Limits of Justice* (Cambridge: Cambridge University Press), 33.

about and discussing issues with other members. Reasoning from the citizen's standpoint, we deny that families are beyond justice, and in explanation of the content of that denial we say two things: (1) families are part of society's basic structure and need to be consistent with and supportive of a just scheme; (2) in justifying family law, public policy, and surrounding institutions that structure the opportunities of men and women, we proceed from the premise that the adult members of families are equal and independent and that children are so in prospect. So we take as a premise that subordination on the basis of gender is wrong, that gender difference ought not to predict social advantage, and that marriage does not fuse two citizens into a single person. When we adopt the citizen's standpoint, we are puzzled when Milton Friedman—who says that a country is "the collection of individuals who compose it"—then also says: "As liberals, we take the freedom of the individual, or perhaps the family, as our ultimate goal in judging social arrangements."[19] What is this "or perhaps the family"? What is the source of hesitation? And what would it mean to be concerned about the freedom of the family but not principally about the freedom of its members?

But now, when we take the standpoint of the member of a family, these same considerations of justice need not (they may, but need not) provide the basis of deliberation and choice. Decisions might be informed by the view that members of a single household have special responsibilities for one another, by feelings of love and attachment, by a conception of one another as partners in a common life, and by the intimate knowledge that comes from close association, but not by the thought: "We ought to treat one another as equals, since we are all equal and independent moral agents." To borrow Bernard Williams's famous line, that's one thought too many.

Okin's initial response to the proposed reconciliation was that I was simply repeating what she had said in *Justice, Gender, and the Family*: namely, that we may expect more than justice from the family, but that is not the same as exempting it from the requirements of justice. I disagreed. I thought that my proposed division of deliberative standpoints was not simply a matter of supplementing the demands of justice with further conditions and that it provided a more compelling way of making sense of

19. Milton Friedman, *Capitalism and Freedom* (Chicago: University of Chicago Press, 1962), 1, 12.

the claim that the family is beyond justice—a way to interpret and accommodate it, not demolish it. And Okin apparently came around to the view that the two-standpoints idea was not simply a restatement of her view. In her last paper, published in the *Fordham Law Review* in 2004, she mentions that Rawls endorses the two-standpoints idea (which he attributes to my review of her book).[20] She criticizes Rawls on this point and goes on to suggest that family decisions should be governed by Rawls's difference principle.[21]

Although I am not sure what it would mean to govern the family by the difference principle, I am inclined to think that some elements of this recent skepticism may be well placed and that my relaxed reconciliation—with its assumed division of deliberative labor—may be too easy. To be sure, it may be attractive to imagine families conducting their lives without explicit reference to norms of political justice, while those norms operate in the background as the basis of law, public policy, and the structuring of social opportunities. But there may be great difficulties in achieving this division of deliberative labor in a just society, parallel to the difficulties that G. A. Cohen has explored in his writings on incentive inequalities.[22]

Cohen intends his point to generalize the feminist thesis that the personal is political. Suppose, then, that we have designed law and policy to ensure the maximum expected well-being of the least advantaged social group. It does not follow that the expected well-being of the least advantaged *is* maximized because citizens with scarce talents may demand incentives—perhaps large incentives—for deploying those talents in socially

---

20. Susan Okin, "Justice and Gender," *Fordham Law Review* 72, 5 (April 2004): 1564–1565; John Rawls, "The Idea of Public Reason Revisited," in *The Law of Peoples* (Cambridge, MA: Harvard University Press, 1999), 159n63.

21. Okin, "Justice and Gender," 1564. Okin seemed to identify the claim that principles of justice apply to the family with the claim that Rawlsian principles apply: thus her claim about the difference principle applying to the allocation of resources among members of the family. An alternative view (also consistent with much that she says) is that there are standards of justice for families, which state what the members of the family owe to one another in virtue of the special relationships that obtain between and among them, but that those standards are different from those that apply to relations among free and equal adults in a well-ordered society. A view of this kind would then—like the two-standpoints view discussed in the text—need to explain the relationship between standards of family justice and standards of justice for the wider society. I am indebted to David Miller for pressing this point.

22. For a statement of the central ideas, see G. A. Cohen, *If You're an Egalitarian, How Come You're So Rich?* (Cambridge, MA: Harvard University Press, 2001).

productive ways. Cohen argues that if these citizens were guided in their
market behavior by the demands of egalitarian justice, then they would not
demand (such large) incentives. And if they did not demand incentives,
then the marginal tax rates could be increased with no substantial labor
supply response, and the less advantaged could then be made better off.
The problem is that the incentive seekers divide their deliberative labor:
they use completely different standards to guide their market and political
conduct. Egalitarian citizens in the state, they remain self-interested maxi-
mizers in the market. And that problem could be quite large. If we confine
egalitarian standards of justice to our institutions, while treating the market
ethos as part of the fixed background for justice, then we might end up in a
society with profound economic inequalities, with islands of great wealth
surrounded by vast seas of misery and destitution. So the division of deliberative labor could have troubling implications.

Consider how a parallel concern might arise in the domestic arena.
The Rawlsian standard of fair equality of opportunity says that people
who are equally motivated and equally able ought to have equal chances
to attain socially desirable positions. But if, as a consequence of domestic
circumstances and upbringing, men and women are very differently motivated, then fair equality permits a deeply gendered society, with substantial differences in life chances for men and women. And if we accept the
division of deliberative labor, and the associated idea that norms of political justice do not have a role in the internal life of the family, aren't we
inviting that result, even if we assume that Rawlsian egalitarianism is the
right theory of justice?

Simply making the principle of fair equality part of the domestic ethos
may not address the concern. Even if it were part of the domestic ethos,
still—as I have just explained—it would permit differences of motivation
to translate into differences of opportunity. So making the principle of fair
equality part of the domestic ethos could leave substantial gender inequality: it is possible to endorse that principle while encouraging differences in motivation and aspiration between boys and girls. What might
also need to be part of the ethos is the underlying idea that men and
women are moral equals, that differences between men and women are
morally contingent, and that those differences ought not to lead to differences in life prospects.

I say "might" because an alternative possibility is also worth considering. Start again with the incentive inequality issue. I said that a society

might have vast inequalities and even destitution, consistent with meeting the principle of maximizing the advantage of the least advantaged, if we hold the social ethos—the ethics of the market, so to speak—fixed.[23] That is a logical possibility, but political philosophy is not about logical possibilities, and how plausible that result is depends both on the dispersion of human capital in a society with the investments in education and training required to ensure fair equality of opportunity and on the motivations that people can be expected to have in a democratic society. As Rawls put it, "the character and interests of individuals themselves . . . are not fixed or given. A theory of justice must take into account how the aims and aspirations of people are formed; and doing this belongs to the wider framework of thought in the light of which a conception of justice is to be explained." Rawls continues:

> An economic regime . . . is not only an institutional scheme for satisfying existing desires and aspirations but a way of fashioning desires and aspirations in the future. More generally, the basic structure shapes the way the social system produces and reproduces over time a certain form of culture shared by persons with certain conceptions of their good.[24]

So maybe a genuinely just society, with political equality and fair equality of opportunity, would dampen incentive demands because members would pervasively see one another as equals. Maybe the hypothetical concern about great dispersion and destitution is not a real concern: perhaps it is located in the space of the logically possible, not the humanly and socially plausible. And if it is not, then the division of deliberative labor—between market and state—is perfectly sensible.

By analogy (an analogy that is in many ways imperfect), in the gender case, it may be that motivations and life aspirations are shaped as much by public norms of equality—in the arenas of education, employment, and politics—as by their domestic assertion or rejection. And if that is right, if parental norms and instruction have as little significance as children claim and as parents fear, then the concern about the reproduction of gender as

23. The discussion that follows draws on Joshua Cohen, "Taking People as They Are?" *Philosophy and Public Affairs* 30, 4 (2002): 363–386.

24. John Rawls, A *Theory of Justice*, rev. ed. (Cambridge, MA: Harvard University Press, 1999), 229; and *Political Liberalism*, 2nd ed. (New York: Columbia University Press, 1996), 269–271.

a consequence of the division of deliberative labor will be at least muted. The issue intersects with the topic I mentioned earlier, about whether the family is the linchpin in the gender system. The less conviction we have that the family is a linchpin, the less worry we have that the division of deliberative labor provides yet another cover for privilege.

Where, then, do things stand with the assertion that the domestic arena is "beyond justice"? Does the elementary feminist thesis demolish that idea? In my review of Okin, I suggested a way to interpret that idea, consistent with acknowledging the priority of justice. I think that that interpretation has much to be said for it and that a society that achieved the division of deliberative labor that I described would have much to recommend it. But its attractions are, of course, no assurance that deliberative labor can be divided along the proposed lines. And although Okin's initial response to me—that I was reasserting her view, in the guise of a criticism—was mistaken, her later suspicion was well-taken. Let's face it: we do not know whether we can achieve an acceptably gender-equal society with a division of deliberative labor any more than we know whether we can achieve an acceptably distributively fair society consistent with a division of deliberative labor between state and market. Moreover, I do not think we have a good grasp of what to do if we cannot. The elementary feminist thesis does not demolish views that suppose that such achievements are possible. But it presents a forceful challenge to the relaxed reconciliation I proposed.

3. Public and Private

The third issue that emerged in Okin's reply to my review concerned the public-private distinction: the issues I have just now been exploring have already put me in these precincts. In reading *Justice, Gender, and the Family*, I was struck by Okin's ambivalence about the public-private distinction: nothing like Catharine MacKinnon's trenchant remark that "the right of privacy is an injury got up as a gift."[25] Okin did express considerable disquiet about the distinction, and she said that it needed to be subjected to a "thorough examination and critique."[26] But she also seemed to embrace it very substantially. Yet at the same time, she balked at my suggestion about the extent of her embrace.

---

25. Catharine A. MacKinnon, *Feminism Unmodified* (Cambridge, MA: Harvard University Press, 1987), 100.
26. *JGF*, 111.

Generally speaking, Okin said that "both the concept of privacy and the existence of a personal sphere of life in which the state's authority is very limited are essential."[27] And her embrace grew even tighter when she shifted from abstract principle to law and policy. Let me explain.

Suppose you think that the public-private distinction has as little to recommend it when it comes to domestic life as when it comes to economic ordering: as little to recommend it when we are thinking about regulating families as when we are thinking about regulating firms. Suppose, too, that you believe that the unequal domestic division of labor is the linchpin in the system of gender inequality—or even if not the linchpin, at least a big part of that system. Then you might well be attracted to—or at least would want to consider—a range of policies for ensuring gender equality that Okin did not explore, and many of which she would, I think, have found repugnant. So, for example, why not make the failure to share in domestic responsibilities an actionable form of sex discrimination, with married partners empowered to bring civil suits against spouses? Or make such sharing a clause—at least a default clause—in marriage contracts? Or why not have a regulatory agency responsible for ensuring a reasonable sharing of domestic responsibilities? Or, if you like market solutions, why not have tradable reduced-domestic-chores permits, which one could buy to get reduced responsibilities?[28] Or why not let children sue a parent for neglect or have him arrested for abuse if that parent is not sharing in the responsibilities? If the family is the linchpin, and one thinks there's nothing—or even not too much—to the public-private distinction, then why not?

But these were not the kinds of solutions that Okin considered. She was troubled by what she described as vulnerability by marriage and troubled,

27. Ibid., 128.

28. In discussion, Joseph Grundfest suggested that some kinds of prenuptial agreements could be interpreted as, in effect, agreements to provide financial compensation for reduced domestic responsibilities. I suspect that Okin would have been unhappy with such agreements for at least three reasons. First, class inequalities would restrict the general availability of the prenuptial solution. Second, the agreements would bring up privacy concerns of the sort noted in the text. Third, and most fundamentally, the agreements might reduce women's vulnerability at the cost of undermining the equal sharing of domestic responsibilities, which is important for the moral education of the next generation. On Okin's story about the family as a school of justice (borrowed substantially from Nancy Chodorow), the crucial point is that domestic responsibilities be shared in ways that are manifest to children. So, a sharply gendered division of domestic labor, even if freely agreed to, would limit the morally educative effects of the family.

too, by the effects of deep inequalities in the division of domestic labor on the moral development of children. But her proposals for reducing that vulnerability and changing that division were virtually all more indirect, more focused on changing the background conditions to reduce imbalances of power and to create possibilities of choice and exit, and focused in particular on the labor market or on income support: flex time, child care support, parental leaves, a framework of divorce law designed to equalize living standards for postdivorce households, and, most directly, an equal splitting of wages between partners.[29]

My diagnosis for this policy focus—rather than a focus on more direct regulatory strategies—was that Okin endorsed a liberal conception of justice, including a public-private distinction, and an associated idea that people ought to be able to form the kinds of families they want and think appropriate in light of their ethical and religious convictions and personal sensibilities—which sometimes will assign the principal domestic responsibility to women. Okin said, more or less, precisely that.[30] But then why wasn't she worried that lots of people would choose to form traditional families, with highly gendered divisions of labor? And worried, too, that if they did, then those choices would serve—through the socialization of children raised in families with gendered divisions of labor—to sustain gender norms and expectations within lots of families and thus a gendered division of labor in the wider society? And that, if such choices reproduced a gendered culture in the wider society, then the gendered culture would make an equality-sustaining division of domestic labor less likely, which in turn would serve to sustain gender inequality in the economy and polity? Because of her liberalism, Okin did not want to regulate these choices. Because her views about vulnerability by marriage and about the moral education of children emphasized the importance of greater equality in the division of domestic labor—expressed in her conviction about the greater justness of "families in which roles and responsibilities are equally shared regardless of sex"[31]—Okin needed to be concerned about those choices.

The answer to the concern, I believe, is that Okin could not believe that, in a world with genuinely fair chances, large numbers of women would

---

29. I am grateful to Deborah Rhode for pressing the importance of Okin's support for income division.

30. See, for example, *JGF*, 180.

31. *JGF*, 183.

choose positions of domestic subordination. The historical prevalence of such subordination was not a product of choices made under fair conditions but one of social constraint: understandable accommodations to unjustly restricted opportunities. Okin's acceptance of a public-private distinction, I thought, was part of her more general hopeful moral-political outlook: we could have our liberty and our equality, too; these political values are not at war; and what underwrites the prospect of their reconciliation is a conception of the kinds of choices people would make under free and fair conditions of a kind that has not thus far obtained. We do not know what those choices are, because we have never lived in those conditions. But we can hope, with reason, that diverse choices about work and family made under fair conditions will not lead to a gendered society.

I found that picture very compelling and could not understand why Okin would feel the disquiet she expressed in her response to my review at my suggestion that she, to a larger extent than she sometimes suggested, endorsed a public-private distinction. Here, I can only speculate about the answer. My speculation is that she felt the fragility of the hope I just described. She was deeply uncertain about how much pressure on personal decisions would be needed to sustain a gender-free society, and how much domestic diversity would really be possible in such a society. So Okin was prepared to say that "the concept of privacy and the existence of a personal sphere of life in which the state's authority is very limited are essential." But she also worried about how that conviction fit with others of comparable importance.

Here, it is worth remembering that Plato was the great hero of Okin's *Women in Western Political Thought*. The most brilliant argument in that book was that Plato was able to take women seriously as human beings— and to consider the possibility of women guardians—only when, in the name of achieving the profound common allegiance required of a just polity, he contemplated the abolition of separate families and private property, and considered a world in which feelings of pleasure and pain would be common, and everyone would say "mine" and "not mine" about the same things. To be sure, Plato contemplated dismantling the family to ensure unity in the ideal republic, not to achieve gender equality. But this dismantling in turn required that Plato suspend the conventional treatment of women by reference to their role in the family:[32] what Okin called

---

32. Here, Okin follows Rousseau's discussion of Plato in *Emile*. See WWPT, 37–38.

the "functional" view of women as wives and mothers, which otherwise dominated the representation of women in western political thought. "Book V of the *Republic*," Okin says, "contains a more remarkable discussion of the socially and politically relevant differences between the sexes than was to appear for more than two thousand years thereafter."[33] The account of women "in the *Republic* is clearly unparalleled in the history of Western thought."[34] True, but also true that Plato would not have said that "the concept of privacy and the existence of a personal sphere of life in which the state's authority is very limited are essential." Nor did his proposals in the *Republic* about regulating the fine details of the public culture—from literature to architecture—suggest any confidence in the choices that people would make under reasonable conditions.

I suggest, then, that Okin was ambivalent about the public-private distinction—she strongly embraced it and yet kept it at a distance—because she was deeply committed to the idea that justice requires a gender-free society; deeply committed to a world of vibrant, diverse, and emotionally committed families; and profoundly uncertain about the prospect of reconciling those fundamental commitments. Her uneasy relationship with the public-private distinction, then, was not a matter of intellectual inconsistency or evasiveness, but may instead have been a way to express the compelling force of these competing convictions and an unwillingness to make an impossible choice between them.

33. *WWPT*, 234.
34. Ibid.

III

GLOBAL JUSTICE

9

MINIMALISM ABOUT HUMAN RIGHTS:
THE MOST WE CAN HOPE FOR?

1. Hope

At the conclusion of his book *Human Rights*, Michael Ignatieff says that "we could do more than we do to stop unmerited suffering and gross physical cruelty." Efforts to halt such suffering and cruelty are, he continues, the "elemental priority of all human rights activism: to stop torture, beatings, killings, rape, and assault to improve, as best we can, the security of ordinary people."[1] Ignatieff describes this focused concern on protecting bodily security as a *minimalist* outlook on human rights. And he distinguishes human rights minimalism from more expansive statements about the content of human rights and more ambitious agendas for their promotion—agendas that might extend both to a richer array of civil and political rights, and to social and economic rights.

The 1948 Universal Declaration of Human Rights presents one such more ambitious agenda. Its account of human rights extends well beyond minimalist assurances of bodily security, to comprise rights associated with the rule of law (Arts. 6–11), political participation (Art. 21), work (Art. 23), education (Art. 26), and culture (Art. 27). And neither of the 1966 covenants on human rights (which entered into force in 1976) is a minimalist charter—certainly not the Covenant on Economic and Social Rights, but

I presented earlier versions of this essay at the fiftieth-anniversary celebration of the MIT Center for International Studies, the Center for Ethics and the Professions at Harvard's John F. Kennedy School of Government, Boalt Hall, the Annual Meeting of the Association of American Law Schools, and as a Romanell–Phi Beta Kappa Lecture at MIT. I am grateful for comments from audiences on all these occasions, and in particular for comments from Charles Beitz, Alyssa Bernstein, Robert Goodin, Donald Horowitz, Michael Ignatieff, Patrizia Nanz, Robert Post, Samuel Scheffler, Judith Thomson, and three anonymous reviewers for *The Journal of Political Philosophy*. I also wish to thank Daniel Munro for research assistance.

1. Michael Ignatieff, *Human Rights as Politics and as Idolatry* (Princeton: Princeton University Press, 2001), 173.

equally not the International Covenant on Civil and Political Rights, with its provisions on self-determination (Art. 1), rights of peaceable assembly and freedom of association (Art. 21, 22), political participation (Art. 25), and equality before the law (Art. 26).[2] In response to the criticism that minimalism is simply a political strategy—and not an especially plausible one—for defusing authoritarian objections to human rights by reminding authoritarians that they do not have to do very much to stay in compliance, Ignatieff denies that minimalism is simply strategic. It is, he says, "the most we can hope for."[3]

In the *Critique of Pure Reason*, Kant says that the three great philosophical questions are: "What can I know?" "What should I to do?" and "What may I hope?" The first question expresses the interests of our reason in its theoretical use; the second question expresses the interests of our reason in its practical use. The third joins the interests of both theoretical and practical reason: given the demands of morality and what we know about how the world does and might work, what sort of world, we ask, is it reasonable to hope for and to strive to achieve?[4] The world that the minimalist imagines—a world without torture and with genuine assurances of bodily security for all—is no small hope, and I do not wish here to dispute Ignatieff's assertion about elemental priorities—about the relative importance of rights of bodily security. But I do wish to dispute the idea that human rights minimalism is "the most we can hope for." Minimalism may be more than we should ever reasonably expect. But hope is not the same as expectation. And human rights minimalism draws the boundaries of hope too narrowly.

This is a large thesis, and I do not propose to argue for it fully. Instead, I will concentrate here on one apparently attractive route to minimalist conclusions. The route I have in mind begins with an emphasis on the value of toleration and an acknowledgement of ethical pluralism and ends in human rights minimalism. Ignatieff suggests this argument, when he says that: "The universal commitments implied by human rights can be compatible with a wide variety of ways of living only if the universalism implied

2. For the Declaration and Covenants, as well as other human rights conventions and charters, see the Annex on Documents in Henry J. Steiner and Philip Alston, *International Human Rights in Context: Law, Politics, Morals*, 2nd ed. (Oxford: Oxford University Press, 2000).

3. Ignatieff, *Human Rights*, 173.

4. Immanuel Kant, *Critique of Pure Reason*, trans. Paul Guyer and Allen Wood (Cambridge: Cambridge University Press, 1998), A805–B833.

is self-consciously minimalist. Human rights can command universal assent only as a decidedly 'thin' theory of what is right, a definition of the minimal conditions for any life at all."[5] If human rights are to apply to all, as basic demands on social and political arrangements, then it seems desirable that they be acceptable to all: that they command "universal assent." And if we want them to be acceptable to all, then—in view of the wide range of religious, philosophical, ethical, and political outlooks that are now endorsed in different societies, and that we can expect to persist into the indefinite future—the content cannot be very demanding, perhaps no more than a statement of the protections required "for any life at all."

This case for human rights minimalism suggests a dilemma for more expansive conceptions of human rights. According to the dilemma, we can be tolerant of fundamentally different outlooks on life or we can be ambitious in our understanding of what human rights demand, but we cannot—contrary to the aims of many human rights activists—be both tolerant and ambitious. Just as some people argue that deep disagreement pushes us to a minimalist conception of democracy, with an emphasis on electoral competition, or a proceduralist view of justice, the suggestion is that, in the case of human rights as well, disagreement dissipates substance. I disagree with the thesis about democracy and justice, and I also want to dispute the thesis about human rights. I deny that more ambitious projects of human rights are bound to be objectionably intolerant.

So the proposed route to minimalism begins in toleration and ends in a very thin set of normative principles. To assess it, I need first to describe it more precisely. And describing it will require a distinction between two views that play a role in theoretical discussions of human rights. Both have a claim to the title "minimalist," but they are very different from one another in content and role.[6]

I will call the first view *substantive minimalism*, which is a position about the content of human rights and, more broadly, about norms of global justice. The central idea of substantive minimalism is that human rights are confined to protections of negative liberty: and, even more particularly, to ensuring against restrictions on negative liberty that take the form of forcible intrusions on bodily security.

---

5. Ignatieff, *Human Rights*, 56.
6. I believe that Ignatieff uses the term "minimalism" to cover both. See *Human Rights*, 55–56.

The second view I will call *justificatory minimalism*. Here, in contrast with substantive minimalism, we have a view about how to present a conception of human rights, as an essential element of a conception of global justice for an ethically pluralistic world—as a basic feature of what I will be referring to as "global public reason." Justificatory minimalism is animated by an acknowledgement of pluralism and embrace of toleration. It aspires to present a conception of human rights without itself connecting that conception to a particular ethical or religious outlook; it minimizes theoretical aspirations in the statement of the conception of human rights with the aim of presenting a conception that is capable of winning broader public allegiance—where the relevant public is global. The conception is presented, as Rawls suggests in his account of overlapping consensus, as a "module," and the case that the module can win support from different ethical and religious traditions is a matter of argument within those traditions, with, of course, different traditions offering different lines of argument.[7] (I will make some remarks later about how such argument might proceed.)

In the service of practical reason, then, the justificatory minimalist minimizes philosophical depth. That ambition is important, but it needs to be properly understood: in section 2 of this essay I will discuss and reject what I will refer to as "skeptical" and "empirical" variants of justificatory minimalism and propose an alternative formulation that does not—contrary to the line of thought sketched above—have substantively minimalist implications.

Of course, justificatory minimalism is not the only proposed route to substantive minimalism, with its focus on rights associated with bodily security. Five considerations are commonly offered for resisting more demanding lists of human rights, for example, social and economic rights, as well as a richer class of civil and political rights:

- They threaten to overtax the resources and disperse the attention required for monitoring and enforcing human rights;
- More expansive lists of social and economic rights cannot be fully realized because their realization is simply too costly, and for that reason are not genuinely speaking lists of *rights*;

7. John Rawls, *Political Liberalism* (New York: Columbia University Press, 1996), 12, 145. My emphasis in this paragraph on how the human rights conception is presented follows Rawls's account of the second feature of a political conception of justice. See *Political Liberalism*, 12.

- Because rights correspond to obligations, and we cannot give determinate content to the obligations associated with social and economic human rights in advance of their institutionalization, there are no economic and social rights;[8]
- Expansive lists threaten an (undesirable) substitution of legal principles for political judgments, of often uncompromising rights claims ("rights talk") for informed and more supple political deliberation and judgment; and (a partly related point);
- Expansive lists threaten to subordinate the political self-determination of peoples (within acceptable limits) to the decisions of outside agents, who justify their interventions in the language of human rights.

Although I will say something about the fourth and fifth of these considerations near the end of this essay, my principal focus here is on the thought that pluralism and toleration, expressed in the idea of justificatory minimalism, lead us to a substantively minimal account of human rights.

2. Justificatory Minimalism

The central idea of justificatory minimalism is that a conception of human rights should be presented autonomously: that is, independent of particular philosophical or religious theories that might be used to explain and justify its content. Jacques Maritain—perhaps the central figure in mid-twentieth-century efforts to reconcile Catholic social thought with democracy and human rights, and who participated in discussions leading to the Universal Declaration—formulated the idea as follows: "Yes, we agree about the rights, but on condition that no one asks us why." The point of developing a conception of human rights, capable of being shared by adherents to different traditions, he said, was to create agreement "not on the basis of common speculative ideas, but on common practical ideas, not on the affirmation of one and the same conception of the world, of man, and of knowledge, but on the affirmation of a single body of beliefs for guidance on action."[9]

8. For discussion of the merits of this line of argument, see Onora O'Neill, *Bounds of Justice* (Cambridge: Cambridge University Press, 2000), chap. 6; Henry Shue, *Basic Rights: Subsistence, Affluence, and U.S. Foreign Policy* (Princeton: Princeton University Press, 1980); Amartya Sen, "Towards a Theory of Human Rights," *Philosophy & Public Affairs* 32, 4 (2004): 315–356.

9. Cited in Mary Ann Glendon, *A World Made New: Eleanor Roosevelt and the Universal Declaration of Human Rights* (New York: Random House, 2001). On the background of

Maritain's point of view makes considerable sense if we think of a conception of human rights as designed to play a certain practical role, to provide "guidance on action," as he puts it. The practical role, as I will understand it, is to provide a broadly shared outlook, across national boundaries, about the standards that political societies, in the first instance, can be held to with respect to the treatment of individuals and groups; and correspondingly, the treatment that individuals and groups can reasonably demand, and perhaps enlist assistance from outside in achieving. Or if not a shared outlook, at least a broadly shared terrain of deliberation about the standards to which political societies can reasonably be held and when they are appropriately subject to external criticism or interference. An account of human rights is one element in an ideal of *public reason* for international society.[10] Because that society comprises adherents to a wide range of distinct ethical and religious outlooks, justificatory minimalism, with its ideal of autonomous formulation or presentation, is an intuitively plausible desideratum. And its point is not simply to avoid a fight where none is necessary; the point is to embrace the value of toleration.

Human Rights: Content, Role, and Rationale

To develop these points more fully, I need first to say something more about what a conception of human rights is and about what I have described as its practical role. Think of such a conception, then, as having three elements.

The first is a statement of a set of rights, of the sort that we find in the Declaration and the Covenants. There are many such statements and substantial disagreement about which rights belong on the list: about whether human rights include social and economic rights, and if so which ones; but also about whether there is a human right to democracy, and, if not, what

---

Maritain's views of human rights in broader efforts to rethink the fundamentals of Catholic social thought—especially the relative significance attached to notions of the human person and the common good—see John T. McGreevy, *Catholicism and American Freedom: A History* (New York: Norton, 2003), chap. 7.

10. Rawls refers to the public reason of the "society of peoples." See *The Law of Peoples* (Cambridge, MA: Harvard University Press, 1999), 54–57. I do not wish here to engage the issue of whether "peoples" are the moral agents in international society. Thus the less theoretically committed term "international society."

kinds of representation and accountability might be matters of basic human right.[11]

Such disagreement is of course the normal situation when it comes to issues of justice: disagreement comes with the territory, and should not be taken as a sign of a deficiency. We can assume that the disagreement is genuine—not simply a matter of people talking past each other, as it would be if different proposed lists of rights represented so many different ways of assigning meaning to the term "human rights." Nor need we interpret the disagreement as showing that statements of human rights are simply ways of presenting power and interest in normatively attractive garb. Instead, there may be broad agreement about the practical role of human rights as global, public standards, disagreement about the content of the rights suited to that role, and a practice of argument that aims to clarify and perhaps narrow the terms of disagreement. Thus global public reason—and the idea of human rights in particular—provides a terrain of deliberation and argument about appropriate norms (specifically, I will suggest below, about the requirements of treating individuals as members), not a determinate and settled doctrine awaiting acceptance or rejection.

Second, the role is to present a set of important standards that all political societies are to be held accountable to in their treatment of their members: it offers, in the language of the Declaration, "a common standard of achievement for all peoples and all nations."[12] A statement of human rights presents, as is commonly said, a set of limits on internal sovereignty, or—perhaps better—presents conditions on which a state's internal sovereignty is acknowledged.[13] The idea that there are such limits on internal sovereignty is often said to be a fundamental departure from the Westphalian conception of sovereignty that prevailed from the mid-17th century until the end of World War II. Stephen Krasner has suggested an alternative view. Krasner points out that the norms of Westphalian sovereignty

11. On the human right to democracy see Thomas Franck, "The Emerging Right to Democratic Governance," *The American Journal of International Law* 86, 1 (1992): 46–91. Rawls rejects the right to democracy as a basic human right in favor of a weaker requirement of organized group consultation.

12. Universal Declaration of Human Rights, in Steiner and Allston, *International Human Rights in Context*, 1376.

13. See Stephen D. Krasner, *Sovereignty: Organized Hypocrisy* (Princeton: Princeton University Press, 1999). I am indebted to Thomas Christensen for discussion of the point in the text.

were persistently violated throughout the period of Westphalian sovereignty by externally guaranteed protections of rights. According to Krasner, the change at the end of World War II is best understood as a shift from abridgements of sovereignty in the name of minority group rights to abridgements in the name of individual rights, rather than a shift in the basic conception of sovereignty itself. Krasner is certainly right to emphasize that protections of minority rights were abridgements of conventional norms of internal sovereignty. But more recent developments seem to have changed the content of the regnant norms and not simply the pattern of "organized hypocrisy" in their abridgements.

In any case, human rights standards represent a partial statement of the content of an ideal of global public reason, a broadly shared set of values and norms for assessing political societies both separately and in their relations: a public reason that is global in reach, inasmuch as it applies to all political societies, and global in its agent, inasmuch as it is presented as the common reason of all peoples, who share responsibility for interpreting its principles, and monitoring and enforcing them. The precise ways of exercising that responsibility—who exercises it (international courts and other institutions, regional bodies, individual states, non-governmental organizations) and with what instruments (ranging from monitoring, to naming and shaming, to sanctions, to force)—vary widely. Often, acting on the principles of global public reason may consist simply in observing the implementation of its principles by separate political societies, or perhaps in assisting in their implementation. The more immediate responsibility for interpreting and implementing the principles will—as the Declaration and Covenants emphasize—typically fall to those political societies themselves, in part—although not only—because of the value of collective self-determination affirmed in Article 1 of the Covenant on Civil and Political Rights.[14]

Now it might be argued that the human rights identified by principles of global public reason are identical in content to the basic natural rights that individuals would have even in a pre-institutional state of nature. But—and here I follow an illuminating discussion by Charles Beitz[15]—

14. Thus Article 2 of the Covenant on Civil and Political Rights requires states to adopt the "legislative and other measures" needed to give effect to the rights. See Steiner and Allston, *International Human Rights in Context*, 1382.

15. Charles Beitz, "Human Rights as a Common Concern," *American Political Science Review* 95, 2 (2001); "What Human Rights Mean," *Daedalus* 132, 1 (Winter 2003): 36–46; and

that claim about identity of content, whatever its merits, should not be presented as issuing directly from a *conceptual* identification of human rights with natural rights. These concepts are fundamentally different, as is evident from the fact that many of the rights enumerated in the Universal Declaration and the 1966 Covenants—including rights to a fair hearing and the right to take part in government—have institutional presuppositions, and thus could not be rights in a pre-institutional state of nature, assuming there are such rights. Instead, a claim about identity of content between human rights and natural rights would need to be defended through a substantive normative argument to the effect that the rights implied by the most reasonable principles for global public reason—the standards of individual treatment appropriate to use in holding political societies accountable—are, contrary to the Declaration, the very same rights that individuals would hold in pre-institutional circumstances. That conclusion, if true, would be surprising. Why should reasonable norms of global responsibility, in a world with separate political societies and substantial interactions—economic, political, cultural—across and among those societies, have the same content as the norms for a very different setting, in which there are no organized political societies and institutions at all?[16] My point here, though, is not to dispute the thesis that human rights are identical in content to natural rights but simply to characterize its status.

A third element in a conception of human rights is an account of why the rights have the content that they have. A conception of human rights is not given simply by a list of rights together with an account of the role of human rights, but also by some view about why certain rights are suited to that role: why it is appropriate to require that political societies ensure those rights. It is here that justificatory minimalism has real bite. Given the practical role of a conception of human rights, we need to avoid formulating the rationale for human rights (as well as their content) by reference to a particular religious or secular moral outlook. So we should avoid

"Human Rights and the Law of Peoples," in Deen K. Chatterjee, ed., *The Ethics of Assistance: Morality and the Distant Needy* (Cambridge: Cambridge University Press, 2004), 193–214.

16. One might argue that human rights are the result of applying natural rights to the circumstances of an organized political society. So, for example, the right to equality before the law might be derived from a natural right to bodily security, along with some reasonable assumptions about the conditions for protecting that right in a society with a legal system. I do not find this argument compelling but cannot pursue the reasons here.

saying that, for example, human rights are preconditions of the autonomous moral agency prized by Kantians, or for fulfilling divinely imposed obligations, whether the preferred statement of the obligations is found in Thomistic or Lockean natural law theory, or some formulation of the shari'ah.

Instead, I propose that human rights norms are best thought of as norms associated with an idea of *membership or inclusion* in an organized political society. The relevant notion of membership is a normative idea—it is not the same as, for example, living in a territory—and the central feature of the normative notion of membership is that a person's interests are taken into account by the political society's basic institutions: to be treated as a member is to have one's interests given due consideration, both in the processes of authoritative decision-making and in the content of those decisions. Correspondingly, disagreements about human rights may be seen as proceeding on a shared terrain of political argument, and can be understood—unlike disputes about the content of natural rights—as disagreements about what is required to ensure membership—about what consideration is due to each person in a political society.

The importance of the notion of membership in an account of human rights is suggested by the breadth and substance of the rights in the Universal Declaration and the Covenants—including rights to education, work, and cultural inclusion, as well as assembly, expression, and participation. To be sure, some human rights (to life and to personal security, for example) are not tied only to membership but are more plausibly associated with demands of basic humanity, irrespective of membership. But the guiding thought behind the more capacious list seems to be that an acceptable political society—one that is above reproach in its treatment of individuals—must attend to the common good of those who are subject to its regulations, on some reasonable conception of that good, and ensure the goods that people in the territory and subject to political rule need in order to take part in the political society. Human rights claims, then, identify goods that are socially important because they are requirements of membership. Failing to give due consideration to the good of members by ensuring access to these goods is tantamount to treating them as outsiders, persons whose good can simply be dismissed in making laws and policies: no-counts, with no part to play in the political society.

One rationale for the emphasis on membership is suggested by the idea of political obligation. Thus, on a plausible account of political obligation, attending to the common good, on some interpretation of that good, is necessary if the requirements that a political society imposes on people under its rule are to have the status of genuine obligations and not mere forcible impositions. If an account of political obligation along these lines is correct—and it certainly is more plausible than a theory of obligation that ties political obligations to justice—then the rights that are required if individuals are to be treated as members would be identical to the rights that are required if the requirements imposed by law and other regulations are to be genuine obligations.

Two final points of clarification. First, in emphasizing that acceptable arrangements acknowledge rights as a way to acknowledge and uphold the status of membership, I do not wish to deny that human rights protections were particularly animated by more specific concerns about genocide, torture, and other extreme forms of cruelty. But as the Declaration and Covenants indicate, the concerns were not confined to those evils, but included other forms of social exclusion, perhaps understood as both objectionable in themselves and as opening the way to more hideous forms of treatment. Second, in associating human rights with membership in an organized political society, I do not mean to exclude the thought that those rights can also be understood as articulating the conditions of membership in a more global society. But much of our lives as "global citizens" continues to be lived within particular political societies, with distinct institutions, even as it is substantially affected by external decisions and practices. So if national and transnational institutions worked to ensure reasonable conditions of membership in organized political societies, they would thereby go some distance to ensuring the rudiments of global membership as well.

A conception of human rights, then, has three elements: a statement of what the rights are; an account of the role of human rights as standards of practical reason that can be used by a range of different agents in assessing all political societies in their treatment of their members; and a view about why the rights are as they are, given that role. The idea of justificatory minimalism is that each of these elements—including the account of membership and affirmation of its importance—should be presented autonomously or independently, so that all can be affirmed by a range of ethical outlooks, for the varying reasons provided by the terms of those different outlooks, and then used as a basis for further argument about and elaboration of the content of human rights.

Justificatory Minimalism: Neither Skeptical nor Empirical

To appreciate the force and plausibility of this requirement of autonomous formulation, we need to distinguish justificatory minimalism from two positions—skeptical and empirical—with which it might be conflated.

The first position is a set of familiar nihilistic or skeptical claims about the need for so-called anti- or post-metaphysical political theorizing. Those claims deny the truth or reasonableness or knowability of traditional views about the foundations of human rights in philosophical theories about human nature or religious conceptions of the human person or right conduct. Thus Richard Rorty describes such views as "human rights foundationalism" and urges that we put such foundationalism behind us— like all other efforts to shore up any of our practices, by suggesting that anything can or should be said on their behalf other than "that's how we do things these days around here," for some suitable specification of "here."[17]

But justificatory minimalism is founded on an acknowledgment of pluralism and a commitment to toleration. Neither *anti*-foundational nor *post*-metaphysical, it simply does not take a position for or against any particular foundational view, whether religious or secular, about the content and importance of human rights, nor does it make any claims about whether such views can (or cannot) be known to be true. It is *unfoundational*, rather than anti-foundationalist. Justificatory minimalism does not require denying anything, whether about truth or knowledge, much less asserting (with Rorty) that pragmatic arguments for human rights should replace metaphysical ones, as though Rortyean pragmatism, or its antecedents in Romantic conceptions of self-creation, is somehow less committal than other metaphysical theories.

Instead, because human rights ideas are intended to provide part of a framework of political deliberation whose practical role, as a partial specification of the content of a global public reason, requires that it be shared among people who endorse very different ethical positions, we ought to free the statement of the outlook from its connection to any one of those views. No unnecessary hurdles should be placed in the way of adherents of different traditions who wish to embrace the ideas. When the Universal Declaration came before the United Nations in 1948, proposals to include

17. Richard Rorty, "Human Rights, Rationality, and Sentimentality," in Stephen Shute and Susan Hurley, eds., *On Human Rights* (New York: Basic Books, 1993), 112–134.

references in the Declaration to God or nature were rejected by the body, at the urging of C. K. Chang.[18] Those views were not rejected as false or outdated. Instead, the Declaration was presented in a way that left adherents of different views to work out the relations between their broader philosophy of life and the account of human rights. And working out those relations is important for adherents, and thus it is of practical importance for the acceptance and efficacy of the human rights idea.

Having said this, I also need—and here I come to the second distinction—to set justificatory minimalism off from the view that ideas of human rights are somehow to be "found" within each religious and moral tradition, or located at the intersection of those different traditions, taking their content as fixed and given: say, in the spirit of H. L. A. Hart's "minimum content of natural law" or the reiterated moral ideas suggested by Michael Walzer's "moral minimalism."[19] Call this the *empirical interpretation* of justificatory minimalism.[20] If this interpretation were correct, then we might plausibly expect substantive minimalism to follow. After all, what more could be expected to lie at the de facto intersection of different ethical traditions than prohibitions on infringing on bodily security—and, more generally, assurances of the conditions of any life at all? If we are looking to assure that a conception of human rights is actually accepted from within a wide range of different traditions—not simply that it be acceptable—then the content is likely to be driven down to a minimum.

But justificatory minimalism is not about locating the de facto intersection of different ethical traditions, taking those traditions as fixed and given. That idea in any case has uncertain content, inasmuch as each ethical tradition has competing formulations, with often sharp contests within the tradition about which formulation is best—a point that is tirelessly reiterated by postmodernists and postcolonialists. Instead, the formulation of a conception of human rights is, as I have said, an independent

18. For discussion, see Glendon, *World Made New*.

19. See H. L. A Hart, *Concept of Law*, 2nd ed. (Oxford: Oxford University Press, 1994), 193–200; Michael Walzer, *Thick and Thin: Moral Argument at Home and Abroad* (South Bend, IN: University of Notre Dame Press, 1994), chap. 1.

20. The empirical interpretation parallels a conventional misunderstanding of Rawls's conception of an overlapping consensus. For discussion of the misunderstanding, see Joshua Cohen, "Moral Pluralism and Political Consensus," in David Copp, Jean Hampton, and John Roemer, eds., *The Idea of Democracy* (Cambridge: Cambridge University Press, 1993), 270–291.

normative enterprise, which aims to present reasonable global norms and standards to which different political societies can be held accountable— more particularly, I have suggested, an account of the conditions of membership. In pursuing that enterprise, we recognize in general terms that global public reason is intended to provide a public reason for people who belong to different ethical traditions. But the specifics of those traditions are not in view. To see the force of the idea that the normative enterprise is independent, suppose—with Rawls's *Law of Peoples*—that we think of the principles of global public reason as the object of an initial compact among different peoples (or among the members of those peoples). Then the idea of justificatory minimalism would be modeled by an agreement made with awareness of the fact that there are fundamentally different religious and ethical traditions, each with competing formulations. But the agreement would not be made with awareness of the content of those traditions or their political distribution.

Because the formulation of the ideas and principles of global public reason is not undertaken with an eye to finding common ground among determinate ethical traditions, the enterprise of showing that those ideas and principles can win support within different ethical traditions may require fresh elaboration of those traditions by their proponents—where it is understood that the point of a fresh elaboration is not simply to fit the tradition to the demands of the world but to provide that tradition with its most compelling statement.

To illustrate this point about fresh elaboration, consider first the fit between constitutional democracy, with its conception of individual rights and principles of religious toleration, and the evolution of Catholic natural law theory associated with Vatican II. With its "Declaration of Religious Freedom," the Catholic Church rejected the traditional doctrine that "error has no rights" (the "exclusive rights of truth"), and the associated thesis that religious toleration is an accommodation to political weakness. Instead, the Church embraced a principled commitment to religious toleration founded on an idea of the "dignity of the human person." The idea of a special dignity owing to our creation in God's image was always a centerpiece of Catholic doctrine. But according to the traditional interpretation of that doctrine, "as a rational and moral being, man is constituted in his proper dignity by his adhesion to what is true and good." Because human dignity was associated with living in the truth, "the erroneous conscience has no right to external social freedom. . . . In particular, it has no right publicly to propagate or disseminate its belief."[21]

To bring a principled commitment to religious toleration into Catholic social thought, it was not possible to deny that the truth lay in Catholic doctrine: thus, as the Declaration on Religious Freedom reaffirms, "God Himself has made known to mankind the way in which men are to serve Him, and thus be saved in Christ and come to blessedness. We believe that this one true religion subsists in the Catholic and apostolic Church."[22] Instead the conception of human dignity needed to be reinterpreted so that human dignity imposed significant limits on how the state could treat those who are not living according to the truth. Thus human dignity was seen as issuing in an account of political legitimacy that imposed principled limits on the state's authority in matters of religious faith and practice. Dignity still is understood to impose a "moral duty" to "seek the truth" and "adhere to the truth." But while the "one true religion subsists in the Catholic and apostolic Church," the pursuit and embrace of truth must—as modern cultural and political experience has brought home—comport with the dignity owing to our nature as free persons "endowed with reason and free will and therefore privileged to bear personal responsibility." And this requires immunity from "external coercion," as well as "psychological freedom." Those who reject the truth are as entitled to this immunity as those who embrace it, and those who embrace the truth must seek it through free inquiry, and follow it "by a personal assent."

Once more, this reinterpretation was not seen—and certainly not expressed—as simply a result of a practical need to accommodate Catholic doctrine to the brute facts of modern political life—in particular, the minority status of Catholicism in most countries—and to encourage trust in Catholic commitment to respecting religious pluralism. Instead it was presented as animated by a need to reformulate political ideas in light of fundamental truths about the human person that modern "cultural

21. John Courtney Murray, "The Problem of Religious Freedom," in *Religious Liberty: Catholic Struggles with Pluralism* (Louisville: Westminster, 1993), 131.

22. See "Declaration on Religious Freedom," in *The Teachings of the Second Vatican Council: Complete Texts of the Constitutions, Decrees, and Declarations* (Westminster, MD: The Newman Press, 1966), 366–367. The quotations in this paragraph all come from the Introduction to the Declaration, and from its first chapter, on the "General Principles of Religious Liberty."

and political experience" had made manifest.[23] To be sure, external circumstance—including the experience of constitutional democracy and stable religious pluralism—prompted the doctrinal changes, and the political ideas about principled religious toleration originated outside Catholicism. For that reason, these ideas might be described as "borrowed" and as pragmatic adjustments. But such descriptions obscure the importance to proponents of presenting the new view as a reasoned doctrinal argument. The changes were argued for as matters of compelling doctrinal evolution and to that extent as matters of internal principle rather than simple external borrowing.

3. Two Illustrations

To illustrate further this point about the fresh elaboration of a doctrine in relation to an autonomously formulated account of human rights, I want to consider two illustrative cases: Confucianism and Islam. My aim is to show how the fundamentals might be interpreted in a way that supports a conception of human rights—and the elaboration of that conception on a shared terrain of argument—although neither view includes rights as fundamental elements.[24] In neither case do I aim to show that the best interpretation of either outlook leads to an endorsement of human rights; that argument proceeds within Confucianism and Islam themselves. And in neither case do I am aim to show that we can identify which rights are human rights by deriving them from within these different doctrines: on the view I sketched earlier, working out the content of human rights is a matter of specifying the preconditions of membership. Instead the aim is to show that the terrain of deliberation about the nature and content of human rights can be occupied by a proponent of these doctrines.[25]

---

23. In the case of revealed religions, a large issue about the relationship between revelation (including the manifestation of truths about human beings) and history looms in the background—about whether the whole truth is revealed at a determinate moment in history or is instead revealed over the course of history. I do not propose to explore this disagreement here.

24. The same of course can be said for utilitarianism and for perfectionist views founded on an Aristotelian understanding of human nature and human flourishing. For proposals about how to bring ideas about rights without parentage in positive legislation into utilitarianism, see John Stuart Mill, *Utilitarianism*, reprinted in *Utilitarianism, Liberty, and Representative Government*, ed. H. B. Acton (New York: E. P. Dutton, 1972), chap. 5; and H. L. A. Hart, "Natural Rights: Bentham and John Stuart Mill," in Hart, *Essays on Bentham* (Oxford: Oxford University Press, 1982), chap. 4.

25. To be sure, we have a strong case that that terrain cannot be occupied if paradigmatic human rights are incompatible with the doctrine.

Confucianism

In a collection on *Confucian Traditions in East Asian Modernity*, Tu Wei-ming says the following two things about Confucianism: that "In its political philosophy the Confucian tradition lacks concepts of liberty, human rights, privacy, and due process of law," and that "the Confucian concern for duty is not at variance with the demand for rights."[26] Putting the two comments together, the point seems to be that although the Confucian tradition does not have a conception of human rights, to be discovered by inspecting its contents—say, reading such classical texts as the *Analects*—such a conception can nevertheless be brought within its sphere. I think that this assertion is correct and want to sketch a way of doing that. If what I say is right, the conclusion would not be that the idea of human rights is essential to Confucian moral and political thought but that the central ideas associated with the Confucian tradition can be presented in a way that supports a conception of human rights. The fundamentals are not hostile to the idea of human rights, at least not when they are understood as aspects of membership in an acceptable political arrangement.

To see why not, think of Confucianism as having three main elements: a philosophical anthropology (theory of human nature), an ethic (understood broadly, to include rules of conduct, appropriate human ends, and ideals of character), and a political conception about the proper role and form of government.[27]

1. The central element in the account of human nature is the idea of human beings as standing in relations of various kinds to others: in particular, relations to others in a family, extending across generations, but also political relations (say, relations between rulers and officials, or officials and those subject to their decisions). Thus persons are not conceived of as free and equal individuals, or as principally choosers of their

---

26. See his "Epilogue," in *Confucian Traditions in East Asian Modernity*, ed. Tu Wei-Ming (Cambridge, MA: Harvard University Press, 1996), 347.

27. My statement of the elements of Confucianism draws on the Four Books (*Analects, Great Learning, Doctrine of the Mean,* and *Mencius*). See *The Four Books,* trans. James Legge (New York: Paragon, 1966); *The Analects of Confucius: A Philosophical Translation,* trans. Roger Ames and Henry Rosemont (New York: Ballantine, 1998). For helpful discussion, see the Introduction by Ames and Rosement to *The Analects,* 1–66; Kwong-Loi Shun, *Mencius and Early Chinese Thought* (Stanford: Stanford University Press, 1997).

ends (as in a comprehensive liberal philosophy of life), but as standing in relations from which their ethical identity and obligations derive.[28]

2. The ethic includes at least four important elements:

(i) An account of the responsibilities associated with human relationships, say, duties of filial piety and brotherly respect that are required to ensure the proper ordering of those relations: "The ruler must rule, the minister minister, the father father, and the son son" (12.11).[29]

(ii) An account of self-cultivation—of education in the broadest sense—that enables the person who stands in these relations to understand and fulfill the responsibilities associated with them. In the case of the political relation, fulfilling these responsibilities may require refusing to serve, when the demands imposed by the ruler are wrong.

(iii) An account of the human virtues—humaneness *(ren)*, wisdom, fidelity, loyalty, and observance of ritual *(li)*—required for conduct that fulfills the responsibilities ingredient in human relationships.

(iv) An ideal of the kind of person we should aspire to be: someone whose cultivation is sufficient to understand the virtues and act on them (the "gentleman" or "exemplary person"). According to Tu Wei-ming, Confucianism also embraces a conception of human dignity associated with the capacity for such cultivation. And, he might have added, in at least some of its formulations, Confucianism assumes this capacity to be widely distributed among human beings.

3. Finally, the political conception includes an account of the responsibilities of political officials to care for the common good of subjects: "Make sure there is sufficient food to eat, sufficient arms for defense, and that the common people have confidence in their leaders" (12.7; also 5.16, 6.30, 12.7, 13.9, 20.2). This responsibility is in part an expression of the duties associated the position of official and the relations of official to subjects, and in part an expression of the requirements of the virtues—in

28. On the view of human nature and its metaphysical background, see Ames and Rosemont, "Introduction," 23–29.

29. I have included all references to the *Analects* in the text, and I cite the Ames and Rosemont translation.

particular the demands of virtue of humaneness *(ren)*—as applied to the case of the official.

As this last observation about the implications of the virtue of humaneness for official conduct indicates, I do not mean to suggest—in separating out the ethical conception from the political—a sharp distinction within Confucianism between personal and political virtues and responsibilities. Confucianism rejects any such fundamental distinction and instead affirms continuity between the virtues associated with familial relations and political virtues: "It is all in filial conduct! Just being filial to your parents and befriending your brothers is carrying out the work of government" (2.21). Or again: "It is a rare thing for someone who has a sense of filial and fraternal responsibility to have a taste for defying authority. And it is unheard of for those who have no taste for defying authority to be keen on initiating rebellion. Exemplary persons *(junzi)* concentrate their efforts on the root, for the root having taken hold, the way will grow therefrom. As for filial and fraternal responsibility, it is, I suspect, the root of authoritative conduct *(ren)*" (1.2).

These elements, of course greatly simplified, enable us to see how Confucianism can be interpreted to support a conception of human rights. Consider the Universal Declaration, in particular, the Articles requiring rights to life, liberty, and security; condemning slavery, torture, degrading treatment, arbitrary arrest and detention; and mandating rights to an adequate standard of living.[30] Three considerations within the Confucian view support such rights.

First, basic human rights can be thought of as conditions for fulfilling the obligations associated with human relationships: slavery, torture, and threats of arbitrary arrest, as well as poor health, lack of education, and absence of sufficient economic means will all infirm the ability of people to confidently fulfill the obligations that flow from their relationships. As a bearer of such obligations, a person can claim both that others *ought to* assure them freedom from arbitrary arrest and detention, and also that those others owe it *to the person* with the obligations to provide such assurance. The essential point is that the relational or role-based obligations, essential to the ethical view, explain why the assurances must be provided.

---

30. On Confucianism and the right to an adequate standard of living, see Stephen Angle, *Human Rights and Chinese Thought: A Cross-Cultural Inquiry* (Cambridge: Cambridge University Press, 2002), 244–245.

The idea is not simply that people benefit from a generalized obligation to be humane and decent, although that is true, too: more than that, they can demand certain kinds of treatment as conditions for fulfilling the obligations they are assumed to have, given their social position and the responsibilities associated with it. They do not make the demands independently from those obligations, but in their name.[31]

To be sure, the need to make such demands on others might be interpreted as a sign of an ethical or political deficiency, as resulting from the failure of officials and others to act according to the ethically appropriate standards for their position: "The master said, 'In hearing cases, I am the same as anyone. What we must strive to do is to rid the courts of cases altogether" (12.13; also 12.17, 12.19, 13.6, 13.13). Moreover, "Exemplary persons (junzi) make demands on themselves, while petty persons make demands on others" (15.21). But under less than ideal conditions—the only conditions we have experienced—the demands can permissibly be made as a way to ensure that one receives proper benefits. "If proper in their own conduct, what difficulty would they [officials] have in governing? But if not able to be proper in their own conduct, how can they demand such conduct of others?" (13.13).[32]

Second, if human worth turns on being in a position to fulfill responsibilities, then people can demand of others—as a condition of acknowledging that worth—that those others assure the conditions required for fulfilling the responsibilities associated with their position. Once more, under ideal conditions the demand will not be necessary: "Exemplary persons (junzi) cherish fairness" (4.11).

Third, the basic human rights flow as well from the responsibility of officials to care for the common good: say, the peace and security of the

31. In this case, the human rights belong, as Rawls puts it, to "an associationist social form . . . which sees persons first as members of groups—associations, corporations, and estates. As such members, persons have rights and liberties enabling them to meet their duties and obligations and to engage in a decent system of social cooperation." Rawls, *Law of Peoples*, 68.

32. The line of argument noted in the text is not the only one available within Confucianism. Angle points to two alternative strategies of early twentieth-century Confucian argument for "ethical aggressiveness: struggling to exercise those abilities and receive those benefits that properly belong to one." See Angle, *Human Rights*, chap. 6. Throughout, Angle rightly distinguishes the idea that doctrinal evolution sometimes represents a response to external provocations from the idea that such evolution consists simply in embracing ideas that are external to an ethical tradition.

people. How, we might ask, can officials fulfill their responsibility of caring for the good of members if they fail to provide the protections required by a code of human rights? Consider in this light Mencius's claim that "If beans and millet were as plentiful as water and fire, such a thing as a bad man would not exist among the people." Or his opposition to an excessive use of conscripted labor and to savage penalties: both in the name of government guided by the virtue of humaneness *(ren)*.

These three considerations suggest reasons for supporting a conception of human rights without relying on a liberal conception of persons as autonomous choosers, but instead drawing on an ethical outlook that understands persons as embedded in social relations and subject to the obligations associated with those relationships. The notions of persons standing in relations and bearing duties associated with positions in those relations remain fundamental: rights are understood to flow from the demands of those duties and an account of the worth of human beings that is tied to their fulfilling social responsibilities. This ethical outlook can be interpreted as providing support for an independently elaborated conception of human rights—developed autonomously, as an account of what is owed to members—without relying on the idea that persons as fundamentally choosers of their aims, or that obligations are self-imposed, or that individuals have special worth or dignity because they posses a capacity to formulate and revise their aims.

A notion from Rawls helps to clarify the point. The various liberalisms, he says, represent individuals as "self-authenticating sources of valid claims"—as agents who are entitled to make claims on their institutions, where those claims are "regarded as having weight of their own apart from being derived from duties and obligations specified by a political conception of justice, for example, from duties and obligations owed to society." Other political conceptions do not embrace the idea of individuals as "self-authenticating sources of valid claims," and hold instead that "claims have no weight except insofar as they can be derived from duties and obligations owed to society, or from their ascribed roles in a social hierarchy justified by religious or aristocratic values."[33] Confucianism appears to be a view of this latter kind, with obligations derived from ascribed roles, although it is

33. Rawls, *Political Liberalism*, 32–33.

not for that reason hostile to rights of the kind incorporated into the Universal Declaration. So the terrain of argument of a global public reason that comprises a conception of human rights is available to its adherents.

The terrain of argument of a global public reason that comprises a conception of human rights, then, seems to be available from within Confucianism. Once more, I do not say that we can "find" a conception of human rights in this ethical tradition. Instead, there are ways of elaborating an ethical outlook that is nonliberal in its conception of the person and political society but that is also consistent with a reasonable conception of standards to which political societies can reasonably be held. Similar elaborations can be (and have been) developed for other ethical traditions.

Islam

Thus consider, more briefly, the case of Islam.[34] Here, in contrast with Confucianism, persons are not conceived of as in the first instance members of groups or a community. Instead, individuals themselves are the ultimate locus of responsibility and accountability: "And fear the day when ye shall be brought back to Allah. Then shall every soul be paid what it earned, and none shall be dealt with unjustly."[35] Or again: "But how will they fare when we gather them together against a day about which there is no doubt. And each soul will be paid out just what it earned" (3:25). And "On the day when every soul will be confronted with all the good it has done and all the evil, it has done, it will wish there were a greater distance between it and its evil" (3:30). Moreover, the fundamental duty of commanding right and forbidding wrong is assigned to individuals: "command right and forbid wrong, and bear patiently whatever may befall thee" (31:17). In his study of this duty, Michael Cook says that it assigns to "each and every legally competent Muslim an executive power of the law of God,"[36] as Lockean natural law theory assigns the executive power of the law of nature to each person.

34. For an illuminating discussion of approaches to interpretation within Islamic law, see Wael B. Hallaq, *A History of Islamic Legal Theories: An Introduction to Sunni Usul Al-Fiqh* (Cambridge: Cambridge University Press, 1997), esp. chap. 6, which describes both contextualist/historicist and holistic styles of interpretation.

35. *Qur'an*, 2:281. I have used *The Holy Qur'an*, trans. Abdullah Yusuf Ali, 10th ed. (Beltsville, MD: Amana Publications, 1999). Hereafter, references are in the text.

36. See Michael Cook, *Commanding Right and Forbidding Wrong in Islamic Thought* (Cambridge: Cambridge University Press, 2000), 583.

Despite the focus on individually responsible agents, trouble for an idea of human rights might be seen as emerging from a way of interpreting the fundamental conception of God as sovereign.[37] Thus suppose we think of God as exercising His authority by setting down strictures (expressed in shari'ah) that provide a fully detailed specification of the right way to live, a dense order of normative requirements that determine, for every possible circumstance of choice, the right way to act.[38] Suppose, too, that God has created human beings with the intellectual capacities required for understanding those requirements and also with the exalted status of vicegerents (2:30), who are assigned among others, an obligation to promote justice: not simply to act rightly, but also to "command right and forbid wrong."

Now it might be argued that fulfilling this obligation, which is assigned to all, actually requires a variety of basic rights: that if individuals are to fulfill the moral demands of vicegerency, by forbidding wrong and promoting justice, they must have rights of expression and association, and perhaps rights of participation, as well as the circumstances of health, education, and security that are preconditions for fulfilling their obligations. But that attractive conclusion does not follow so easily. For the contents of right and wrong are given in the first instance by the densely ordered strictures of this non-latitudinarian God. So the submission to God's will that is Islam arguably consists in individual rectitude and an enforcement of the rectitude of others, where rectitude involves compliance with those strictures, as expressed in some formulation of shari'ah. And although God "careth for all" and is "truly the cherisher of all," "Allah loveth not those who do wrong" (3:57).[39]

This line of thought suggests, in barest outline, a case from within Islam that works against the idea that political societies must ensure conditions of social membership for each person. It seems instead to favor

37. I have been helped in my discussion here by Khaled Abou El Fadl, *Islam and the Challenge of Democracy* (Princeton: Princeton University Press, 2004).

38. See Kevin Reinhart's Introduction to Laleh Baktiar, *Encyclopedia of Islamic Law: A Compendium of the Major Schools* (Chicago: KAZI Publications, 1996), xxxiii.

39. Qutb's account of freedom of conscience and responsibility seems to be of this kind. See Sayyid Qutb, *Social Justice in Islam*, trans. John B. Hardie (Oneonta, NY: Islamic Publications International, 1953). Thus freedom of conscience is a matter of, among other things, freedom from false worship, fear (of death, injury, and humiliation), and false social values (53–68). The fundamental metaphysical idea in Qutb's view—a particular interpretation of the absolute unity of existence *(tawhid)*—appears to limit any role for basic human rights.

extending basic rights only for those who can be expected to act rightly—
freedom of opinion for those with correct opinions, freedom of assembly
for those who assemble to forbid the wrong. So it might be said that each
person has a determinate personal responsibility under the law to "cleanse
and purify" his appetites and "make them follow the path of righteousness,"
and that there is no case for rights that permit departures from that path.[40]

But an alternative elaboration of these fundamentals suggests a different conclusion. Three points are essential to the alternative. The first is
a distinction between the true propositions of law—that is, standards of
right conduct—as set down by God and the historically-situated human
interpretation of those laws, which is both fallible and contextual. Failure to acknowledge and give sufficient weight to the distinction between
law and human interpretation is a form of idolatry, a failure to distinguish sovereign and vicegerent. But drawing the distinction creates
space for the disagreement and error that inevitably comes with the territory of human interpretive activity, and also for efforts to improve understanding of right conduct and reinterpret those requirements under
changed conditions.

The second is a distinction between human responsibility and God's
responsibility. The human responsibility is to seek to understand what is
right and provide moral instruction, whereas God is responsible for entering final judgment on the sincerity of belief and righteousness of conduct.
Associated with this distinction is the principle that there is to be "no
compulsion in religion" (2:256). Usurping final judgment—and compulsion in religion is a form of usurpation—is another form of idolatry: "can
they, if Allah wills some penalty for me, remove his penalty? Or if he wills
some grace for me, can they keep back His grace" (39:38). By accepting
these two distinctions—while also acknowledging the commanding responsibility to command right and forbid wrong—we have a case for wider
assurances of basic rights, as conditions of membership and of the appropriate exercise of responsibility, rather than for extending them only to
those who have what are presumed to have correct beliefs, as given by
some interpretation of shari'ah.

The third idea is that a diversity of religious communities is a natural
human condition: "To each among you have We prescribed a law and an

40. Qutb, *Social Justice*, 80.

open way. If Allah had so willed he would have made you a single people. But His plan is to test you in what He hath given you; so strive as in a race in all virtues. The goal of you all is to Allah; it is He that will show you the truth of the matters in which ye dispute" (5:48). If the first two points suggest a basis for a wider extension of rights within an Islamic community, with diverse interpretations of the law, the third—joined to the rejection of compulsion in religion and the idea that Allah cherishes all, loves all who do good, and "means no injustice to any of His creatures" (3:108)—suggests a basis for supporting a conception of human rights as part of a public reason of global reach.

Once more, then, the terrain of global public reason is available. That terrain is not the exclusive property of the "network of free-thinking, autonomy-asserting individualists," who belong to the party of "Lockian [sic] individual liberty," and to insist otherwise is both an intellectual error (for the reasons sketched above in the remarks on Vatican II, Confucianism, and Islam) and an objectionable form of intolerance.[41]

4. Substantive Minimalism

I have been sketching a way to interpret the idea of justificatory minimalism as neither skeptical nor empirical and showing how the autonomous presentation of a conception of human rights might enable that conception to win support from a range of ethical and religious outlooks: as my examples should make clear, the autonomously presented conception is not simply *consistent with* those outlooks, but is supported by certain interpretations of them. What then about substantive minimalism? Does autonomous formulation lead to the minimalist focus on rights associated with personal security?

I have provided the beginning of an answer already by distinguishing justificatory minimalism from a search for de facto points of overlap. Substantive minimalism may seem straightforwardly plausible as a statement about the overlap of competing ethical outlooks—as an account of normative strands that run through all of them (recall, once again, Hart's "minimum content of natural law" or Walzer's "moral minimalism"). But its plausibility diminishes on the account of justificatory minimalism I have suggested here. The content of human rights is left open to an independent

41. See Thomas M. Franck, "Are Human Rights Universal?" *Foreign Affairs* 80, 1 (2001): 195.

argument about conditions of membership that proceeds on the terrain of global public reason.

To pursue the question further, however, I first need a point of clarification. I have been identifying substantive minimalism with the view that human rights are essentially confined to rights of bodily security, or, more generally, to the rights that are required "for any kind of life at all."[42] Minimalism, thus understood, is not identical to the view—endorsed, for example, by Rawls in *Law of Peoples*—that human rights are only a "proper subset" of the rights embraced by any of the reasonable views of justice for a democratic society.[43] More precisely, substantive minimalism is one instance of the proper subset view, but other instances embrace more expansive sets of rights than minimalism—say, rights to an adequate standard of living, to adequate levels of health, education, and housing, and to some form of political representation and accountability—though not a full complement of liberal-democratic rights, including full equality of political rights.

There are, I think, good reasons for endorsing the proper subset view— for thinking that standards of human rights should differ from and be less demanding than standards that we endorse for our own society. But these reasons operate from within an autonomously presented conception of human rights, and reflect the political values associated with that conception: in particular, the elements of a reasonable conception of membership and its demands. They are not the results of a search for de facto points of intersection or common normative strands among competing ethical outlooks. And they do not lead to substantive minimalism. I do not propose to make a specific case here about what they lead to: instead, my aim is simply to sketch some reasons for endorsing the proper subset view that do not carry us to substantive minimalism and that also are not founded on the skeptical or empirical interpretations of justificatory minimalism.

Suppose then, by way of example, that you endorse the first principle of Rawls's theory of justice, requiring equal liberties of conscience, expression, association, and participation. You might still, for three reasons, resist the idea that this principle of justice should be an element of global public reason, that it should be applied to the whole world as a human

42. Ignatieff, *Human Rights*, 56.
43. Rawls, *Law of Peoples*, 78–81.

rights principle, so that a society must satisfy it to be beyond reproach—
that is, for three reasons think that different norms are suited to different
cases of political association, and that, for example, an Islamic democracy
with restrictions on office-holding or political party formation would not
violate, for that very reason, human rights, even if it were unjust.

First, a plausible element of any conception of human rights is a principle of collective self-determination, of a kind stated in Article 1 of the
Covenant on Civil and Political Rights. The satisfaction of this principle
requires that collective decisions be based on a process that represents the
interests and opinions of all those who are subject to the society's laws and
regulations. Suppose that that principle is satisfied, and, moreover, that
the outcomes of the process do not produce gross infringements of other
fundamental interests. Then we should resist the idea that the political
society should be held to a standard of justice that is rejected by its own
members and may have no real resonance in the culture, even if we think
that that standard represents the truth about justice.

But the case for this conclusion—that the society, though unjust, is beyond reproach from the point of view of global public reason—seems
stronger to the extent that the political society can plausibly claim that it
does accommodate and advance the good of all those subject to its laws
and regulations, by providing more than minimalist guarantees of bodily
security—say assurances of decent levels of health, education, and economic security, and some form of political accountability. That is, the case
is stronger to the extent that the society can be seen to provide the basis
for some recognizable form of collective self-determination and not to be
simply a form of group domination (even if the group domination exists
alongside minimalist assurances).

A second consideration turns on the distinction between what justice
requires and what people in a society have an obligation to do. It is widely
agreed—in political philosophy and in life—that the members of a society
have obligations to obey regulations even when those regulations are not
fully just. But now suppose the members of a society have an obligation to
obey—that is, the institutions meet the normative standards, whatever
they are, that suffice for political obligation but fall short of justice. Then
outsiders ought to show some reluctance to pressure for changes, and certainly a reluctance to intervene more forcefully or forcibly in the name of
the more demanding norms of justice. Surely it is not permissible for outsiders to forcibly intervene to change arrangements with which members

are obliged to comply. So if human rights standards are standards for treating members whose violation warrants stringent external criticism (and perhaps intervention), then the distinction between standards of justice and standards of obligation exerts some additional downward pressure on the content of those standards.

A third point concerns toleration. If you endorse a liberal principle of equal liberties, such as Rawls's first principle, then you think that non-liberal political arrangements—such as an ideal Islamic democracy—are unjust. But you also endorse the idea that, on complex normative issues, reasonable people disagree: a commitment to toleration is another part of your political outlook. The idea of tolerating reasonable differences suggests that the standards to which all political societies are to be held accountable will need to be less demanding than the standards of justice one endorses. This point about toleration does not imply relativism about justice: the point is not that justice is relative to circumstance, or consists, as Michael Walzer once said, in fidelity to local cultural understandings. Instead, the point is that a political society can, within limits, be unjust but beyond reproach, from the point of view of an acceptable global public reason. Of course there are limits on toleration, and an aim of the conception of human rights is to set out those limits. But the observation here is simply that, once we take into consideration the value of toleration, we will be more inclined to accept differences between what we take to be the correct standards of justice—and the rights ingredient in those standards—and the human rights standards to which all political societies are to be held accountable.

Of course the value of toleration is not absolute, but it is profoundly important. Its importance owes in part to the connections between the respect shown to a political society, when it is treated in global public reason as beyond reproach, and the respect shown to members of that society, who ordinarily will have some identification with that political society and its way of life. Not extending toleration has serious costs, and those costs must sometimes be paid. But the costs are real: in Rawls's forceful words, "lapsing into contempt on the one side, and bitterness and resentment on the other, can only cause damage."[44] "Only" puts the point too strongly. But the point remains: the presence of these costs operates to cre-

44. Ibid., 62.

ate some distance between the requirements of justice and the rights that are part of a doctrine of human rights.

But although these three considerations all work to limit the requirements of human rights to a proper subset of the requirements of justice, none of the three leads to substantive minimalism. Indeed the first point—about collective self-determination—suggests something very different and much more demanding: that the rationale for not insisting that international standards match standards of liberal justice is that such insistence would be incompatible with collective self-determination. But as I indicated earlier, the requirements of collective self-determination—whatever their precise content, and while they are less demanding than norms of democracy—extend well beyond the demands of minimalism. For example, any reasonable conception of collective self-determination that is consistent with the fundamental value of membership and inclusion, will—as with the Declaration and the Covenant on Political and Civil Rights—require some processes of interest representation and official accountability, even if not equal political rights for all.

5. Conclusion

To conclude: justificatory minimalism aims to avoid imposing unnecessary hurdles on accepting an account of human rights (and justice), by intolerantly tying its formulation to a particular ethical tradition. It is left to different traditions—each with internal complexities, debates, competing and conflicting traditions of argument, and (in some cases) canonical texts—to elaborate the bases of a shared view of human rights within their own terms. To be sure, it is desirable that that view be capable of winning wide support, from different ethical traditions, and that it be acceptable from within those traditions, even if it is not accepted by them in their historically prominent formulations. As An-Na'im says, "If international human rights standards are to be implemented in a manner consistent with their own rationale, the people (who are to implement these standards) must perceive the concept of human rights and its content as their own. To be committed to carrying out human rights standards, people must hold these standards as emanating from their worldview and values."[45]

---

45. Abdullahi Ahmed An-Na'im, "Conclusion," in *Human Rights in Cross-Cultural Perspectives: A Quest for Consensus*, ed. Abdullahi Ahmed An-Na'im (Philadelphia: University of Pennsylvania Press, 1992), 431.

But we do not specify the concept or the content of a human rights conception by looking to worldviews and values, taking them as determinate, fixed, and given, and searching for points of de facto agreement. Instead, we hope that—as is so often the case—different traditions can find resources for fresh elaboration that support a conception of justice and human rights that seems independently plausible as a common standard of achievement with global reach. That, and not substantive minimalism, is the best we can hope for. Or at least that wide acceptability is something we may reasonably hope for, consistent with a theoretical knowledge of human pluralism and a moral commitment to respecting it.

10

IS THERE A HUMAN RIGHT TO DEMOCRACY?

Is there a human right to democracy? My answer, in brief, is "No." Five interconnected claims will play a role in my argument for this conclusion:

1. Justice requires democracy.
2. Human rights are a proper subset of the rights founded on justice, so a society that fully protects human rights is not ipso facto just.
3. A conception of human rights is part of an ideal of global public reason, a shared basis for political argument that expresses a *common reason* that adherents of conflicting religious, philosophical, and ethical traditions can reasonably be expected to share.
4. That conception includes an account of membership, and human rights are entitlements that serve to ensure the bases of membership.
5. The democracy that justice requires is associated with a demanding conception of equality, more demanding than the idea of membership associated with human rights.

An underlying thought that runs through the argument is that democracy is a demanding political ideal. The thesis that there is a human right to democracy—although it may seem to elevate democracy—threatens to strip away its demanding substance.

I presented earlier versions of this chapter to the Harvard-MIT Joint Seminar on Political Development (JOSPOD), the University of Connecticut Philosophy Department, the Stanford University Political Science Department, and my political philosophy seminar in the spring of 2004. I am grateful to audiences on all three occasions for their comments and criticisms. I also wish to thank Alyssa Bernstein, Annabelle Lever, Frank Michelman, and Christine Sypnowich for comments.

1. The Question

I will start with some comments aimed at clarifying my question about whether democracy is a matter of human right. A variety of things are commonly said on behalf of democracy:

- Democracy is good for peace, at least to the extent that countries with democratic political regimes do not fight each other.[1]
- Democracy, joined with a free press, prevents famines.[2]
- Democracy helps to protect such basic personal liberties as liberty of conscience and speech.

These claims each have some plausibility, and each, if true, would be reason enough for welcoming democracy's wider reach.[3] But none of these arguments for democracy on grounds of their very desirable consequences

---

1. The thesis in the text is one of a family of claims about the relevance of regime type to war: that democracies do not fight wars against other democracies (either because democratic institutions empower those who bear the costs of war or because of the regnant norms in a democracy), that democracies win their wars more frequently than non-democracies (either because they are better at mobilizing the population or better at picking their fights), and that democracies are less likely to use unacceptable methods in fighting wars. Moreover, claims about democracy and war are part of a larger family of anti-realist theses about the importance of factors other than the distribution of power—for example, economic and institutional cooperation—in shaping international politics. All these claims are disputed by realists, who see the conduct of states under conditions of anarchy and associated insecurity as driven by the underlying distribution of power, which is assumed to be more fundamental than ("second image") differences in regime type. See M. E. Brown, S. M. Lynn-Jones, and S. E. Miller, eds., *Debating the Democratic Peace* (Cambridge, MA: MIT Press, 1996), and Michael Desch, "Democracy and Victory: Why Regime Type Hardly Matters," *International Security* 27, 2 (2002): 5–47. See Kenneth Waltz, *A Theory of International Politics* (Reading, MA: Addison-Wesley, 1979), and John Mearsheimer, *The Tragedy of Great Power Politics* (New York: W. W. Norton, 2001), for general statements of realist skepticism about the relevance of regime type to the conduct of international politics. See B. Russett, J. Oneal, and M. Berbaum, "Causes of Peace: Democracy, Interdependence, and International Organizations, 1886–1992," *International Studies Quarterly* 47, 3 (2003): 371–393, for a recent defense of the democratic peace theory, along with allied ideas about the relevance of trade and international institutions to peace.

2. Amartya Sen, *Development as Freedom* (New York: Knopf, 1999), chap. 7.

3. Although reasons for caution would remain. As Edward Mansfield and Jack Snyder argue, even if democracy is good for peace, democratization may not be. They argue that democratization, absent strong political institutions (rule of law, executive authority), often generates belligerently nationalist mobilization and conflict. See Edward Mansfield and Jack Snyder's *Electing to Fight: Why Emerging Democracies Go to War* (Cambridge, MA: MIT Press, 2007). If this view is right, the case for outside intervention in the name of a human right to democracy (assuming there is such a right) would be extremely tenuous. Democracy-promoting intervention would require that outside agents help to establish the strong institu-

depend on the premise that—or imply the conclusion that—democracy is the object of a human right.

It is sometimes also said that democracy is a demand of justice: that justice comprises a right to democracy—more particularly, an equal right of individuals to political participation, including equal rights of suffrage, office-holding, association, assembly, and expression. But the thesis that democracy is an aspect of justice does not settle the human rights issue, except on the view—not widely shared—that all rights required by justice are also human rights.

Consider—as an illustration of the distinction between a right founded on justice and a human right—John Rawls's account of justice as fairness and of the law of peoples. Justice as fairness includes, as part of its first principle, an equal right to participate in the processes of authoritative collective decision-making. According to this principle of participation, "all citizens are to have an equal right to take part in, and to determine the outcome of, the constitutional process that establishes the laws with which they are to comply."[4] Here we have a right to democracy—more particularly, a collection of individual rights that require democratic processes of collective decision-making—founded on justice. Rawls's proposed law of peoples,[5] in contrast, has a relatively short list of human rights that does not include either an equal right of participation or an equal liberty of conscience.

This distinction between the rights that must be assured in a just political society and human rights is associated with Rawls's distinction between liberal and decent but non-liberal peoples.[6] A liberal people endorses some form of political liberalism, all forms of which assign priority to a set of equal basic liberties, including equal rights of participation. A decent but non-liberal people has a legal system founded on a "common good" conception of justice that includes protection of human rights and imposes genuine obligations on everyone in the territory. Associated with

---

tional preconditions—and there are many reasons for skepticism about that ability, not the least being the limited staying power of outside agents.

4. John Rawls, A *Theory of Justice*, rev. ed. (Cambridge, MA: Harvard University Press, 1999), 194.

5. John Rawls, *The Law of Peoples* (Cambridge, MA: Harvard University Press, 1999), 78–81.

6. Ibid., 64–72.

this common good conception of justice—and helping to ensure that its conditions are met—is a "consultative" scheme of political decision-making that permits the expression of a range of opinions (including political dissent) and ensures representation of the fundamental interests of all. But consultation—joined with human rights, a rule of law, and arrangements that serve the common good—does not suffice for democracy.

Thus a political society with an official religion, as well as religious restrictions on office-holding and positions of influence, could in principle be decent and protect human rights, including liberty of conscience. And its decency would qualify it as a member in good standing in the global society of peoples—an equal member, beyond reproach by reference to the standards suited to cooperation across peoples and to which different peoples may reasonably hold one another accountable (the law of peoples), and owed justifications by reference to reasons that we can expect both liberal and decent peoples to reasonably accept.[7] But although beyond reproach (in the sense just specified), the decent society would nevertheless be unjust in virtue of the inequalities of rights that violate (among other things) the principle of participation.

Details aside, the essential idea—that a society might protect human rights (and be in other respects decent) while falling short of justice because it fails to ensure all the rights that justice demands[8]—is, I think, widely shared: it is, for example, rare to see an argument for an account of human rights that proceeds simply by providing an account of the rights ingredient in a just society.[9]

I will not say more about Rawls's view, although I will return later to the distinction between rights founded on justice and human rights. I mention the difference between his conception of the requirements of justice as fairness—and other politically liberal views—and of the law of peoples

7. Ibid., 59.

8. Without the clause that begins with "because," the claim would be fairly trivial: a society might protect all the human rights and yet fail to be just because justice requires more than protection of rights.

9. The idea that human rights are a special subset of rights—not simply to be identified with rights founded on justice—is endorsed by theorists who embrace expansive sets of human social and economic rights, and is not confined to human rights minimalists, who believe that human rights are confined to rights of bodily security. See, for example, Amartya Sen, "Elements of a Theory of Human Rights," *Philosophy and Public Affairs* 32, 4 (2004): 315–356, in which he emphasizes that human rights are associated with freedoms of a particular importance.

because it crisply illustrates my initial point: that the thesis that there is a human right to democracy represents a distinctive normative case for democracy, different on its face from (although of course consistent with) both consequentialist arguments about the merits of democracy as a way to forestall great evils such as war, famine, and tyranny, and arguments for democracy that appeal to rights required in a just society. I want to consider whether there is a compelling case of this kind.

To be clear: I am not asking whether, when all the relevant considerations are in, there is a compelling case for democracy, but instead what kind of case there might be, and, more specifically, whether a case of a particular type—a human rights case—is available. Investigations of this kind, characteristic of philosophy, often provoke an impatient response, because they are not about, bottom line, all-things-considered political judgments, but about the force and implications of particular lines of argument. I do not share this impatience because I think that normative-political argument is itself an important feature of political life. What matters are not simply the conclusions we arrive at but how we arrive at them.

2. Human Rights: Neither Maximal nor Minimal

I have not yet explained how I understand "human rights" as a distinct normative category.[10] As a preliminary, then, I will say that human rights have three features:

- They are *universal* in being owed by every political society and owed to all individuals.
- They are requirements of political morality whose force as such does not depend on their expression in enforceable law.[11]
- They are especially *urgent* requirements of political morality.

These features are suggested by the remark in the Universal Declaration of Human Rights, that human rights are "a common standard of achievement for all peoples and all nations."[12]

---

10. This section draws on and extends Joshua Cohen, "Minimalism about Human Rights: The Most We Can Hope For?" *Journal of Political Philosophy* 12, 2 (2004): 190–213 (reprinted as Chapter 9 in this volume). That companion essay also contains a range of references that I have not included here, for reasons of space.

11. See Sen, "Elements of a Theory of Human Rights," for discussion of this point.

12. The Universal Declaration, as well as other human rights conventions and charters, are printed in the Annex on Documents in Henry Steiner and Philip Alston, *International*

I also make two methodological assumptions. First, I assume that an account of human rights must meet a condition of *fidelity*: if there are human rights, then at least some substantial range of the rights identified by the principal human rights instruments—especially the Universal Declaration—are among them. The rights identified in those instruments represent "provisional fixed points" in our reflection on the nature and content of human rights. Second, I assume a condition of *open-endedness*. Thus any proposed enumeration of human rights—as in the Declaration or the Covenants on Civil and Political Rights and on Economic and Social Rights[13]—is open-ended in at least two ways that parallel the open-endedness of rights embodied in law: (1) we can, through normative reasoning, argue in support of human rights that were not previously identified or enumerated; and (2) moreover, such rights as are identified are expressed in abstract language whose application requires interpretation.

I will say more later about these five general features—universality, non-juridification, urgency, fidelity, and open-endedness. With these as background, I want to now expand on my earlier comments about the nature and distinctiveness of a human rights case for democracy. To clarify the point, I will distinguish two stylized views about human rights: *maximalist* and *minimalist*. Maximalism holds that human rights are coextensive with rights founded on justice and that the case for a human right to democracy is correspondingly straightforward—assuming (as I do) that an equal right to participation is a matter of justice. Minimalism confines human rights to protections of bodily security and thus denies a human right to democracy (except derivatively, if democracy turns out to be the unique way to ensure the right to bodily security). If we reject both minimalism and maximalism about human rights, the issue is correspondingly less straightforward.

A popular case for minimalism is founded on an interpretation of the value of toleration.[14] This case presents a minimal set of human rights as the lowest common denominator of distinct ethical and religious traditions—as their ethical intersection. As Ignatieff summarizes it: "Human

---

Human Rights in Context: Law, Politics, Morals, 2nd ed. (Oxford: Oxford University Press, 2000).

13. See the Annex to Steiner and Alston, *International Human Rights in Context.*

14. I discuss this argument in some detail in Cohen, "Minimalism about Human Rights."

rights can command universal assent only as a decidedly 'thin' theory of what is right, a definition of the minimal conditions for any life at all."[15]

But this rationale for minimalism misconceives toleration. Toleration, in this domain, requires that a conception of human rights be formulated and defended independently of particular ethical and religious traditions, and that the autonomously formulated conception be capable of eliciting support from adherents of different and conflicting ethical and religious traditions reasoning within the terms of their tradition. However, such support may require a reformulation of the tradition—some form of doctrinal evolution. Toleration does not require, as Ignatieff suggests, "universal assent" or acceptance, but a certain kind of broad acceptability. Once we reject the lowest-common-denominator conception, the case for a minimalist account of human rights based on toleration is no longer so clear.

Six other considerations are commonly offered against more demanding lists of human rights, including a richer class of civil and political rights as well as some social and economic rights:

- They threaten to overtax the resources and disperse the attention required for monitoring and enforcing human rights.
- More expansive lists cannot be fully realized because their realization is simply too costly or burdensome and for that reason are not genuinely speaking lists of rights.
- Because rights correspond to obligations, and we cannot give determinate content to the obligations associated with an expansive class of rights in advance of their legal institutionalization, rights are limited in scope.
- Expansive lists threaten to substitute legal principles for political judgments—often uncompromising rights claims for informed and more supple political deliberation and judgment.
- Expansive lists threaten to subordinate legitimate political self-determination to the decisions of outside agents, who justify their interventions in the language of human rights.

For reasons that I will discuss later, the sixth consideration—collective self-determination—is not at all plausible as a basis for minimalism. As for

15. Michael Ignatieff, *Human Rights as Politics and as Idolatry* (Princeton: Princeton University Press, 2001), 56.

the others, suffice it to say that each has some force, but none presents a robust case for the minimalist's narrow circumscription of human rights.

You might, finally, arrive at minimalist conclusions if you begin with the premise that human rights are Lockean natural rights, understood as moral rights that individuals would have even in a pre-institutional state of nature.[16] Because of the non-institutional setting, the content of natural rights is necessarily relatively restricted, and on a conception that identifies natural and human rights, the latter would inherit that limitation. So it would be difficult, for example, to explain the human right to fair legal process—a right that presupposes an institutional context—on the theory that a human right is a Lockean natural right.[17]

But the concepts of natural right and human right are fundamentally different, as is evident from the institutional presuppositions of many of the rights enumerated in the Universal Declaration and the 1966 Covenants— including rights to a fair hearing, to equality before the law, and to take part in government, none of which could obtain in a pre-institutional state of nature. Unless the authors of the Declaration were conceptually confused in their enumeration of human rights, or believed that the institutionally specified human rights in the Declaration can be derived by applying non-institutional natural rights to institutional conditions, the argument for minimalism premised on an identification of human and natural rights is deficient. The idea that they were conceptually confused is implausible and defeated by considerations of fidelity; and the idea that all the institutionally specified human rights—for example, the right to fair legal protections—are simply instruments for protecting pre-institutional natural rights is nowhere suggested in the arguments for the declared rights, which seem to be answerable to considerations of a different kind. Human rights are not rights that people are endowed with independent of

16. In *A Theory of Justice*, Rawls mentions a different, non-Lockean conception of natural rights, freed from the idea that natural rights are rights that individuals would have in a pre-institutional state of nature. According to this conception, natural rights are fundamental rights of persons, founded on justice, rather than on law or custom. See Rawls, *A Theory of Justice*, 442–443n30. The point in the text applies only to the Lockean idea. I am grateful to Valentina Urbanek for emphasizing the importance of this alternative conception.

17. I draw here on Charles Beitz, "Human Rights as a Common Concern," *American Political Science Review* 95, 2 (2001): 269–282; "What Human Rights Mean," *Daedalus* 132, 1 (Winter 2003): 36–46; and "Human Rights and the Law of Peoples," in Deen K. Chatterjee, ed., *The Ethics of Assistance: Morality and the Distant Needy* (Cambridge: Cambridge University Press, 2004), 193–214.

the conditions of social and political life, but rights that are owed by all political societies in light of basic human interests and the characteristic threats and opportunities that political societies present to those interests. They are, in ways I will explain later, conditions of membership or inclusion in such societies.

Shifting attention from minimalism to maximalism: I said earlier that human rights are not as expansive as rights founded on justice, that they are only a "proper subset" of the rights required by justice. Minimalism—with rights limited to bodily security—is an extreme version of the proper subset view. Other versions embrace more expansive sets of rights than minimalism—say, rights to an adequate standard of living, to adequate levels of health, education, and housing, and to forms of political representation and accountability that suffice for collective self-determination, although not a full complement of democratic rights, including full equality of political rights.

Whereas we should resist the pressure to the minimalist extreme, the proper subset view has much to be said for it. I want to present three considerations that recommend it: arguments based on self-determination, obligation, and toleration. To make the discussion a little less abstract, it will help to have a specific norm of justice at hand. So I will assume that justice requires, inter alia, rights to equal liberties of conscience, expression, association, and participation. Even if you embrace this principle as a requirement of justice, however, you might still resist its extension to the whole world as a human rights principle. Intuitively, the reason for such resistance is that human rights have, as I have said, a particular urgency, which transcends the urgency that surrounds considerations of justice generally. The three considerations here represent different ways of articulating that urgency.

First, a plausible element of any conception of human rights is a requirement of collective self-determination, which I understand to be a normative requirement, but less demanding than a requirement of democracy, which is one form of collective self-determination. In particular, let us say that collective self-determination requires that: (1) binding collective decisions result from, and are accountable to, a political process that represents the diverse interests and opinions of those who are subject to the society's laws and regulations and expected to comply with them. The representation may, for example, be organized territorially, functionally, or ascriptively; but however it is organized, it may—consistent with collective self-determination—assign special weight to the interests of some social groups; (2) rights to dissent from, and appeal, those collective decisions are assured for all; and (3) government normally provides public explanations for its decisions, and those explanations—intended to show why the decisions are justified—are founded on a conception of the common good of the whole society.

These three conditions of collective self-determination are politically important, and commonly violated, but they can be satisfied by an undemocratic political arrangement. Thus a society that meets the conditions of collective self-determination may still have an official religion endorsed by a preponderance of the population. Moreover, it may be that only adherents of that religion are permitted to hold official positions, that special privileges and assignments of resources are associated with the organizations of the official religion (although other religious groups are politically represented), and that the selection of representatives is made through separate social groups and not through competitive party elections.

Suppose now that the three conditions of collective self-determination are satisfied, and, in part for that reason, the political process does not result in gross infringements of other fundamental interests. But suppose, too, that democratic ideas lack substantial resonance in the political culture, or the history and traditions of the country. Then the value of collective self-determination itself recommends resistance to the idea that the political society should be required to meet the standard expressed in a principle of equal basic liberties, even if we think that that standard represents the truth about justice. I want to emphasize, though, that the case for this conclusion is stronger to the extent that the political society does accommodate and advance the good of all those subject to its laws and regulations, by providing, say, assurances of decent levels of health, education, and economic security, and some form of political accountability, as well as protections of personal security: assurances that extend well beyond a minimalist program of human rights. That is, the argument from self-determination to the proper subset view is stronger to the extent that the political society can—by embracing a more than minimal class of human rights—meet the charge that, in the name of collective self-determination, it establishes and enforces a form of group domination. So the value of self-determination is important, and provides a basis for more than minimalist rights, but does not imply maximalism.

A second consideration turns on the distinction between justice and political obligation. It is widely agreed that the members of a society have obligations to obey regulations even when those regulations are not fully just and/or do not emerge from just institutions: something less normatively demanding than justice is sufficient for an obligation to obey.[18] Now suppose the members of a society have an obligation to obey—that is, the institutions meet the normative standards, whatever they are, that suffice for political obligation but fall short of the more demanding standards of justice. Then outsiders ought to show some reluctance to pressure for changes and certainly a reluctance to intervene more forcefully or forcibly in the name of justice. Surely it is impermissible for outsiders to forcibly intervene to change arrangements with which members themselves are obliged to comply. So if human rights standards are urgent standards of political morality whose violation warrants external reproach (and in extreme cases sanctions and intervention), the distinction between norms of justice and norms of political obligation exerts some downward pressure, away from maximalism, on the content of those human rights standards.

A third point concerns toleration. If you accept a principle of equal public and private liberties as one requirement of justice, you think that non-liberal political arrangements—arrangements that are undemocratic but that nevertheless meet the three conditions for collective self-determination—are unjust. But you also endorse the idea that, on complex normative issues, reasonable people disagree: a commitment to toleration is another part of your political outlook. The idea of tolerating reasonable differences strongly suggests that the standards to which all political societies are to be held accountable—the appropriate common standards of achievement—will need to be less demanding than the standards of justice one endorses. In making this point—to underscore what should by now be clear—I am not endorsing a relativist view of justice, which has the fundamental requirements of justice varying with circumstance.[19] Instead, the point is that a political society can, within

---

18. See A. J. Simmons, *Moral Principles and Political Obligations* (Princeton: Princeton University Press, 1979) and Ronald Dworkin, *Law's Empire* (Cambridge, MA: Harvard University Press, 1986), chap. 6, especially 202–206, for discussion of obligations within unjust arrangements.

19. Walzer embraces a form of relativism about justice when he says that a society is just when it is "faithful to the shared understandings of the members." See Michael Walzer, *Spheres of Justice* (New York: Basic Books, 1983).

limits, be unjust but beyond reproach from the point of view of a global public reason (an idea I will explain soon).

Of course the requirements of toleration are not obvious. Later, I will be connecting human rights, as standards of global public reason in judging organized political societies, to conditions of membership or inclusion in an organized political society. In effect, I propose—as a substantive normative thesis, not as an analysis of the concept of reasonableness—that political conceptions and doctrines count as reasonable within global public reason (as distinct from what counts as reasonable within other settings) only if they accept the norms of membership, and that they need not endorse the democratic idea of society as an association of equals. To be sure, the value of toleration is not absolute. But it is a profoundly important value, and its importance in the current setting owes in part to the connections between the respect shown to a political society and the respect shown to members of that society, who ordinarily will have some identification with that political society and its way of life, even if they are critical of the society, its ethos, and its practices. Not extending toleration has serious costs, and those costs must sometimes be paid. But the costs are real: in Rawls's forceful words: "Lapsing into contempt on the one side, and bitterness and resentment on the other, can only cause damage."[20] "Only" puts the point too strongly. But the point remains: the presence of these costs operates to create some distance between the requirements of justice and the rights that are part of a doctrine of human rights.

If the human right to democracy is neither excluded (as with minimalism) nor demanded (as with maximalism), we need to determine whether the right to democracy—that is, an equal individual right to political participation—lies in the range of rights comprised by a reasonable conception of human rights, where the range includes more than a minimalist guarantee of bodily security but not everything required by justice. To address this issue, I will need to say more about the bases of human rights—building on the earlier points about how human rights norms are universal, urgent standards of political morality that need not be legally expressed and that are open-ended, although their content must broadly fit with settled understandings—and then about democracy.

20. Rawls, *Law of Peoples*, 62.

First, then, a conception of human rights—as I said earlier—presents a set of especially important, urgent standards that are universal in that all political societies are to be held accountable to them in their treatment of members. As a way to interpret this idea, I suggest that we think of the conception as a partial statement of the content of an ideal of what I will call global public reason. Generally speaking, global public reason comprises a set of political values, principles, and norms for assessing political societies, both separately and in their relations, that can be widely shared.

Global public reason is global in its reach, inasmuch as it applies to all political societies, and global *in its agent*, inasmuch as it is presented as the common reason of all peoples, who share responsibility for interpreting its principles and monitoring and enforcing them. Because it is presented as the common reason of all peoples in a deeply pluralistic world, as a reason whose content can be shared, it needs to be formulated autonomously from different and conflicting religious, philosophical, and ethical traditions—as a conception of reasons that adherents of different traditions can reasonably be expected to share. It is public in its use, in that it provides terms of argument and justification used in discussing the conduct of different political societies.

The precise ways of exercising the responsibility of interpretation, monitoring, and enforcement—who exercises it (international courts and other institutions, regional bodies, individual states, non-governmental organizations) and with what instruments (ranging from monitoring, to naming and shaming, to sanctions, to force)—vary widely. Although the agent and reach of the reason are global, often acting on the principles of global public reason may consist principally in observing the implementation of its principles by separate political societies or perhaps in assisting in their implementation.

The more immediate responsibility for interpreting and implementing the principles will—as the Declaration and Covenants emphasize—typically fall to separate political societies themselves, in part, although not only, because of the value of collective self-determination affirmed in Article 1 of the Covenant on Civil and Political Rights.

Second, part of a conception of human rights is an account (a normative theory) of why the rights have the content that they have and how the content of the conception may be extended, interpreted, and revised: the open-endedness that I mentioned earlier requires such an account. Thus, although a conception of human rights needs to be expressed, at least provisionally, in a definite statement of rights, it is not given simply by an enumeration of rights, much less an enumeration of highly specific rights—a kind of rule book of enumerated rights—but also includes an account about what rights belong on the list and how to interpret the rights when their content needs application to an issue. Global public reason is better understood as a terrain of reflection and argument than as a list of determinate rules: that is part of the force of the term "reason."

At the same time, because the conception of human rights belongs to global public reason, the rationale for human rights needs to be formulated in terms that can plausibly be shared, which means that it cannot be formulated by reference to a particular religious or secular moral outlook.[21] So we should not present, as the underlying rationale, the theory that, for example, human rights are preconditions for the autonomous moral agency prized by Kantians and the special dignity owing to the capacity for such agency; or that they are necessary for fulfilling divinely imposed obligations, whether the preferred statement of the obligations is found in Thomistic or Lockean natural law theory, or some formulation of shari'ah; or that they are required for the full expression of human powers associated with Aristotelian ethical views.

Instead, I propose that human rights norms are best thought of as norms founded on an idea of membership or inclusion in an organized political society and not on a deeper outlook about the proper conduct of a good or righteous life. The relevant notion of membership is a normative idea—distinct, for example, from living in a territory. The central feature of the normative notion of membership is that a person's good is to be taken into account by the political society's basic institutions: to be treated as a member is to have one's good given due consideration, both in the processes of arriving at authoritative collective decisions and in the content of those decisions. For this reason, an idea of collective self-determination of a kind that I mentioned earlier is a natural correlate of the requirement of treating all as members (especially because of the first two features of collective self-determination). And although human rights

21. See Hedley Bull, *The Anarchical Society: A Study in World Order*, 3rd ed. (New York: Columbia University Press, 2002), especially 41–43, for a suggestive discussion of related ideas. Thus Bull distinguishes cases in which a power has its own moral rationale for its conduct from cases in which that rationale is founded on ideas that provide a common terrain. Only in the latter case do we have, in Bull's special sense, an international society.

are not confined to matters of process, the prerequisites of a process of collective self-determination—including rights of dissent, expression, and conscience—are among the human rights.

Correspondingly, disagreements about the scope of human rights may be seen as proceeding on a shared terrain of political argument—the terrain of global public reason—and not (or not only) as disputes among different moral and political traditions themselves. They can be understood, in contrast with disputes about the content of natural rights, as disagreements about what is required to ensure membership—about what consideration is due to each person in a political society, and how to ensure that consideration under particular circumstances.

In emphasizing the connection between human rights and membership, I mean to affirm a view more or less precisely opposite to the classical Bentham–Marx critique of rights. Rights are not excluding, dividing, atomizing, and community-defeating, but instead a partial expression of norms of social and political inclusion.

I referred earlier to a condition of fidelity on a conception of human rights: it must be broadly faithful to the content of the rights as laid out in the standard statements, in particular the Universal Declaration. The membership theory, I believe, meets this test of fit. The importance of the notion of membership in an account of human rights is suggested by the breadth and substance of the rights in the Universal Declaration and the Covenants—including rights to education, work, and cultural inclusion, as well as assembly, expression, and participation. To be sure, some human rights (e.g., to life and to personal security) are not tied only to membership but are also more plausibly associated with demands of basic humanity, irrespective of membership in an organized political society. But the guiding thought behind the more capacious lists in the principal human rights instruments seems to be that an acceptable political society—one that is above reproach in its treatment of individuals—must attend to the common good of those who are subject to its regulations, on some reasonable conception of that good, and ensure the goods and opportunities that people in the territory and those subject to political rule need in order to take part in the political society. Human rights claims, then, identify goods and opportunities that are socially important because they are requirements of membership (and that are not provided as a matter of course, if they are provided at all). Failing to give due consideration to the good of members by ensuring access to such goods and opportunities is tantamount to treating those members as outsiders, persons whose good can simply be dismissed in making laws and policies: no-counts, with no part to play in the political society.

One reason for emphasizing membership in this way—apart from considerations of fidelity—is suggested by the idea of political obligation. Thus, on a plausible account of political obligation, attending to the common good, on some interpretation of that good, is necessary if the requirements that a political society imposes on people under its rule are to have the status of genuine obligations and not mere forcible impositions. Regulations cannot impose obligations of compliance on those who are subject to them unless the regulations reflect a concern with their good. If an account of political obligation along these lines is correct—and it is more plausible than a theory of obligation that makes the justness of processes and outcomes a necessary condition for political obligations—the rights that are required if individuals are to be treated as members would be identical to those that are required if the requirements imposed by law and other regulations are to be genuine obligations.

3. Equality and Democracy

Having said some things about a conception of human rights, I now need to introduce a conception of democracy. Simplifying a vast terrain: the essential point for addressing the question about human rights and democracy is that an idea of equality plays a central role in any reasonable normative conception of democracy. In fact, disagreements in normative democratic theory are typically disagreements about what is required in treating those subject to the rules (laws and regulations) as equals under the rules that apply to all and with which all are expected to comply.

One way to bring out the special importance of an idea of equality in any plausible conception of democracy is to note that the term "democratic" is sometimes used to characterize a form of politics, and also used more broadly to describe a type of society, characterized, broadly speaking, by conditions of equality—a society of equals, with equal rights and equal status, whose members relate to one another as equals. When Tocqueville discusses the democratic revolution in his *Democracy in America,* and the replacement of an aristocratic by a democratic society, he has in mind a transformation of the social hierarchy characteristic of feudalism into equality of condition and not the emergence of electoral competition or widespread suffrage rights.[22]

Similarly, Rawls says that his two principles of justice as fairness express the underlying "democratic conception of society as a system of cooperation among equal persons," and the idea of "democracy in judging each other's aims," meaning that members of a just society do not—"for the purposes of justice"—assess the "relative value of one another's way of life." He also describes his conception of equal opportunity and fair distribution—his difference principle—as a conception of democratic equality.[23]

Two ideas are essential in the characterization of a society as democratic, as a society of equals. First, each member is understood as entitled to be treated with equal respect, and therefore as entitled to the same basic rights, regardless of social position. An aristocratic or caste society, or some other society with fixed social orders, requires equal respect (and equal rights) within social ranks but differential respect (and rights) across ranks. Second, the basis of equality lies, in particular, in what I will refer to as political capacity: we owe equal respect to those who have sufficient capacity to understand the requirements of mutually beneficial and fair cooperation, grasp their rationale, and follow them in their conduct. So the basis of equality in a society of equals lies in the capacity to understand and follow the requirements that provide the fundamental standards of public life—a capacity that appears to be more or less universally characteristic of human beings (even though its basis, either in a particular mental module or in more generalized powers of reflective thought, is not well understood).

The fact that "democracy" has these two applications—to a form of society and a form of political regime—expresses an insight, not an equivocation: the insight that a democratic political arrangement expresses in the design of its institutions, in particular at the supreme level of political authority, the conception of the members as equal persons owed equal

22. See *Democracy in America*, trans. and ed. Harvey C. Mansfield and Delba Winthrop (Chicago: University of Chicago Press, 2000).

23. This paragraph and the next three draw on Joshua Cohen, "For a Democratic Society," in Samuel Freeman, ed., *Cambridge Companion to Rawls* (Cambridge: Cambridge University Press, 2002), 86–138 (reprinted as Chapter 5 in this volume).

respect. Moreover, the connections between a democratic society and democratic political arrangement run in both directions.

Thus, once the institutions of political democracy are in place, it is natural to regard the members of society as equals, with a broader claim to equal concern and respect in the arrangements of society: that is, natural to endorse the democratic conception of society. It is natural inasmuch as the conception of members as equal persons is itself suggested by the practices associated with democratic politics. For those practices entitle individuals—irrespective of class position or place in the distribution of natural assets—to bring their interests and their judgments of what is politically right to bear on supremely authoritative collective decisions. They provide that entitlement in the form of rights of participation, association, and expression: not just any rights, but equal rights to participate in making fundamental judgments about society's future course. "The instant the people is legitimately assembled as a sovereign body," Rousseau says, "all jurisdiction of the government ceases, the executive power is suspended, and the person of the humblest citizen is as sacred and inviolable as that of the first magistrate."[24]

At the same time, once the members of society are regarded as free and equal individuals—once we reject the idea of a fixed aristocratic hierarchy of unequal worth and entitlement and accept the idea of a sufficient equality of political capacity—it is natural to conclude that there ought to be widespread suffrage and elected government under conditions of political contestation, with protections of the relevant liberties (of participation, expression, and association). For the extension of political (and other) liberties expresses the respect owed to persons as equals, with political capacity: Dahl calls this extension of the idea of a society of equals to political arrangements "the logic of equality."[25] The thought is that once a democratic society is in place, with its ideas of equal standing and equal respect, a political democracy is a natural concomitant, inasmuch as its gives public expression—manifest and crystallized in institutions—to the idea of equality and equal respect and provides that expression in the basic design of the essential arrangements of collective decision-making. Martin Luther King, Jr. said that the "great glory of American democracy

24. Jean-Jacques Rousseau, *The Social Contract and Other Later Political Writings*, ed. and trans. Victor Gourevitch (Cambridge: Cambridge University Press, 1997), book 3, chap. 14.
25. Robert Dahl, *On Democracy* (New Haven: Yale University Press, 2000), 10.

is the right to protest for right"—that citizens have a right to bring not only their interests but also their sense of justice to bear on matters of common concern: a right to exercise what I have called their political capacity. So the emergence of a democratic society fosters the emergence of a political democracy, with the basic liberties of citizenship secured for all adult members—fosters, at least in the sense that it provides a forceful rationale for a democratic political society.

Three dimensions of a right to participate are suggested by an account of democracy founded on this conception of persons as equals:

1. *equal rights of participation*, including rights of voting, association, and office-holding, as well as rights of political expression;
2. a strong presumption in favor of *equally weighted votes*; and
3. *equal opportunities for effective political influence.*

I want to make a brief comment on the third element, because it helps to bring out the underlying rationale of the right to participate in a conception of free and equal persons.[26] Thus democracy's right to participate demands equal opportunity for effective political influence rather than equality of influence. The simple demand for influence—irrespective of one's own actions or of the considered convictions of others—is unreasonable. That is because a compelling interpretation of the idea of political equality, in a society of equals who are endowed with political capacity, must ensure a place for individual responsibility. Members of a democratic society are represented as free and equal. As free, they are to be treated as responsible for the exercise of their political capacity, and that must be reflected in the content of the equal right to participate. If I demand influence irrespective of my conduct or the judgments of others, I deny the importance of such responsibility.

The importance of equal opportunity for political influence is obscured by the fact that much democratic theory in the "elite" tradition, which endorses a more minimalist conception of democracy and the associated political rights, casts persons principally in the role of audience, with a fundamental interest in listening to debates, acquiring information through both formal political communications and more informal processes of discussion,

26. See Joshua Cohen, "Money, Politics, Political Equality," in Alex Byrne, Robert Stalnaker, and Ralph Wedgwood, eds., *Facts and Values* (Cambridge, MA: MIT Press, 2001), 47–80, for further discussion on the idea of equal opportunity for political influence.

arriving at judgments about policies and candidates, and acting as political agents when they express those judgments at the polls, making informed judgments among competing candidates. But as the conception of persons as free and equal in virtue of possessing political capacities suggests, citizens are also agents, participants, speakers, who may aim to reshape both the terms of political debate and its results, by running for office and seeking to influence the views of candidates, the outcomes of elections, and the inter-election conduct of politics. A requirement of equal opportunity for political influence aims to ensure that they are in a position to play that role, should they wish to take it on.

4. A Human Right to Democracy?

In asking whether there is a human right to democracy, then, I am asking two related questions: Is the equal right to participate that I have associated with democracy a human right? And is the democratic conception of persons as free and equal—the conception that underlies the equal right—a plausible component of a conception of human rights comprised within global public reason?[27] We know that the conception of persons as free and equal is not universally accepted by different ethical and religious outlooks, but that is not the relevant question: as I indicated in my earlier remarks about toleration, some conceptions may need to be adjusted to the terms of an acceptable global public reason.

I want to discuss three considerations that might be advanced in support of the thesis that there is a human right to democracy, and respond critically to each. I am unconvinced that there is a human right to democracy, because I do not find these considerations compelling.

1. *Truth.* In support of the claim that the conception of persons as free and equal—and the associated equal right to participation—is a plausible element of a conception of human rights, it might be argued that it represents the truth about human beings and our moral standing: not a truth acknowledged by all, but one that has, like virtually all interesting truths,

---

27. It might be objected that I have loaded the dice against a human right to democracy by presenting a conception of democracy more demanding than the minimalist idea of democracy as a system in which regular, competitive elections decide who runs the government. The objection would say that, on a less demanding view, there is a human right to democracy. I am not convinced that the assertion in the previous sentence is true. But even if it were, the point would remain that the democracy and associated rights required by justice are more demanding than the democracy and rights required by a conception of human rights.

come to be understood over the course of history. But I have proposed that we think of a conception of human rights as part of a conception of global public reason. The aim of a conception of global public reason is to present standards that one can reasonably expect others to accept: to present reasons that can be shared and that provide a common standard of achievement and a basis for common responsibility. What is true and what is reasonable to believe are distinct: the former is singular and the latter is plural; incompatible views can each be reasonable to believe, although they cannot both be true.

Now it is objectionably intolerant to hold that everyone must acknowledge the normative truth and that a conception qualifies as an element of public reason simply in virtue of its truth. I am not here denying the truth of the view that persons are free and equal and entitled to be treated as such as a matter of justice. To the contrary, I believe that individuals are free and equal and that they have an equal right to participate, from which it follows—since believing is believing true—that I believe that these propositions are true. Nor am I suggesting that political argument should exhibit the indifference to truth and falsity that Frankfurt claims is the essence of bullshit.[28] Instead I am affirming the distinction between what is true and what it is reasonable to expect people to believe in the setting of global public reason and am emphasizing that the truth of a proposition does not suffice to win it a place as an element in global public reason. A conception of persons as equals is true, and it may have such a place, but it does not gain entry simply by virtue of being true—any more than claims about divine creation gain entry by virtue of being true (if they are true).

2. *Bootstrapping.* It might be said instead that this conception of persons is not only true but also implicit in global public reason because some (open-ended) account of human rights is part of global public reason and—here is the controversial claim—all human rights depend for their justification on the conception of persons as free and equal. If this latter claim were true, the equal right to participation would not be in any way normatively distinctive: it could not be cabined off from other rights but would be best understood as part of a single normative structure with a common rationale. Assume that there are some human rights, that, as I have suggested, human rights are not simply given by a list, but have a rationale

---

28. Harry Frankfurt, *On Bullshit* (Princeton: Princeton University Press, 2005).

that is itself part of the terrain of global public reason, and that the rationale includes a conception of persons as free and equal. Then there would be a right to democracy. The right to democracy could not, on the best account of human rights, be separated off, because the democratic conception of a society of equals, and the political norms associated with it, would be implicit in all human rights discourse and an appropriate guide to its interpretation and thus to the extension of human rights beyond those that are already settled.

But this argument does not seem right. I cannot explore the issues in detail here, but in a companion piece (reprinted as Chapter 9 in this volume), I sketch interpretations of arguments within Confucianism and Islam that accept the importance of membership, and support a more-than-minimalist conception of human rights, but neither of which depends on the democratic conception of society or of persons as free and equal. The Islamic conception is founded on obligations given by law, and it interprets rights as preconditions for fulfilling the obligations. But it may not extend to the idea of an equal political capacity. Similarly, the Confucian view illustrates the idea that rights may be founded on responsibilities associated with positions in social relations: in this case, the rights are extended as preconditions for fulfilling those responsibilities, which are differentiated across individuals. But there is no conception of persons as free and equal and of a moral-political capacity possessed in sufficient degree by all to provide the basis of equal political standing and equal political opportunity.

More generally, I proposed earlier that we think of human rights as partial assurances of membership or inclusion, rather than as founded on an idea of persons as free and equal. The latter conception is associated with membership specifically in a democratic society, understood as a society of equals, and not with membership and the possession of rights as such.

3. *Unacceptable Conditions.* A third argument—which shades back into the instrumental conceptions that I mentioned at the outset—points to unacceptable conditions commonly associated with the absence of democracy: unacceptable consequences (war, famine, and tyranny) and the unacceptable subordination associated with an absence of equal political standing. The claim, then, is that these conditions—quite apart from any *independent* force of the idea of persons as free and equal—provide the case for including an equal right to participate as a human right and thus for including the idea of persons as free and equal, which is associated with that right.

I have two responses. First, if democracy is a requirement for avoiding unacceptable circumstances, we do have a case for it, although it may also be hard to achieve democracy when the political culture is deeply at odds with the underlying rationale for it, in a conception of persons as free and equal. We may hope, with Zakaria, that if people practice it long enough they will start preaching it, but there may be large hurdles to establishing and consolidating the practice.[29]

Second, it is not clear how strong a case we have for the claim that a society that ensured a relatively rich set of human rights, including conditions of collective self-determination short of democracy, would nevertheless be so clearly unacceptable as to bear so much argumentative weight in the case for a human right to democracy. Terrible evils are correlated with the absence of democracy, including expansionist foreign policy, famine, tyranny, and cruel subordination. But the same cases are also typically associated with an absence of collective self-determination, which is less demanding than democracy; with a weak or absent rule of law; and with weak protections for speech, press, and association. Isolating and assessing the grossly objectionable implications that flow specifically from an absence of democracy as distinct from these other conditions are difficult. Thus Sen famously observes that democracies do not have famines and points out the terrible Chinese famine after the Great Leap Forward.[30] But in the period after the Great Leap Forward, China also lacked collective self-determination, the rule of law, and (as Sen emphasizes) protections of speech, press, and assembly. It is hard to know whether to lay the responsibility specifically on the doorstep of democracy.

5. Conclusion

I have argued that there is no human right to democracy. But is this view not deeply patronizing? Does it not suggest, in the name of tolerance, that democracy is good for "us" but not for "them"—that benighted peoples, who have not yet received full illumination from enlightenment's bright candle and fully understood human moral powers, do not have the right to be treated as equals in their political arrangements? Surely toleration has its limits.

---

29. Fareed Zakaria, *The Future of Freedom: Illiberal Democracy at Home and Abroad* (New York: W. W. Norton, 2003), esp. 150.
30. Sen, *Develoment as Freedom*, chap. 7.

Surely it does. And an essential point of a conception of human rights is to describe those limits. But this blunt observation about toleration carries no argumentative weight. The issue is not whether to tolerate genocide, slavery, torture, group starvation, enforced illiteracy, or imprisonment without trial, or persecution for religious or political convictions. The question is whether a system with unequal political rights should be tolerated—on the assumption that it ensures collective self-determination and protects a reasonably wide range of other human rights and thus provides the bases of membership. The answer to that question is not aided by sweeping platitudes about the limits of toleration.

More fundamentally, the objection on grounds of patronizing insult is entirely misconceived. The position I have presented implies no asymmetry in rights to democracy. Justice requires democracy: that is true for everyone, for "us"—so to speak—as well as for "them." Democracy is not required as a matter of human rights: that too is true for "us" and "them." A world with more democracy would be a more just world because it gives people the treatment as equals to which all are entitled. But democracy, with its equal right to participate, is not part of the common standard of achievement, defensible on the terrain of global public reason, to which global public responsibility extends.

Protecting human rights is then a less-demanding standard than assuring justice and the democracy it requires. Less demanding, but let us not forget that the world would be unimaginably different—many hundreds of millions of lives would be immeasurably better—if this less-demanding but exacting standard were ever achieved.

11

EXTRA REMPUBLICAM NULLA JUSTITIA?

WITH CHARLES SABEL

In a world of rivalrous states whose peoples are connected ever more directly by globalization, Thomas Nagel has forcefully reasserted a classical thesis of early modern political thought: outside the state, Nagel argues, there is no justice.[1] From this it follows, given the absence of a global state, that there can be no global justice.[2]

Apart from this striking conclusion, however, little in Nagel's argument echoes the Hobbesian variant of the early modern tradition to which he appeals. Even in our globally stateless condition, Nagel assumes, a humanitarian morality, including protections of basic, universal human rights, imposes obligations across borders, although these obligations fall short of requirements of justice. He acknowledges, too, the growing importance to the lives of individuals the world over of global forms of cooperation organized by specialized institutions that commonly

A reply to Thomas Nagel, "The Problem of Global Justice," *Philosophy & Public Affairs* 33 (2005): 113–147. We have placed page references to Nagel's article in the text. The authors thank Josiah Ober and Denis Feeney for assistance with the title. We are grateful for comments on an earlier draft from Suzanne Berger, John Ferejohn, Barbara Fried, Robert Keohane, Gerald Neuman, Josiah Ober, Mathias Risse, Debra Satz, Joanne Scott, William Simon, Jonathan Zeitlin, and the Editors of *Philosophy & Public Affairs*.

1. Nagel notes the parallels between his conclusions and those in Michael Blake's important article, "Distributive Justice, State Coercion and Autonomy," *Philosophy & Public Affairs* 30 (2001): 257–296. But there are also large philosophical differences. Although Blake, like Nagel, thinks that state boundaries make a large difference to moral requirements, in particular, that concerns about "relative deprivation" are confined to relations between co-citizens, Blake sees domestic and global political moralities as resulting from the application of liberal ideas of autonomy and "egalitarian justice" to different institutional settings. So Blake is not a skeptic about global justice and appears to embrace a comprehensive moral liberalism rather than the kind of political conception that Nagel endorses.

2. At least none that cannot be reduced to the domestic justice of the separate parts.

operate with substantial independence from their initial sovereign authors.[3]

Despite this assumption and acknowledgment, Nagel argues that a normative order beyond humanitarianism's moral minimum emerges only within states whose central authority coercively enforces rules made in the name of everyone subject to those rules: only, that is, when individuals are both subjects in law's empire and citizens in law's republic. More particularly, Nagel traces the political morality of egalitarian justice to this co-authorship of coercive law, and correspondingly confines its exacting requirements to the circle of co-authors. Thus the arresting and puzzling novelty of Nagel's argument, which:

1. Affirms, against Hobbes and his realist descendants, that the world outside the state is a normative order;
2. Endorses, in constructivist spirit, the view that norms of political morality need to be political in the generic sense of being sensitive to the circumstances of human engagement, the "different cases or types of relation" (p. 123), for which they are formulated,[4] and that changed relations among people can therefore generate "a new moral situation" (p. 133) with new normative requirements;
3. Acknowledges that the global space outside the state, the space of global politics, is incomparably richer in interdependence, cooperation, rule making, regimes, institutions, debate, social movements, and political contest than in Hobbes's day;
4. But concludes that normative requirements beyond humanitarianism only emerge with the state.

We endorse premises (1) through (3), but reject Nagel's "strong statist" conclusion (4). We will start by explaining the force of Strong Statism by distinguishing it from several alternative normative conceptions that are arguably suited to what we will be calling "the conditions of global poli-

---

3. This assumption is suggested by Nagel's discussion at 136–143. For a useful if slightly dated description of the organizational terrain, see Cheryl Shanks, Harold K. Jacobson, and Jeffrey H. Kaplan, "Inertia and Change in the Constellation of International Governmental Organizations," *International Organization* 50 (1996): 593–627. Note in particular that 70 percent of intergovernmental organizations (IGOs) are "emanations," that is, IGOs created by other IGOs (594).

4. He cites approvingly the generic idea that, as Rawls put it, "the correct regulative principle for a thing depends on the nature of that thing" (122).

tics," the features that seem especially salient for reflection on norms of justice that apply beyond the state (section 1). We then discuss Nagel's defense of Strong Statism, and explain why we are unpersuaded (section 2). Finally, we sketch the conditions of global politics, and explain why we think that they generate new norms, both procedural and substantive (section 3).

Our criticisms are not founded on a commitment, associated with some formulations of cosmopolitanism, to a globe-circling, egalitarian-democratic political morality. Indeed, part of our point is that discussion of global justice should move past the intellectually and politically limiting debate between cosmopolitanism and its nationalist or statist antithesis. Instead, we argue that a political morality can be political in a capacious sense, that is, sensitive to the circumstances and associative conditions, to the "different cases or types of relation" for which it is formulated, without being statist. We propose in particular that reflection on the political morality suited to global politics is aided by attending to the general class of justice-generating political relations of which the relation of co-citizen is one particular (and important) case. However intimate the connection may have been between justice and the state in the world that Hobbes (as well as Rousseau, Hegel, Mill, and Morgenthau) occupied; and whatever we may think of the victory of modern accounts of sovereignty and justice over a tradition of "associative justice" (*Genossenschaftsrecht*), which rooted norms in a variety of forms of human association not confined to the state,[5] it is now a mistake to assign the state so fundamental a role in political morality.

In making the case that global politics provides a terrain of moral-political argument, we will suggest that an idea of inclusion, both procedural and substantive, is central to the domain of global justice. Conceptions of global justice offer accounts of human rights, standards of fair governance, and norms of fair distributions (including access to such basic goods as health and education). Competing conceptions can be understood, then, as advancing alternative accounts of what inclusion demands: of the kind of respect and concern that is owed by the variety of agencies, organizations, and institutions (including states) that operate on the terrain

---

5. See Otto von Gierke, *Natural Law and the Theory of Society* (Boston: Beacon Press, 1960); Paul Hirst, ed., *The Pluralist Theory of the State: Selected Writings of G. D. Cole, J. N. Figgis, and H. J. Laski* (New York: Routledge, 1990).

of global politics. One such conception of global justice may be correct, but we should of course expect that alternative conceptions will always compete for attention. In any case, our aim here is neither to defend any particular interpretation of inclusion or of global justice, nor even to evaluate political philosophy's aptitude for working out a compelling account of global justice. The debate about what justice demands beyond the state does not belong only to political philosophy; it is already part of the world of global politics. Nagel turns philosophical argument against that debate. "Fighting philosophy with philosophy," we write to defend the debate.[6]

1. Statism

Nagel assigns special normative importance to the state. That importance can be understood in at least two distinct ways, however, one much stronger than the other, and Nagel defends not only the weaker claim but the stronger one as well:[7]

Weak Statism: The existence of a state is necessary and sufficient to trigger norms of egalitarian justice, where those norms are understood to require, generally speaking, that individuals be given equal consideration in collective decisions. A mark of egalitarianism, thus understood, is a concern with relative well-being, expressed in the requirement that inequalities in well-being, at least inequalities that trace to collective decisions about rules, be given an especially compelling justification.

Strong Statism: The existence of a state is necessary and sufficient to trigger *any* norms beyond humanitarianism's moral minimum.

Strong Statism is a strong claim. To see just how strong, lets distinguish a practical interpretation of it, which Nagel suggests, from the philosophical interpretation that he defends. Nagel's skepticism about global justice sometimes reads as a counsel of patience. Today's inchoate global institu-

6. The phrase comes from John Rawls's unpublished lectures on Bishop Butler.

7. All combinations of affirmation and rejection of Strong and Weak Statism are possible. Cosmopolitans, who think that the state does not make a difference to the requirements of justice, reject both. Nagel, who thinks that the existence of a state changes the normative terrain by shifting us from humanitarianism to egalitarianism, accepts both. Classical liberals, who reject the claim that the state triggers egalitarianism and thus reject Weak Statism, might accept Strong Statism. We suspect that many egalitarians accept Weak Statism while believing, against the Strong Statist, that requirements of justice shift with increased interdependence or cooperation.

tions, established to provide public goods, may, he suggests, eventually mature into some approximation of a global state, which can then be commandeered for nobler purposes. But reason's magic takes time. For now the powerful should be given a relatively free hand to create and shape global arrangements, and people who care about global justice must resist the temptation to impose premature demands for justice on still-fragile supranational institutions. Those efforts—say, to incorporate strong labor or human rights standards such as a right to freedom of association into the "international standards" deployed by the World Trade Organization (WTO) in assessing trade barriers—are likely to obstruct the construction of stronger institutions and thus to be morally counterproductive.[8] With global justice as with love: you just have to wait.

But Nagel's Strong Statism is first and foremost philosophically ambitious, not practically prudent: absent a global state, he says, we cannot "even form an intelligible ideal of global justice." Strong Statism is founded on the thesis that norms of justice only apply to people who stand to one another in certain relations: in particular, as members of a single state, subject to the same coercively enforced rules, and presented as sharing responsibility for those rules. Outside a state, in the absence of those norm-generating relations, justice simply does not impose determinate requirements for anyone to (fail to) fulfill.[9] Appeals to global justice are, then, not pragmatically premature demands on emerging institutions but a kind of high-minded badgering, or, even worse, an effort to protect the powerful and advantaged by keeping the less powerful and less advantaged out of the club until they meet impossibly demanding conditions.

8. Article 2.4 of the WTO's Technical Barriers to Trade (TBT) Agreement requires that member states use "international standards" as the "basis" for technical regulations. Labor and human rights standards are not now understood to be among the relevant "international standards."

9. Nagel asserts in effect that attributions of justice presuppose a particular relationship. Thus the injunction to act justly is best understood as, roughly, the following injunction: act toward those persons to whom you stand in a certain relation, namely that of common citizenship, in a way that is appropriate to that relation. So the injunction to act justly is like the injunction to be a good mother, which requires that you act toward those persons *to whom you stand in the relation mother-of* in a way that is appropriate to that relation. The relational character of the norm is simply closer to the surface in the latter case. It is different with the injunction to be maternal, which says that you should act toward people in a way that is appropriate to the relation of a mother to child. Although you can in principle be maternal toward anyone (even irritated strangers), you can only be a good mother with your children. Similarly, Nagel's point is that you can be humane or charitable toward any person, but only just to those to whom you bear the relation of *co*-citizenship.

To clarify this ambitious thesis, we make four background points, each of which will play a role in our criticism of Strong Statism.

Content

Weak Statism asserts that we are required, as a matter of justice, to give equal consideration—"equal concern, equal respect, equal opportunity" (125)—to others when and only when we and those others are members of a common state. It conflicts with "monistic" theories of morality—utilitarianism is the classical example, but cosmopolitan egalitarianism may be another—according to which a single set of fundamental norms of justice always applies to individuals, even if the implications of those norms vary with circumstance.[10] But it is essential to understanding the force of the designation "statism" to see that Weak Statism belongs to the family of nonmonistic views, which includes nonstatist members, as well as the Strong Statism we discuss later. All members of the family are political in accepting that we owe equal consideration only when certain social or political background conditions are in place, but the nonstatist relatives reject the idea that a state with coercive authority is among the relevant conditions.

Consider three such views:

Weak Institutionalism: the existence of an institution with responsibilities for distributing a particular good (education, or health, or decent wages and working conditions, for example) is necessary and

---

10. We say that cosmopolitan egalitarianism "may be" monistic because some cosmopolitans think that egalitarian principles apply globally *because* of the nature of global politics, not irrespective of that nature. Thus one of Charles Beitz's main arguments in his *Political Theory and International Relations* (Princeton: Princeton University Press, 1979) is that the presence of a global "basic structure" triggers a global difference principle (see especially 151). Nagel offers Thomas Pogge as an example of a cosmopolitan. But some of Pogge's work depends on the assertion that there are coercive global institutions that trigger norms more demanding than those that would hold even in the absence of such institutions. And some of what he writes about global justice is not founded on egalitarianism but on the relatively weak *normative* premise that we are morally required not to harm others, together with strong (and highly contentious) *positive* claims about the extent to which current global arrangements, including the rights to command resources that are associated with sovereignty, harm people who are badly off. See his *World Poverty and Human Rights* (Cambridge: Blackwell Publishing, 2002). It might be argued that Pogge's use of the harm principle depends on a strongly egalitarian baseline relative to which worsenings count as harms. Absent such an argument, however, it is not clear that Pogge counts as a cosmopolitan, on Nagel's understanding.

sufficient to require that institution to meet the obligation of equal
concern in fulfilling its responsibility;[11]

Weak Cooperativism: the existence of a consequential scheme of
organized, mutually beneficial cooperation under rules (a regime)[12]
is necessary and sufficient to trigger equal concern.[13]

Weak Interdependence: equal concern is owed whenever the fate of
people in one place depends substantially on the collective decisions
taken by people in another place, and the fate of people in that latter
place depends substantially on the collective decisions of people in
the former.

Suppose we understand cosmopolitanism as requiring equal concern,
equal respect, equal opportunity regardless of background conditions. Then
doubts about cosmopolitanism do not select between Weak Statism and any
of these other members of the noncosmopolitan family.

But our interest here is in Strong Statism, and we report on the weak
branch of the noncosmopolitan family only to highlight the distance from
Weak Statism to its Strong Statism cousin. Notice that each of the three
views just stated has a strong analog (Strong Institutionalism, Strong Cooperativism, Strong Interdependence). What defines each of these analogs is that some condition less demanding than common political authority suffices to trigger norms more demanding than humanitarianism
but less demanding than egalitarianism, with its requirement of "equal
concern, equal status, and equal opportunity."

Strong Cooperativism, for example, says that cooperation in the shadow
of a consequential scheme of rules, with significant effects on conduct and
well-being, suffices to trigger norms of justice more demanding than humanitarianism, and that nothing less involving suffices. One variant might

11. See Thomas M. Scanlon, "When Does Equality Matter?" (unpublished), especially his
discussion of institutional agents with responsibilities for distributing a particular good: "In at
least some cases, if an agency is obligated to deliver some good to various beneficiaries, it
must, absent special justification, deliver it in equal measure to all of them" (12).

12. When we say that the rules are consequential, we mean both that they increase level of
cooperation over what it would otherwise be and that the increased level of cooperation has
normatively relevant consequences for social welfare or for the protection of rights. Whether
or not regimes are in this sense consequential remains a matter of live controversy. On the
case of the trade regime, see Judith Goldstein, Douglas Rivers, and Michael Tomz, "Institutions in International Relations: Understanding the Effects of GATT and the WTO on World
Trade" (unpublished paper, March 2005).

13. Beitz, *Political Theory and International Relations*, suggests a view of this kind.

include the claim that it is unjust when, in a world that operates in the shadow of rule-making and cooperating-organizing trade and financial regimes, the circumstances of people who are badly off are not improving at all, although the circumstances of others who are vastly better off are improving a great deal. The focus of concern is not distinctively egalitarian: not that some people are better off than others, nor that some improvements are larger than others; nor is there any assumption that all inequality requires an especially compelling justification. Instead, on this variant of Strong Cooperativism, it is unjust when—against the background of a cooperation-organizing regime that makes rules but could have made different rules, where the different rules would have produced differences in conduct and well-being—the very urgent needs of some people are going unaddressed, although they could be addressed without large costs to others, whose circumstances are improving a great deal.[14] More simply stated, people who are badly off are not getting an acceptable share, decent opportunities, or reasonable improvements, on any conception of acceptable, decent, or reasonable. The concern expressed by this variant of Strong Cooperativism is not with a failure to treat them as equals, owed equal concern, status, and opportunity, but with *inclusion.* Some people are treated by consequential rule-making processes as if, beyond the humanitarian minimum owed even in the absence of any cooperation, they count for nothing. Whatever the more precise content of inclusion (and the content varies across cooperative relations), the norm of inclusion (the requirement of treating people as members, whose good counts for something) requires more than humanitarianism but need not be egalitarian.[15]

Cosmopolitanism, understood as egalitarianism regardless of background conditions, appears to be Nagel's principal target, but in arguing against it, he rejects all of these "Strong" alternatives as well. For him, the

14. The reference to "urgency" and "large costs to others" does not make the concern comparative or focus attention on relative well-being, any more than a humanitarian duty of rescue is made comparative as soon as it says something about the urgency of the need for rescue and the burdens of meeting that need.

15. Consider Rawls's idea of a decent hierarchical society. Such a society is not founded on an idea of equal concern and respect but is guided by a common-good conception of justice that requires attention to the good of members beyond what humanitarian concern already commands. We are of course not proposing the idea of a decent hierarchical society as a model of global justice but observing instead that the notion of a common-good conception of justice provides one way to understand a normative terrain that is neither basic humanitarianism nor egalitarianism. See John Rawls, *Law of Peoples* (Cambridge, MA: Harvard University Press, 1999).

state is the unique normative trigger: unique in establishing the conditions not only for egalitarianism but also for the validity of any norms of justice more demanding than humanitarianism.

Specifically Normative

Strong Statism has affinities with the normatively skeptical variant of realism that once dominated the study of international politics.[16] But it differs from such realism in two ways. First, Strong Statism holds that humanitarian morality is binding even in the absence of a state. Hence global politics is never the moral vacuum, with states moved only by national interest, that realism (an ultra-Strong Statism) takes it to be.

A second, related difference is more important. Strong Statism is meant to be neutral in the debate between realists and their institutionalist and constructivist opponents about the empirical importance of international regimes and more formal institutions in organizing and shaping cooperation in areas of trade, finance, environment, labor standards, human rights, and security, among others.[17] In particular, Strong Statism is not founded on the empirical-realist claim that the underlying distribution of power among states explains everything worth explaining in global politics.[18] It accepts that, or at least is meant to be consistent with the claim that, organized cooperation at the global level is positively consequential: for example, that trade regimes do not simply reflect and codify the underlying distribution of power across states, that they promote continuing mutual adjustment among states, and that such adjustment can increase trade flows and improve social welfare. Although acknowledging such

16. See Hans Morgenthau, *Politics among Nations* (New York: McGraw-Hill, 1985); Kenneth Waltz, *The Theory of International Politics* (Boston: McGraw-Hill, 1979); John Mearsheimer, *The Tragedy of Great Power Politics* (New York: Norton, 2003).

17. For the germinal argument on the importance of regimes in international political economy, see Robert Keohane, *After Hegemony: Cooperation and Discord in the World Political Economy* (Princeton: Princeton University Press, 1984). For a crisp statement of realist skepticism, see John Mearsheimer, "The False Promise of International Institutions," *International Security* 19 (1994/1995): 5–49. Mearsheimer is especially skeptical about the capacity of international institutions to reduce threats of violent conflict. But because military power depends on resources, states have to be concerned about the distribution of the benefits of cooperation on economic and environmental issues as well, and that "relative gains" concern, he argues, will vex other forms of cooperation as well.

18. The realist view of transnational regimes and institutions sometimes takes an epiphenomenalist form and sometimes an intervening-variable form. The epiphenomenalist claim is that regimes have no causal importance; the intervening-variable form says that regimes are one of the ways that national power is expressed and exerted.

possibilities, Strong Statism affirms a sharp and *specifically normative discontinuity* between a world without an overarching coercive authority—the world of humanitarian morality—and a world with such an authority—the world of egalitarian political morality.

Generality

Although Nagel's case for Strong Statism focuses exclusively on norms of "socioeconomic justice" (114), the implications are completely general and apply with equal force to political-process norms, which apply to the governance of supranational arrangements. Thus if we assume that justice requires a state, and put aside the implausible and unmotivated idea that in the absence of a state suprahumanitarian norms of justice apply, but exclusively to processes of rule making, then current debate about the justice or injustice of forms of global governance is misguided: there are no such norms because the conditions for evaluating arrangements as just or unjust are simply absent. So normatively motivated worries about whether global institutions are fair, or accountable and relatively transparent, or democratic, or about how to structure greater participation or representation in their decision-making are all misguided.[19] This relaxed attitude about governance norms is surprising in view of the second point of disagreement with realism. Assume that transnational institutions with distributive responsibilities or transnational regimes are positively consequential: that they foster cooperation by helping to pool information, providing a sharper definition of property rights, enabling bargaining over the distribution of the benefits of cooperation, or sanctioning violations of agreements; that such cooperation has important welfare implications; and that such arrangements generate expectations about future cooperation or shape political mobilization. Against this backdrop, maintaining a relaxed attitude about governance norms depends on the claim that even if institutions or less formal regimes have significant effects on cooperation, and those effects on cooperation have significant welfare effects, and those welfare effects would be very different under different rules, the institutions do not shift the normative terrain.

19. See, among many others, Robert Keohane, *Power and Governance in a Partially Globalized World* (London: Routledge, 2002), chaps. 10, 11; David Held, *Global Covenant* (Cambridge, MA: Polity Press, 2004); Benedict Kingsbury, Nico Krisch, and Richard B. Stewart, "The Emergence of Global Administrative Law," *Law and Contemporary Problems* 68, 3 (2005): 15–61.

Voluntarist Exception

An apparent exception to the fixity of the normative terrain outside the state is that new norms may be added by states when they make voluntary agreements. But Nagel thinks that voluntary agreement is not simply a "passing trait"[20] of institutions and regimes, a fact about their historical origins but irrelevant to their normative consequences. Instead, originating conventions (and continuing agreement) fix the content of the suprahumanitarian norms to which they give rise. So if states agree to an institution, the new norms to which they are subject are those, and only those, determined by their agreement.[21]

This persistently voluntary or contractual character of agreements (and agreements derived from agreements) among states contrasts sharply with the norm-generative power that Strong Statism assigns to the state. When individuals are members of a state they acquire a normatively new status and are required to treat other members as equals, *even if the state originates in an equality-denying convention.* Justice does not permit nightwatchman states, even if they originate in expressly nightwatchman conventions. When it comes to states, but only states, conventionality is a passing trait and equality is always in the fine print of any originating social compact.[22] Put otherwise, in the case of the state, the regulative political-moral norms are fixed *by the nature of the relationship that people have entered,* not by its origins.

So when Nagel says that voluntary agreements among states create new norms whose content is exhausted by the terms of their agreement, he is not simply describing the origins of cooperation, or simply affirming one implication of a general voluntarist normative outlook, but reaffirming

20. We borrow the phrase from Quine: "Conventionality is a passing trait. Significant for classifying terms on the moving front of science, but useless for classifying terms behind the lines," W. V. O. Quine, *The Philosophy of Rudolph Carnap*, ed. Paul Schlipp (LaSalle, IL: Open Court, 1963), 395.

21. A difficulty with this position that we will not explore here is that such agreements are not only inevitably open-ended, but also often intentionally vague because precision would defeat the possibility of future flexibility and indeed of any agreement at all. So some method of subsequent elaboration of commitments is always needed, and those subsequent elaborations do not always require consensus.

22. Hegel rejected a contractualist theory of the state for more or less precisely this reason: he thought that the normative demands that states make on their members could not be explained by reference to a voluntary agreement. For discussion of the objection and a response to it, see John Rawls, *Political Liberalism* (New York: Columbia University Press, 1996), 285–288.

that the relationships engendered by those agreements are not independently norm-generating, in contrast with the relationships among the members of a state.

2. Why Statism?

Since the early nineteenth century a familiar argument for Strong Statism has taken the nation state to be uniquely propitious for solidarity. Underlying this solidaristic form of statism is the idea—elements of which are suggested in Hegel and Durkheim, in the 1980s communitarianism of Michael Walzer and Michael Sandel, and in current arguments of Euroskeptical social democrats and some U.S. constitutionalists deeply indebted to the legacy of the New Deal—that suprahumanitarian norms (especially norms of distributive justice) depend on prior group solidarities.[23] Such norms are founded on and express a shared sense of membership in particular groups (cultural, religious, ethnic), each less encompassing than humanity.

But if group solidarities, a sense of a "we" that shares a common fate, lie at the root of norms, what is so special about the state? After all, there are lots of groups, many less encompassing than the state. According to the solidaristic statist, the state is important in part because it provides the setting in which a plurality of solidary groups can sustain their distinct identities and practices. The solidaristic statist goes further, however: the special moral significance of the state ultimately is founded on the fundamental importance of a person's identity as a member of a nation or people associated with a particular state. The normative requirements on the laws of that state are rooted in what we, as members of a particular national group subject to a common authority, owe to one another. But, the solidaristic statist argues, the content of those requirements becomes determinate only when they are crystallized in legal regulations, which express the identity of the demos. Outside the state there is no justice, then, because outside the state and its laws, we have no way to determine what any solidary group, the nation in particular, requires of its members.

Nagel scants this tradition (see 143–144). His aim is to explain the special normative importance of the state without founding it on antecedent group solidarity: norms of justice do not express a sense of pre-political

23. For an especially illuminating discussion of national identity and political morality, see David Miller, *On Nationality* (Oxford: Oxford University Press, 1995).

group membership or identity but are founded on the distinctive relations that persons bear to one another as members of a state.

Nagel's case for statism, then, starts with a rejection of cosmopolitanism and the broader family of "monistic" theories of morality that deny that particular relations among persons generate new moral requirements. Conceptually, however, the alternative to monism is, as Nagel observes, not dualism (one set of norms for individuals, another to govern the relations among members of a state) but pluralism (122): the idea that there are distinct normative principles appropriate to different types of relations depending on some normatively salient features of those relations. John Locke's distinction between the moralities of the natural condition (interaction between independent and equal persons), family (ties of birth and affection), and state (coercive authority) is a form of pluralism, as is Michael Walzer's idea of distinct spheres of justice associated with distinct goods, and John Rawls's distinction between principles of justice for a single society and principles for the foreign policy of a liberal society in a society of distinct peoples. But Nagel's Strong Statism *is* a form of dualism, and his defense of it proceeds in two steps: he argues, first, that the "complex" combination of centralized coercion and co-authorship of laws distinctive of sovereignty does trigger new norms, in particular, requirements of egalitarian justice, but that, second, various forms of global association that might be thought to have that effect do not trigger any new norms at all. Thus he rejects Strong Interdependence, Institutionalism and Cooperativism, so that pluralism in practice reduces to Strong Statism.

Why, then, does the state "move us past humanitarianism"? Nagel suggests two answers. The first is that the state triggers new norms because cooperation triggers new norms and the state, with its coercive powers, is necessary to sustain a willingness to cooperate by assuring cooperators that their willingness to do their part will not be exploited by others. More particularly, the theory might be that cooperation triggers norms of reciprocity and fairness, which require that beneficiaries of the cooperative self-restraint of others must contribute to the joint effort by a like restraint in order to deserve a fair share of the benefits. On this first answer, the state comes into the picture derivatively: without a third-party enforcer in the background, norm-generative cooperation cannot be sustained.

This answer shades into and is decisively reinforced by a second: that states not only foster cooperation by coercively enforcing rules but implicate the will of those subject to their coercive authority by making, in the name of all, regulations that apply to them all and with which they all are (normatively) expected to comply. Because the regulations are represented as authorized by all—as generally willed and thus as the object of collective responsibility—the content of the regulations is normatively constrained: the regulations must be a possible object of joint authorization. The central idea in this "involvement of will" theory is that it is impermissible to speak in someone's name (and therefore in the name of all) unless that person (and therefore all) is (are) given equal consideration in making the regulations, which are represented as jointly authorized. Thus the regulations made by the state must comply with standards that can be justified to their co-authors.

And not just any justification will do. The justification must speak to each individual in whose name the coercion is exercised and on whom the laws impose obligations: the justification must treat each person to whom justification is owed—each in whose name the coercion is exercised—as an equal.[24] So the state's claim to speak in the name of a law-generating general will—to treat all the subjects of its regulations as their co-authors—generates the new normative standards with which the laws and institutions are to comply. In short, egalitarian justice is the internal morality of the association of equals that is formed by a legal order in which the subjects of the law are represented as its authors.[25]

We will return to this line of thought later. Assume for now that the "complex fact" (128) of coercion plus co-authorship, "that we are both putative joint authors of the coercively imposed system, and subject to its norms" (128), is necessary and sufficient for equal consideration. We come now to the second step: we need to know why coercion and co-authorship of a kind that we associate with the state are required to trigger any norms

---

24. Coercion by itself does not produce the demand for such special justification: wars are the ultimate coercive projects, and there is a morality of war, but that morality is not founded on the idea that members of the opposing state are owed equal consideration. Instead, the roots of the requirement of treating people as equals lie, Nagel argues, in the conjunction of coercion and the claim of collective authorization.

25. As Gerald Neuman observed in comments on a previous draft, this argument leaves some large questions unanswered: What happens when the state is populated in part by resident noncitizens? What moral requirements apply to lawmaking by subunits in a federal system? Do they owe equal concern to citizens from other subunits (say, Texas)? Do the answers to the previous two questions vary with the subject matter of the laws? Could it be that everyone gets equal concern when it comes to criminal procedure but not when it comes to social provision? We share Neuman's suspicion that the plausibility of Strong Statism diminishes with reflection on these questions.

more demanding than humanitarianism, for example, the norm of inclusion that we mentioned earlier. Nagel recognizes the concern. It follows from his explicit recognition that pluralist non-monism, as distinct from dualism, "is a natural suggestion, in light of the general theory that morality is multilayered" (141). But if monism is wrong, if morality is multilayered, and new requirements can emerge with new kinds of relations, then why does nothing other than a state, with its distinctive mix of coercion and co-authorship, actually generate new moral requirements? Nagel seems to have two reasons for rejecting a non-dualist pluralism: an argument founded on voluntarism and one founded on arbitrariness.[26]

We mentioned the argument from voluntarism earlier. It says that justice does not apply "to a voluntary association or contract among independent parties concerned to advance their common interests" (140). Thus intergovernmental agreements or other forms of supra-national arrangement can give rise to new normative requirements, but the content of those requirements is exhausted by the agreements or conventions: the relations themselves do not trigger norms, only the agreements do. But the idea that voluntary agreements can extend obligations is already part of the minimal humanitarian morality, which may be understood to include the principle that "pacts must be respected." So we need something more to get us to equality.

This point about voluntary membership will not do. Pointing to ideas about network governance and delegation, Nagel acknowledges that the "traditional model of international organizations based on treaties between sovereign states has been transcended" (139). So we need an account of why these other "newer forms of international governance" are not norm-generative, why they do not give rise to a new set of social and political relationships among agents subject to them that, although different from the state, suffice to generate new norms whose content cannot be fully explained by reference to the authorizing conventions.

Nagel's answer is that, even with these newer forms of governance, the relationship of individuals to the supranational bodies is completely mediated by governments.[27] So those bodies do not speak in the name of all,

---

26. These two arguments correspond respectively to Sections VIII and IX of Nagel's article.

27. For a crisp assertion to the contrary, see Sabino Cassese, "Shrimps, Turtles, and Procedures: Global Standards for National Administrations," Institute for International Law and Justice Working Paper 2004/4, 19.

their conduct is not authorized by individuals, and the wills of those individuals are not implicated. In the next section of the essay we will suggest that this is not obviously true, even in the case of organizations that, like the WTO, are formally intergovernmental.

The second case for step two in the defense of Strong Statism is an argument from arbitrariness, suggested in Nagel's distinction between "continuous" and "discontinuous" political conceptions. On the continuous view, which he rejects, there is a "sliding scale of degrees of co-membership in a nested or sometimes overlapping set of governing institutions. . . . [and] a corresponding spectrum of degrees of egalitarian justice that we owe to our fellow participants in these collective structures" (140–141). This conception argues for a difference of degree, but not kind, between the norms governing Nagel's relations to the Brazilian who grows his coffee and the American who picks his lettuce or irons his shirt (to borrow his examples). On the discontinuous view, which he favors, he owes nothing beyond humanitarianism to those with whom he shares no state.

In reference to the continuous view, Nagel asks: "But if those institutions [that are not a state but that foster global economic cooperation] do not act in the name of all the individuals concerned, and are sustained by those individuals only through the agency of their respective governments or branches of those governments, what is the characteristic in virtue of which they create obligations of justice and presumptions *in favor of equal consideration* for all those individuals?" (142; emphasis added). Nagel answers: "If the default really is basic humanitarianism, permitting voluntary actions for the pursuit of common interests, then something more is needed to move us up to the *higher standard of equal consideration*. It will not emerge merely from cooperation and the conventions that make cooperation possible" (142–143; emphasis added).

Both question and answer are misleading, and the earlier distinction between Strong and Weak Statism explains why. The Strong Statist thesis that the state is the unique normative trigger is much stronger than the claim that the state is necessary to trigger equal consideration in particular. Consider again the Strong Cooperativist, who says that norms more demanding than humanitarianism, even if not egalitarian, emerge with cooperation that is fostered by rules that are decided by a rule-making body and could be decided differently, with different consequences for affected parties, say, a norm requiring that such rule-making bodies give special weight in their decisions to particularly urgent needs. So the right question is, "What is the characteristic in virtue of which they create obligations of justice and *greater normative demands than humanitarianism?*" And the right way to state Nagel's answer, "If the default really is basic humanitarianism, permitting voluntary actions for the pursuit of common interests, then something more is needed to *move us past humanitarianism.* Norms more demanding than humanitarianism, which is always binding, will not emerge merely from cooperation and the conventions that make cooperation possible."

But why not? Nagel's point seems to be that we lack any plausible explanation for why norms become gradually more demanding as our lives become gradually more intertwined, even when the intertwining is the product of consequential rule choices. The Strong Statist points to the complex fact of coercively enforced, co-authorized rules as the source of the transcendence of simple humanitarianism. In contrast, the more pluralistic, continuous view asserts that forms of connection that do not require a state suffice to trigger norms beyond humanitarianism, for example, norms of the kind expressed in labor codes, requiring "minimum compensation, fair labor practices, and protection of worker health and safety" (141), as well as restrictions on overtime and freedom of association, all expressing the general norm that attention is owed to the interests of workers. But it lacks, according to the argument from arbitrariness, a coherent moral story to support that assertion.

We disagree. We think that global politics does implicate more demanding norms and think that the rationale lies in a mix of the factors suggested by Strong Interdependence, Cooperativism, and Institutionalism, as well as a degree of involvement of will on the global scale that is more extensive than Nagel's argument suggests.

3. Global Justice

In this section we explore two arguments for the conclusion that global politics implicates norms that are more demanding than humanitarianism, although not expressly egalitarian. The first draws on Nagel's claims about the involvement of will and its normative implications and suggests that the requisite involvement of will does not require a state. A second proceeds more intuitively, and asks, by reference to some examples, whether the mix of coercion and co-authorship associated with the state should really be made to bear the normative load that Nagel assigns to them: whether it is really plausible that the world of global politics leaves the normative terrain untouched. We consider these arguments in turn. But as both presume the same broad characterization of the conditions of contemporary global politics, much of which would win general agreement among informed observers, we begin with a brief statement of this characterization:

1. Economic integration, as measured by communication and transportation costs, trade and trade dependence, and movements of capital, has made the global economy a substantial presence in the economic lives of virtually all states.

2. Cultures, economic circumstances, and political institutions and traditions vary widely and much more widely between states than within them.

3. Although states remain essential players, to a considerable and growing extent, rule making, as well as rule elaboration and application, especially in the arena of economic regulation, but also in areas of security, labor standards, environment, rights, food safety standards, product standards among others, are taking place in global settings that, even if established by states (and many regulatory functions are provided by private or public–private bodies), conduct their activities of making, elaborating, and applying rules activities with some de facto decision-making independence from their creators.

4. The rules made in those settings are consequential for the conduct and welfare of individuals, firms, and states, in part because they provide standards for coordinated action and in part (although not only) because national rule-making itself proceeds subject to rules, standards, and principles established beyond the national level.

5. Those settings are the focus of a transnational politics of movements and organizations, and not only an intergovernmental politics between states, that contest and aim to reshape the activities of supranational rule-making bodies, in part through protest, in part by representing interests to those bodies.[28]

28. Mary Kaldor, *Global Civil Society: An Answer to War* (Cambridge, MA: Polity Press, 2003); John Keane, *Global Civil Society?* (Cambridge: Cambridge University Press, 2003); John Ruggie, "Taking Embedded Liberalism Global: The Corporate Connection," in David Held and Mathias Koenig-Archibugi, eds., *Taming Globalization* (Cambridge: Cambridge University Press, 2003).

6. Whatever the origins of these rule-making bodies, they are expected, by states, firms, individuals, and organizations, to continue
to exist, and to make consequential decisions, so that agents (including states, firms, and nongovernmental organizations) and movements need to take them into account in making decisions and
pursuing goals.

7. Even when rule-making and applying bodies lack their own independent power to impose sanctions through coercion, they have the
capacity to encourage conduct by providing incentives and permitting the imposition of sanctions; moreover withdrawing from them
may be costly to members (if only because of the sometimes considerable loss of benefits).

Global politics is thus not an occasional matter of sparse agreements;
while much is changing quickly, it seems to be enduring and institutionally dense. Confining attention to intergovernmental organizations with
permanent administrative staffs, the world's least integrated country is a
formal member of fourteen organizations, and virtually all other countries are formal members of more than a hundred organizations. In addition, there are agreements that establish rights and obligations but do not
create administrative capacity.[29] So in contemporary global politics we
have a mix of precisely the conditions of interdependence, cooperation,
and institutions that have justice-generating implications according to
Strong Interdependence, Cooperativism, and Institutionalism. These
three views offer different explanations for *why* the conditions of global
politics carry such implications, but they converge on the conclusion that
they do.

Of course global politics as sketched does not require a global state, even
a nascent one. But its features are sufficiently important to throw into question, in two ways, the Strong Statist claim that the normative terrain has
not been enriched beyond the "pre-political" humanitarian baseline.

A first approach to the Strong Statist conclusion is to ask whether global
politics meets Nagel's norm-triggering conditions of involvement of will
and co-authorship. To respond, of course, we need some rough gauge of the
scope of involvement of will, of the conditions under which the exercise of
coercive, rule-making authority implicates the will of those it coerces. Nagel

29. See Shanks, Jacobson, and Kaplan, "Inertia and Change."

offers an expansive account of these conditions. In particular, he supposes that a colonial or occupying power, at least if it "claims political authority over a population . . . [and] . . . purports not to rule by force alone" (129n14), makes regulations in the name of, and "intended to serve the interests" of, those over whom it exercises authority. Therefore the legitimate occupying power or colonizer must make regulations that treat its subjects as equals. Even though the subjects do not have rights to participate in making the laws, they are expected to comply; and by complying, and especially by paying taxes, they lend their support to the laws and are normatively expected to do so. Because of these normative expectations of compliance and support, those subject to the laws bear some responsibility for the laws. It is not simply that the laws affect them. Their will is implicated, and they are therefore owed a special justification: "Since their normative engagement is required, there is a sense in which it is being imposed in their name" (129n14).[30]

But this same line of argument appears to extend to international regimes and institutions. Suppose the International Monetary Fund (IMF) will lend structural adjustment funds to a country on the brink of economic chaos only if the borrower agrees, as a condition of the loan, to reduce regulatory barriers to trade, and improve its courts and other rule-of-law institutions, whose current deficiencies make it impossible to enforce any regulatory reform. IMF officials insist emphatically, and are indeed wholly convinced, that both sets of measures will enhance the freedom and well-being of citizens in the borrower country (and they have a set of theories, about how conditionality is essential given weak institutions and about how good institutions provide the commitment devices needed to bind the hands of decision makers, to support their case). Why not say in these cases that the wills of debtor-state citizens are implicated? That the regulations their government is forced to make are made in all their names, and must therefore pass some normative test beyond humanitarianism?

30. Several commentators on an earlier draft worried that we were making too much of Nagel's remarks about the moral requirements on imposed regimes. But his treatment of these cases seems natural, given other elements of the view. If the absence of a state, with co-authorization by citizens, leaves us with nothing more than humanitarianism, then colonial or occupying powers would be more or less free to do as they wished, unless they were operating subject to more demanding restrictions imposed by a treaty-based international organization or, as Nagel supposes, bound by requirements of justice rooted in their claim to act in the name of the people they rule.

The people in the country may have a complaint against the government for creating the disaster, or they may think that the current government should resist the plan, but there appears to be sufficient involvement of will for people also to think that the plan, and its institutional background, is unjust, and not to blame the government for making the best of a bad thing. Or imagine that the WTO approves trade sanctions on a country that has adopted some nontariff trade barriers. Or, perhaps more to the point, assume that a country changes its trade policies to remain in compliance with WTO agreements, which are binding on all member states. Why not say that citizens in member states are expected to take account of WTO decisions, which have binding legal force: that they ought not to oppose a new trade regulation that is made pursuant to a WTO finding? Of course in all these cases the citizens of the affected states are not consulted. But the same is true with the occupying power.

To be sure, people may want to complain that the IMF impositions or the WTO decisions are illegitimate either because the procedures of rulemaking are not accountable or because neither organization takes itself to be bound by suprahumanitarian norms. But these complaints do not defeat our point; they give voice to it. The fact that the impositions and rules are binding on them adds strength to their claim that the rulemaking process needs to conform to more demanding procedural and substantive standards.

Still, it might be said that any complaint against global rule-making bodies should really be directed against the state for accepting their directives: that if citizens object to the WTO agreements that have binding force, or to sardine standards devised by the Codex Alimentarius Commission that the WTO uses as a baseline for national regulations,[31] their complaint should be directed against the government for joining, or against their fellow citizens for authorizing the membership, and that the relationship to the rule-making bodies is entirely mediated by the state's decisions and thus insufficiently direct to trigger new norms.

But this point seems almost facetious. Opting out is not a real option (the WTO is a "take it or leave it" arrangement, without even the formal option of picking and choosing the parts to comply with), and given that it is not, and that everyone knows it is not, there is a direct rule-making

---

31. For example, see *European Communities—Trade Description of Sardines* (WT/DS231R, 29 May 2002 and WT/DS231/AB/R, 26 November 2002).

relationship between the global bodies and the citizens of different states. In an attenuated but significant way, our wills—the wills of all subject to the rule-making authority—have been implicated, sufficiently much that rules of this type can only be imposed with a special justification, although whether that justification must be egalitarian, instead of, say, merely inclusive, is, as we will now see, another matter.[32]

The very malleability of the involvement-of-will idea that allows for this extension reveals, however, a fugitive aspect to the concept that may provoke unease about using it as a cornerstone in an argument about when our relations to one another suffice to trigger requirements of justice, and whether such relations obtain in the world of global politics. So a second strategy is to ask more directly about the plausibility of the thesis that global politics, with its conditions of interdependence, cooperation, and institutional responsibility, does not trigger requirements of justice, either procedural or substantive, more demanding than humanitarianism. How, for example, could it be that when a decision-making body operating in the conditions of global politics makes consequential rule choices, fully aware that the choices could have been different, and that body has a distinct area of responsibility (and is subjected to pressures from movements and states in the exercise of that responsibility), that the processes of rule-making and the substance of the rules are entirely at the discretion of the agency? Nagel focuses on distributive norms, but a conception of global justice includes concerns about distribution (including access to basic goods), governance, and human rights. And Nagel's argument, as our earlier discussion of "generality" indicated, limits the normative terrain to humanitarianism in each of these areas.

Consider first, then, the case of governance norms. Suppose, for example, that the International Labor Organization (ILO) announced that, although its rule-making activities were important for ensuring decent standards for child labor as well as adult compensation and working conditions (a disputable proposition), it would, in the future, shift away from its traditional tripartite political process, with independent representation from governments, employers, and workers in its standard-setting deliberations, and develop and review compliance with labor standards with no mechanisms for the representation of labor, and no way for organizations of workers to

32. Nagel disagrees: see the last paragraph of Section VIII (140).

hold it accountable. Whatever one's doubts about the institutional strength of the ILO, and the magnitude of the effects of its decisions on compensation and working conditions, this proposal is surely objectionable. If the ILO takes on responsibility for formulating labor standards, asserts that its formulations are consequential, accepts that a different formulation would have different consequences, understands that withdrawal from the organization would have costs, and appreciates that no comparable institution will emerge to take its place, it cannot permissibly deny that there are any process norms it must meet—norms for the fair representation of affected interests—so long as it conforms to the demands of basic humanitarianism.

But what is true of governance norms is surely true as well of norms focused on outcomes. Consider again the ILO. In 1998, the ILO announced a shift to a focus on "core labor rights" and away from detailed codes of rights. In the 1998 Declaration on Fundamental Principles and Rights at Work, the ILO announced that all 177 member states are obligated, as part of implicit ILO constitutional principles and regardless of whether they have ratified specific ILO conventions, to promote freedom of expression and collective bargaining, eliminate forced labor, abolish child labor, and end discrimination.[33] Suppose that the ILO now publishes a report announcing that this new regulatory strategy has had a desirable impact on wages and working conditions, except in the informal sector, where workers have been hurt by the new regime. Suppose it announces, too, that the injury to workers in the informal sector is insufficient to trigger humanitarian concern and therefore a matter of moral indifference: that outside the state the only morality is humanitarian, and the ILO has no obligation to attend to the interests of workers in the informal sector. This would rightly be condemned as an entirely arbitrary distinction. The fact that the ILO is not a state does not mean that it can, as a matter of political morality, permissibly make whatever collective decisions it wishes to, so long as those decisions respect the humanitarian minimum. Its concern needs to be more inclusive. It cannot say that workers in the informal sector do not matter, so that the ILO's own policies need not take them into account, except when those policies raise humanitarian concern.

---

33. For debate about the merits of the new ILO direction, see Philip Alston, "Core Labor Standards and the Transformation of the International Labour Rights Regime," *European Journal of International Law* 15 (2004): 457–521; Brian Langille, "Core Labour Rights: The True Story," *European Journal of International Law* 16 (2005): 409–437.

This point might seem special to the ILO because of its distinctive history and self-conceived mission,[34] as someone might say that, having announced a concern for the human impact of Bank-sponsored dam projects, or the role of gender in development, the World Bank should carry through on those announced concerns, particularly when a set of expectations builds up around them, even if it is assumed that the concerns were initially optional.[35] But the way in which the WTO directly and through decisions by the Appellate Body (AB), its highest judicial instance, fixes the rules of international trade strengthens this claim about the normative implications of consequential rule-making by bodies with distinct responsibilities. The WTO's chief purpose is, of course, to foment world trade by (de-)regulatory reform of barriers to it. Many supporters of the WTO desire that it pursue this goal to the exclusion of all others; many of its opponents are convinced that this is precisely what it does. Are such bodies, as Nagel supposes, morally unencumbered? "International treaties or conventions, such as those that set up the rules of trade," he writes, "have a quite different moral character from contracts between self-interested parties within a sovereign state." Whereas the "latter may be part of a just socioeconomic system because of the background of collectively imposed property and tax law in which they are embedded," trade agreements among sovereign states, lacking this background, are "'pure' contracts, and nothing guarantees the justice of their results."[36]

But in fact the WTO anticipates that trade rules will frequently conflict with, and need to be modified to accommodate, a wide range of normative concerns embodied in the domestic laws and regulations of those trading in world markets. These conflicts are chiefly regulated in the WTO Technical Barriers to Trade (TBT) Agreement, which applies to a broad class of domestic regulations, except those concerning agricultural health and safety regulation, which fall under the WTO Agreement on Sanitary and Phytosanitary Measures (SPS).[37] Both agreements permit

---

34. As stated in the Preamble to the ILO constitution, http://www.ilo.org/public/english/about/iloconst.htm#preñ.

35. We are not here endorsing the claim that the concerns were initially normatively discretionary.

36. "Nothing guarantees the justice of their results" is an odd way of expressing skepticism about the applicability of norms of justice to the procedures or outputs of the organization. After all, nothing guarantees the justice of anything.

37. The TBT (along with SPS) "represents as big a paradigm shift to international economic law as, say, the prohibition on the use of force and the introduction of the Security

member states to make domestic rules regarding products and production processes, animated, say, by a concern for public health or product safety, that have the effect of inhibiting trade on condition that the inhibiting rules conform to the agreements. With TBT, such conformity requires that the rules have a "basis" in international standards (where such standards exist), which means, roughly, that states must either use those standards or show through an acceptable rule-making process that the domestic rules are a reasonable departure from those standards, motivated, for example, by an assessment of health risks.

To be sure, central aspects of these agreements are still indeterminate, in flux, and subject to conflicting interpretation, above all, the idea of having a basis in international standards. Still, at the limit, the WTO could conceivably make continuing approximation of domestic rules to international standards a condition of participation in world trade, while at the same time recognizing as valid only those global standards that make reasonable accommodations for national or regional particularities as determined through broad engagement of concerned parties. The system of deregulation could become a forum for global reregulation, with a requirement that global standards be attentive to the local diversity that partly defines the conditions of global politics, while also disciplining rule-making in those diverse settings by evolving international standards.

What matters for our argument, however, is not the eventual jurisprudence of the AB or the outcome of the many debates surrounding the TBT and SPS Agreements but that these controversies are occurring at all. Disputes about how much, and in what way, to modify trade rules or permit deviations from them in order to accommodate other values important to those who will eventually be subject to those rules take for granted that the rule-makers consider themselves obligated to give some weight to the reasonable concerns of the rule-takers (who are themselves assumed to have a responsibility to show concern for the interests of their own citizens), that the rule-takers, who are subject to global rules, see themselves as entitled to a say in establishing what the rules will be

---

Council with binding resolution and police powers represented within the classical world of international law." These agreements produce "an internationally determined normativity." Henrik Horn and Joseph H. H. Weiler, *"European Communities—Trade Description of Sardines:* Textualism and Its Discontents," in Henrik Horn and Petros C. Mavroidis, eds., *The WTO Case Law of 2002: The American Law Institute Reporters' Studies* (Cambridge: Cambridge University Press, 2005), 250.

(although the precise form of that say, and the agents entitled to provide it, are contested). We take this combination of obligation and entitlement in the formulation of global trade rules to be expressing a norm of inclusion: In joining the WTO in order to participate as fully as possible in the global economy, member states are not agreeing to substitute the domestic rules that they have settled on with the universal laws of efficient commerce. Rather, they are agreeing to remake their rules, in domain after domain, in light of the efforts, recorded in international standards regimes, of all the others to reconcile distinctive domestic regulations with general standards that are also attentive to the interests of others elsewhere. Of course, the practice of intergovernmental and transnational bodies is not normatively authoritative, but the fact that they (and their critics) do not take themselves to be operating in a normative vacuum, or in a world of pure humanitarian morality, is at least suggestive.

What is true for governance and distribution is also true for human rights. The thesis that humanitarianism exhausts the normative terrain outside the state suggests the idea that human rights are confined to the pre-institutional, negative rights that individuals could legitimately claim against each other even in a world with no social or political relations. On this view, claims for more institutionally dependent human rights, civil and political as well as social and economic, for example, rights to participation, education, or access to basic health care, are expressions of interest disguised as assertions of rights. If this account of human rights is correct, then much of the debate about and since Universal Declaration about the nature and content of human rights has been badly misguided, since that debate has often assumed a wide range of institutionally dependent human rights, even as disagreement persists about the precise content of that set.

An alternative account of human rights is that they are, inter alia, claims for inclusion in a political society that operates on the terrain of global politics and that can be held accountable by others operating on that terrain for ensuring the conditions of inclusion. On this view, human rights are not as such confined to negative rights that can be specified apart from institutions but may include claims for institutionally defined goods and opportunities required for inclusion or membership in an organized political society. Here, membership is a normative idea, and a person is treated as a member if only if the person's good is given due consideration in law and policy.[38] In turn, debates about the content and scope of human rights can be understood as disagreements about the requirements of inclusion: about what it takes for a political society to treat people as members, about what consideration is due, and about which agents are best positioned to ensure that those rights are secured.[39]

We cannot resolve here the disagreement between these accounts of human rights. Suffice it to say that the latter seems more faithful to the debate about the content and implementation of human rights. Moreover, the theory that human rights are claims to inclusion in the world of global politics—by, in the first instance, being treated as a member of one of the political societies operating on that terrain—does not exclude the thesis that human rights are confined to pre-institutional rights against interference. But it requires that that thesis be defended as the best account of the conditions of inclusion, not as an immediate consequence of the claim that justice presupposes a state.

These concerns about inclusion point in a second and complementary direction as well. In addition to suggesting more determinate norms—of mutual regard and the requirements for openness and reason-giving that this entails—the idea of inclusion, in both its procedural and substantive aspects, calls attention to a process: the reflective exploration, by a variety of actors in the setting of global politics, of the character of the moral norms, both procedural and substantive, that are suited to the forms of association that already connect them. If Nagel's dualistic political conception is right, this will be a short discussion: until we have a state, there is nothing to talk about, and the role of reflective moral thought will be to police the boundaries between the authentic normative demands that emerge with co-citizenship and the "bawling upon paper" (and in the streets) that now passes for reflection on global justice.[40]

---

38. Giving equal respect and concern is a special case of giving due consideration, which is what inclusion requires.

39. See Joshua Cohen, "Minimalism about Human Rights: The Most We Can Hope For?" *Journal of Political Philosophy* 12 (2004): 190–213; and Cohen, "A Human Right to Democracy?" in Christine Sypnowich, ed., *The Egalitarian Conscience: Essays in Honour of G. A. Cohen* (Oxford: Oxford University Press, 2006), 226–248 (reprinted as Chapters 9 and 10 in this volume).

40. "Bawling upon paper" was Bentham's phrase for declarations claiming natural and inalienable rights. See Jeremy Bentham, "Anarchical Fallacies," in *The Works of Jeremy Bentham*, vol. 2, ed. John Bowring (Edinburgh: Tait; London: Simpkin, Marshall, 1843), 494.

If the pluralist version of non-monism is right, however, the spread of new relations and novel forms of association should trigger such further exploration of a range of demanding questions of political morality. Who is to be included in the concerns of rule-making bodies: everyone in the world, or only citizens of member states of intergovernmental or transnational organizations? What are the implications of inclusion: to what kind of concern does it entitle people (individually or in groups), both procedurally and substantively? And who, in the world of global politics, bears responsibility for ensuring inclusion?

In addressing these questions, the conventional points of reference are absent: there is neither a demos nor any other solidary group reflecting on how to keep faith with its identity, nor a state claiming a legitimate monopoly on the achievement of justice in a territory. Yet the questions are of commanding importance, and political philosophy has a role to play in addressing them. In times of transformation of fundamental human relations, political philosophy can tell us where, in the space ranging from humanitarian obligation to egalitarian justice, to look for answers, and can suggest what we might find. But, as ever, its first task is to respond to the skeptics.

ACKNOWLEDGMENTS

INDEX

ACKNOWLEDGMENTS

The essays collected in this book were written between 1983 and 2006. Their footnotes express the many intellectual debts I accumulated in writing each of them. I wish here to add a few acknowledgments that apply to the whole collection.

I thank Jessica Sequeira for her summer 2009 assistance in getting the volume into shape.

I very much appreciate the advice and encouragement of Lindsay Waters in bringing this collection together.

The essays were all written while I was a member of the MIT faculty. I am grateful to the many undergraduates and graduate students I had the privilege to teach there, to my remarkable colleagues in philosophy and political science, to my friends in the departments and Dean's office (among others, Helen Ray, Sue Mannett, Grace Mitchell, Pam Clements, Susan Twarog, Paula Kreutzer, Mary Grenham, Doug Pfeiffer, Janet Sahlstrom, and Anne-Marie Michel), and to the wonderful members of the MIT administration (including Philip Khoury, Chuck Vest, and Bob Brown) for making MIT an exemplary intellectual and human community.

As in the previous volume, I have included papers jointly authored with my friends and longtime intellectual companions, Joel Rogers and Chuck Sabel.

My principal intellectual debt is to my late friend and teacher John Rawls, and I dedicate the volume to his memory.

Finally, I want to thank Robert and Alene Cohen, Ellen Eisen, Daniel Cohen, and Isabel Cohen for their constant love and for their boundless patience with my preoccupations.

The essays, other than the first, are reprinted without significant change. I have expanded "The Arc of the Moral Universe" by restoring some material that I needed to cut for the purposes of publishing it as a journal article. The essays appeared in the following publications, and I thank the publishers for their permission to reprint.

Essay 1: "The Arc of the Moral Universe," *Philosophy and Public Affairs* 26, 2 (1997): 91–134, by Wiley-Blackwell Publishing.

Essay 2: "Structure, Choice, and Legitimacy: Locke's Theory of the State," *Philosophy and Public Affairs* 15, 4 (1986): 301–324, by Wiley-Blackwell Publishing.

Essay 3: "Democratic Equality," *Ethics* 99 (July 1989): 727–751. Copyright © 1989 by the University of Chicago Press.

Essay 4: "A More Democratic Liberalism," *Michigan Law Review* 92, 6 (May 1994): 1503–1546. Copyright 1994 by Joshua Cohen.

Essay 5: "For a Democratic Society," in Samuel Freeman, ed., *The Cambridge Companion to Rawls*, pp. 86–138. Copyright © Cambridge University Press 2003. Reprinted with the permission of Cambridge University Press.

Essay 6: "Knowledge, Morality and Hope: The Social Thought of Noam Chomsky" (with Joel Rogers), *New Left Review* 1, 187 (May–June 1991): 5–27, by New Left Review.

Essay 7: "Reflections on Habermas on Democracy," *Ratio Juris*, 12, 4 (1999): 385–416, by Wiley-Blackwell Publishing.

Essay 8: "A Matter of Demolition? Susan Okin on Justice and Gender," in Debra Satz and Robert Reich, eds., *Toward a Humanist Justice: The Political Philosophy of Susan Moller Okin* (2009), pp. 41–54. By permission of Oxford University Press.

Essay 9: "Minimalism about Human Rights: The Most We Can Hope For?" *Journal of Political Philosophy* 12, 2 (2004): 190–213, by Wiley-Blackwell Publishing.

Essay 10: "Is There a Human Right to Democracy?" in *The Egalitarian Conscience: Essays in Honour of G. A. Cohen*, edited by Christine Sypnowich (2006), pp. 226–248. By permission of Oxford University Press.

Essay 11: "Extra Rempublicam Nulla Justitia?" (with Charles Sabel), *Philosophy and Public Affairs* 34, 2 (2006): 147–175, by Wiley-Blackwell Publishing.

INDEX

Abolitionists, 59

Abortion rights, 170–171

Acquisition of sense of justice: maximin and, 120, 122; well-ordered society and, 120; reciprocity and, 121–123; at positions above minimum, 122–123; account of, 149n89; in contrast with acquisition of moral ideas, 162–163

Afro-Baptism, 40

Anarchism: as historical tendency, 238–239; Chomsky's, 238–245; coercion-free system, 239–242; as social order, 239–242; dispersed-coercion system, 240–242; weaknesses of, 242–245; Habermas and, 262n2

Antinomianism, 42

Arendt, Hannah, 211

Aristotelian principle, 124–126; companion effect of, 125–126

Aristotle, 38, 63, 124–126

Associative obligations, 304

Authority: legitimate, 11–12; of slaves, 36; property versus, 81–82; political, 83, 98; distribution, 101

Autonomy: slave, 36, 45, 47–48, 50–52, 55; political, 219, 223, 283; restricted, 224–225; fundamental interest in, 232; of political argument, 262; of political reason, 262; discourse principle and, 264; political philosophy and, 266; civic, 266–267; private, 266–277; normative understanding of, 284–285; value of, 285; empirical content of, 289. *See also* Private autonomy; Public autonomy

Average utility, 105

"Backroom Boys," 252–253

Barry, Brian, 141, 281

Bibb, Henry, 37

Blake, Michael, 373n1

Bootstrapping, 369–370

Brent, Linda, 48

Capitalist democracy, 246, 255

Chomsky, Noam: radical democracy and, 8; linguistics work, 231, 233n9, 234–235; fundamental ideas, 231–232; hope offered by, 232, 245–259; rationalism romanticized by, 233–238; anarchism of, 238–245; expanded domain of freedom and, 256–259. *See also* Propaganda model

Citizens: political conception of, 151–157, 163, 165–167; free, 157–158; competing views of, 158; critical discourse and, 172–173; in constitutional democracy, 188; representatives judged by, 199; moral powers of, 204–205; liberties advancing good of, 205; autonomous political reason and, 262; communicative relation among, 263; self-ruled, 264; political power of, 273; policy judgments of, 286; direct problem solving by, 291; participating in radical democracy, 291; global, 329

Class exclusion, 179, 195

Cleburne, Patrick, 63

Coercion: in states, 239–242; dispersed, 240–242; co-authorship and, 374, 385–386, 391–392; law and, 374

Collective action: of slaves, 65; in state of nature, 86